THE BLUE AND GRAY ALMANAC

THE BLUE AND GRAY ALMANAC

The Civil War in Facts and Figures, Recipes and Slang

ALBERT A. NOFI

CASEMATE

Philadelphia & Oxford

Published in the United States of America and Great Britain in 2017 by
CASEMATE PUBLISHERS
1950 Lawrence Road, Havertown, PA 19083, USA
and
The Old Music Hall, 106–108 Cowley Road, Oxford OX4 1JE, UK

Copyright 2017 © Albert A. Nofi

Hardback Edition: ISBN 978-1-61200-552-2
Digital Edition: ISBN 978-1-61200-555-3

Portions of this work previously appeared in whole or part in *North & South* © 1997–2013, used with permission, or on *StrategyPage* © 1998–2017, used with permission, or in some of the author's earlier works.

Unless otherwise credited, images and maps are from my own collection or from *The Annals of the War Written by Leading Participants North and South*, edited by Alexander K. McClure (Washington, DC: Times Publishing, 1879), which is out of copyright.

A CIP record for this book is available from the British Library

Printed and bound in the United States of America
Typeset in India by Lapiz Digital Services, Chennai

For a complete list of Casemate titles, please contact:

CASEMATE PUBLISHERS (US)
Telephone (610) 853-9131
Fax (610) 853-9146
Email: casemate@casematepublishers.com
www.casematepublishers.com

CASEMATE PUBLISHERS (UK)
Telephone (01865) 241249
Fax (01865) 794449
Email: casemate-uk@casematepublishers.co.uk
www.casematepublishers.co.uk

For
Marilyn J. Spencer
and
Lori Fawcett,
in loving memory

Acknowledgments

As is often the case, many people helped in various ways during the writing of this book.

Keith Poulter merits thanks for granting permission to use some items that appeared, in whole or part, in the late and much lamented *North & South*. In 1997, with "buffs" and scholars alike looking ahead to the sesquicentennial of the Civil War, Poulter, formerly editor and publisher of *Strategy & Tactics* magazine, brought out the first issue of *North & South*, an innovative journal of Civil War history. Called by historian James M. McPherson "an outstanding source of information on the Civil War, and an invaluable acquisition for anyone interested in the war," *North & South* bridged the occasionally yawning gap between Civil War buffs and re-enactors, serious amateur students, and professional historians. The magazine's content encompassed an eclectic range of subjects, from traditional "drums and bugles" military history to detailed analyses of particular events, ideas, battles, or campaigns, looks at life on the home fronts, profiles of generals and other notables, debates among scholars about critical questions in the study of the conflict, and occasional special issues devoted to particular events or ideas. Many of the articles that appeared in *North & South*, by the likes of James M. McPherson, Gordon Rhea, Stephen W. Sears, Geoffrey Perret, Craig Symonds, Thomas P. Lowry, Gregory Urwin, Harold Holzer, Allen C. Guelzo, and many other noted specialists, threw fresh light on people or events, often breaking new ground in the study of America's great national trauma. For a time the leading popular publication on the Civil War, the demise of *North & South* was in part—and ironically—a result of rising competition due to the advent of the 150th anniversary of the war, and in part due to the loss of over-the-counter sales as a result of the closing of a major book-selling chain. *North & South* ceased publication in 2013, bringing to an end a venue where the student and scholar of the Civil War could "meet" comfortably with the interested layman, the buff, and the novice. A valuable resource for anyone interested in the Civil War, although no longer being published, *North & South* remains accessible in a digital edition of the entire run of the journal, available at http://www.northsouthmag-sales.com/.

Thanks are also in order for my associates at *StrategyPage* (www.strategypage.com), James F. Dunnigan, Austin Bay, Dan Masterson, and Annabelle Bay, for permission to use some items that had previously appeared on its pages. Founded in 1997, *StrategyPage*, to which the present writer is a contributing editor, is an online journal of contemporary strategy and military affairs within a historical framework, and also has historical features, book, film, and simulation reviews, and more.

Members of the "buff" community have often provided useful insights into various aspects of the Civil War, from unraveling genealogical details of potential interest to providing tips on useful anecdotes or helpful references. In this regard the denizens of the Study of the Civil War, Civil War Society, and several other online communities, were particularly generous with their advice, ideas, and leads.

Over the years, a number of re-enactors have been of great help in demonstrating the more practical aspects of tactics, drill, and soldiering, which has helped this writer reach a better understanding of why some things sometimes happened as they did on the battlefield, in particular the personnel of the recreated 15th New York Engineers, Co. A of the 124th New York Volunteers, Clark's Battery (B, 1st New Jersey Artillery), the 1st New Jersey Cavalry, and the 14th Brooklyn.

Chuck Lyons, Diana Medalie, Mike Markowitz, William Horn, Thomas Lowry, and Diana G. Mathieson are due my thanks for helping provide valuable tips, ideas, or technical advice.

Special thanks are in order for Matilda Virgilio Clark, who graciously provided access to family records that helped document the interesting career of Surgeon Augustus M. Clark.

The National Park Service and several state park services should also be thanked for their excellent work in preserving historic sites, as there's nothing like walking the field or examining an artifact to help one develop an understanding of how the fight went or the people of the day lived and worked.

Despite the proliferation of electronic resources, there's lots more valuable material lurking in genuine brick and mortar book hoards, documentary repositories, the occasional county clerk's office, many a musty attic, and similar places, where one can find the revealing anecdote, the elusive name, or the amusing factoid in its native habitat. Of particular importance for the present work were the New York Public Library and the Perry-Castañeda Library at the University of Texas at Austin, as well as the National Archives, the library of the New-York Historical Society, and the New York City Municipal Archives.

Particular thanks are in order to Ruth Sheppard, Clare Litt, Michaela Goff and Hannah McAdams of Casemate Publishers.

Cassie also merits some thanks, for usually refraining from walking across the keyboard while trying to get my attention.

And very special thanks are in order to MSN, who has to put up with these projects.

Albert A. Nofi
Austin, TX
Austin—Brooklyn—Austin

Contents

Introduction

The great national epic in American history is not, as in many countries, the War for Independence, but rather the Civil War. Consider the seemingly unending flood of new books on the subject, which according to one tally had reached some 70,000 works by the onset of the twenty-first century and if anything seems to be increasing.[1] This book is about that war. It is not, however, a history of the war, though Chapter 3 will give the reader a quick overview of the nation's most devastating conflict. And although there is a lot about soldiers and soldiering in it, the reader will not find a lot about battles here, because the Civil War wasn't about battles. The Civil War was about the nation's people living and dying as they struggled over the meaning, promise, and nature of America, and whether, in the words of Lincoln, it could endure "half slave and half free."

This book looks at America and Americans and their war not as a narrative, but rather more like a commonplace book, a collection of useful, interesting, or entertaining information—factoids, essays, poems, anecdotes, lists, profiles, and what not—that help throw light on various aspects of the war, from its origins through its battles and people. It tries to offer a look at how the war affected America and Americans, then and down to the present, looking at the ways in which we remember and memorialize those people and events. Naturally some things may be omitted or given less attention than what some people might consider necessary, depending on their views of the events and the war, but it's always worth keeping in mind that no single volume, no matter how carefully done, can ever include everything.

There may be some surprises in the book, because much of what we "know" about the Civil War is not necessarily true. Ulysses S. Grant noted in his *Memoirs*, "Wars produce many stories of fiction, some of which are told until they are believed to be true,"[2] and that certainly applies to the Civil War even more than most, because unlike most wars—even the Revolutionary War—the Civil War continues to provoke lively controversy. Indeed, the Civil War is the perhaps the best proof of William Faulkner's oft misquoted phrase, "The past is never dead. It's not even past."

Why do we call it "The Civil War"?

"Civil War" sounds like an oxymoron; how can a war be civil? But the word "civil" has many meanings. In modern American usage "civil" is most often taken as meaning something more or less like "polite", or perhaps "thoughtful", as in "that's very civil of you" or "civil amenities." But that's not how the word began.

The English word "civil" derives from the Latin *cives*, which denoted a Roman citizen, a sense preserved in the phrases "civil rights" or "civil liberties," that is, the rights and liberties of the citizen. A "civil" war is one between the citizens, and can be as brutal and horrific as any other kind of war, if not more so. During the long Secession Crisis, the Secession Winter, and into the early years of the war, the term "civil war" was often used by both sides, as, for example, when Confederate Secretary of State Robert Toombs (1810–85)—although as ardent a secessionist as any—warned Jefferson Davis that firing on Fort Sumter "will inaugurate a civil war greater than any the world has yet seen." And in fact, a search of newspapers and other publications shows that "civil war" was in common usage in both North and South during the war, although lagging behind "The Rebellion" and variants thereof in the North. In the years after the war, however, Confederate sympathizers preferred not to use the phrase "civil war."

There are many other names for the war, some of which are given here.[3]

- The War of the Rebellion
- The War for Separation
- The War of the Sections
- The War for Constitutional Liberty
- The Confederate War
- Mr. Davis' War
- Mr. Lincoln's War
- The War for Southern Independence
- The Southern Rebellion
- The Great Rebellion
- The War for Southern Rights
- The Slaveholders' Rebellion
- The War of Northern Aggression
- The Reb Time
- The War of Secession
- The War Between the States
- The Late Unpleasantness
- The War for Abolition
- The War for Southern Liberty
- The Second American Revolution
- The War of Yankee Arrogance
- The War of the 1860s

"The War of the Rebellion" or the "Slaveholders' Rebellion" were common in the North throughout the war, and the first is the actual name of the conflict by act of Congress, used in many official documents and publications, such as the monumental documentary collections *The War of the Rebellion: A Compilation of the Official Records of the Union and Confederate Armies* and *Official Records of the Union and Confederate Navies in the War of the Rebellion*, as well as in newspapers and common usage at the time, but it waned in popularity over the decades following the war.

"Mr. Lincoln's War" and "Mr. Davis's War" were at times used by their political enemies during the war, which seems hardly fair to either gentleman.

Most of the other names appear only rarely in wartime newspapers, speeches, or other publications, including variants of "War of Southern Independence" or "Second American Revolution." "The War Between the States" can occasionally be found in wartime literature, usually without the capital letters, but grew much more popular after the war, though it has been in decline in recent years.

Many of the names were actually coined after the war, usually to make political points. The "War of Northern Agression," for example, first seems to have appeared in 1948, during the Dixiecrat secession from the Democratic Party, one of several names intended to assert the right-eousness of the Confederate "cause," such as "the War for Constitutional Liberty" or "the War of Yankee Arrogance." Several of the alternative names were coined to smooth over feelings, such as the "War of the Sections"; the wonderfully innocuous "War of the 1860s," coined during the centennial years of the 1960s by a publisher who hoped to sell his somewhat antiseptic American history texts in both North and South; and "The Late Unpleasantness," often found in the South, perhaps the most curious name of all, suggesting it was all an unfortunate mistake. "The Reb Time" was a common name in African American oral tra-dition about the war. Arguably the most accurate name, "the War of Secession" has never found much favor among Americans, though it sometimes occurs in foreign works touching on American history, such as in French, Spanish, or German.

CHAPTER I

The "House Divided"

The American Civil War was long in coming. The question at issue was a simple one: secession, the separation of a state from the Union of States, a subject on which the Constitution of 1789 is silent. But secession only became a divisive issue because there developed significant social, cultural, and economic differences between the Southern states and the rest of the nation. In the decades following American independence, the South—rural, agricultural, and aristocratic—saw its interests threatened as the rest of the nation was, relatively speaking, becoming increasingly urban, industrial, and democratic. There were disputes over tariffs, over government-sponsored internal improvements, and over the distribution of public land, all of which the Northerners and Westerners generally favored, and which the Southerners generally opposed. Complicating the issue was the fact that the population of the North and the West grew at a rate faster than did that of the South, a development itself largely as a result of the divergent character of the regions; immigrants mostly settled in the Northern and Western states. This trend led to a decline in Southern influence in the Congress, as the House of Representatives took on an increasingly Northern character. Then, Southern influence in the Senate began to be threatened, as new states tended towards a Northern or Western socio-economic culture. Even without further complicating factors, the differences between the sections would have been sufficient to raise tensions, though it is hardly likely that these tensions would have led to an open break. There was, however, one major difference between the regions that was simultaneously at the root of and more important than all the other issues taken together: slavery.

Slavery in America

In colonial times, slavery was legal in all the states, and several Northern states had substantial slave populations. But even then, there were voices protesting slavery, particularly among members of religious groups, notably the Mennonites and the Quakers, who were joined after the Protestant "Great Awakening" of the early eighteenth century by some of the Presbyterians, Baptists, and Methodists.

Although many of the "Founding Fathers" were themselves slaveholders, the War for Independence (1775–83) gave impetus to the notion that slavery was incompatible with the new nation's founding principles. Beginning in 1777 with Vermont (actually not yet a state but acting as an autonomous republic), by war's end Pennsylvania and Massachusetts had initiated steps to abolish slavery, while others, such as Rhode Island and New York, granted freedom to slaves who had served in the war. By the time the United States Constitution was adopted in 1789, nearly half the states had completed or initiated abolition, while by unanimous vote Congress had barred slavery from the Northwest Territories, which would eventually become six new states.

The trend toward abolition was supported to a greater or lesser extent by many of the Founding Fathers, including Benjamin Franklin, George Washington, Thomas Jefferson, John Jay, James Madison, Alexander Hamilton, and others, some of them slave owners and some not, though they often differed over the means and moment. By 1801, virtually all of the Northern states had either abolished slavery or initiated abolition, while in other states emancipation of individual slaves was relatively common, notably in Virginia and Maryland, and particularly in Delaware. In addition, all states save South Carolina had banned the importation of slaves from abroad. In 1807, Congress voted to ban the further importation of slaves into the country, with only the delegates from South Carolina dissenting, and this was followed in 1819 by

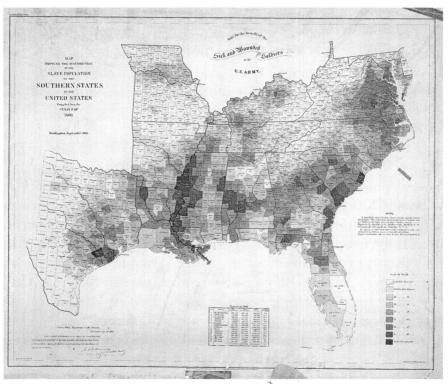

The slave population of the United States, 1860. Compiled from the census of 1860, this map was published for sale to raise money for soldiers' relief. (Library of Congress)

Congressional action declaring the Atlantic slave trade an act of piracy, punishable by death.

This trend toward abolition didn't take root in the South, particularly after the introduction of the cotton gin, which turned a secondary crop into a major one, yielding enormous profits not just to Southern planters. So, while the rest of the Western world was abandoning slavery, most of the white people of the South, relatively few of whom actually owned slaves, had come to view the institution as vital to their economic survival, a perspective with which many in the North could sympathize. Largely overlooked today is the Northern involvement in slavery. Northern banks provided loans to planters, often with slaves as collateral, while insurance companies wrote policies on the lives of slaves. Northern ship owners profited from transporting the cotton, and even helped smuggle slaves into the country, while some Northern entrepreneurs produced "slave goods" such as clothing, footwear, and shackles, and at times even owned slaves and plantations in the South.[1] By 1840, the United States was the only major Western country in which slavery was still legal.

Slave resistance

Slave resistance was surprisingly common, but not necessarily in ways we think of when the word "resistance" is used. Most slave resistance was passive, in the form of behaviors or subversive actions, a pattern common in all slave cultures. Feigning illness, stupidity, or ignorance, concealing inventiveness, suppressing initiative, stealing, telling lies, sabotaging tools or machinery, and so forth were all forms of slave resistance.

Of course, not all slave resistance was passive: there were instances of violence by slaves toward their masters. But this is actually very hard to quantify. There are many confirmed cases in which an individual slave harmed a master or other white person in a momentary rage, but no one seems to have ever tallied such incidents. There were also cases of slaves, especially "house servants," executed for poisoning their masters, but no way to sort out real instances of poisoning from accidental ones; before modern sanitation and refrigeration, waterborne diseases and food poisoning were hardly rare.[2]

And of course, there were more overt forms of resistance.

Escape

Escape is very hard to quantify. Most escape attempts were unsuccessful, and probably went unreported. Many were spontaneous responses to sudden opportunity, while others were well planned. Some slaves, of course, did manage to get away, which is why there was a national Fugitive Slave Act. Although in 1850 one pro-slavery advocate claimed 100,000 people had escaped over the previous four decades, the census suggests that between 1840 and 1860, on the eve of the Civil War, about

15,000 slaves succeeded in escaping to freedom, an average of about 750 a year. This estimate is probably reliable, as slave owners had an incentive to report escapees, because slaves were taxed as livestock, and masters often had "escape" insurance.[3]

Escape was often facilitated by the "Underground Rail Road" (UGRR). The UGRR was essentially an informal network of people—white and black, slave and free, and even slaveholders—who for various reasons abetted fugitives. The story of the UGRR actually can never really be told, as there was no real organization and very little accurate information survives. Aside from the memoirs of some escapees or people who abetted them, there's little evidence of how the system worked. And not all the memoirs, nor much of the oral tradition, are reliable.

Slave rebellions

In his pioneering works *Negro Slave Revolts in the United States, 1526–1860* (1939) and *American Negro Slave Revolts* (1943), Herbert Aptheker enumerated some 250 slave uprisings or conspiracies involving at least ten persons on the territory of the United States. While his work was criticized on many grounds, not least because he was an avowed communist, Aptheker is generally reliable, although he did make some mistakes. He tended to accept as accurate several cases in which the evidence has since been shown to have been rather murky. Hysterical whites often conjured up slave plots on the slenderest pretexts, such as rude remarks, perceived slights, or even accidents, and such suspicions might be readily confirmed by some poor souls who could be tortured into confessing. So at times, it's hard to tell whether a slave conspiracy existed or not.

Certainly there were many actual slave uprisings or plots, such as the New York Slave Rebellion of 1712, the Stono Slave Rebellion—"Cato's Conspiracy"—in South Carolina in 1739, Gabriel's Conspiracy in Richmond, Virginia, in 1800, and Nat Turner's Rebellion in 1831, near Southampton, Virginia. Nat Turner's rebellion, the subject of the award-winning 2016 film *The Birth of a Nation*, was the last major outbreak, during which some sixty whites died while perhaps as many as

A lurid 1831 woodcut print purporting to show events during Nat Turner's rebellion, depicting the murder of an unnamed white woman and her children (1), Turner's "master", Joseph Travis (2), and a "Mr. Barrow" who attempted to resist the rebels (3). (Library of Congress)

200 African Americans, free or slave, rebellious or not, were killed in the fighting or by execution.[4]

But there are also cases in which a "servile rebellion" existed largely in the paranoid imaginings of the slave owners. Some examples:[5]

- 1741, New York City: Rumors that Catholic priests were suborning slaves to rebel led to the execution of some blacks and several priests.
- 1856, Dover, Stewart, and Montgomery counties, TN: Rumors that some of the thousands of enslaved blacks working in the local iron industry were plotting an uprising led to the torture of scores of people and the execution of about thirty.
- 1860, "The Texas Terror": With July temperatures hitting 114°F, many fires broke out in homes and businesses across the Dallas area. While this was probably the result of spontaneous combustion of the primitive matches of the day, many whites believed the fires were part of a slave conspiracy organized by the proverbial "outside agitators," leading to many arrests and a number of executions.
- 1860–61, the "Second Creek Slave Conspiracy": During the Secession Winter, rumors of an abolitionist–inspired slave conspiracy in the vicinity of Natchez, TN, caused whites to go on a rampage trying to root out the conspirators and the "outside agitators" supposedly stirring them up, during which as many as 400 African Americans and some whites were lynched.

In each of these cases, the only evidence that a conspiracy existed was what could be tortured out of various unfortunates, whites as well as blacks, which led to numerous deaths, either by mob violence or execution.

Determining whether a slave conspiracy was real or merely conjured up by white paranoia can perhaps be best illustrated by the case of Denmark Vesey (c. 1767–-1822). Vesey was a skilled carpenter who had brought his freedom and become a leader of the small free African American community in Charleston, SC, and was one of the founders of the famous Emanuel African Methodist Episcopal Church, widely known as "Mother Emanuel," site of a murderous attack by a white racist terrorist in 2015. In 1822, Vesey was accused of organizing an insurrection by thousands of slaves. Supposedly, the conspiracy was betrayed by a slave who was devoted to his master. Word spread quickly, inspiring fear among the whites of South Carolina, a state in which over half the population was enslaved, and positive hysteria in Charleston, where blacks—slave and free—comprised three-fifths of the 25,000 inhabitants. The militia was called out, Vesey and more than a hundred others were arrested, including some whites. Through torture, three men were induced to "confess" and implicated literally hundreds of others, in return for which they were sentenced to "transportation" out of South Carolina. Many whites testified to slights or remarks by their slaves that they now interpreted as hints of the coming uprising. In the end brief, irregular trials sent Vesey and thirty-five other black men to the gallows for "servile insurrection," thirty-one others to "transportation," and the four whites to fines and short jail sentences.

Reviewing the Vesey case, some historians have noted serious flaws in the received account. For example, despite supposed meticulous planning, no stockpiles of weapons were found, certainly a necessity for any insurrection, and there were significant contradictions in the trial transcripts, not to mention many missing documents and procedural errors. So, was there a "conspiracy" or was one constructed by hysterical whites?[6]

The battle over slavery

Serious sectional arguments over slavery only began to emerge during the "Era of Good Feeling," the years that followed the War of 1812. By

1820, the Union comprised 22 states, half of which had abolished or were in the process of abolishing slavery, while the other half remained slave states. In that year, the "Missouri Compromise" was concluded, with Missouri admitted to the Union as a slave state and Maine, detached from Massachusetts, as a free state, and specifying that new states formed from territories north of latitude 36°30' be free, while those formed south of that would be slave.[7]

The compromise confirmed the influence of the slave states in Congress; although over 60 percent of whites lived in the North, the "three-fifths" clause of the Constitution, by granting slave states representation for that proportion of their slave population, gave the slave states nearly half of all the seats in the House of Representatives, and thus a significant proportion of Electors in presidential elections.

The era of "Manifest Destiny"

"Am I not a man, and a brother?". The seal of the Society for the Abolition of Slavery in England, adopted in the 1780s, and here seen on a tract issued by the American Anti-Slavery Society in 1837. (Library of Congress)

In the two decades following the Missouri Compromise, only two new states entered the Union, Arkansas, a slave state, and Michigan, a free state, thus preserving the balance between slave and free. But at that point, there was virtually no land south of latitude 36°30' from which new states could be formed. This fed the already great sense among many Americans that the United States should expand to the Pacific Ocean, what came to be known as "Manifest Destiny." Manifest Destiny essentially cloaked territorial—and racial—expansion with an aura of divine providence, that is, that American institutions and the

American branch of the Anglo-Saxon race had a God-given mission to "civilize" the Continent.[8]

The Mexican War

Arguably the most notable victim of Manifest Destiny was Mexico, independent since 1821, but highly unstable. In 1835, the Mexican state of Texas, into which the Mexican government had unwisely invited Americans to settle, rose in revolt, native *Tejanos* and immigrant English-speaking Texians alike uniting against the dictatorial regime of Antonio Lopez de Santa Ana, and in an upset victory secured independence.[9] The Republic attracted more settlers from the United States and secured foreign recognition and financial support, but never established an effective government, running up enormous debts, while proving unable to cope with occasional incursions by the Mexican Army, banditry, and Indian raids. Attempts to secure annexation by the United States bore fruit at the end of 1845. This sparked the Mexican-American War, which was opposed by many, including Abraham Lincoln and Ulysses S. Grant, as an unjust conflict.

In 1846–47, Brig. Gen. Zachary Taylor advanced from Texas and secured control of much of northern Mexico, while the Navy and Army in combination captured California. Then, in March 1847, General-in-Chief Winfield Scott effected an amphibious landing at Vera Cruz, quickly captured the fortress-city, and then marched on Mexico City, which fell in mid-September after a series of hard-fought battles. During the war, many officers who would later become famous distinguished themselves, including Ulysses S. Grant, Robert E. Lee, George B. McClellan, George Thomas, Jefferson Davis, Joseph E. Johnston, and Thomas J. Jackson.

The war with Mexico established the Rio Grande as a boundary for Texas, and transferred to the United States territory comprising what are now California, Nevada, and Utah, most of Arizona, about half of New Mexico, and parts of Wyoming and Colorado, in return for a direct payment of $15 million plus the assumption of $3.25 million in claims by American citizens against Mexico. It also reopened the sectional conflict over slavery.[10]

The Compromise of 1850

Much of the new territory annexed by the United States from Mexico was south of latitude 36°30', and thus reserved for slave states according to the Compromise of 1820. Controversy erupted almost immediately, over California.

The discovery of gold in California on January 24, 1848 touched off the "Gold Rush." California's population, 6,500–7,500 Hispanic *Californios* and some 700–800 others, mostly from the United States, plus about 150,000 Native Americans, exploded in a year as another 100,000 people arrived, mostly from the United States, but some from other places, including China. San Francisco soared from a village of about 1,000 to a city of some 25,000, placing it among the two dozen largest cities in the United States. California quickly developed a lively economic, civil, and political life. In September 1849, a provisional state government was established which petitioned for statehood, with a proposed state constitution that explicitly barred slavery, despite the fact that much of the state was south of latitude 36°30'.

California statehood dominated the national political scene in 1849 and 1850, as pro- and anti-slavery proponents took stands and offered "compromises," a matter complicated by Texas politicians claiming "historic rights" to additional territories, including much of what is now New Mexico. After much fiery debate, Kentuckian Henry Clay (1777–1852) worked out a compromise that was acceptable to slavery advocate John C. Calhoun (1782–1850) of South Carolina and abolitionist Daniel Webster (1782–1852) of Massachusetts. The "Compromise of 1850"[11] had six major provisions, each embodied in a separate act:

1. California was admitted as a free state.
2. The buying and selling of slaves was abolished in the District of Columbia, though slavery remained legal there.
3. A "Territory of Utah" was organized with the proviso that the residents could determine whether the territory was free or open to

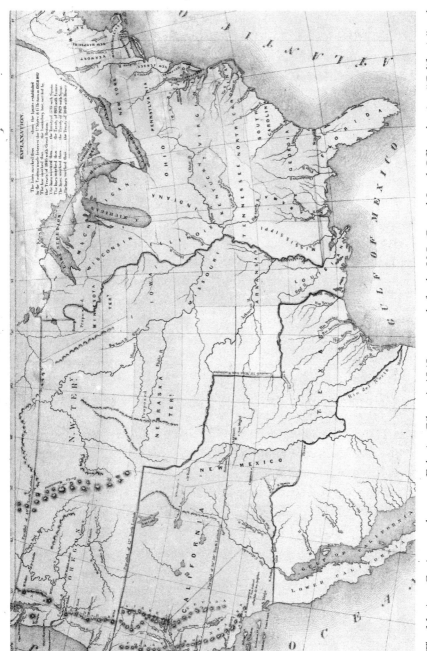

The Mexican Cession, as shown on Ephraim Gilman's 1848 map made for the U.S. General Land Office, showing "California" and "New Mexico" as acquired by the United States. Note the "Missouri Compromise" line of 36°30'. (National Archives)

slavery, known as "popular sovereignty," cancelling the Compromise of 1820, as the territory lay north of latitude 36°30'.

4. A "Territory of New Mexico" was organized on the same terms, to include most of the present New Mexico and Arizona.

5. A new "Fugitive Slave Act" was passed.

6. Texas ceded the portion of the state north of latitude 36°30' (*c.* 5,700 square miles), which became the Oklahoma panhandle, and abandoned its dubious claim to New Mexico east of the Rio Grande, in return for $10 million in U.S. 5 percent bonds to pay off the debt of the former Republic.

Two of the provisions of the Compromise quickly proved contentious.

Popular sovereignty

In accordance with the Compromise of 1850, in 1854 Congress passed the Kansas-Nebraska Act, organizing two new territories and leaving the question of slavery up to the inhabitants. Pro- and anti-slavery advocates began encouraging like-minded folks to move to the new territories, in order to influence the ultimate vote on the slavery issue. Along with legitimate settlers seeking a better life, there came radical extremists. From the South, and especially Missouri, armed bands of pro-slavery "Border Ruffians" entered Kansas, to be countered by similar bands of armed anti-slavery "Jayhawkers" from the North.

Kansas in particular soon became the scene of bloody violence, arson, and murder. At least fifty-six people are know to have died in "Bleeding Kansas" before the disorders were surpressed by military intervention in 1859. By then, after four tries marred by fraud, intimidation, violence, and occasional interference by pro-slavery President Franklin Pierce, Kansans, mostly settlers from the North, finally approved a state constitution with a strong anti-slavery component, but their application for statehood was blocked by pro-slavery members of the U.S. Senate. "Popular sovereignty" had not settled the question of slavery, but merely inflamed it.

The Fugitive Slave Act of 1850

The Constitution required states to cooperate in returning fugitive slaves to bondage, and in 1793 a national fugitive slave law was enacted. This allowed slave owners to assert claims to fugitives in state courts and regain possession upon presentation of evidence, and also prescribed penalties for persons knowingly aiding or abetting anyone escaping from slavery. During early nineteenth century, most Northern states passed legislation to protect suspected fugitives, requiring cases against purported fugitives to be tried before a jury; in 1847, Abraham Lincoln famously represented a Kentucky slave-owner in such a case, which he lost. Northern law enforcement and judicial authorities were reluctant to take cases involving fugitive slaves, often putting obstacles in the path of persons trying to assert claims to fugitives. This was the reason the Compromise of 1850 included the Fugitive Slave Law.[12] It had many provisions that many Northerners found highly objectionable, whatever their views on slavery:

- Federal officials were empowered to enforce the law, and could impress citizens into a posse or even call out federal troops to assist them.
- A slave owner's affidavit claiming a person as a fugitive was sufficient to oblige a Federal marshal or state law enforcement officer to detain the person, to be held for adjudication.
- The slave owner's claim was to be adjudicated by a special federally appointed commissioner.
- Law enforcement officers aiding slave owners in the successful recovery of fugitives were rewarded $10, easily two weeks' pay for most Americans at the time, but only $5 if the case went against the claimant.
- Officials refusing to carry out the arrest of a claimed runaway slave were liable to a fine of $1,000, an enormous sum for the day.
- Anyone aiding a fugitive in any way was subject to up to 6 months' imprisonment and a $1,000 fine.

The Fugitive Slave Act was a gross violation of states' rights; Southerners, the staunch champions of states' rights, were perfectly willing to increase federal authority when it came to recovering fugitive slaves. It was, in the words of historian Eric Foner, "the most powerful exercise of federal authority within the United States in the whole era before the

Civil War."[13] The law also violated the right to trial by jury embodied in Article III of the Constitution and the judicial protections embodied in the Fifth, Sixth, and Seventh amendments. Despite this enormous enlargement of federal power and disregard for the Constitution, there were no speeches in the legislatures, of South Carolina and the other bastions of state rights, protesting "federal tyranny."

Worse, the law was at times used to kidnap free blacks into slavery; without the right of a trial, accused "fugitives" could not prove they were free. That $10 reward seems to have tempted some law enforcement officers to bend over backwards, as there certainly were cases in which freed or free-born African Americans, at times persons of standing in their communities, suddenly found themselves "claimed" as someone's property, sparking the flight of many free blacks to Canada. Moreover, since some fugitives of mixed race were found passing as white, many whites otherwise indifferent to slavery came to realize that under the terms of the law, almost literally anyone could be claimed as a runaway on the word of a slave owner.

Resistance to enforcement of the Fugitive Slave Act was widespread in the North, including "jury nullification" in cases brought against free people charged with violating the act, and in some instances irate citizens rioted or even stormed courthouses or jails in efforts to free purported fugitives, often with success. Perhaps most famously, in 1854, when a court ordered 21-year-old Anthony Burns to be returned to slavery from Boston, some 1,600 U.S. marshals, soldiers, and marines, as well as some Massachusetts militiamen—others refused to serve—and paid volunteers had to escort him through an angry crowd claimed to number 50,000 to a revenue cutter that was to take him south.

Anthony Burns being returned to slavery. (Courtesy Wikipedia Commons)

Although the pro-slavery interests were strongly in favor of the Fugitive Slave Act, it was a tactical mistake. Many northerners were indifferent to slavery, but were just as staunch believers in states' rights as Southerners claimed to be. As Eric Foner put it, "the whole process, under the Fugitive Slave Law, of the federal government seizing people galvanized opinion in the North in a way that the abstract question of slavery may not have done."[14]

The filibusters

Filibusters were a curious phenomenon of nineteenth-century political life.[15] Although the usage is obsolete, in the early nineteenth century filibusters were freelance military adventurers who organized expeditions to take over part or all of a country, usually for their own profit, but occasionally for some loftier objective, such as to liberate a colony from bondage. In the aftermath of the Mexican-American War, a number of filibustering expeditions or conspiracies were undertaken by Americans seeking to grab territories that might eventually be annexed to the United States, primarily in support of the expansion of slavery. Expeditions were undertaken or proposed to capture Cuba, various parts of Mexico, Honduras, Guatemala, Costa Rica, Nicaragua, the British Miskito Coast protectorate, Santo Domingo, Haiti, and even the Galapagos Islands and Hawaii. One historian estimated that Americans—mostly Southerners, but often backed by Northerners with financial ties to the South— organized at least one filibustering expedition every year from 1848 through to the outbreak of the Civil War.

The most famous American filibuster was William Walker (1824–60). Tennessean Walker was quite short—5ft. by some accounts—but unusually well educated, with a bachelor's from the University of Nashville, an M.D. from the University of Pennsylvania, and an advanced medical certificate from France. He worked as a physician and journalist in New Orleans for a time, and then became involved in filibustering. In 1853, Walker invaded Mexico and established a short-lived republic in Baja California and Sonora, before being ousted by Mexican forces in 1854. The next year, he went to Nicaragua to support one side in a civil war, but soon seized power and established a pro-slavery government.

While pressing for annexation to the U.S., he invaded Costa Rica, but the Costa Ricans rallied and, aided by exiled Nicaraguans and with some support from other Central American countries, defeated him and he fled to the United States.

In August 1860, Walker tried invading Honduras, but the expedition was a disaster. Walker and his "army" got lost, and blundered into the British territory of the Miskito Coast. The British arrested the lot, and turned them over to the Honduran government; on September 20, 1860, Walker—the "Grey-eyed child of destiny"—was executed by firing squad.

William Walker, self-proclaimed general and President of Nicaragua, from his obituary in Harper's Weekly, *October 13, 1860. (Library of Congress)*

Walker's expeditions had a lot of support. Millionaire Cornelius Vanderbilt, who wanted to build a transcontinental railroad in Nicaragua, backed him in that county, though the two subsequently had a falling out, while Southern politicians such as Joseph Brown, Alexander H. Stevens, Thomas L. Clingman, and Robert Toombs, all of whom would hold high positions in the Confederacy, endorsed his efforts. Although arrested several times by federal authorities for violations of American neutrality laws, sympathetic jurors always got him off.

A number of filibusters rose to some prominence in the Civil War, including several who became brigadier generals: Isaac H. Duval and Thomas A. Smyth in blue and Robert C. Tyler, Birkett Davenport Fry, and Allison Nelson in gray, plus a score or more who became colonels. Filibuster organizers attempted to recruit a number of other men, who turned them down; how different might the events of 1861–65 have been if Jefferson Davis, Robert E. Lee, or Pierre G. T. Beauregard, all of whom were approached by filibusters, had shared Walker's fate?[16]

The Dred Scott case

Perhaps the final blow to a compromise settlement of the slavery issue came in 1857, with the Dred Scott case. Born in slavery, in the mid-1830s Dred Scott (c. 1799–1858) was sold in Missouri to John Emerson, an assistant surgeon in the U.S. Army. Scott went with Emerson as he was transferred from Missouri to Illinois, the Wisconsin territory, Louisiana, and back to Missouri, where Emerson left the Army in 1842.

In 1846, by which time Emerson had died, Scott sued Mrs. Emerson for his freedom, citing, among other grounds his residence in Illinois and Wisconsin, where slavery had been prohibited by the Northwest Ordinance of 1787, arguing that he was free under a Missouri precedent that held that prolonged residence in a Free State made a slave free. In addition, Scott noted that while in Wisconsin, he had been married by a justice of the peace, which further proved that he was free, since slaves could not contract legal marriages. In 1847 the Missouri court ruled against Scott on a technicality, but the presiding judge called for a retrial, and in 1850 a jury found for Scott. Irene Emerson appealed, and in 1852 a split Missouri Supreme Court declared the 28-year-old "Prolonged Residence" precedent invalid, returning Scott to slavery. Mrs. Emerson then transferred Scott's ownership to her brother John F. A. Sanford. As Sanford was a legal resident of New York, in 1853 Scott—who had a lot of legal help from abolitionists—brought his case in federal court, on the grounds that if free, he would be a legal resident of Missouri, and thus his suit was an interstate one. Scott's case made its way through the federal courts, finally reaching the Supreme Court, overseen by Chief Justice Roger B. Taney (1777–1864). Although generally pro-slavery, Taney had freed his own slaves, and had earlier concurred in the 1841 *Amistad* case, finding for enslaved Africans who had mutinied and captured the ship that was illegally carrying them across the Atlantic. Nevertheless, on March 6, 1857, Taney delivered the six to two majority opinion denying Scott's claim to freedom on the grounds that it would violate his master's Fifth Amendment rights to the security of his property without due process of law. Then, apparently wishing to settle once and for all the issue of slavery, Taney declared that:

- Persons descended from Africans, whether slave or free, could not be citizens of the United States.
- The Northwest Ordinance of 1787 did not confer either freedom or citizenship within the Northwest Territory to non-white individuals.
- The Missouri Compromise was void, since it exceeded the powers of Congress in excluding slavery and granting freedom and citizenship to non-white persons in the northern part of the Louisiana Purchase.

Taney's ruling was essentially opinion, with virtually no constitutional basis, as the Constitution says nothing about race as a qualification for citizenship and the Northwest Ordinance predated the Constitution by several years. Moreover, the decision also negated the Compromise of 1850.

Celebrated as a victory by the Slavocrats, in the Free States, Taney's ruling was viewed as unconstitutional and a gross violation both of states' rights and civil liberties. Arguably, Taney made slavery legal everywhere: what happened if a slave owner settled in a Free State with his "property"?—a frightening prospect for poor working class whites, who might otherwise have been indifferent or even hostile to abolition. Although Taney sought to settle the issue of slavery for all time, he only made things worse.

John Brown's raid

On October 16, 1859, radical abolitionist John Brown (1800–59), who had acquired a reputation for brutality fighting the equally brutal pro-slavery elements in Kansas, attempted to spark a massive slave uprising across the South. With twenty-one followers, including five African Americans and three of his sons, he attacked Harper's Ferry, in western Virginia, quickly capturing much of the town, taking some hostages and collecting arms, at the cost of three local men killed, one a free African American. But if Brown was right about the need to abolish slavery, he was severely mistaken about the means to attain that end. Brown's choice of Harper's Ferry to start his rebellion was less than ideal; there were relatively few slaves in the vicinity, and those were mostly domestic servants or craft workers, rather than brutalized masses of field hands on vast plantations possibly willing to make a desperate bid for freedom. Although Frederick Douglass found the plan foolish, Brown did attract the backing of some white radical abolitionists. Brown also totally underestimated the speed with which the local authorities could mobilize lawmen and militiamen to suppress any outbreak. His uprising proved a disaster.

Aside from two male slaves who joined Brown's band—or were coerced into joining—the attack attracted no support from the local African American population, while local whites quickly armed themselves and offered resistance, and were soon reinforced by local militiamen. By the morning of the 17th, more militia companies arrived, with still more expected, and Brown, realizing there was no escape, withdrew his band into the building housing the Federal arsenal's fire engine, to make a stand.

Meanwhile, overnight, word of the incident had reached Washington. On orders from President James Buchanan, Lt. Col. Robert E. Lee,

Dred Scott, in an engraving made for The Century Magazine, 1887. (Library of Congress)

Chief Justice Roger Taney, in a Brady image taken sometime between 1855 and his death in 1864. (Library of Congress)

in town on private business, took command of a detachment of U.S. Marines and, accompanied by several other officers, headed for Harper's Ferry by train. Arriving there on the 17th, Lee tried to negotiate with Brown, but then ordered the Marines to storm the Engine House. Almost all of Brown's men were killed or captured, at the cost of two Marines wounded, one of whom later died. Lee directed security operations around Harper's Ferry for several days. Of twenty-three raiders, ten were killed during the raid, including Brown's two eldest sons, and eight (including Brown) were captured in the Engine House or shortly afterwards, while five escaped completely, including Brown's third son, all of whom subsequently served in the Union Army.

Brown and the other captured raiders were found guilty of treason against the Commonwealth of Virginia, first-degree murder, and inciting servile insurrection and were sentenced to death. On December 2, 1859, after delivering an eloquent indictment of slavery and a prediction of more bloodshed to follow, John Brown was hanged at Charlestown, VA.

Brown's raid and his subsequent execution caused much ink to be spilled. Although some abolitionists praised him, in general most people, including most abolitionists, condemned him for resorting to violence, which, many argued, rightfully, only hardened the slaveholders' resolve. Just days after Brown's hanging, the Alabama legislature authorized the raising of 8,000 volunteers and establishment of a military college, arsenal, powder works, and munitions factory, ostensibly to prepare the state to suppress slave rebellions, even if they occurred beyond the state—measures soon matched by other states, including Mississippi and Virginia—which were violations of Article I, Section 10 of the Constitution, barring states from keeping "Troops ... of War in time of Peace," and were arguably a deliberate step in anticipation of secession.[17]

"The Portent"

Brown inspired an interesting meditative poem by Herman Melville (1819–91). Melville had gained fame as the author of the novels *Typee* (1846) and *Omoo* (1847), his memoir of service in the U.S. Navy, *White*

Jacket (1850), and some short stories. But when *Moby Dick* came out in 1851, it met with a cool reception, and his subsequent works did poorly as well. By the time Brown and his band descended on Harper's Ferry, Melville was working as a customs inspector in New York. During the war, Melville wrote a number of poems, which were published in 1866 as *Battle-Pieces and Aspects of the War*, with a dedication: "To the Memory of the Three Hundred Thousand Who in the War For the Maintenance of the Union Fell Devotedly Under the Flag of Their Country." The collection opens with "The Portent," on John Brown.

John Brown, without the iconic beard, which he only grew to help disguise himself during the preparations for the attack on Harper's Ferry. (National Archives)

The Portent
(1859)

Hanging from the beam,
   Slowly swaying (such the law),
Gaunt the shadow on your green,
   Shenandoah!
The cut is on the crown
   (Lo, John Brown),
And the stabs shall heal no more.

Hidden in the cap
   Is the anguish none can draw;
So your future veils its face,
   Shenandoah!
But the streaming beard is shown
   (Weird John Brown),
The meteor of the war.[18]

Although dated 1859, "The Portent" was written during the Civil War, as suggested by the reference to the ominous fate of the Shenandoah Valley, in which armies in blue and gray would fight and march back and forth for nearly 4 years.

Battle-Pieces and Aspects of the War received mixed reviews, and sold poorly (only 486 copies in its first two years), not enough to cover half the publishing costs. In a rather sympathetic obituary of Melville on October 2, 1891, *The New York Times* noted that the work "fell flat," and added that despite the merits of his early sea stories, Melville "has died an absolutely forgotten man." As with *Moby Dick*, the true worth of *Battle-Pieces and Aspects of the War* would not be recognized until long after Melville's death.

Signs of the times

From the inception of the transatlantic slave trade in the early sixteenth century to its abolition in the mid-19th, between 12.5 million and 17.5 million Africans were kidnapped to the Americas, of whom about 12 percent died during the voyage. Most of these people were landed in the Caribbean or South America, but an estimated 500,000 or so landed in areas that eventually constituted the United States.

Early in the eighteenth century, South Carolina's militia law required service by able-bodied black men, free or slave, the latter to serve in companies commanded by their masters (who would receive their pay and be compensated their purchase price if they died in service), a requirement that was abolished after Cato's Conspiracy.[19]

After executing Nat Turner for his role in the Great Southampton Slave Revolt of 1830, the Commonwealth of Virginia paid the estate of his late master $375 for the loss of "property," equivalent to perhaps $100,000 today on the "unskilled labor" scale.[20]

Although John C. Calhoun, arguably the father of secession, and other states' rights champions claimed that tariffs favored Northern industries, thus supposedly harming Southerners by forcing them to pay more for foreign goods, they were notably silent about tariffs that protected Southern products such as cotton, tobacco, rice, and sugar, imports of which were taxed at 30 percent or more, rising to an amazing 375 percent for some items, such as sugar candies.[21]

During its brief existence, the Republic of Texas (1835–45) ran up a national debt of almost $12.5 million, nearly as much as the U.S. had accumulated since 1775, approximately $15.9 million, which was assumed by the U.S. government under the Compromise of 1850; the U.S. per capita debt in 1845 was about $0.81, that for Texas about $100, equal to about ten weeks' pay for a master carpenter in New England.[22]

On Monday, September 3, 1838, wearing sailor's clothing and using a borrowed set of seaman's papers the identified him as an American citizen, Frederick Douglass "stole" himself from his master by the simple expedient of taking a train from Baltimore to Wilmington, DE, and a steam ferry to Philadelphia and freedom.[23]

Jefferson Davis once armed a group of slaves as part of a posse against a gang of white marauders who were raiding plantations in western Mississippi, demonstrating a curious loophole in the otherwise stringent Southern restrictions regarding slaves and weapons, and blacks harming whites.[24]

In 1841, Solomon Northup (c. 1808–c. 1863), a freeborn black New Yorker, was kidnapped into slavery in Louisiana, until identified and rescued in 1853, about which he wrote in *Twelve Years a Slave*. The latter was made into a motion picture in 2013, with Chiwetel Ejiofor and Benedict Cumberbatch, which won three Academy Awards.[25]

Formed in 1846 from some 550 or so members of the Latter Day Saints, the Mormon Battalion—the only religiously segregated unit in American military history—marched from Fort Leavenworth to San Diego, nearly 2,000 miles across Kansas, New Mexico, and Arizona, to support the conquest of California from Mexico.[26]

In 1847, while on his way to organize the invasion of Mexico, Winfield Scott dallied in New Orleans long enough to be beaten at chess by one Paul Morphy, which did not go down at all well with the General-in-Chief, as his opponent was only 9.[27]

Frederick Douglass (1818–95), fugitive slave, crusading journalist, influential abolitionist, and presidential counselor. (National Archives)

Harriet Beecher Stowe, author of Uncle Tom's Cabin, *which so enraged the slaveholders that Lincoln called her "the little lady who made this big war." (National Archives)*

At the end of the Mexican-American War, Maj. Gen. Winfield Scott wrote a commendation for 1st Lt. Ulysses S. Grant, which was delivered by 1st Lt. John Pemberton. The two later met again in different circumstances at Vicksburg on July 4, 1863, when Pemberton, a Confederate lieutenant general, surrendered the city and his army to Grant, a Union major general.

After escaping from slavery in Maryland in 1849, Harriet Tubman (c. 1822–1913) made thirteen expeditions into the South, bringing out at least 70 people and possibly more than 300, while providing advice that permitted the escape of several score more. Slave-owners put rewards of as much as $12,000 for her capture, the equivalent of 40 years income for most Americans of the day.[28]

Published in 1852, Harriet Beecher Stowe's *Uncle Tom's Cabin* sold 300,000 copies in its first year in print, and another 100,000 over the following 6 months, sales that even today would make it a best seller.

During the Kansas troubles, radical abolitionists shipped arms to anti-slavery settlers in Kansas in crates bearing innocuous labels

Harriet Tubman, in an image made about 10 years after the Civil War by photographer Harvey B. Lindsley. (Library of Congress)

such as "tools," "machinery," and even "books," prompting wags to nickname the Sharps rifle the "Beecher's Bible," because New England clergyman Henry Ward Beecher had said "there was more moral power in one of those instruments, so far as the slaveholders of Kansas are concerned, than in a hundred Bibles."[29]

By 1860, about 13 percent of the population of the U.S. was foreign born, of whom more than half had arrived since 1850. Nearly half of the residents of New York, Chicago, and St. Louis were foreign born, as were about a quarter of those of New Orleans, most being Irish or German.[30]

Although today largely forgotten—or deliberately ignored— religious and ethnic bigotry was common in the antebellum era. From the end of the War for Independence through the eve of the Civil War, there were more than fifty riots in New York State alone in which "Nativists"—Protestant Anglo-Saxons—attacked immigrants, particularly Germans and Irish, who were often Catholics as well, and the record in other states was no better.[31]

Between 1810 and 1860, the Royal Navy captured some 1,500 slave ships in the Atlantic, liberating an estimated 160,000 people, while from 1819 the U.S. Navy captured more than 100 slavers, freeing about 10,000 people.[32]

For tax purposes, on the eve of the Civil War, Virginia assessed property at $4 per $1,000 of valuation, except for "animate property," including horses, cows, hogs, and slaves, assessed at $1.20 per $1,000 of valuation.[33]

By 1861, the average price for a slave in the United States was $800, easily equivalent to about $150,000 today, with even small children priced at as much as $400.[34]

In the antebellum South, slave ownership was far more pervasive than capitalist enterprise in America during the 1950s, when only 2 percent of American families owned corporate stocks equal in value to the comparable purchasing power of the average price for a slave in 1860 (when about a third of Southern families owned slaves, amounting to about 10 percent of all American families).[35]

CHAPTER 2

From Secession to Civil War

By the late 1850s, tensions over slavery had risen to the point where violence between pro- and anti-slavery advocates was commonplace, with virtual open warfare in Kansas. Even Congress was not immune. On May 22, 1856, South Carolina Representative Preston S. Brooks, entered the Senate chamber, and brutally beat Massachusetts Senator Charles Sumner with a cane for an alleged "insult" offered to his cousin, Senator Andrew Butler of South Carolina, during a speech. Sumner was seated at the time, and two other Southern congressmen kept people from rendering him aid. Brooks was widely praised across the allegedly "Gallant South".

When the 36th Congress convened, in December 1859, sectional tensions were so high that Senator James Hammond of South Carolina claimed, "Every man on the floor of both Houses is armed with a revolver, some with two revolvers and a Bowie knife."[1] The following year, 1860, was a presidential election year.

The election of 1860

Arguably, the outcome of the election was decided not at the ballot box, but at the Democratic nominating convention, because tensions over slavery led to the dissolution of the Democratic Party. The most prominent Democrat, Senator Stephen A. Douglas (1813–61) of Illinois, was generally regarded as the front-runner for the nomination. A "moderate" on

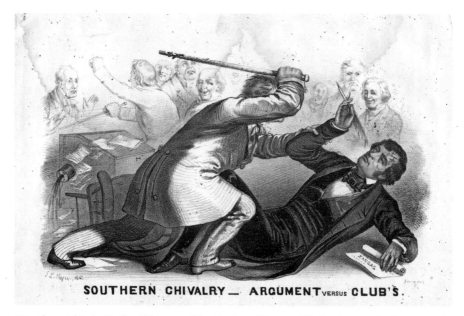

SOUTHERN CHIVALRY — ARGUMENT versus CLUB'S.

"Southern Chivalry," a fanciful image of the Caning of Senator Charles Sumner by Representative Preston Brooks. The image correctly depicts Brooks' henchmen wielding canes to keep anyone from aiding Sumner, but fails to show that the senator was trapped by his desk and unable to offer resistance. (Library of Congress)

slavery, Douglas was a major supporter of "popular sovereignty." During the famous series of senatorial election debates with Abraham Lincoln in 1858, however, Douglas had expressed some reservations about the Dred Scott decision, making him unpopular with the pro-slavery element in the party. So, even before the Democratic national convention met in Charleston, South Carolina, on April 23, 1860, pro-slavery "Fire-Eater" William Yancey (1814–63) of Alabama convened a clandestine meeting of the delegates from Alabama, Arkansas, Florida, Georgia, Louisiana, Mississippi, and Texas to organize a "stop Douglas" movement.

Under the influence of Yancey and other Fire-Eaters, the party platform committee produced a strongly pro-slavery program. Northern delegates pointed out that the platform would cost the party the election, and on April 30 proposed an alternative which omitted the pro-slavery planks. This was adopted by a vote of 165 to 138, and it split the party, as fifty slave-state delegates left, including every one from Alabama, Florida, Georgia, Louisiana, Mississippi, and Texas, to hold their own convention elsewhere in the city.

The remaining delegates, still a majority of the party's representatives, attempted to nominate a presidential candidate. But after fifty-seven ballots, in all of which Douglas led, with a decided, but never decisive margin, on May 3 the convention adjourned, to meet again in Baltimore 6 weeks later.

Meanwhile, on May 9, the newly formed Constitutional Union Party held its convention, in Baltimore, and nominated for president Senator John Bell (1796–1869) of Tennessee, a strongly Unionist former Whig, on a platform apparently designed to neither offend nor please anyone. A week later, the Republicans gathered in Chicago for their own convention. There were several prospective candidates, and New York Senator William Seward (1801–72) led on the first two ballots, but was completely edged out by Illinois attorney Abraham Lincoln on the third. The convention wrapped up its business in just 3 days, adjourning on the 18th.

That same June 18, the Democrats reconvened in Baltimore, but many delegates from the South promptly seceded, to hold their own convention. So, while Douglas was nominated by a wide majority of the official convention, in another part of Baltimore the dissident Southern delegates nominated Vice President John C. Breckinridge (1821–75) for president, with a platform that even included the reopening of the African slave trade.

On election day, November 6, 1860, the turnout was 81.2 percent, the highest ever attained to that time.[2] Abraham Lincoln lost the popular vote by a wide margin, but won in the Electoral College, thus becoming president-elect.

Table 1: November 1860 election

Candidate	Popular vote	States	Electors
Lincoln	1,865,908 (39.8 percent)	18	180
Breckinridge	848,019 (18.1 percent)	11	72
Bell	590,901 (12.6 percent)	3	39
Douglas	1,380,202 (29.5 percent)	1	12

Had the Democrats not split over the question of slavery, Stephen A. Douglas would almost certainly have been elected President in 1860. So in breaking the Democratic Party over the issue of slavery, the Slavocrats insured the election of a man they perceived as strongly anti-slavery.

From secession to the Confederacy

Lincoln's election virtually insured secession. Although a moderate on slavery, he was opposed to its expansion (as were most Northern whites even if they were not abolitionists), and hopeful of its ultimate extinction, but did not dispute its legality. Nevertheless, he was considered too radical by the most ardent Slavocrats, to whom any reservations about their "peculiar institution" (the preferred euphemism for slavery) amounted to radical abolitionism.

Secession was—and arguably is—one of the thorniest of constitutional questions. While the Constitution provides for a number of contingencies, such as the formation of new states, or the merger or division of existing ones, it's silent on secession. Some argue that secession is implicit in the Tenth Amendment, which reserves unstated powers to the States, but that would seem to run up against the "Supremacy Clause" of Article VI, which makes the Constitution "the supreme Law of the Land; and the Judges in every State shall be bound thereby, any Thing in the Constitution or Laws of any State to the Contrary notwithstanding." During South Carolina's attempt to "nullify" the tariff in 1832–33, President Andrew Jackson—hardly weak on state rights, arguing that the Constitution was "the perpetual bond of our Union"—secured from Congress authorization to "employ such part of the land or naval forces, or militia of the United States" to enforce the law. Finding no support even among the other Southern states, South Carolina conceded, as Congress enacted a token modification of the tariff.

Nevertheless, pushed by fanatical pro-slavery advocates like John C. Calhoun of South Carolina, Southerners continued to champion the ideas of nullification and secession as legitimate tools for the preservation of the Southern way of life, and in particular its "peculiar institution".

On December 20, 1860, South Carolina—in which slaves outnumbered freemen and nearly half of all free families owned slaves—passed an Ordinance of Secession, followed four days later with a Declaration of Secession, which read in part:[3]

> an increasing hostility on the part of the non-slaveholding States to the institution of slavery ... the election of a man to the high office of President of the United States, whose opinions and purposes are hostile to slavery. He is to be entrusted with the administration of the common Government, because he has declared that that "Government cannot endure permanently half slave, half free," and that the public mind must rest in the belief that slavery is in the course of ultimate extinction.

By February 2, 1861, Mississippi, Florida, Alabama, Georgia, Louisiana, and Texas had followed South Carolina into secession. Five of these states prepared their own justifications for secession. In each case, the perceived threat to the institution of slavery was the primary—usually the only—reason cited for secession. The seven states that seceded during that winter had the highest rate of slave ownership in the nation, averaging 36.7 percent slave-owning families. In both South Carolina and Mississippi, slaves outnumbered free persons of any color, while in Louisiana almost half the population was in slavery; in those three states African Americans, free and slave, outnumbered whites.

When delegates from these states met in Montgomery, Alabama, on February 4, 1861, to create a Confederate States of America, slavery was the fundamental principle of their proposed new government. Where the authors of the Constitution of the United States, embarrassed by the existence of slavery in their new nation, used phrases like "all other persons" (Article I, Section 2, Clause 3) and "Person held to Service or Labour" (Article IV, Section 2, Clause 2) to avoid "slaves" or "slavery," the Founding Fathers of the Confederacy had no such reservations. They wrote a constitution that not only guarantees "the right of property in negro slaves" but bans the "Confederal" government from abolishing that right (Article I, Section 9, Clause 4), and essentially bars individual states from doing so as well (Article IV, Section 1, Clause 2), a gross violation of the vaunted notion of states' rights.

Vice President Alexander H. Stevens of the Confederacy. (National Archives)

Well before the Civil War, Jefferson Davis declared "African slavery, as it exists in the United States, a moral, a social, and a political blessing,"[4] a sentiment repeated on March 21, 1861, shortly after the adoption of the Confederate Constitution, when Alexander Stevens, Provisional Vice President of the Confederate States, said: "Our new government is founded upon exactly the opposite idea [of "all men are created equal"]; its foundations are laid, its cornerstone rests, upon the great truth that the negro is not equal to the white man; that slavery, subordination to the superior race, is his natural and normal condition."[5]

Searching for compromise

As the Secession Crisis deepened, political leaders began making proposals for a compromise that would bring the seceded states back into the fold. During the Congressional session that began in December 1860 and ran through inauguration day (March 4, 1861), some fifty-seven proposed constitutional amendments intended to assuage pro-slavery elements were submitted to Congress, as well as scores of resolutions on the subject. Mississippi Democratic Senator Jefferson Davis, who did not resign from the Senate until January 21, 1861, 12 days *after* his state seceded, proposed one that explicitly protected property rights in slaves.

Kentucky Senator John J. Crittenden (1787–1863) suggested a series of amendments that reaffirmed the 36°30' line between slave and free territories and prohibited Congress from abolishing slavery on federal properties in Slave States, as well as a flock of other measures favorable to the slaveholding interests, including a ban on repeal of the amendment, all of which were rejected by Congress. Even New York Senator William H. Seward, a decidedly anti-slavery man, and Thomas Corwin (1794–1865), a Representative from Ohio, submitted a proposed constitutional amendment reading: "No amendment shall be made to the Constitution which will authorize or give to Congress the power to abolish or interfere, within any State, with the domestic institutions thereof, including that of persons held to labor or service by the laws of said State."

Jefferson F. Davis, a prewar image by Mathew B. Brady. (National Archives)

Although the delegates from the seceded states were missing, Congress approved the proposed amendment and it was submitted to the states for ratification on March 2, 1861, just 2 days before the presidential inauguration; in his inaugural address, Lincoln endorsed the proposal. But ratification required approval by three-fourths of the states, effectively twenty-four out of thirty-four, as the secessionist states were still legally part of the Union. This figure could only attained if the seven secessionist states abandoned secession, joining their votes with those of the eight slave states still loyal and those of any eight Free states, a figure very probably attainable. Since the seceded states did not return to loyalty, what would have been the Thirteenth Amendment never passed.

As the fate of the Corwin Amendment shows, had the secessionist states remained in the Union, they would have continued to hold the balance of power in Congress and with their Northern allies would have been able to block any legislation or constitutional amendment aimed at abolishing slavery. In fact, assuming slavery survived to the present day in the fifteen states in which it existed in 1860, it would still be impossible to pass a constitutional amendment abolishing the institution, since an amendment requires ratification by thirty-eight states.

Reviewing the events, historian Mark L. Lause gave what is perhaps the best summary of how secession came to pass:

> Secession had grown from the fiction that the mere election in 1860 of a president critical of slavery represented an attack on the rights of the slaveholders. The founders of the Confederacy had taken unilateral preemptive action to forestall an anticipated radicalization of the Federal Union on the subject of slavery. Acting on these unrealized fears paradoxically insured their realization.[6]

During President James Buchanan's final months in office, seven states had declared themselves separated from the Union, seized federal installations—forts, customs houses, mints, arsenals, naval bases—and formed a new confederacy, military and naval officers had left the service in droves (and many of those who remained were of suspect loyalties), while secession fever seemed to be growing in the remaining Slave States, and the smell of war was in the air. Buchanan believed secession was unconstitutional, but curiously he did not believe the government had the power to use force to prevent it, despite the Constitution's authority to use military force and the militia "to execute the Laws of the Union, suppress Insurrections and repel Invasions," and the example of Andrew Jackson's stand against nullification. While historians' judgments on Buchanan's are generally harsh, some argue that he tried to keep things calm, rather that take any action that might tie the hands of the incoming administration.

Lincoln assumes the presidency

Lincoln took the inaugural oath on March 4, 1861, under threat of assassination, amidst the greatest security measures ever taken.

Lincoln's principle objective was to preserve the Union, and his actions were based on the premise that secession was unconstitutional and the assumption—albeit an erroneous one—that the mass of Southern citizens were fundamentally loyal and would, in time, return to the Union peacefully. So, he acted with considerable caution. By the time of his inauguration, the several seceded states had already begun raising troops, and on March 6, 1861, just 2 days into his presidency, the Confederate Provisional Congress authorized the Provisional President to call out the militia for 6 months and accept 100,000 one-year volunteers, while establishing a Regular Army of 10,600 men, but Lincoln deliberately avoided initiating any military preparations.[7] He also communicated with political leaders in some of the seceded states, while avoiding direct contact with officials of the Confederate government. Nevertheless, despite his caution, Lincoln was determined to preserve whatever remained of federal authority in the seceded states, which comprised just three isolated forts: Pickens, off Pensacola, Taylor in the Florida Keys, and Sumter in Charleston Harbor. It was at Sumter where things came to a head.

The Capitol was still under construction when Lincoln was inaugurated. Asked if construction should be suspended to save money for the war, he replied: "If people see the Capitol going on, it is a sign we intend the Union shall go on." (Library of Congress)

Fort Sumter

In late 1860, the garrison of the Charleston harbor forts consisted of two companies of the 1st Artillery, altogether ten officers, about sixty-five men, and eight bandsmen, under the overall command of Kentuckian and sometime slave owner Maj. Robert Anderson. Almost all these troops were at Fort Moultrie. When South Carolina seceded, on December 20, state officials and militiamen began occupying federal installations, including the arsenal in Charleston, the Office of the Collector of the Port, post offices, and so forth, and the outlying coast defense installations around Charleston Harbor, which had "garrisons" of as few as one sergeant. Anderson realized that Fort Moultrie, a "water battery" fortified only on the seaward side, was indefensible from land attack. So on the night after Christmas, he moved his troops to Fort Sumter, on a rocky outcrop in the middle of Charleston Harbor. A three-story pentagonal masonry fortress, Sumter been under construction for 32 years, and was only about 80 percent complete, but was already a formidable position, requiring only the mounting of its heavy artillery.[8]

Anderson's move sparked outrage in South Carolina and across the South. The state's governor, Francis W. Pickens, protested to President James Buchanan, who refused to order Anderson back to Moultrie. A stand-off ensued, and as Anderson and his men settled into Sumter, South Carolina militiamen manned forts Moultrie and Pinckney and began erecting additional batteries directed at Sumter.

Although on January 9, 1861 the South Carolina batteries fired on the steamer *Star of the West*, carrying supplies and 250 reinforcements for Sumter, which drew off after being lightly damaged by three hits—traditionally regarded as the "first shots of the Civil War"—the stand-off was otherwise peaceful, and even friendly. The Confederates permitted food to be sent to the fort and kept Anderson's officers supplied with cigars and port, while visitors were allowed to enter, among them various dignitaries and their wives, as before secession Anderson and his officers were distinguished members of Charleston society. One visitor was the major's wife.

A native North Carolinian, Eliza Bayard Anderson (although in poor health) feared for her husband's safety and sought out Peter Hart, a New York City policeman, formerly a sergeant with Anderson's battery in the Mexican-American War, and convinced him to accompany her to South Carolina. Arriving in Charleston by rail, she asked Governor Pickens, a friend of her late father Col. Duncan L. Clinch, for permission to visit her husband, and leave Hart with him. Pickens agreed to her visit, but at refused to let Hart enter the fort, only giving in after she scornfully asked if South Carolina, aspiring to be a sovereign power among the nations of the earth, would be endangered by the addition of one man to so tiny a garrison. Mrs. Anderson had a 2-hour visit with her husband, who was "reinforced" by Peter Hart; during the bombardment, Hart proved invaluable, inspiring the troops, fighting fires, helping mount cannon, and even climbing up a damaged flag pole to restore "Old Glory" to its proper position after it had been knocked down by a shell.[9]

Such friendly relations couldn't last. South Carolina—and the Confederacy—needed Fort Sumter as a symbol of Southern independence, and the Union could not concede it without effectively recognizing that independence. Early in April, Lincoln dispatched two emissaries to inform Governor Pickens that he intended to reprovision Sumter, specifying that neither arms nor troops would be landed. Pickens informed Jefferson Davis.

Davis realized that Lincoln was playing a waiting game. Lincoln wanted to stave off hostilities as long as possible, to keep the northern tier of Slave States—North Carolina, Virginia, Tennessee, Arkansas, Missouri, Maryland, Kentucky, and Delaware—within the Union. While Lincoln believed, erroneously, that most of the citizens of the seceded states were essentially loyal to the Union, and given time would come to their senses and return to the fold peacefully, if things came to a fight, he wanted the onus of starting hostilities firmly on the Confederacy, to unify the North in support of war. Davis was well aware of this. But he also realized that the Confederacy could not be a viable nation without the upper tier of Slave States, and that Sumter raised questions about the legitimacy of the Confederacy's claim to stand among the nations of the earth while a "foreign" fortress stood in one of its premier harbors. Davis ordered Sumter captured as soon as possible.

On April 7, Brig. Gen. Pierre G. T. Beauregard, commanding Confederate troops in Charleston, halted food supplies to the fort. Two days later, the Confederate cabinet endorsed Davis' decision to use force with one dissenting voice: Secretary of State Robert Toombs, as ardent a secessionist as any, objected, presciently saying, "firing on that fort will inaugurate a civil war greater than any the world has yet seen ... It will lose us every friend at the North. You will only strike a hornet's nest ... Legions now quiet will swarm out and sting us to death. It is unnecessary. It puts us in the wrong. It is fatal."[10]

Major Anderson rejecting the Confederate demand for the surrender of Ft. Sumter.

The interior of Fort Sumter, in an image reportedly taken on April 14, 1861, shortly after the surrender, with the "Stars and Bars" on the flag pole. (National Archives)

On April 11, Beauregard dispatched emissaries with an ultimatum demanding that Anderson surrender or hostilities would commence. Anderson refused to do so. Shortly before midnight, Beauregard dispatched Col. James Chesnut (former governor of Virginia and husband of the later famous diarist Mary Chesnut), Capt. Stephen D. Lee (later a lieutenant general, who had carried the earlier message to the fort), and Col. Alexander R. Chisolm to inform Anderson that unless he surrendered, the bombardment would commence immediately. Arriving at the fort shortly after midnight on the 12th, they handed Anderson their message. He managed to delay his response until 3:15 a.m., when he replied negatively. Told the bombardment would begin in an hour, according to Col. Chisolm, Anderson replied, "Gentlemen, I shall await the first shot, and if you do not batter us to pieces, we shall be starved out in a few days," a comment that was totally disregarded.[11]

The bombardment of Sumter began at 4:30 a.m. on April 12, shortly after which the first of the supply ships arrived off the harbor entrance, to lie offshore as thousands of rounds began raining down on the fort. Anderson agreed to surrender on the 14th.

Lincoln's call for volunteers

On April 15, 1861, even as the formal surrender of Fort Sumter was taking place, Lincoln issued a call for 75,000 volunteers.[12] Proponents of secession asserted that Lincoln had no legal right to issue such a call, but in his proclamation, he echoed the words of the Constitution, which recognizes the possibility of "rebellion" or "insurrection" against the United States, authorizes Congress to establish a process for "calling forth the Militia to execute the Laws of the Union, suppress Insurrections, and repel Invasion" and appoints the President as "Commander in Chief" of "the Militia of the several States, when called into the actual Service of the United States." These provisions were codified in the Militia Acts of 1792 and 1795, the later of which reads in part:

> whenever the laws of the United States shall be opposed, or the execution thereof obstructed, in any state, by combinations too powerful to be suppressed by the ordinary course of judicial proceedings, or by the powers vested in the marshals

by this act, it shall be lawful for the President of the United States to call forth the militia of such state, or of any other state or states, as may be necessary to suppress such combinations, and to cause the laws to be duly executed; and the use of militia so to be called forth may be continued, if necessary, until the expiration of thirty days after the commencement of the then next session of Congress.

Oddly, when Lincoln issued his call for troops, he did not cite the previous occasions when a president made use of this authority, notably the Whiskey Rebellion of 1794, the Louisiana Purchase of 1803, and the *Caroline* Affair and Canadian border disorders of 1837–39.

Since the 36th Congress (1859–61) had adjourned shortly after his inauguration, in accordance with the requirements of the Militia Act, Lincoln called for Congress to convene on July 4, "to consider and determine such measures as in their wisdom the public safety and interest may seem to demand." The date was dictated by the fact that, depending on the state, elections for the 37th Congress, to sit in 1861–63, had begun in August 1860 and in some cases could not be completed until September 1861, since Congress did not normally convene until December.

Of course, even though Lincoln's call for volunteers was legal, it was rejected by most of the Slave States still in the Union.

The North rallies around the flag

Although strongly Unionist, most Northerners seem to have been uncertain as to what to do about Secession. Even Horace Greeley, editor of the *New-York Daily Tribune* and a devout abolitionist, said, "Let them go," adding: "we do not see how we could take the other side without coming in direct conflict with those Rights of Man which we hold paramount to all political arrangements."[13] But the firing on Fort Sumter changed that. As John Adams Dix, an old soldier who had served as Buchanan's Secretary of the Treasury during the Secession Winter and returned to duty during the Civil War put it in his memoirs:

It is by no means improbable that if a separation had been sought by the slave-holding States persistently, and through peaceful means alone, it might have been ultimately conceded by the Northern States in preference to a bloody civil war, with all its miseries and demoralization. But the forcible seizure of arsenals, mints, revenue-cutters, and other property of the common government, and the attack and capture of Fort Sumter, put an end to argument as well as to the spirit of conciliation, and aroused a feeling of exasperation which nothing but the arbitrament of arms could overcome.[14]

The "firing on the flag" at Sumter caused an almost universal outpouring of patriotic ardor. Over 92,000 men responded to Lincoln's call on the states for 75,000 volunteers, and that despite the fact that only Delaware and Missouri of the eight still loyal Slave States supplied any troops at all; Lincoln's follow-up call for 500,000 more troops, on May 3, 1861, ultimately yielded over 700,000 men.

Although secession had troubled many in the Free States, the South had some staunch friends in the North, such as senators Benjamin F. Butler of Massachusetts, long a political ally of Jefferson Davis, and John A. McClernand and John A. Logan of Illinois, as well as New York City Mayor Fernando Wood, who during the Secession Winter had proposed his city secede and grow rich trading between North and South. Ardent secessionists believed that Northern Democrats, long favorable to "Southern Rights," would oppose efforts to suppress secession by force. This proved not to be the case. The "firing on the flag" revealed that most Southern sympathizers in the North were ardent Unionists.

What the secessionists missed was that the Southern-sympathizing Northern politicians and the people who voted for them saw the Union as more important than slavery. During the debate over the Compromise of 1850, President Millard Fillmore wrote to abolitionist Daniel Webster: "God knows I detest slavery, but it is an existing evil, for which we are not responsible, and we must endure it and give it such protection as is guaranteed by the constitution, till we get rid of it without destroying the last hope of free government in the world."[15] Benjamin Butler, criticized for supporting Davis' candidacy for the Democratic presidential nomination in 1860, would later write, "I voted for Davis in 1860 with the intent to preserve the Union, believing him disinclined to support secession."[16] Once the South chose to break the Union over slavery, the sympathies of most of the pro-Southern Northerners turned firmly to the preservation of the Union, and men such as Fillmore, Butler, Logan, McClernand, and Wood supported Lincoln's effort to restore the Union by force of arms.

Similarly, many in the South believed Northern financial interests would support them. After all, Northern banks profited greatly from the cotton business, at times even providing covert financing for illegal slave smuggling, and had made enormous investments in the South in the form of loans. Although there is considerable uncertainly as to the extent of Southern indebtedness to the North at the beginning of the war—estimates range from $200 million to $500 million—secessionist "Fire-Eaters" believed the banks would hardly wish to put such enormous sums at risk by opposing Southern separatism. But the secessionists lost that support fairly quickly. Even before secession, some Northern bankers, fearing that with secession would come repudiation of debts owed them, seem to have been cutting back on loans to the South. The seceding states all prohibited repayment of loans to the North, pledging resumption of payment upon recognition of their independence by the United States, but there was no guarantee that the South would honor this promise, and as *The New York Times* reported, fearing devastating financial loss, Northern banks and financiers rallied to the Union. On April 19, 1861, the New York City Chamber of Commerce passed a resolution calling for donations to support the war effort, and within 10 minutes the members present had donated $21,000, arguably more than $8 million today based on comparable standards of wealth, and by the end of the year banks in the city had lent Uncle Sam more than $200 million.[17]

The border states

Lincoln's call for volunteers precipitated the secession of Virginia on April 17, followed by Arkansas, North Carolina, and finally Tennessee, while Maryland, Kentucky, and Missouri wavered in their loyalty. In some of these states there was considerable popular support for secession, but in others secession was achieved through chicanery and terror, while in others secession failed.[18]

Virginia

A secesson resolution had been defeated weeks before Sumter by a special convention. On Lincoln's call for troops the delegates reconvened, on April 17, and opted for secession pending ratification by the voters. But by then, the state had already been taken out of the Union by a *coup d'état*. On April 16, former Governor Henry Wise directed a cabal of secessionist officials and militiamen to seize the arsenal at Harper's Ferry and the Navy Yard in Norfolk. On May 7, 1861, Virginia was admitted to the Confederacy, which immediately transferred its capital to Richmond. By the time the secession referendum was held on May 23, Virginia was already firmly in the Confederate camp. About 155,000 Virginians fought for the Confederacy, while about 33,000 white and at least 6,000 black Virginians fought for the Union.

Arkansas

Amidst widespread pro-secessionist violence, including an attempt to seize the federal arsenal at Little Rock, a specially elected convention voted against secession by a narrow margin, deferring the question to a referendum to be held in August. On Lincoln's call for volunteers and the governor's rejection of it, the convention reconvened on May 6, and voted almost unanimously for secession. The August referendum was never held. About 45,000 Arkansans fought for the Confederacy, and more than 8,000 white and at least 5,500 black Arkansans fought for the Union.

North Carolina

An election on February 28, 1861 rejected holding a secession convention, but by only about 650 votes out of 94,000. A new election held after Lincoln's call for volunteers yielded 120 delegates (100 of whom were slave owners, with an average of twenty-one human beings listed as their property) for a convention on May 20, and they voted unanimously for secession, rejecting a proposal for a popular vote. About 127,000 North Carolinians fought for the Confederacy, while about 3,000 white and at least 5,000 black North Carolinians fought for the Union.[19]

Tennessee

In January, ardent secessionist Governor Isham G. Harris called for elections to hold a secession convention, openly abetted secessionist harassment of Unionists, which caused many to flee the state (nearly a quarter of the 22,623 residents of Memphis among them), ordered the militia to seize federal installations, and dispatched delegates to the Confederate government. Following Sumter, Harris rejected Lincoln's call for volunteers, and on May 6 the legislature voted for secession, which was confirmed by popular vote on June 8. About 115,000 Tennesseans fought for the Confederacy, while 31,000 white and 20,000 black Tennesseans fought for the Union.[20]

Delaware

With only a handful of slaves (c. 1,800 out of an African American population of about 20,000), and a decidedly Unionist governor, the legislature overwhelmingly defeated a proposal to secede and never wavered. About 11,250 white and about 1,000 black Delawareans fought for the Union, and about 1,200 for the Confederacy.

Maryland

Although mostly Unionist, secessionists dominated the eastern regions, which included the capital, Annapolis, and largest city, Baltimore, where pro-slavery mobs attacked troops en route to Washington, notably on April 18 and 19, 1861, which resulted in bloodshed when the 6th Massachusetts retaliated. The governor cut rail lines to the north of Baltimore to prevent movement of Union volunteers to Washington, but under orders from General-in-Chief Winfield Scott, Massachusetts's Brig. Gen. Benjamin Butler, moving by ferry on the Chesapeake Bay, occupied Annapolis with Northern militiamen, opening a safe route for reinforcements to reach the capital, and in May quietly took control of Baltimore. Lincoln suspended habeas corpus in portions of Maryland, notably along the rail lines north, and later detained some members of the state legislature thought to be plotting a secessionist coup. A meeting of the legislature in Unionist Frederick, rather than Annapolis, voted unanimously against secession. Some 20,000 white Marylanders may have joined the Confederacy, while nearly 34,000 fought for the Union, as did over 8,500 black Marylanders.

Missouri

Governor Claiborne Fox Jackson called for a vote to hold a state secession convention on his first day in office, January 3. The vote went heavily against secession, but many delegates were "Conditional Unionists," wishing to wait and see how the national crisis worked out.

The 6th Massachusetts retaliates against secessionist rioters in Baltimore, April 19, 1861.

Agitation over secession spawned violence, as secessionists, supported by the governor, and Unionists, who included many slave owners and most of the state's large German immigrant population, began arming. After Sumter, Jackson rejected Lincoln's call for volunteers, entered into secret correspondence with Jefferson Davis, and planned to take Missouri out of the Union in a coup by selected elements of the militia and hastily organized volunteers. Regular Army Capt. Nathaniel Lyon, dispatched by Secretary of War Simon Cameron to supersede the irresolute and superannuated Brig. Gen. William S. Harney, armed Unionist volunteers, secured federal installations, and even captured the secessionist volunteers encamped near St. Louis, with some deaths. Backed by some regulars and many volunteers, Lyon proceeded to take control of much of the state, including the capital, Jefferson City, where a Unionist government was installed. In October, Governor Jackson and a rump faction of the state legislature issued a declaration of secession, and the Confederacy admitted Missouri as a state, but only 30,000–40,000 white Missourians entered Confederate service, while about 150,000 served the Union as volunteers or militiamen, as well as some 8,000 black men from the state.

Kentucky

Given the state's strongly Unionist population, pro-slavery Governor Beriah Magoffin, offered "compromises" during the Secession Crisis, all of which would have given the Slave States a veto over national policy, and responded to Lincoln's call for volunteers by wiring, "I will send not a man nor a dollar for the wicked purpose of subduing my sister Southern states." He declared the state's neutrality, a policy supported by elder statesman and sometime U.S. Attorney General John J. Crittenden and many others. This arguably suited both sides; from Lincoln's perspective it kept the state in the Union, which he considered a major strategic objective ("I hope to have God on my side, but I must have Kentucky"), while for the Confederacy it constituted a buffer that protected Tennessee and the Southern heartland from Union military movements south from Ohio, Indiana, and Illinois. Both sides engaged in covert recruiting in the state, while concentrating forces on its frontiers.

Elections for Congress in June and the state legislature in August returned heavily Unionist delegations. With prospects for secession fading, on September 4, 1861, Confederate Maj. Gen. Leonidas Polk invaded Kentucky from Tennessee, capturing Columbus, which prompted the then obscure Brig. Gen. Ulysses S. Grant, commanding at Cairo, IL, to occupy Paducah on the 6th. The next day, the legislature ordered the Confederates out of the state, putting Kentucky in the Unionist camp. Although on November 18, 1861, a kangaroo legislature enacted an ordinance of secession, and the Confederate Congress formally claimed Kentucky as a state, only about 25,000—some estimates put it as high as 50,000—white Kentuckians fought for the Confederacy, while some 75,000 white and nearly 25,000 African American Kentuckians served the Union.

Secession and the Army and Navy

In late 1860, the United States had two military services, the Army and the Navy, the latter including a small Marine Corps. In addition, there was the paramilitary Revenue Marine or Revenue Cutter Service, primarily a customs enforcement and anti-piracy agency, and the Light House Service and the Coast Survey, essentially civilian agencies partially officered by military and naval officers. Together, these totaled about 2,400 officers and nearly 25,000 other ranks.[21]

Many of the officers were quite old, as there was no retirement system; John de Barth Walbach, a veteran of the French Army, had joined the U.S. Army in 1799 and died on active duty as colonel and commander of the 4th Artillery in 1857, at the age of 93.

The Army

There were 1,080 officers on active duty at the onset of the "Secession Winter," plus about 15,000 enlisted men. The Army had ten regiments of infantry, five of mounted troops, four of artillery, plus a small engineering component and a number of staff corps. On the eve of the war, 183 of the 198 companies (92.4 percent) in the Army were stationed west of the Mississippi, so that there was one regular soldier for every 120 square miles west of the great river, but only one for every 1,300 square miles east of it. Despite the motion picture industry, although some of these men had Southern roots, most had been recruited in the North, and about half of all recruits for the Army from about the Mexican-American War onwards were Irish or German immigrants.[22] Of the officers, 821 (76 percent) had been commissioned from West Point, and 259 (24 percent) had received direct commissions from civil life, a ratio of approximately 3:1.

Four hundred and sixty of the officers were from Slave States, of whom 330 had entered the service through West Point (c. 72 percent), and 130 (c. 28 percent) by direct commission, including the army's most senior officer, Maj. Gen. Winfield Scott, a ratio of 2.5:1.

Six hundred and twenty of the officers were from Free States, approximately 62 percent, of whom 491 (c. 60 percent), were commissioned via West Point and 129 (40 percent) from civil life, a ratio of 3.8:1.

Secession resulted in the separation of 313 officers from the Army, slightly less than 30 percent, either by resignation or dismissal for desertion or other causes. Only sixteen of these officers were Northerners, all West Point graduates who had married into Southern families. The other 297 were Southerners, of whom 168 were West Point graduates and 129 had been commissioned from civil life. While only one Southern-born officer commissioned from civil life remained loyal, General-in-Chief Scott, nearly half of Southern graduates from West Point did so.

Not all of the officers who left the Army during the Secession Crisis and early days of the war fought for the Confederacy. Some took advantage of Congress's passage of a retirement act in 1861, while others were unwilling to either fight for or against the "Old Flag" or had been disgraced for peculation or other crimes.

The enlisted men were far more likely to remain loyal to the Union than their officers. During the Secession Winter and early months of the war, there were several army posts on the frontier that were devoid of officers due to resignations, which nevertheless continued to function under the command of senior non-commissioned officers. Perhaps 500 Army-enlisted men deserted to join the Confederacy, about three percent, including some captured in Texas at the start of the war and coerced into Confederate service, many of whom deserted back to the Union at the first opportunity.

The Navy

On the eve of the war, the Navy had 1,094 officers of the line, engineering, or the staff, including commissioned midshipmen, who would today be ranked as ensigns, and about 7,600 enlisted men. As in the Army, most of the enlisted men were of northern origins, and many were immigrants. Of the officers, 243 resigned or were dismissed from the service, about 22 percent, but only 126 of these men served the Confederacy, as some of those who left the service did so by reason of age or health, and a number actually ended up serving in the Union's Volunteer Army.

Of the 253 officers of Southern origins in the Navy, 126 (48 percent) resigned to join the Confederacy, a rate significantly lower than that for southern-born army officers (c. 64 percent).

Of 257 Acting Midshipmen (i.e. cadets) at Annapolis, 111 resigned or were dismissed (42 percent), but only seventy-seven entered Confederate service, many of the remaining thirty-four entering the Volunteer Army or the Volunteer Navy as officers.

An unknown number of enlisted naval personnel eventually joined the Confederacy. But enlisted service in the Navy was different from that in the Army—men almost always were enlisted for a cruise, rather than a set period of years—so it's difficult to determine how many active enlisted men joined the Confederacy.

The Marine Corps

Legally a branch of the Navy, there were only forty-eight officers and about 1,000 enlisted men in the Marines. Of the officers, twenty-seven (c. 56 percent), left the service. Three of these men entered the Union's Volunteer Army, twenty-one entered Confederate service, mostly in the Confederate States Marine Corps, but several in the Provisional Army, one of whom, erstwhile 1st Lt. William W. Kirkland (1833–1915), became a brigadier general, while three men retired to civil life.

A handful of enlisted marines entered Confederate service.

The Revenue Marine, Light House Service, and Coast Survey.

The Revenue Marine and the Light House Service, precursors of the Coast Guard, had some 200 officers and about 1,200 enlisted men on the eve of the war. About sixty (30 percent) of the officers resigned from the service on the outbreak of the war, not all of whom joined the Confederacy, some entering the Union's volunteer services. About a dozen revenue cutters or light house tenders were seized by the secessionist states, some willingly surrendered by their officers. The Coast Survey had several dozen officers seconded from the Army and Navy, all but seven of whom appear to have remained loyal to the Union, and are included in the numbers for their respective services.

Signs of the times

Soon after South Carolina Representative Preston Brooks' brutal beating of abolitionist Senator Charles Sumner on the floor of Congress, he was publicly insulted by Representative Anson Burlingame of Massachusetts, and demanded satisfaction, to which the latter readily agreed. The duel never took place, however, because Brooks learned that Burlingame was a crack shot, and the "gallant" Southern gentleman chickened out.[23]

Until late in the nineteenth century, most Americans voted by "party ballot" issued by a political party, listing its candidates, which the voter deposited in the ballot box. As each party issued ballots in different colors, this meant that one's vote was known to anyone watching, and often led to harassment or even violence at the polls. Not until 1888 did New York and Massachusetts introduce the "Australian ballot," an official state ballot listing all candidates, a practice that spread rapidly across the nation.[24]

Since custom required candidates modestly to refrain from appearing to actually want to be President, when Lincoln went to the polls on November 6, 1860, thinking it inappropriate to vote for himself, on the advice of his law partner William Herndon, he cut the names of the Republican presidential electors off his ballot and voted for the rest of the ticket.[25]

Lincoln received no votes in Alabama, Arkansas, Florida, Georgia, Louisiana, Mississippi, North Carolina, Tennessee, and Texas, as no Republican ballots were distributed in those states, nor in South Carolina, where there was no popular vote for President, the state's electors being picked by the legislature until 1868, during Reconstruction.

Of the four major presidential candidates Abraham Lincoln, Stephen A. Douglas, John C. Breckinridge, and John Bell, only the last carried his home county in the election.[26]

Only three of the eleven clergymen living in Springfield, Illinois, in 1860, voted for Lincoln, a matter which seems to have caused the president-elect some dismay.[27]

The results of a plebiscite on the question of secession held in Georgia on January 2, 1861 were never published, because about 48 percent of the voters opposed leaving the Union, and in some areas as many as 75 percent; the state seceded on January 19.[28]

By curious coincidence, as the Texas Secession Convention convened on January 28, 1861, the U.S. Treasury was making its annual payment toward the retirement of the former Republic's $12.5 million debt, which had been assumed by the federal government as part of the Compromise of 1850.[29]

Reportedly, at one point during the Secession Winter president-elect Lincoln, hearing a rumor that President James Buchanan had ordered Major John Anderson to surrender Fort Sumter if attacked, cried out, "If that is true they ought to hang him!"[30]

Of fifty delegates who participated in the Confederate Constitutional Convention, in Montgomery, AL (February 4–March 11, 1861), forty-nine were slave owners, of whom twenty-one had at least twenty slaves and one had 473.[31]

On February 11, 1861, Abraham Lincoln left his home in Springfield, IL to travel to Washington for his inauguration as President of the United States, while Jefferson Davis left his home, on the Mississippi just south of Vicksburg, to travel to Montgomery, AL, for his inauguration as Provisional President of the Confederate States.

From the election of November 6, 1860 through the inauguration of March 4, 1861, General-in-Chief Winfield Scott received over 130 letters threatening his life should he "allow" Abraham Lincoln to become president.[32]

Reassured of her safety when South Carolina militiamen replaced "Old Glory" over Fort Moultrie with the state's palmetto flag on December 27, 1860, 15-year-old Kate Skillen, daughter of the post custodian, replied: "I am not crying because I am afraid, I am crying because you have put that miserable rag up there."[33]

When Lincoln proposed calling for 75,000 volunteers, Secretary of War Simon Cameron, though widely regarded as both inept and corrupt, urged him to ask for 500,000.[34]

Following Lincoln's initial call for volunteers on April 15, 1861, spontaneous patriotic demonstrations broke out all across the North, so that just 3 days later, *The Detroit Free Press* reported "the supply of bunting is rapidly becoming scarce."[35]

On April 22, 1861, Governer Henry M. Rector of Arkansas replied to Lincoln's call for troops by writing: "In answer to your requisition for troops from Arkansas, to subjugate the Southern

States, I have to say that none will be furnished … The people of this Commonwealth are freemen, not slaves, and will defend to the last extremity their honour, lives, and property against Northern mendacity and usurpation," overlooking the fact that over 25 percent of the people of Arkansas *were* slaves.[36]

During the period of Kentucky's "neutrality," U.S. Army purchasing agents bought mules in the state, regularly paying $125 a head, well above market price, as part of Lincoln's effort to keep the state loyal.[37]

When the Union reoccupied Fort Sumter, on April 15, 1865, Brig. Gen. and brevet Maj. Gen. Robert Anderson raised the same flag that been lowered in surrender 4 years earlier to the day, accompanied by his wife and the faithful Sgt. Peter Hart.

CHAPTER 3

The Civil War in 11,000 Words

With the outbreak of war, men North and South were quick to answer the call, desirous of taking part in the great adventure, whether to save the Union or secure "Southern Rights." Most believed the war would be short. A few suggested in vain that it would be long and hard, among them aged Winfield Scott, hero of the wars of 1812 and with Mexico, now a brevet lieutenant general and still General-in-Chief of the Army.

1861: the beginning

It started in small ways. There were relatively bloody riots in Baltimore (sixteen killed) and St. Louis (around forty-five), and virtually bloodless battles at Fairfax Courthouse (two), Philippi (eight), Big Bethel (nineteen), and Mathias Point (one) in Virginia, and Booneville (ten) and Carthage (about twenty-five) in Missouri. Although the numbers of dead from this fighting pales in comparison to what would come later, they seemed quite high at the time, and many of these small actions were touted as great victories by one side or the other. Meanwhile, large forces were concentrating, notably in the Washington area, in northern Virginia, and in Missouri. The war began begin in earnest on July 21, at Bull Run, a small creek near Manassas in northern Virginia.

Brevet Lt. Gen. Winfield Scott, nicknamed "Old Fuss and Feathers." Scott was old and stout and unable to mount a horse, and although he retired in late 1861, he essentially outlined the strategy that would win the war. (National Archives)

The Confederacy's Gen. Pierre G. T. Beauregard, who had captured Fort Sumter and won the First Battle of Bull Run, was little employed for most of the war, due largely to personal differences with President Jefferson Davis. (National Archives)

The East

Called by William T. Sherman "one of the best planned battles of the war, but one of the worst fought," Bull Run was an ill-managed, hard-fought battle between two hastily assembled armies lacking serious training, extensive experience, or even uniformity of dress, equipment, or drill.[1] Everyone was very green and very brave. Confederate forces under Brig. Gen. Pierre G. T. Beauregard, reinforced to about 32,000 by a timely rail movement of nearly 10,000 men from the Shenandoah Valley—one of the earliest strategic movements by rail in warfare—defeated 35,000 Union troops led by Brig. Gen. Irvin McDowell. Deaths, both sides taken together, totaled some 875, plus some 2,600 wounded, at the time seemingly horrendous losses, but even these casualty rates that would soon be eclipsed by the butcher's bills to come.

In the East, both sides pulled back, the Confederates as disorganized in victory as the Federals in defeat. Each sought to strengthen itself for the future. Though numerous skirmishes would follow in northern Virginia through the end of 1861, there were few operations of importance. Camp and cabinet were where the decisions were being made. A new man became head of the Union forces, Maj. Gen. George B. McClellan, who began to create a real army out of the inchoate mass of volunteers concentrating around Washington, while a scant 50 miles away in Virginia his Confederate counterpart, Gen. Joseph E. Johnston, undertook the same task. The result was the creation of two armies fated to be eternally linked: the Union's Army of the Potomac and the Confederacy's Army of Northern Virginia.

The West

As the armies in the East settled into a quiet routine of drills and exercises punctuated by an occasional skirmish, in the West things grew hotter, with major clashes in Missouri at Wilson's Creek (August 10, 1861)—where the men of the 1st Iowa gallantly held their fire when a brave Texan rode out between the lines to retrieve a fallen flag—and Lexington (September 12–20, 1861) and smaller fights at other places. The Union slowly gained the upper hand, securing control of most of Missouri, while Kentucky, vainly trying to maintain "neutrality," found itself drawn into the struggle by an ill-conceived invasion from the South, which prompted the intervention of Union forces, as Ulysses S. Grant, a former Regular Army officer returned to duty and recently promoted to brigadier general, advanced from Cairo, IL, into the state to capture Paducah without a shot.

It had been a decisive year, 1861, though not as one normally understands "decisive;" neither secession nor slavery were decided, but rather the shape of the war, though many still thought otherwise, would be long, hard, and bloody. Through the winter that followed, men on both sides learned to soldier, in the peculiar half-professional half-amateur fashion that has always characterized the American volunteer, at least initially, until hard campaigning turned him into a veteran.

President Lincoln, Maj. Gen. George B. McClellan, and members of the cabinet, late 1861, from a period engraving.

The waters

Right from the start, both sides quickly began building up their naval forces, the Union starting with a small number of useful ships and many seasoned seamen, while the Confederacy had to build literally from nothing, with only a handful of former naval officers and improvised crews. As the U.S. Navy began somewhat feebly to impose a blockade on the South, the Confederacy began sending privateers and raiders to sea to impede Union commerce. Most importantly, very early, despite the difficulties of expansion, the U.S. Navy in cooperation with the Army, began to flex Uncle Sam's amphibious muscle, with the capture of Hatteras Inlet in North Carolina (August 27–29, 1861), while sustaining the isolated garrisons at Fort Pickens in Pensacola Harbor and Fort Zachary Taylor at Key West.

The diplomatic front

The principal foreign policy goal of the Confederacy was to secure recognition from Britain and France, which might lead to their intervention and ultimately confirm Southern independence. Naturally, the Union was determined to prevent this. Although many in Britain and France, and some other countries, were sympathetic to the Confederacy, at times to the point of violating neutrality, foreign recognition and intervention was never achieved, the closest call occurring in late 1861.

In November 1861, the steam frigate USS *San Jacinto*, commanded by Capt. Charles Wilkes (1798–1877), intercepted the British mail packet *Trent* and removed two Confederate agents who were aboard her, James M. Mason (1798–1871) and John Slidell (1793–1871). Although many in the Union applauded Wilkes, his action violated international law. Despite public outcry on both sides of the Atlantic, and calls for war in some circles in Britain, quiet diplomacy ultimately smoothed away the issue, aided by the intervention of Prince Albert, consort to Queen Victoria, who at his request toned down one British diplomatic message. The State Department shortly notified the British Foreign Secretary that Wilkes had acted without orders, and then the Confederate agents were released to the British on December 26, 1861. Despite this, tempers remained inflamed, especially in Britain, which dispatched troops to Canada—though in a conciliatory gesture, when their passage through the Saint Lawrence River was blocked by ice, Secretary of State William Seward permitted some of them to land in Maine and proceed by rail to Montreal, further diffusing the crisis.

Never again did the Confederacy come so close to securing foreign support, and all hope of such would vanish with the Emancipation Proclamation.

1862: grappling

Both sides prepared for 1862 with enormous energy, improvising great armies, as it was expected that it would be the year of decision. The Union adopted a realistic strategy, first outlined by old Gen. Scott. Derided at the time as the "Anaconda Plan," Scott proposed to strangle the Confederacy with a naval blockade, while one great army advanced down the Mississippi River to cut the Confederacy in two, and another seized Richmond, capital of the rebellion. In a sense, the Confederacy adopted no strategy at all, counting on winning by avoiding defeat—arguably the policy of the American Patriots during the War for Independence. But this required that the Federal forces be beaten back wherever they advanced. In the West, the new armies were largely concentrated in Missouri, Tennessee, and Kentucky, while in the East they concentrated in Virginia and Maryland and around Washington. When the armies began to move in early 1862, the troops on both sides were well equipped with what a later President would call the "instrumentalities of war," but were only half-trained, and led by officers and even generals hardly better prepared, though all were as enthusiastic for a fight as only green troops can be, leading to enormous casualties. Years later, Confederate veteran Lt. Gen. Daniel H. Hill would recall, "We were lavish of blood in those days, and it was thought to be a great thing to charge a battery of artillery or an earthwork lined with infantry."[2]

For the Confederacy, 1862 promised Union offensives on all fronts, but the enlistments of many of the men who had volunteered in 1861 were soon to expire and the flow of volunteers into the ranks had been declining. After much debate, in April the Confederate Congress introduced conscription "for the duration" for all men of military age, and also extended by fiat the enlistments of the men already in the ranks, to a 3-year term, a move that caused some grumbling and desertions, and still later extended them "for the duration."

Although officially only 21 percent of Confederate manpower was obtained through the draft, by legislative fiat the Confederate Congress twice prolonged the enlistments of the volunteers of '61, so in fact the majority of Confederate troops served under compulsion.

The West

An obscure, but able, Union brigadier general named Ulysses S. Grant initiated operations with a successful winter offensive, in cooperation with a small naval squadron. Moving upstream from central Kentucky on the Tennessee and Cumberland rivers into Tennessee, he secured the critical Confederate positions at forts Henry (February 6) and Donelson (February 16), taking thousands of prisoners, and garnering fame as "Unconditional Surrender Grant." Much of western and central Tennessee were quickly cleared of Confederate forces. Advancing south along the Tennessee River, Grant was surprised at Shiloh Church by Confederate troops under Gen. Albert Sidney Johnston on April 6. After a brutal 2-day fight by the largely unseasoned armies, Grant, somewhat reinforced, beat off the attackers. Casualties were enormous, Johnston himself falling at the head of his men.

Some weeks later, on April 25, a Union naval squadron boldly swept up the Mississippi to seize New Orleans. Commanding the squadron was

Flag Officer David Glasgow Farragut, who perched himself in the ship's rigging and through shot and shell urged on his men, crying "Don't flinch from that fire, boys! There's hotter fire than that for those who don't do their duty."[3] With the Union in control of both ends of the great river, the stage was set for an advance that would cut the Confederacy in two.

Following Shiloh, Grant was supplanted in command by Maj. Gen. Henry Halleck, widely respected for his knowledge of military history, theory, and practice. But Halleck lacked the will and skill to put his knowledge to good use. Despite outnumbering Gen. Pierre G. T. Beauregard, the victor of Sumter and Bull Run, by about 120,000 to 65,000, Halleck took a month to capture the critical road junction at Corinth, in northern Mississippi, only

Ulysses S. Grant, who had the most impressive rise of any American, from obscurity to the presidency in just 8 years. This image, by Mathew B. Brady, was taken after he had become famous. (National Archives)

about 20 miles south of Shiloh. Halleck was soon replaced by Grant, who began operations against Vicksburg, a small city high on a bluff at a bend on the east side of the Mississippi, which controlled movement on the river. During the summer and autumn of 1862, Grant essayed several offensives in northern Mississippi, trying to get close to Vicksburg. A series of battles, raids, and skirmishes resulted, in which Confederate Maj. Gen. Earl Van Dorn demonstrated that an overland approach was unworkable by striking at Grant's lines of supply. Grant altered his strategy. In late December, his capable subordinate Maj. Gen. William Tecumseh Sherman advanced down the Mississippi with the idea of landing near Vicksburg and taking the city by storm. The effort failed. But rather than withdraw Sherman's men up river, Grant left them in position on the Mississippi in northern Louisiana, just across from Vicksburg, where they settled down for the winter. Meanwhile, great battles were being fought in the heartland.

General Braxton Bragg was a most contentious Confederate general, though a confidant of Jefferson Davis. (Wikimedia Commons)

Major General William S. Rosecrans, who did well against Bragg, until Chickamauga. (Library of Congress)

During the summer of 1862, a Confederate army under the able but contentious, Gen. Braxton Bragg invaded Kentucky, partially in the hope that the state would rise for the South and partially as a strategic diversion to draw Federal attention from the vulnerable line of the Mississippi. Considerable maneuvering resulted, as Union forces sought to pin Bragg down and destroy him. Union Maj. Gen. William S. Rosecrans finally cornered Bragg at Murfreesboro, TN. Bragg, although somewhat outnumbered, attacked on December 31. One of the hottest battles of the war, when it finally ended, on January 2, 1863 with a Confederate retreat, a soldier in the 64th Ohio intoned, "Praise God, From Whom all blessings flow," which was taken up by the rest of the regiment and then by much of the Union Army.[4] Both sides had taken heavy losses. After months of maneuvering and enormous bloodshed the situation was much as it had been before Bragg's offensive. Meanwhile, the armies in the East had not been idle.

The East: the Peninsula Campaign

After Bull Run there had been a long lull in the East, as the armies made ready. The Confederate forces defending Richmond were under Gen.

Joseph E. Johnston, while Union forces around Washington were under 34-year-old Maj. Gen. George B. McClellan. Confident, talented and energetic, a brilliant planner and organizer, McClellan created the Army of the Potomac, but lacked the instinct and will to lead it to victory. As the spring of 1862 approached, anticipation of a Federal offensive rose. But McClellan dithered, demanding more men and more equipment, while Lincoln prodded him to take some aggressive action, reportedly even saying, "If General McClellan does not intend to use his army, may I borrow it?" Yet McClellan did conceive a brilliant plan, one made possible by Union command of the seas.

The Confederacy had attempted to break the Union naval blockade by introducing a radical new warship, the ironclad *Virginia*, rebuilt from the hulk of the old wooden steam frigate *Merrimac*. The ironclad wreaked havoc among the blockaders in Hampton Roads, VA on March 8, 1862. But that night an even more radical new warship arrived, the USS *Monitor*, basically an iron raft with a rotating turret. The next day, the two fought to a draw, which was a strategic win for the Union, for the action not only sustained the blockade, but also set the stage for the next phase of the land war. In early April, McClellan made his move.

A brilliantly executed amphibious operation placed more than 100,000 men on the coast of Virginia between the James and York rivers, in anticipation of an advance on Richmond before Confederate forces in northern Virginia could be redeployed. Swift movement toward the Confederate capital might have proven decisive. But McClellan lost his nerve, frittering away a month in unnecessary operations before Yorktown against inferior Confederate forces under John B. Magruder. This gave Gen. Joseph E. Johnston, commanding the main Confederate forces in Virginia, time to shift his forces and turn what might have been a spectacular Union victory into failure. While Brig. Gen. Thomas "Stonewall" Jackson covered Johnston's exposed rear in a brilliant diversionary campaign in the Shenandoah Valley, Johnston held McClellan away from Richmond. But Johnston's attempts to inflict a major defeat on the Union forces were frustrated by inexperience, a confused Confederate command structure, and some remarkably hard fighting by Union troops. Johnston, wounded

General Robert E. Lee, in an image made by Matthew Brady shortly after the surrender at Appomattox in 1865. (National Archives)

Although Maj. Gen. George B. McClellan, shown here posing as the "Young Napoleon," could conceive brilliant plans, his lack of will prevented him from carrying them out. (National Archives)

in the Battle of Seven Pines (May 31), was replaced by Gen. Robert E. Lee on June 1.

With McClellan not 10 miles from Richmond, Lee hastily made plans. On June 26, he began a series of brilliant, if costly, counterattacks resulting in the successive battles of Oak Grove, Mechanicsville, Gaines's Mill, Garnett's and Golding's Farm, Savage's Station, Glendale, White Oak Swamp, and Malvern Hill, known collectively as the Seven Days' Battles. The Union actually won most of the battles tactically; of Lee's approximately 92,000 troops, some 20,000 were killed, wounded, or missing compared with about 19,000 of McClellan's 92,000 troops, in fighting so intense a young Georgia soldier wrote, "I have seen, heard, and felt many things in the last week that I never want to see, hear, nor feel again."[5] Despite doing well in most of the actions, after each fight McClellan took counsel of his fears and pulled the Army of the Potomac back, until it was ensconced in a fortified camp against the James River, where it was supported by the Navy. Of course, the Union troops had not been defeated, only McClellan, who made banal comments like, "If we have lost today, we have yet preserved our honor." He had performed poorly, though his retreat to the James was superb, and he remained remarkably popular with the troops.

The Trans-Mississippi

Perhaps the most forgotten operations of the war were those that took place in the vast Trans-Mississippi theater, encompassing Kansas, Missouri, Arkansas, western Louisiana, Texas, and the Indian Territory (Oklahoma), with the Arizona–New Mexico territories as an appendix. By early 1862, the Union had secured control of most of Missouri and had frustrated a Confederate invasion of Arizona and New Mexico, which was ultimately aimed at carrying the war to California.

Thereafter, the war in the Trans-Mississippi largely found the Union seeking to expand its control into Arkansas, western Louisiana, the Indian Territory, and Texas, while securing the areas already under federal control. This met with mixed success.

In Missouri and Kansas, operations by Confederate partisans sparked a brutal guerrilla conflict that was never quite suppressed, although a major raid by Confederate forces from Arkansas under Maj. Gen. Sterling Price in September–October 1864 was soundly defeated. In Arkansas itself, Union forces generally expanded their control, taking Little Rock in mid-1863, but never completely bringing the state under federal authority.

Union efforts against Texas and western Louisiana were largely unsuccessful. Although Galveston, the largest city in Texas, was captured in October 1862, the Confederacy retook it on January 1, 1863. An attempt to capture Sabine Pass was defeated on September 8, 1863, and a major offensive up Louisiana's Red River nearly came to a disastrous end after the Confederate victory at Mansfield (April 8, 1864).

In the Indian Territory, Confederate sympathizing Indians initiated the war by attacking their Unionist counterparts in September 1861. Fighting continued, each side gaining at best temporary advantage, until the Battle of Honey Springs (July 17, 1863), when a Union force of about 3,000, including white, black, and Native American troops, defeated a

Confederate Indian column of about 6,000. This largely secured the Indian Territory for the Union, but guerrilla operations continued until the end of the war.

Commanders on both sides in the Trans-Mississippi were hampered by a lack of resources, as senior political and military leaders in Washington and Richmond seriously neglected the theater. In fact, the Confederate high command several times transferred substantial forces from the Trans-Mississippi to take part in fighting further east.

The East: Second Bull Run and Antietam

Faced with defeat in the Peninsula, Lincoln attempted to recover with an advance by the forces remaining near Washington. On June 26, even as Lee began his counteroffensive, Lincoln had created the Union Army of Virginia, under Maj. Gen. John Pope, who had successfully cleared Confederate forces from the vicinity of New Madrid and Island Number Ten on the Mississippi River earlier in the year.

Pope advanced south from Washington on July 14. Alerted to the threat to his rear, Lee dispatched Stonewall Jackson north, who dealt Pope's leading army corps a heavy blow at Cedar Mountain on August 9. Pope fell back, and was reinforced by sea from the Army of the

Lieutenant General Thomas "Stonewall" Jackson. (Wikimedia Commons)

Lieutenant General James "Old Pete" Longstreet. (Library of Congress)

Potomac. On August 28, Lee boldly undertook an envelopment against Pope's larger army, baiting his trap with Jackson's corps while Lt. Gen. James Longstreet delivered a nearly fatal blow at Second Bull Run, the campaign costing the Union over 14,000 casualties, and the Confederacy only about half that. Confederate battlefield leadership seemed superior.

So far, Lee's victories had been won on the strategic defensive, very much on the model of the War for Independence. But Lee believed that to secure victory and independence from the Union, the war had to be carried into the North, and convinced Jefferson Davis to approve an offensive into Maryland, partially in the hope that the state harbored thousands of Confederate sympathizers who would reinforce Lee. On September 4, 1862, Lee took his Army of Northern Virginia across the Potomac into Maryland. By June 7, he was concentrating his troops near Frederick, in western Maryland, from which he could threaten both Washington, 40 miles to the southeast, or Baltimore, about 50 miles to the east. Things had gone well for him, though the anticipated thousands of volunteers was unrealized, as only a few hundred men enlisted.

Desperate, Lincoln recalled McClellan to the Army of the Potomac, into which Pope's army had been merged. McClellan advanced cautiously. He missed an opportunity to cut Lee's army in two on September 13, when by a remarkable stroke of luck he captured a copy of Lee's orders, but he did manage to keep his forces concentrated. A series of small battles resulted. Lee began to fall back. On the evening of September 16, Lee held an ambiguous position near Sharpsburg in western Maryland, along Antietam Creek. While the terrain tended to favor the defense and the creek partially covered his front, Lee had his back to the Potomac. Worse, a quarter of his troops were miles south of the river and there was only one available crossing, which put his army at risk. Someone bolder than McClellan would have made Lee pay dearly, but the "Young Napoleon" proved true to form. At Antietam on September 17—"artillery hell," according to Confederate gunner Stephen D. Lee[6]—McClellan had no overall plan. He threw army corps after army corps into a series of ill-coordinated, poorly supervised, piecemeal attacks that did not take advantage of his superiority in numbers. This permitted Lee to shift his slender resources from one part of his front to another as the situation dictated. Nevertheless, the Union forces almost won a smashing victory. Lee was saved at about 4:40 p.m., when his last arriving division delivered a counterattack against Union Maj. Gen. Ambrose E. Burnside's army corps, which was driving into Lee's right. This threw Burnsides' troops into disarray, and fighting soon tapered off. The battle was over, though the armies faced each other through the 18th. That night, Lee slipped across the Potomac into Virginia.

Antietam was the bloodiest day in the history of American arms. The 2,108 Union soldiers who died that day still stand as the highest single loss in one day in the history of the U.S. Army, and Confederate deaths were even higher, at 2,700. The battle had been a remarkable defensive success for Lee. But the Union could also claim victory, for strategically the Confederates had been ousted from Maryland, and, perhaps more importantly, Lee was seen to have lost a battle. This was sufficient to give Lincoln the opportunity to more clearly define Union war aims by issuing the preliminary Emancipation Proclamation on September 22.

After Antietam both armies withdrew to recuperate. The Army of Northern Virginia was reinforced, reorganized, and re-equipped. McClellan put the Army of the Potomac through the same drill, while feuding by telegraph with his superiors in Washington, who wanted him to advance at the earliest. As Secretary of War Edwin M. Stanton put it, "Fight, fight—be whipped if you must, but fight on."[7] There was some maneuvering by both armies in late October, but nothing decisive resulted. Finally, exasperated with McClellan's "slows," Lincoln replaced him with the reluctant Ambrose E. Burnside on November 7.

The East: Fredericksburg

Appointed commander of the Army of the Potomac in November 1862, Ambrose E. Burnside had a number of modest successes under his belt, and had not performed noticeably worse than anyone else, but lacked confidence in himself, and said so. Nevertheless, he immediately undertook an offensive, commencing a series of maneuvers that by November 17 saw his forces concentrating north of the Rappahannock River, across from Fredericksburg, on Lee's right. Burnside planned to cross the river into Lee's rear, but a shortage of pontoons delayed the crossing, giving

Lincoln with Allan Pinkerton and Maj. Gen. John A. McClernand, visiting the Antietam battlefield on October 3, 1862, in an image by Alexander Gardner. (Library of Congress)

Lee time to gather his forces. Burnside got much of his army across the Rappahannock on December 11–12, against light resistance. His attack the next day was intended to be a rather sophisticated envelopment of the Confederate right. But the operation was poorly handled, and it degenerated into a series of costly frontal attacks against Lee's well-entrenched left, which beat off fourteen separate attacks by seven divisions over several hours. In one spirited assault, New York's Irish Brigade closed to within 20 yards, of the Confederate lines—closer than any other Federal unit—with losses of about 60 percent. Fredericksburg was a one-sided Confederate victory; the Union's 13,000 killed, wounded, and missing was nearly triple Lee's 5,000. Burnside withdrew. Surveying the battlefield, Lee is supposed to have said, "It is well war is so terrible; we should grow too fond of it."

Thus ended 1862. For the Confederacy it had seemed a successful year. Despite some losses in the West, the Union armies in the East had repeatedly been beaten back. But the price had been high. For the Union, the year had seemed disastrous, the victories in the West appearing small alongside the failures in the East. Yet the West was far more decisive a theater than most realized, and the performance of the Federal armies there had demonstrated that it was not the troops who were at fault but their leaders. The men on both sides had performed admirably.

1863: decision in the balance

The winter of 1862/63 saw both sides once again preparing for another year's fighting. Both were fully mobilized, conscription having replenished the ranks of the Confederacy, while those of the Union were still being sustained, with some difficulty, by volunteers. The armies were well trained and well equipped, and both had a strong contingent of veterans tempered in the hardest of schools. Enthusiasm and confidence were high.

The year opened with a major political coup by the Union: the implementation of the Emancipation Proclamation. This headed off virtually any possibility of foreign intervention on behalf of the Confederacy, while making available to the Union a deep pool of African American recruits; by war's end, black men comprised some 10 to 12 percent of those serving in blue. But hard fighting would still be needed to settle the issue.

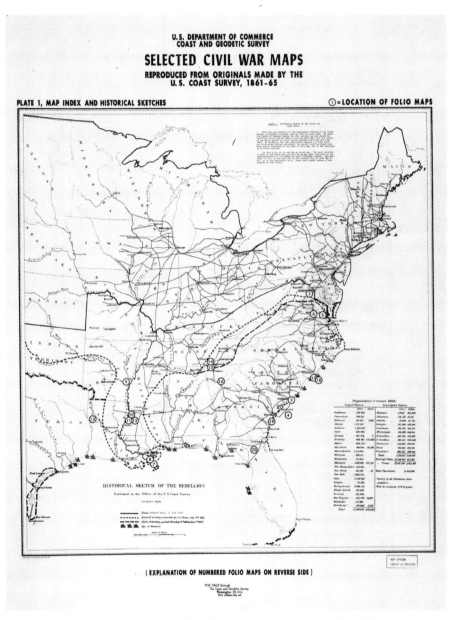

The general course of the war. (From Selected Civil War Maps: Reproduced from Originals Made by the U.S. Coast Survey, 1861–65*)*

Early in 1863, things were quiet. Through the winter there were many small-scale actions—guerrilla operations, raids, reconaissances—in all theaters, while at sea there were spectacular deeds by Confederate commerce raiders, and, ominously, the everyday affrays of the persistent and ever-tightening Union naval blockade. But then larger forces began to move.

The West: Vicksburg

As was the case in 1862, when the fighting began in 1863, it began in the West, where Ulysses S. Grant resumed Union operations to secure control of the Mississippi, focused on the capture of Vicksburg. In March, Grant launched the first of five attempts to outflank the Confederate bastion high on the east bank of the river, by trying to use the many swamps and bayous in the area as routes to get his troops into central Mississippi. Each attempt failed, as much frustrated by geography and the forces of nature as by Confederate resistance. The effort, however, left him with strong forces in northern Louisiana, across the great river from Vicksburg. In April, he arranged for the river fleet under Rear Adm. David Dixon Porter, a tough sea dog with a remarkable sense of humor, to run upstream from New Orleans past batteries south of Vicksburg. The fleet picked up Grant's army and transferred it to the east bank of the Mississippi at Grand Gulf, some 25 miles south of Vicksburg, on April 29. Grant then advanced east into the heart of Mississippi, abandoning his supply lines to live off the land. This befuddled his Confederate opponent, Lt. Gen. John Pemberton. A Northerner who had "married South," Pemberton wasted days trying to sever Grant's nonexistent line of supply. As Grant inflicted a number of reverses on Pemberton, he moved eastward to secure control of central Mississippi, defeating a Rebel relief column under Gen. Joseph E. Johnston at Jackson on May 14. Then Grant turned on Pemberton, hitting him hard at Champion Hill (May 16) and the Big Black River Bridge (May 17).

On orders from President Davis to hold Vicksburg at all costs, Pemberton fell back into the fortified city, a major strategic error. Grant bottled Pemberton up on May 18, along with some 30,000 of the South's best troops, and initiated a long, hard siege. Then it was merely a matter of time. One Union soldier wrote:

Every man ... became an army engineer ... soldiers worked at digging narrow, zigzag approaches to the rebel works. Entrenchments, rifle pits, and dirt caves were made in every conceivable direction. When entrenchments were safe and finished, still others yet farther in advance were made, as if by magic in a single night ... foot by foot, yard by yard [our troops] approached nearer the strongly armed rebel works. The soldiers ... with a spade in one hand and a gun in the other.[8]

Vicksburg surrendered on July 4. It was an Independence Day on which the Union had much to celebrate, for success had crowned its arms elsewhere as well.

The East: Chancellorsville

Early in 1863, Lincoln appointed Maj. Gen. Joseph Hooker to command the Army of the Potomac. The army was in terrible shape. Desertion was common, morale low, equipment deteriorating, and its organization clumsy. Hooker re-equipped the army, improved its organization, created an intelligence service, and introduced a rational leave policy for the first time. Morale soared and desertion fell. Having proven himself an even abler administrator than McClellan, Hooker went on to demonstrate that he was an even bolder planner, devising a brilliant scheme to crush Lee's Army of Northern Virginia.

With part of Lee's army temporarily transferred for an operation further south, in early April, Hooker concentrated the Army of the Potomac on the Rappahannock, near the old Fredericksburg battlefield. He undertook a number of diversionary attacks to draw Lee's attention to the lower Rappahannock. Then he struck, sending the bulk of his forces west, to cross the Rappahannock on April 29. Soon Hooker had a large force in Lee's rear, near Chancellorsville, with another strong force in front of Lee at Fredericksburg. With but 60,000 troops, Lee seemed trapped between two strong Union forces totaling 110,000. Lee's options appeared limited: he could accept battle at very long odds, risking annihilation, or abandon the line of the Rappahannock and retreat further into Virginia. But in a desperate situation, Lee took desperate measures. On May 1, leaving a small rearguard behind to screen the Fredericksburg front, Lee began to shift forces to confront Hooker. It was a highly risky maneuver, as a determined Federal advance would have forced him to accept battle on unfavorable terms or retreat, abandoning the Rappahannock, one of the best defensive lines in Virginia. But that Union advance never came. Lee then divided what remained of his main body, sending "Stonewall" Jackson to turn the Union right flank late on May 2, while a smaller force held Hooker's attention in front. When Jackson hit Hooker's flank, it collapsed in disorder. But as the evening deepened and Jackson pressed his advantage, he was wounded by one of his own men in the confusion. The Confederate drive was halted, and it was still possible that Lee might be crushed.

At this critical moment, a cannon shot struck the porch on which Hooker was standing. A post fell on the general, knocking him unconscious. Suffering from a concussion, over the next few hours he issued confusing and illogical orders. Neither his second-in-command nor his chief medical officer saw fit to relieve him. The Army of the Potomac was effectively leaderless. Lee's position was still precarious—his army was now in three segments, each greatly inferior to the Union forces before it. Despite the lack of decisive leadership, the Union troops were recovering their cohesion and putting up a stiff fight in the gathering darkness. About the night battle, one Confederate officer wrote:

> We knew nothing, could see nothing, hedged in by the matted mass of trees. Night engagements are always dreadful, but this was the worst I ever knew ... to hear shells whizzing and bursting over you, to hear shrapnel and iron fragments slapping the trees and cracking off limbs, and not know from whence death comes to you, trying beyond all things.[9]

A bold move by the Union forces might have turned Lee's masterful holding action into a disaster. It did not happen. Hooker, still in command despite his incapacity, pulled back on the afternoon of May 3.

Chancellorsville was a spectacular victory for the Confederacy. An apparently unbeatable Union offensive had been turned back and the situation in the Eastern Theater had been restored, though at great cost; Confederate dead were more numerous than Union, and among them was Jackson, who succumbed to his wounds and pneumonia.

The East: Gettysburg

Even before Chancellorsville, the Confederacy's increasingly desperate situation in the Mississippi Valley had led to calls for Lee to take some of his troops west and help restore the situation. Lee however, demurred, unwilling to leave the defense of Virginia in other hands. Observing that, "There is no better way of defending a long line than by moving into the enemy's territory," Lee convinced President Davis that an invasion of the North might be a better way to take pressure off Vicksburg, by threatening Washington, initiating the Gettysburg Campaign.

In early June, Lee led the reorganized and reinforced Army of Northern Virginia rapidly through the Shenandoah Valley, emerging in central Pennsylvania. Hooker followed at a leisurely pace. By June 28, Confederate forces were foraging over a broad swathe of central Pennsylvania, reaching right up to Harrisburg, on the Susquehanna River, with only about a hundred miles to Philadelphia on the southeast, or to Washington, actually to the south. Desperate, Lincoln sacked Hooker, and appointed Maj. Gen. George Meade to command the Army of the Potomac. Meade, a successful corps commander who was popular with his new subordinates, began to close up on Lee.

At this critical moment, Lee's eyes—his cavalry—failed him. Its commander, Maj. Gen. J. E. B. Stuart, supposedly scouting for the army, disobeyed orders to maintain contact in order to go on a raid, which brought his troopers to the suburbs of Washington, and then near disaster as Union forces closed in on him, while leaving Lee without effective reconnaissance. Thus, not until Maj. Gen. Henry Heth's division, foraging toward Gettysburg, ran into some Union cavalrymen northwest of the town early

An incident during the cavalry action at Fleetwood, June 9, 1863, one of several clashes between Union and Confederate cavalry comprising the Battle of Brandy Station, in which the Union troopers proved a match for J. E. B. Stuart's men.

on July 1 did Lee learn that the Army of the Potomac was at hand. The battle that erupted among the verdant hills, rich fields, and sparkling brooks around Gettysburg lasted three days, the largest and bloodiest ever in the Western Hemisphere.

On the first day, after a stout fight, Lee crushed the Union advance guard north and west of the town, driving it back onto Cemetery Ridge. The next day, his ablest subordinate, Lt. Gen. James Longstreet, led a smashing assault on the Union left wing, south and west of the ridge; when his troops cheered as they went into the attack, Longstreet called out, "Cheer less, men; fight more!"[10] Despite hard fighting and heroic sacrifice, the Union lines broke. Only a desperate stand on a small mountain named Little Round Top, and virtuoso performances by several officers—Gouverneur K. Warren, Strong Vincent, and Joshua Lawrence Chamberlain—as well as several regiments—notably the 1st Minnesota and the 20th Maine—averted total disaster for the Union. One Confederate officer said the mountain "resembled a volcano in eruption."[11]

Major General George G. Meade, an able officer who consistently performed well, though he was ultimately surpassed by Ulysses S. Grant. (National Archives)

Union Maj. Gen. John Reynolds performed notably well rallying hard-pressed Union troops on the first day at Gettysburg, but was killed in action, as depicted in this rather imaginative engraving.

On the third day, after the heaviest bombardment in the history of the Western Hemisphere, Lee hurled some 12,000 men across nearly a mile of open ground against the Union center atop Cemetery Ridge, in an attack known ever after as "Pickett's Charge," after Maj. Gen. George E. Pickett, who commanded one of the assault divisions.

Frank A. Haskell, a young lieutenant among the troops on the receiving end of the attack, at "the Angle" atop Cemetery Ridge, later wrote his brother:

> More than a half mile their front extends, more than a thousand yards the dull gray masses deploy, man touching man, rank pressing rank, and line supporting line. The red flags wave. Their horsemen gallop up and down; the arms of eighteen thousand men, barrel and bayonet, gleam in the sun, a sloping forest of flashing steel. Right on they move as with one soul, in perfect order, without impediment of ditch or wall or stream, over ridge and slope, through orchard and meadow, and cornfield, magnificent, grim, irresistible.[12]

The slaughter was great and, though some, a gallant few, scaled the crest of Cemetery Ridge to break into the Union lines, they were a forlorn hope and quickly overwhelmed. The bloodied survivors fell back.

Lee waited through July 4, the most fateful Independence Day since 1776, hoping Meade would strike back. Innately cautious, and having

Little Round Top under fire, July 2, 1863.

An artist's impression of Pickett's Charge at Gettysburg, July 3, 1863.

seen the outcome of Lee's attack, Meade held back. On July 5, Lee slipped away in a driving rainstorm. Meade's pursuit was cautious, and by the end of the month, the armies were back on the Rappahannock. That November, in dedicating the national cemetery at Gettysburg, Lincoln restated the nation's war aims: "That government of the people, by the people, and for the people, shall not perish from the earth."

The West: Tullahoma, Chickamauga, Chattanooga

After months of preparation, in late June Union Maj. Gen. William S. Rosecrans undertook the Tullahoma Campaign. In a series of brilliant operations in central Tennessee he drove Confederate Gen. Braxton Bragg's Army of Tennessee back over a hundred miles by a combination of clever deceptions and careful maneuvers, in one of the most flawlessly executed movements of the war, securing Chattanooga in early September after a virtually bloodless campaign. But then the tables turned. In a well-managed move, Confederate Lt. Gen. James Longstreet brought his corps of the Army of Northern Virginia by rail to Tennessee to strengthen Bragg for a counterblow. By the fortunes of war, Rosecrans' army had become dispersed in the aftermath of the capture of Chattanooga, and this offered the Confederacy an opportunity. In a two-day battle (September 19–20), Bragg fell on Rosecrans' dispersed forces along Chickamauga Creek. Using Longstreet's corps as a battering ram, he slammed into Rosecrans' army, fortuitously striking its front just where a confusion in orders had left a gap. It was a battle in which "the musketry rattled incessantly," as one Confederate soldier said. Captain James R. Carnahan, of the 86th Indiana, wrote:

> [there] came to our ears the sound of that mighty tempest of war—volley after volley of musketry rolling in waves of dreadful sound, one upon the other, to which was added the deep sounding crash of the artillery, like mighty thunder peals through the roar of the tempest, making the ground under your feet tremble as it came and went, each wave more terrible than the former.[13]

Assistant Secretary of War Charles A. Dana, an eyewitness, saw "our lines break and melt away like leaves before the wind," shattered by hard fighting and bad luck, and then, seeing Rosecrans, a devout Catholic, crossing himself, thought, "we are in a desperate situation. Moments later, turning to his staff, Rosecrans said,' Gentlemen, if you care to live any longer, get away from here.'"[14] The broken Union forces fell back on Chattanooga.

The Union reacted swiftly. Major General George Thomas, ever after nicknamed "The Rock of Chickamauga" for his steadiness at the head of the rearguard that day, assumed command and the army was reinforced by the victors of Vicksburg, under Ulysses S. Grant. The situation at Chattanooga was for a time desperate, but Thomas counterattacked on November 25, leading a massive breakout. Then, without orders, the troops—including the 24th Wisconsin led by 19-year-old Arthur MacArthur—went on to storm the seemingly impregnable Missionary Ridge. Asked by Grant if he had ordered the attack, Brig. Gen. Gordon Granger said, "No, they started up without orders. When those fellows get started all hell can't stop them."[15] The Confederate Army of Tennessee was soon streaming to the rear.

The year ended with both armies settling into winter quarters. It had gone well for the Union, but despite serious reverses, Confederate morale remained surprisingly sound, promising that the new year would bring yet more hard fighting.

1864: year of decision

Militarily, 1863 had decisively shifted the initiative to the Union, which was growing ever stronger as new volunteers, including an increasing number of African Americans, brought its armies to over 800,000 men, while the South could muster only rather more than half that. The Confederacy had seen vast territories come under Union control, its foreign commerce virtually choked off by the blockade, and its logistical situation growing increasingly desperate, despite heroic and surprisingly successful efforts at improvisation. As defeat in the field loomed, the Confederacy had already lost the war on the diplomatic front, as any hope of securing foreign recognition—and perhaps intervention—largely faded with the Emancipation Proclamation. Nevertheless, popular support for the war remained rather strong in much of the Confederacy. The Deep South had yet to feel the tread of Union troops, and strong Confederate armies under able commanders were still in the field. Many in the South believed the war could yet be won politically. War weariness and defeatism seemed widespread in the North, and 1864 was an election year. If the Confederacy could stave off defeat until November, political disaffection in the North might eject Lincoln from Washington, bringing in his place someone inclined to a compromise peace. It was a slender reed upon which to lean, but by 1864 the Confederacy had few options.

In March 1864, Lincoln called the most consistently successful Union commander to the East. Promoted to lieutenant general—the first since George Washington—Ulysses S. Grant was made general-in-chief. Grant possessed two excellent qualities: common sense and tenacity. With Lincoln, Grant and his right-hand man William Tecumseh Sherman shaped Union strategy for the coming year. Meanwhile, the U.S. Navy tightened the blockade and sealed off the remaining Confederate ports, most notably Mobile Bay (where in August Adm. David G. Farragut would cry, "Damn the torpedoes! ... Go ahead! ... Full speed!"), the Army would undertake two grand offensives.

In the East, the Army of the Potomac would hit Robert E. Lee and his Army of Northern Virginia with a series of hammer blows

and maneuvers designed to pin them against Richmond, where they could be destroyed. Meanwhile, in the West, Sherman would conduct an offensive from southeastern Tennessee into Georgia, smashing the Confederate Army of Tennessee, capturing Atlanta, and cutting the Confederacy in two yet again by marching to the sea. It would be a grim year; as Sherman put it, "All that has gone before is mere skirmishing."

Rear Admiral David G. Farragut at Mobile Bay (August 5, 1864), in his favorite perch when in action. (Naval Historical Collection)

The East: the Overland Campaign

Asked by an inquisitive citizen how soon he would get to Richmond, Grant replied, "in about four days, that is, if

General Lee becomes a party to the agreement, but if he objects, the trip will undoubtedly be prolonged."[16] Grant expected Lee to object, of course. His orders to Maj. Gen. George G. Meade, still commanding the Army of the Potomac, were simple: "Wherever Lee goes, there you will also go."[17] The army crossed the Rappahannock on May 3, 1864, to engage Lee's Army of Northern Virginia, little more than half its strength. In the Battle of the Wilderness (May 5–6), Grant tried to turn Lee's right in the dense growth below the Rappahannock, the site of the Battle of Chancellorsville a year earlier. Lee blocked the effort by a series of swift maneuvers and counterattacks, culminating in a devastating blow by James Longstreet's corps on the afternoon of the 6th, which almost shattered Maj. Gen. Winfield Scott Hancock's Second Army Corps. Waiting to go into action, Pvt. Homan Melcher, of the famous 20th Maine, observed:

> the dropping of our comrades from the charging line as they rushed across the fatal field with breasts bared to the terrible storm of leaden hail, and we knew that it would soon be our turn to run this fire.[18]

The Wilderness was a costly stalemate. Grant's offensive seemed to be going the way earlier Union offensives in the East had unfolded— stopped in a bloody battle. Previously, at this point, Union commanders had pulled back, to rebuild and reorganize and prepare another try. But having taken Grant's measure, Lee sensed this was not going to happen, saying, "We must make up our minds to get into line of battle and to stay there, for that man will fight us every day and every hour until the end of the war."[19] And so it was.

On the evening of May 7, Grant pulled the Army of the Potomac out of the lines and marched it south, once again maneuvering to turn Lee's right. It was stunningly simple. Grant had come south to fight and he intended to stay in the field until a decision was reached. As they took the roads south, despite knowing they faced more days and weeks of battle and sacrifice, the blue-clad veterans cheered, knowing this time there would be no turning back.

Thus began a series of bloody engagements, as Grant tried to maneuver Lee into battle on unfavorable terms, while Lee kept trying to avoid entrapment. The resulting battles were often costly tactical reverses for

Grant, but even costlier strategic defeats for Lee, who was forced to fight repeated defensive actions. The Wilderness was followed by Spotsylvania Courthouse (May 8–19), a fight so desperate 1st Lt. Stoddard Robertson of the 93rd New York called it "a boiling, bubbling, and hissing cauldron of death," while Nelson A. Miles wrote: "it was the first time during the war that I had actually seen bayonets crossed in mortal combat; it was a crash and a terrible scene … the only ground that I ever saw … that was so completely covered with dead and wounded that it was impossible to walk over it without stepping on dead bodies."[20]

Then there was the North Anna River (May 23–26), and Cold Harbor (June 3), where one Union soldier reported, "We formed in line and charged the enemy over the earth-works, and our men fell in heaps," a battle so grim men pinned their addresses to their coats so that their families could be notified of their deaths.[21] Each time the Rebels did well, but each time Grant pressed them closer to Richmond. Finally, aided by a movement of the Army of the James from the Virginia coast, Grant arrived before Richmond in mid-June.

A burial detail at Fredericksburg, VA, after the Wilderness Campaign, May 1864, photographed by Timothy H. O'Sullivan. (National Archives)

The Union incurred from 40,000 to 60,000 men killed, wounded, or missing out of some 105,000–125,000 engaged during the 6-week campaign, while Confederate losses were 30,000 to 40,000 out of per-haps 65,000 initially engaged.[22] Grant has been accused of using attrition to wear down the Confederates. Yet his casualties were lower than the cumulative losses of the repeated series of unsuccessful Union offensives from 1861 through 1863, which totaled fewer days of combat. To be sure, he had failed to destroy the Army of Northern Virginia in the field by maneuver and battle, but he had pinned Lee against Richmond. Lee lost his ability to maneuver. Although the defensive abilities of Lee's army remained high, it could no longer deliver the lightning surprise attacks that had characterized its earlier performance.

Lieutenant General Ulysses S. Grant looks over Maj. Gen. George G. Meade's shoulder while discussing a map, near Massaponax Church, VA, May 21, 1864. Note the pews, removed from the church. The photograph was taken by Timothy H. O'Sullivan. (National Archives)

For strategic and logistical reasons Grant shifted his front, bringing the Army of the Potomac south of the James River to invest Petersburg, 20 miles south of Richmond. This put his back to the sea, and a secure line of supply, while positioning him to threaten Lee's lines of supply, which ran south and west from the town. After several fruitless attempts to break the Confederate defenses, including the explosion of an enormous mine under the trenches on July 30—the Battle of the Crater—that began spectacularly and ended disastrously, the armies settled into positional warfare. Grant, who earlier in the campaign had said, "I propose to fight it out on this line, if it takes all summer" now found himself conducting a protracted siege of Petersburg that would last into the next spring, and increasingly come to resemble the brutal trench warfare that would characterize the First World War.[23] Meanwhile, the war went on in the West.

The West: Atlanta

By the spring of 1864, "Cump" Sherman had concentrated a large army in the vicinity of Chattanooga. On May 6, Sherman, with the armies of the Cumberland, the Ohio, and the Tennessee, some 100,000 men, began operations against Atlanta, about 100 miles to the southeast. The defense of Atlanta was in the hands of the Confederate Army of Tennessee under Gen. Joseph E. Johnston, who had replaced Braxton Bragg, with some 55,000 to 65,000 troops. What followed was a protracted duel between two talented commanders, who engaged in a complex series of marches and countermarches and nearly a dozen major battles. On balance, Sherman won, as he moved ever closer to Atlanta. But so did Johnston, for it took Sherman 2 months to reach the vicinity of Atlanta.

Wary of his opponent's superior numbers, Johnston kept his forces in motion, preferring maneuver to battle, thereby preserving his army. Johnston had conducted a brilliant campaign. But it was not viewed as such in Richmond. Personally disliking the little general anyway, on July 17, Jefferson Davis replaced Johnston with John B. Hood, "a man who will fight."

Hood did fight. But Sherman won all the battles. There were seven major engagements around Atlanta between July 20 and August 31, and

"Contrabands." Taking advantage of the presence of Union troops, in every theater large numbers of people fled enslavement, often entire families together, as in this sketch made on May 29, 1864 by Union war artist Edwin Forbes. (Library of Congress)

Sherman won every one. These were often desperate, bloody fighting, prompting one Union soldier to write, "I am tired of seeing such butchery."[24] Sherman's noose tightened around Atlanta. Fearing he would become bottled up there, Hood evacuated the city on September 1, in the process putting to the torch military equipment and cotton, which caused much of the town to burn as well. Some days later, Sherman ejected the remaining inhabitants and burned what was left. For about a month things were quiet, as Hood desperately tried to rebuild his army, and Sherman tried to work out some serious logistical problems, caused by Confederate cavalry raids on his long line of supply back into Tennessee.

The West: Tennessee

In a desperate attempt to regain the strategic initiative, Hood, having managed to rebuild the Confederate Army of Tennessee, decided to avoid Sherman's army and attack his line of supply through Tennessee.

General Joseph E. Johnston. Although nicknamed by personal enemies "the great retreater," he never suffered a major defeat, and was widely respected and feared by his Union opponents. (National Archives)

Acting General John Bell Hood. Called a "man who will fight," he was certainly not a man to command an army. (National Archives)

He was surprisingly successful. By mid–October, he was threatening Chattanooga. Sherman initially tried to pin Hood down. But when Hood proved elusive, with Grant's permission, Sherman abandoned the chase. Rather than worry about his lines of supply, he would ignore them altogether and march on Savannah, ordering his troops to "forage liberally from the country."

Meanwhile, Hood decided to undertake an invasion of Tennessee and Kentucky, hoping to draw Sherman away from Georgia. By the end of October, both armies were marching away from each other. Initially successful, Hood's offensive became a disaster, as Union forces under Maj. Gen. George Thomas confronted him. A series of spectacular marches resulted in pyrrhic victories at Spring Hill (November 29) and Franklin (November 30), perhaps the most horrendous battle of the war. The Confederate assault at Franklin dwarfed the more famous Pickett's Charge at Gettysburg, and was repulsed with even bloodier results. One Confederate soldier said, "to go over the works was certain death ... to run to the rear ... of almost equal hazard."[25] Thomas held Hood near Nashville on December 2. This set Hood up for a shattering defeat

Major General George Thomas, nicknamed the "Rock of Chickamauga," "Slow Trot," or just "Pap," was alongside Grant and Sherman as the best the Union had. (National Archives)

Major General William Tecumseh Sherman was a tough campaigner, who set out to "make Georgia howl."

when Thomas attacked in turn on December 15–16, almost totally destroying the Confederate Army of Tennessee, the remnants of which fled eastwards.

The West: the March to the Sea

While the Confederate Army of Tennessee was marching to its doom, Sherman began his "March to the Sea" on November 12. Abandoning his lines of supply, he took his army and 20 days' rations and set out to "make Georgia howl." Making no effort to occupy Confederate territory, the army advanced on a broad front. While cavalry covered the flanks and rear and scouted ahead, each army corps drove east on separate but parallel lines of advance, tactics portending the blitzkrieg of the Second World War. Enormous damage was inflicted upon the Georgia countryside. Though Sherman's men concentrated on military objectives, mostly destroying factories, railroads, munitions stores, and Confederate government property, there was other damage as well. As Sherman said to one general, "See here, Cox, burn a few barns occasionally, as you go along. I can't understand those signal flags, but I know what smoke means."[26] And the host of camp followers, refugees, fugitive slaves, and deserters from both armies that followed in the wake of the army wrought further destruction. There was relatively little fighting, as there were few Confederate troops available. On December 22, Sherman telegraphed Lincoln: "I beg to present you as a Christmas gift the city of Savannah."[27]

The year ended disastrously for the Confederacy. The failure of Southern arms had helped re-elect Lincoln in November. With that, the Confederacy was doomed. But the South had invested too much in blood and treasure and will to quit. So the armies spent yet another winter in the field or in camp. Throughout the South there was terrible hardship, even in areas that had not been marched and fought over.

1865: peace

The winter of 1864/65 did not give the Confederacy a reprieve from its death sentence. Union military operations continued, little diminished by the elements. As the naval blockade grew ever tighter, Sherman's armies marched north from Savannah, taking Charleston, while further south, after an unsuccessful attempt in December, on January 15, a combined Army–Navy operation culminated in the storming of Fort Fisher, on the Cape Fear River, thereby cutting the Confederacy's last port off from the sea. Union troops under Maj. Gen. Philip Sheridan swept through the Shenandoah Valley, bringing sword and fire to Lee's most important source of supplies.

Meanwhile, masses of Union cavalry raided virtually unhindered right across Alabama, the Mississippi Valley was held in an ever stronger Union grip, and in the long trenches stretching around Richmond and Petersburg the daily raids and affrays and sniping never ceased as the Army of Northern Virginia held to its defenses before the increasingly stronger Army of the Potomac. As Sherman ground his way through South Carolina and into North Carolina, Grant prepared to deliver the final blow.

To Appomattox

The end came quickly. Late in March, Grant began to extend his left flank southward to turn Lee's right and sever his rail links with what remained

Phil Sheridan rallies his troops during the Battle of Cedar Creek, October 19, 1864.

The Confederacy's Lt. Gen. Richard Taylor, son of the late President Zachary Taylor, toasting the end of the war with Union Maj. Gen. Edward Canby and his staff, to whom he had just surrendered, at Citronelle, AL, May 4, 1865, to the strains of "Hail Columbia" and "Dixie."

of the Confederacy. Lee fought back, and a series of desperate battles resulted, culminating in Five Forks (April 2, 1865). Unable to maintain his lines of communication, on the night of April 2/3, 1865, Lee evacuated Richmond. A deadly foot race ensued, as Lee tried to escape south, where the tattered Confederate Army of Tennessee, once more under Joseph E. Johnston, was trying to impede Sherman's march through the Carolinas. If the two armies could unite, they might be able to make a final stand. But Grant's pursuit was too close. Lee was unable to shake him.

Grant cornered Lee at Appomattox, southwest of Richmond, on April 9. There was a brief battle. Then, saying, "there is nothing left for me to do but go and see General Grant, and I would rather die a thousand deaths," Lee surrendered. On April 12, as his last brigade completed laying down its arms, the escorting Union troops, hitherto silent, saluted their erstwhile foes.

The surrender at Appomattox hastened the collapse of the Confederate forces remaining in the field. The last organized body of troops to lay down their arms comprised the men of the 1st Indian Brigade, under Brig. Gen. Stand Watie (1806–71), a Cherokee chief, who surrendered on June 23, 1865 at Doaksville in what is now Oklahoma. But in the far off Pacific, the cruiser *Shenandoah* continued sinking ships, and did not learn of the war's end until August, whereupon she sailed for Liverpool, and surrendered to the British on November 6, 1865. It was the final act of what Lincoln had called "the nightmare."

Tragedy

Well before the surrender of the *Shenandoah*, the nation had undergone one more calamity. On Good Friday, April 14, even as the last Confederate forces were still surrendering, the actor John Wilkes Booth—seeking vengeance for the defeat of secession and the abolition of slavery—mortally wounded Lincoln, who died early the following morning. Lincoln's passing was widely mourned, not only in the North. Learning of it on April 19, 1865 at Charlotte, NC, while in flight south to escape capture, Jefferson Davis said: "It is sad news. I certainly had no special regard for Mr. Lincoln, but there are a great many men whose end I would much rather have heard than his. I fear it will be disastrous for our people, and I deeply regret it."[28] Not far off, near Durham, NC, Confederate Gen. Joseph E. Johnston was told of the assassination by William T. Sherman, with whom he was negotiating surrender terms, and became so angry he resorted to "strong language" which included the phrase "a disgrace to the age."[29] They were right, for Lincoln's passing would dramatically affect the postwar years.

Reconstruction

With the war over, what was to become of the South and how were the millions of former slaves to fit into American society? Lincoln had called for the "re-construction" of Southern society, favoring a policy of leniency toward the defeated Confederates, with the restoration of civil government in the erstwhile secessionist states when 10 percent of the prewar voters had taken an oath of allegiance, so long as each state abolished slavery and provided for the civil rights of the freedmen, including suffrage for African American veterans. But Lincoln was dead. His successor, Andrew Johnson, not only lacked Lincoln's political and moral strength, but was by no means favorably inclined to African Americans.

Almost as soon as civil government was restored in several states, the white-dominated legislatures began enacting "Black Codes" restricting the freedom of African Americans, imposing a degree of second-class citizenship matched by some of the severest restrictions on free blacks in the antebellum era, enforced not only by legal means, but by mob violence from "night riders" such as the Ku Klux Klan. Johnson took no action, and as a result barely escaped being removed from office through impeachment, and continued feuding with Congress until the end of his term. In the election of 1868, Ulysses S. Grant was swept into office with the help of the veteran and freedman, and the "Radical Republicans"—essentially anyone who supported the idea that the black man had some rights—came to dominate government policy. A new, more vigorous reconstruction policy was imposed, in some cases returning states to military occupation.

Reconstruction, was—and is—depicted by Confederate sympathizers as a disastrously oppressive, corruption-ridden conspiracy to wreak vengeance upon the South. It was hardly that. It was not even particularly rigorous, at best a half-hearted attempt to establish a niche for the newly liberated African Americans in the South, and it certainly was the least brutal "punishment" ever imposed by a nation in the aftermath of a rebellion. While former Confederate political and military officials were stripped of their civil rights, in every case these were restored immediately upon individual petition. There were no treason trials nor mass executions, in fact there was only one war-related execution, of Capt. Henry Wirz (1823–65), the former commandant of Andersonville Prison. While some individuals were imprisoned, only Jefferson Davis was held for more than a few months.

Reconstruction policies were poorly designed. A Bureau of Refugees, Freedmen, and Abandoned Lands was established to relieve the great suffering of whites as well as blacks as a result of the war, and Bureau agents distributed food, opened schools, provided medical care, and performed other services. But the Bureau, directed by Maj. Gen. Oliver O. Howard, was largely managed by army officers, some of whom acted mean-spiritedly toward the former Confederates, while others were perhaps less inclined to help African Americans than the nature of the agency required.

The most important aim of reconstruction, and its most notable failure, was the attempt to secure the civil rights of African Americans. For a time, there was serious progress in helping newly liberated men and women in adapting to freedom. A few African Americans gained election to public office, though in no state did blacks actually dominate the government. There was, of course, corruption during reconstruction, but that was hardly something new in the nation, even in the South.

Reconstruction ultimately failed, due in part to what can only be described as an insurgency waged by the Ku Klux Klan, the White Leagues, and similar organizations. This insurgency was not aimed at reversing the decision over secession that had been reached on the battlefield, but to insure that white supremacy was reestablished; and the insurgents won, in large measure due to the loss of interest in the rights of the freedmen by Northerners. The political deal that resolved the disputed election of 1876 in favor of Rutherford B. Hayes, a former Union major general with an outstanding war record, included an implicit agreement to end reconstruction.

The end of reconstruction saw the start of a protracted decline in the fortunes of black Americans. It was slow because for many years after reconstruction, the leadership of the South was provided by the old aristocratic class, the former slaveholders themselves, who curiously often found political support among their former bondsmen as well as among the poor whites whom they had led in the war. But this was an unstable arrangement. As the rest of the nation—which itself had never committed to racial equality—gradually lost interest in the war and the freedmen, the leadership of the South passed into new hands and the political situation of black citizens deteriorated. It was a long process, and well into the 1890s there were still some elected black officials in some Southern states. The nadir was reached in the first quarter of the twentieth century, when during the administration of Woodrow Wilson, who as a child grew up in a slaveholding family, federal offices were segregated for the first time, the Ku Klux Klan enjoyed enormous popularity, and black men in the uniform of their country returning from the First World War were even lynched with impunity.[30]

Signs of the times

On November 9, 1861, well after war had broken out, the U.S. Marshal and police in New Bedford, MA, impounded the 330-ton whaler *Margaret Scott*, which had secretly been fitting out as a slaver; the ship was sunk as part of the "Stone Fleet" to block Charleston Harbor on January 20, 1862.[31]

An old tale has it that one night late in 1861, pickets of the 3rd New York Artillery took into custody a coach spotted proceeding suspiciously through one of the army camps about Washington, only to discover to their dismay that they had arrested the President of the United States, the Secretary of State, and the commander of the Army of the Potomac.[32]

Watching Union gunboats bearing down on Fort Donelson on February 12, 1862, Confederate Col. Nathan Bedford Forrest reportedly called out to Major D. C. Kelly, an ordained minister, "Parson, for God's sake Pray! Nothing but God Almighty can save that fort."[33]

General Pierre G. T. Beauregard and his chief-of-staff Thomas Jordan claimed to have consulted Napoleon's orders for Waterloo (June 18, 1815) during the planning for the Battle of Shiloh (April 6–7, 1862)—which, considering the outcome of the earlier fight, hardly suggests that it was a good model to follow.[34]

At the Battle of Malvern Hill (June 1, 1862), Lt. Col. Nelson A. Miles of the 61st New York, later a noted Indian fighter, heard a Confederate colonel cry, "Come on! Come on! Do you want to live forever?" as he led his regiment against the Union lines.[35]

At Fredericksburg on December 13, 1862, the Irish Brigade undertook a desperate attack on the Confederate lines, which were held by current foemen but fellow Irishmen of the 24th Georgia, who cried out, "Oh, God, what a pity! Here comes Meagher's fellows!"[36]

Following an unsuccessful attack at Vicksburg on May 19, 1863, the regimental colors of the Unionist 11th Missouri were found to have eighteen bullet holes in the flag itself plus two canister balls and a musket ball stuck to the staff, with four more bullet holes in the clothing of the color bearer, while the national colors had no less than fifty-six holes and a staff in three pieces.[37]

Incensed by the depredations of some of Lee's troops, on June 16, 1863, a group of irate citizens in Greencastle, PA, ambushed at gunpoint some Confederate troops from Maj. Gen. Robert E. Rodes' division who were escorting looted grain and livestock south, and thereby liberated thirty to forty African American women and children who were being carried off into slavery in Virginia.[38]

Mrs. Margery Clark of Lafayette County, MI, lost her husband and both sons in Pickett's Charge at Gettysburg.[39]

As some Confederate troops were preparing to go into action at the Battle of Chickamauga (September 19, 1863), their chaplain exhorted them to do their best for the cause, concluding, "Remember, boys, that he who is killed will sup tonight in paradise," whereupon one of the men replied, "Come along and take supper with us."[40]

By 1864, for every 100,000 troops Uncle Sam had in service, he also had approximately 27,000 cavalry and artillery horses, and 20,000 wagon mules, plus about 4,500 horses and mules in hospitals.[41]

Surprised preparing supper on the night of May 9, 1864 by a Union attack during the Battle of Spotsylvania, the men of the 3rd Arkansas rallied rapidly and went into action behind their commanding officer, Col. Robert S. Taylor, who led a counterattack wielding a frying pan, which was splattering hot grease in all directions.[42]

Reportedly, on July 4, 1864, as the Union's Maryland Brigade held trenches before Petersburg, their band struck up "Hail Columbia" to celebrate the occasion, whereupon the troops of a North Carolina regiment in the Rebel lines opposite jumped up on their parapet and gave a great cheer.[43]

By one reckoning, during 1864, Florida supplied the Confederate armies an estimated 25 million rations of beef and three million of pork.[44]

Seeking to inspire the wavering ranks of the 28th North Carolina during the Second Battle of Ream's Station (August 24, 1864), Maj. Gen. Henry Heth attempted to go forward with the regimental colors, only to discover that color bearer Thomas Minton refused to relinquish them, so that both men carried them as they stormed a Federal breastworks.[45]

Colonel Rutherford B. Hayes' orderly, Pvt. Billy Crump, was perhaps the ablest forager in the war, once returning from a 20-mile excursion with fifty chickens, two turkeys, a goose, some two dozen eggs, and nearly 30 pounds of butter, all rather untidily draped about his horse. During Hayes' presidency, Crump served as White House Chief Steward.[46]

Accepting the surrender of the 5th Company of the famed Washington Artillery of New Orleans at the end of the war, Union Maj. Gen. Edward Canby remarked upon the demeanor of the troops, noting that they had turned in their equipment in perfect order as if "to be used … for immediate action," added, "There is the noblest body of men that ever lived."[47]

By April 1865, Washington was surrounded by some 20 miles of entrenchments, liberally seasoned with ninety-three fortified artillery batteries and sixty-eight forts, all but one of which had been built since the outbreak of the war.[48]

On July 4, 1865, Brig. Gen. Joseph O. Shelby, commanding several hundred Confederate cavalrymen in Texas and having vowed never to surrender, sank his flags in the Rio Grande near Eagle Pass, and then crossed the river into Mexico to take service with the Emperor Maximilian against Benito Juarez's Republicans.[49]

CHAPTER 4

Armies Blue and Gray

When the Confederate batteries opened fire on Fort Sumter on April 12, 1861, the Regular Army of the United States numbered little more than 16,000, and could hardly concentrate a thousand men in one place. Surprisingly, at that moment, the Confederacy already had perhaps as many as 80,000 men enrolled in either the Confederate Regular Army or the Provisional Army of the Confederate States or various state forces, though no more than about 45,000 seem to have had any training or equipment, and even fewer still were ready for active service.[1] Of course, on the 15th, Lincoln issued his call for 75,000 volunteers. Both sides would soon make greater and greater calls for troops.

As men poured into recruiting stations North and South alike, there were difficulties turning them into soldiers. There were shortages of arms, uniforms, tents, and all sorts of other equipment, particularly in the South. Experienced drill instructors were in such short supply during the early months of the war that cadets from the Virginia Military Institute and similar schools, some as young as 13, trained some 15,000 Confederate troops at Richmond, while in Philadelphia Elizabeth Cooper Vernon (1833–65), whose stage act included firearms demonstrations and the manual of arms, was engaged to drill volunteers.[2]

The men in these armies were much alike. They had enlisted for many reasons: belief in a cause, desire to prove their manhood, local pride, or even, in the words of John N. Opie, teenaged son of a prosperous Virginia farmer, because going to war seemed the only way to avoid "vainly wrestling with a proposition in analytic geometry."[3] By the end of the war, most Southern white men of military age—and quite a few who were younger or older—had served in the Confederate Army, along with some Indians and a even a handful of blacks. Altogether, over 1 million men served in the Confederate ranks, an astonishing turnout. In addition, over 100,000 Southern white men served the Union, helping to bring the number of men in blue to perhaps 2.3 million, of whom about 8 percent were African American, the latter recruited largely in the South.

Remarkably, all of the men in both armies were initially volunteers. Both North and South militia units and newly raised volunteer companies stepped forward to sign up. By the spring of 1862, however, with volunteering in decline and confronted by the imminent expiration of the 1-year enlistments of many men who had joined in 1861, the Confederacy not only introduced conscription "for the duration," but extended by fiat the enlistments of the men already in the ranks, which caused some grumbling and desertions. By the following spring, the Union was also feeling a manpower pinch, and introduced federal conscription. In both cases, conscription regulations provided for certain exemptions and also provided for men to avoid service by furnishing someone willing to serve in their place, known as "substitution," or by paying a substantial sum in lieu of service, which caused some resentment and occasional disorder.

As the principal commanders on both sides were West Point graduates—as was Confederate President Jefferson F. Davis—both armies were raised, organized, and trained in much the same fashion. Troops were usually recruited by the states and then enrolled in either the Provisional Army of the Confederate States or the Volunteer Army of the United States. Most soldiers would have agreed with Pvt. William Watson, 3rd Louisiana Volunteers, who said, "Our home was the regiment, and the farther we got from our native state the more we became attached to it."[4] Infantry regiments were supposed to run about 1,100 men, but disease, casualties, and desertion quickly reduced them.

Union regiments tended to waste away, as fresh troops usually went to form new regiments, rather than to strengthen old ones, the usual Confederate practice. So Confederate infantry regiments tended to be larger than Union ones, which was reflected in the size of brigades, divisions, and army corps, at least until the Confederacy began running out of manpower.

The men were armed much alike. Rifles were just then coming into use, and as the war went on most of the troops were equipped with them. They had greater range and accuracy than smooth-bore weapons, which tended to lead to heavier casualties, but probably not as significantly as is often thought. A musically inclined Union soldier in the Army of the Potomac reported that as a rifle ball passed overhead, one heard "a swell from E flat to F, and as it passed into the distance and lost its velocity, receded to D—a pretty change."[5] Perhaps, but the half-ounce bullets caused horrendous injuries.

Strength of the armies

Attempting to ascertain and compare the strengths of the armies at various moments in the war is not as easy as one might think. While the total number of men enrolled at any given time is not hard to determine, the number of troops actually available for operations is much less so. For example, in early June 1863, on the eve of the Gettysburg Campaign, *on paper* the Confederacy's Army of Northern Virginia had about 135,000 men, while the Union's Army of the Potomac numbered nearly 200,000. Yet when the two clashed at Gettysburg on July 1–3, the Army of Northern Virginia committed some 75,000–77,000 men to the fight, and the Army of the Potomac between 88,000 and 95,000, more precise figures being difficult to calculate since both sides were reinforced during the battle, while some troops didn't take part in the fighting.

There are several reasons for the great discrepancy. Both armies suffered a great deal from desertion. By some estimates, 300,000 Yanks and 200,000 Rebels went over the hill during the war, and possibly far more: in the Confederate Army some troops would desert during the winter and return to duty in the spring. There were also numbers of men assigned to detached duty, who at times were still being carried on the rolls of their "home" regiments, as well as men in hospitals or on recuperation leave, again, still officially on the rolls of their regiments, but not available for duty.

In addition, the two armies counted men in different ways. Both began using the same standards, as follows:

- "Present", sometimes called the "ration strength," included all troops for whom rations had to be issued, whether they were physically with their commands or not.
- "Present for Duty" excluded personnel on sick call or recuperating from wounds and those under arrest, but included musicians, and teamsters, hospital personnel, and other uniformed non-combatants.

At the next level, when it came to determining how many men could go into battle, the two sides used the following:

- Union Army: "Present for Duty Equipped," which included only combat-ready enlisted men and their officers, that is, men armed and ready to fight, which excluded field musicians, teamsters, hospital personnel, and some other personnel.
- Confederate Army: "Effectives," which applied only to enlisted men present and under arms, thus excluding officers, as well as field musicians and various uniformed non-combatants.

But these are not necessarily reliable. In both armies, field musicians were an important part of the combat force, passing orders to the troops. The Confederate exclusion of field musicians and officers means about 7 percent of an army's combat strength was not counted. So, although at times, as in Table 2 below, we see remarkably precise figures for numbers of troops, it's always important to keep in mind that even these are only approximations.

Table 2: Troop strengths 1861–65

Date	Union armies			Confederate armies			CS:US ratio	
	Enrolled	Present	Present as %	Enrolled	Present	Present as %	Enrolled	Present
Jan 1, 1861	16,367	14,663	89.6%	8,500	7,000	82.4%	51.9%	47.7%
Apr 1, 1861	16,028	14,324	89.4%	80,000	45,000	56.3%	499.1%	314.2%
Jul 1, 1861	186,751	183,588	98.3%	116,000	112,040	96.6%	62.1%	61.0%
Jan 1, 1862	575,917	527,204	91.5%	326,768	235,273	72.0%	56.7%	44.6%
Apr 1, 1862	637,126	533,984	83.8%	401,395	301,046	75.0%	63.0%	56.4%
Jan 1, 1863	918,191	698,802	76.1%	449,439	305,619	68.0%	48.9%	43.7%
Jan 1, 1864	860,737	611,250	71.0%	464,646	278,788	60.0%	54.0%	45.6%
Jan 1, 1865	959,460	620,924	64.7%	445,203	218,149	49.0%	46.4%	35.1%
Apr 1, 1865	980,086	657,747	67.1%	358,692	160,198	44.7%	36.6%	24.4%
May 1, 1865	1,000,516	787,807	78.7%	—	—	—	—	—

Notes:

"Enrolled" includes everyone who was carried on the books of the armies on the date given.

"Present" excludes deserters and men in hospitals.

"Present as %" is the proportion of those "Enrolled" listed as "Present".

"CS:US Ratio" gives the strength of the Confederate armies as a percentage of the Union's forces.

Precise figures are from official accountings, while rounded figures are estimates based on incomplete data.

The January 1, 1861 figures for the Confederacy are for the South Carolina militia and volunteers, and those for April 1, 1861 are for troops already mustered into Confederate service, including some 5,000 at Charleston and about 2,000 at Pensacola, plus many troops still under state jurisdiction. Union figures for these two dates are for the Regular Army only, as no call for new troops had been made.

Although by January 1863 the Union had arguably achieved an over-whelming numerical superiority, it's worth keeping in mind that over 200,000 troops were required for garrison duty and line of communications security as Union forces advanced, to keep an eye on Confederate raiders and guerrillas, and to secure the Carolina coasts and offshore posts along the Gulf Coast, at Pensacola, Key West, Ship Island and elsewhere. This was one reason that the Confederacy was usually able to muster 75 to 80 percent of Union strength in most battles, despite the considerably greater Union manpower.[6]

The sea services

Compared to the armies, the manpower of the sea services—navy, marines, revenue service—was relatively insignificant. Officially, there were 132,544 enlistments in Union sea services, but the Navy peaked at some 50,100 men at the end of the war, including about 3,500 marines. Total enlistments in the Confederate sea services were probably between 12,000 and 15,000 men, although the peak strength of the Confederate Navy appears to have been about 5,000, plus about 1,000 marines, attained in early 1864.

Raising the 5th Alabama

On both sides, almost all of the regiments that served were raised for the war by the individual states, and then "mustered into service" in either the Confederate Provisional Army or the Union's volunteer army. The case of the 5th Alabama was more or less typical of how this worked.[7]

One could credit John Brown with providing the impetus for the raising of the 5th Alabama, as his raid at Harper's Ferry led to the formation of many new militia companies in the South. Among these were the Warrior Guards of Tuscaloosa, Alabama, formed little more than a month after his raid, and commanded by Robert E. Rodes. A native of Virginia, Rodes had graduated from the Virginia Military Institute in 1848, and remained there as an instructor until 1851, when he began working as a civil engineer in railroading. By 1859, Rodes was Chief Engineer for the Northeast & Southwest Alabama Rail Road at an impressive $3,000 a year, about ten times what an urban factory worker was likely to earn.

Under Rodes' command, the Warrior Guards proved one of the best militia companies in Alabama, and in November of 1860 won honors for proficiency in a drill competition, a common entertainment of the day. By then, of course, Lincoln had been elected and secession fever was beginning to sweep the South. Anticipating secession, the Warrior Guards were soon drilling daily, as were many other militia companies in the state. Secession came on January 11, 1861, and the Warrior Guards were soon occupying Fort Morgan on Mobile Bay, which had been seized days earlier by secessionists. The company remained at Fort Morgan until March, when their 90-day militia obligation expired and they returned to Tuscaloosa. Over the next weeks, as tensions rose towards war, the company recruited more personnel, and was equipped by popular subscription. In May, Rodes took the company to Montgomery, and, on May 11, at Camp Jefferson Davis, on the state fair grounds, it became Company H of the new 5th Alabama Infantry. The ten companies of the new regiment had been recruited mostly in the central and southwestern part of the state. Some were militia units of long standing, such as the Mobile Continentals, formed in 1836, which for many years sported a uniform that would not have been out of place at Valley Forge, before adopting a more modern one, in blue, just weeks earlier; other companies, like the Warrior Guards, were of more recent formation, some literally only weeks old.

When they arrived at Camp Jefferson Davis, all of the companies had their own officers, elected by the troops, a custom with roots deep in colonial times. While the idea of electing officers seems silly, with a shortage of trained officers, it at least gave rank to men who had some respect among the troops, albeit that some of these instant officers proved inept or corrupt. Surprisingly, the troops usually chose wisely, picking men with some military experience or known character, though there were always some martinets or scoundrels among them. Early in the war, hearing his men protest the strict discipline imposed by their officers, Col. Thomas P. August of the 15th Virginia replied: "The officers of the companies have been elected by yourselves, and if you have failed in your selection you have no one to blame but yourselves."[8] Once the regiment was formed, new elections were held for regimental officers. As a result, Capt. Rodes of Company H,

Table 3: 5th Alabama Infantry companies

Company	Raised as	County
A	Grove Hill Guards	Clarke
B	Livingston Rifles	Sumter
C	Pickensville Blues	Pickens
D	Monroe Guards	Monroe
E	Talladega Artillery	Talladega
F	Sumter Rifles	Sumter
G	Cahaba Rifles	Cahaba
H	Warrior Guards★	Tuscaloosa
I	Greensboro Guards	Hale
K	Mobile Continentals★★	Mobile

Notes:

★ Reorganized as artillery in December 1861.

★★ Reorganized as Company A, Alabama State Artillery, in July, 1861; replaced by the Barbour Grays, from Barbour County.

became colonel and regimental commander, with Capt. Adam C. Jones of Company I as lieutenant colonel and Capt. John T. Morgan of Company G as major. This led to a new round of elections in the three companies to replace these officers.

On May 12, seven companies totaling about 480 men departed from Montgomery to Pensacola, FL, where a defiant Union garrison was holding out in Fort Pickens, just off the coast. At Pensacola, the regiment was mustered into Confederate service for one year. Over the next few weeks, the remaining companies rejoined, and additional personnel arrived, bringing the regiment to about 1,000 strong. In June, the 5th Alabama was ordered to Virginia.

During the war, the 5th Alabama acquired a distinguished record, fighting with what became the Army of Northern Virginia in numerous battles from First Bull Run until Appomattox. Of 1,719 men who served in its ranks, some 300 were killed in action or died of wounds and 240 others died of disease. Three veterans of the regiment became generals, an impressive feat; overall, only one out of every 2,300 Confederate soldiers became a general, while for the 5th Alabama it was one in 573.

Rising stars of the 5th Alabama

Robert E. Rodes (1824–64), who led the 5th at First Bull Run, rose to become the first non-West Pointer to command a division in Lee's army. He was mortally wounded on September 19, 1864, during the Battle of Opequon.

John Tyler Morgan (1824–1907), an attorney, rose from private in the Cahaba Rifles to brigadier, becoming a noted cavalryman. Late in the war, an advocate for raising black troops, he afterwards became a Grand Dragon in the Ku Klux Klan, while serving six terms representing Alabama in the U.S. Senate.

Charles Miller Shelley (1833–1907), an architect and building contractor, began the war as a lieutenant in the Talladega Artillery, later became commander of the 30th Alabama, and ended the war as a brigadier general.

Although most regiments, North and South, were formed pretty much in the same way as the 5th Alabama, there were some with unusual origins. On the outbreak of the war, volunteers from many different ethnic groups began raising regiments from among their fellow countrymen. For example, in New York recruiting began for the Italian Legion, the Hungarian Regiment, the Polish Legion, the German 1st Foreign Rifles, the Netherlands Legion, and some other units. But there were not enough men from each group to form whole regiments, so they were merged into one, as the 39th New York. Known as "The Garibaldi Guard" after the Italian liberal revolutionary hero, it was one of the most polyglot units in the entire war, with troops of at least fifteen different nationalities. The men were formed into companies by language, so there were four speaking German (including one of Swiss), three Hungarian, one each Italian and French, and one of both Spanish and Portuguese speakers, including a number of Latin Americans. The 13th Louisiana, recruited in New Orleans, had similar roots, and its personnel included Louisiana Creoles, immigrant Frenchmen and Italians, and reportedly even some Chinese men.

Company G, 114th Pennsylvania Infantry (Collis' Zouaves), one of a series of company photographs taken in August 1864, on the Petersburg lines in Virginia. Surprisingly, given the lateness of the date, the men are still in Zouave garb. Raised in August 1862, and numbering about 1,000 men, the regiment had served in the Fredericksburg, Chancellorsville, Gettysburg, and Overland campaigns before arriving at Petersburg, where it was assigned to Provost Guard duty. Although 67 men had died in combat and 38 from disease, by the time this picture was taken the regiment numbered only about 350 men, as men were discharged due to wounds or illness, or deserted (Library of Congress)

War horses and dangerous steeds

Horses and mules were critical military resources, so much so that Lincoln banned their export as of May 13, 1862.[9] The U.S. census of 1860 lists 5.9 million horses and mules in the nation, 4.2 million in the future loyal states and 1.7 million in the future rebellious ones. About a million of these animals died during the war.[10] War was harder on horses and mules than on men. Over 65 years after the war, retired cavalryman John J. Pershing, hearing some of his old comrades bemoaning the motorization of the army, would write: "Horses and mules, if they understood the significance, would rejoice whenever a mounted unit is mechanized."[11]

Horses served in many ways. The most obvious was in combat, carrying cavalrymen and officers or hauling artillery. But horses and mules were even more important for the movement of supplies. By the autumn of 1862, the Army of the Potomac had about 120,000 troops present for duty, out of something over 130,000 on its rolls, and 3,798 wagons with about 22,000 horses or mules to move supplies and equipment, or about one wagon and six animals for every thirty-two men without counting animals used as mounts and to haul artillery. Although the Army of Northern Virginia is generally thought of as traveling light, it was almost as burdened with transport wagons as its perennial opponent, having about 90,000 troops on paper, and some 2,500 wagons with about 15,000 horses and mules to pull them, or about one wagon and six animals for every thirty-six men.

From March through October of 1863, the thirty-six cavalry regiments in the Army of the Potomac required 35,380 remounts, or roughly 2.5 per trooper, and overall it is estimated that the average horse in military service during the war lasted about 7½ months before it was killed, died from disease or overwork, or was otherwise rendered unfit for duty.[12] Although disease and overwork took the heaviest toll, horses were much more likely to become casualties than men, despite the motion picture industry, which rarely portrays them as being injured or killed: a horse presents a target that's about five times bigger than a man, and horses rarely can find cover on the battlefield. At Gettysburg the two sides together lost between 3,500 and 5,000 horses killed, plus thousands more rendered unfit for further service, out of perhaps 30,000–35,000 present.

Horses, of course, were important perquisites and symbols of command. During the Civil War there were many famous mounts, such as Robert E. Lee's Traveler, Ulysses S. Grant's Cincinnati, Phil Sheridan's Rienzi, and Jeb Stuart's Virginia, intrepid steeds that saw many a fight. George G. Meade's Old Baldy, whom he acquired shortly before First Bull Run in July 1861, carried him safely through numerous battles, until Globe Tavern in mid–August 1864, when, having received his fourteenth wound, the courageous beast was honorably retired to a farm in Pennsylvania. "Stonewall" Jackson, who was a poor horseman, famously rode Little Sorrel, an intrepid, if distinctly unimpressive beast until his death; in 1997, the horse's remains were interred at the base of the general's statue on the parade ground of the Virginia Military Institute.

Officers' horses took a heavy beating, some generals losing several in the course of a single battle, and some accumulated impressive records: the Union's George Armstrong Custer seems to have lost eleven during the war, while the Confederacy's Joseph O. Shelby lost twenty-four and Nathan Bedford Forrest at least twenty-seven, possibly thirty, and by some accounts as many as thirty-nine.

Of course, while being mounted enabled an officer to get around the battlefield quickly to oversee the fighting, by raising him above the heads of the troops the horse also exposed him to injury or death by enemy action, one reason officers had a high casualty rate. It was while they were mounted that the Confederacy's Gen. Albert Sidney Johnston was mortally wounded at Shiloh and the Union's Maj. Gen. John Reynolds killed at Gettysburg.

But enemy action was not the only way a mounted soldier might be killed or injured. Riding was dangerous, and many officers were killed or injured in riding mishaps, including several generals.[13]

- Brig. Gen. William C. Baldwin (1827–64), C.S.A.: Riding in Mobile, AL on February 19, 1864, a stirrup broke, throwing him to the ground, so severely injuring his right shoulder that he died several hours later.
- Maj. Gen. Louis Blenker (1812–63), U.S.: Commanding a division in the Battle of Cross Keys (June 8, 1862), his horse balked, causing him to fall to the ground, suffering internal injuries that rendered him unfit for further service.
- Brig. Gen. Michael Corcoran (1827–63), U.S.: Commanding his division in the defenses of Washington, he was riding near Fairfax, VA, on December 21, 1863, when his horse became unruly,

throwing him to the ground; he suffered a fractured skull and died the next day.

- Maj. Gen. Ulysses S. Grant (1822–85), U.S.: Although a noted horseman, Grant was injured several times by his mount. In 1960, historian and novelist MacKinlay Kantor used such an incident as the pivot point of his alternative history novel *If the South Had Won the Civil War.*
  - □ April 4, 1862: two days before the Battle of Shiloh, his mount slipped in the rain and fell, pinning his left leg to the ground, resulting in severe swelling that caused him to use crutches for the next few days.
  - □ September 4, 1863: during a military review near Vicksburg, his mount was apparently frightened by a locomotive and lost its footing. Grant was thrown to the ground and briefly rendered unconscious, while his left leg swelled "almost to the point of bursting," causing him to be confined to bed for a week.
  - □ October 23, 1863: Grant's mount slipped while coming down a steep incline, once again injuring his left leg.
- Maj. Gen. Thomas J. "Stonewall" Jackson (1824–63), C.S.A.: While commanding Lee's "Left Wing" during the Maryland Campaign, his favorite horse Little Sorrel was stolen. On September 6, 1862, a secessionist Marylander gave him a horse. Although details vary depending upon the source, when the general, not noted for his horsemanship, mounted the unfamiliar animal for the first time, it reared, throwing him to the ground, which wrenched his back so badly he had to ride in an ambulance for some days. Fortunately, Little Sorrell was recovered soon after.
- Gen. Robert E. Lee. (1807–70), C.S.A.: On August 31, 1862, Lee paused at Stewart's Farm, near Bull Run Creek, to observe the Union lines opposite. According to biographer Douglas Southall Freeman, "He was standing by Traveler, with the reins on the animal's neck. Suddenly a cry was raised, 'Yankee cavalry!' Traveler started at the sudden commotion, and Lee stepped forward to catch the bridle. As he did so he tripped in his long overalls and fell forward. He caught himself on both hands and was up in an instant, but it was soon apparent that he was hurt." Lee had broken a small bone

in one hand and the other was badly sprained, causing both to be put in splints. Unable to ride, Lee had to use an ambulance to get about for almost 2 weeks.[14]

Although we rarely seem to hear of instances in which riders were injured or even killed in riding accidents, this handful of cases suggests it was by no means a rare event. Even so excellent a horseman as Grant, or an otherwise reliable mount such as Traveler, could have a bad moment.

Chaplains in blue and gray

Both governments attempted to meet the spiritual needs of their servicemen, prescribing a chaplain for every regiment, ship, and installation, but neither was actually able to fulfill that goal.[15]

Chaplains often did more than provide spiritual guidance for the troops. They were usually entrusted with the education of drummer boys, and those serving with the U.S. Colored Troops often taught reading and writing to the men. In addition, they were often strong proponents of temperance, helping to keep the troops sober, usually assisted with the wounded, and of course frequently encouraged the troops in combat, on occasion taking part in the fighting themselves.

Confederate chaplains

In May 1861, the Confederate Congress authorized the President to appoint chaplains for both the Army and Navy. Chaplains were to be treated as officers without specific rank.

Apparently 938 men of "recognized denominations" served as chaplains, some being appointed more than once so that a total of 1,308 appointments were actually made. There were not enough chaplains to go around. Most units never had a formally appointed chaplain, but managed nicely since many clergymen and lay preachers were serving in the ranks; they would take a break from their military duties to perform religious services, the most notable cases being Lt. Gen. Leonidas Polk, who was the Episcopal Bishop of Louisiana, and Brig. Gen. William N. Pendleton, an Episcopal priest. Almost all Confederate chaplains were Protestants of various stripes.

Table 4: Confederate chaplain denominations

Denomination	%
Methodist	47
Presbyterian	18
Baptist	16
Episcopalian	10
Catholics	3
Other	5

The number of Confederate chaplains who became casualties during the war is not known. At least thirty-two died of disease while in the service, and seventeen were reported, without much evidence, to have been killed just in 1861–62, but there are no figures for other years.[16] Father Emmeran M. Bliemel (1831–64)—one of about thirty Roman Catholics serving as chaplains for the Confederacy—is often cited as the first American chaplain to have been killed in the line of duty; he was decapitated by a cannonball while giving the last rites to Irish-born Col. William Grace of the 10th Tennessee, during the Battle of Jonesboro, GA. However, that "distinction" seems unlikely, given the late date, August 31, 1864.

In May 1861, pay for chaplains was set as that of a lieutenant in the Army, $85 a month, plus one ration a day. Although this was considerably less than what clergymen could earn in civilian life, and even less than what some states paid chaplains in their militia, the $85 proved controversial (some fiscally conservative members of Congress argued that it was too much, since chaplains only worked one day a week.) So just three weeks later, the Congress slashed chaplains' pay to $50 a month plus one ration a day.[17] This made recruiting chaplains rather difficult, and by early 1862 nearly half of all regiments in the Army lacked a chaplain, so pay was raised to $80 in April 1862, plus one ration. Later in the war, chaplains with the troops in the field were also authorized fodder for one horse, if they had one. In addition to their pay, chaplains in the Confederate Navy were authorized to draw quarters and firewood, or monetary commutation as for Army lieutenants and captains.

No uniform was prescribed for chaplains. Some served in appropriate civilian dress, while others improvised uniforms from various bits of military clothing, adorning it with a religious symbol in lieu of insignia, such as a Latin cross, cross pattée, or Maltese cross. A few chaplains seem to have outfitted themselves rather splendidly. Reportedly, during the

First Battle of Bull Run, Brig. Gen. Theophilus T. Holmes encountered a rather showily uniformed chaplain very close to the fighting and told him, "Go back, sir, this is no place for you; take off that sash, retire to the grove, and besiege a Throne of Grace."[18]

Union chaplains

The Union, of course, already had a military chaplaincy. Only Protestant chaplains had been appointed prewar, though a handful of Roman Catholics were given temporary appointments during the Mexican-American War, a measure pushed by General-in-Chief Winfield Scott, to help allay Mexican fears of a "Protestant Crusade."

During the Civil War, at least 2,398 ministers, priests, rabbis, and lay preachers served as chaplains, mostly in the Army, with some score in the Navy, though apparently only about 600 chaplains were on active duty at any one time. As in Confederate service, clergymen serving in the ranks or lay preachers often pitched in to provide religious services.[19]

Some mainstream Protestants objected to the appointment of Catholics, and despite the fact that about 15 percent of the troops were Catholic, only forty priests were appointed as chaplains; at times Fr. William Corby (1833–97), of the Irish Brigade, was the only priest in the Army of the Potomac, despite the presence of literally tens of thousands of Catholic troops. Many Protestants made even more objection to Unitarians and Jews, as they denied the divinity of Christ. Unitarians could not be avoided, since several New England regiments elected Unitarian chaplains, who were subsequently approved by their state governors. Securing Jewish chaplains was more difficult. Not until July 1862, after much prodding by Lincoln and not a little vicious anti-Semitic outpouring from some religious fundamentalists, did Congress enact legislation to permit Jewish chaplains in the service; as only three actual rabbis were formally appointed, in accordance with Jewish tradition laymen often presided at services.

From available evidence it seems that the Catholic and Jewish clergymen were better educated than many of their Protestant counterparts, since applicants from these faiths were subject to much stiffer scrutiny,

Table 5: Union chaplain denominations

Denomination	%
Methodist	38
Presbyterian	17
Baptist	12
Episcopalian	10
Congregational	9
Unitarian/Universalist	4
Catholics	3
Lutheran	2
Other	4

given the extremely biased religious attitudes of the times; in any case, they had already been rather rigorously trained by their "faith group" in order to qualify as clergymen, in contrast to Protestants, many of whom were essentially self-ordained.

As is the case with the Confederacy, the number of Union chaplains who became casualties is unknown. There were at least eighty-eight deaths, seventy-three due to non-combat causes, mostly disease, and fifteen were killed in action or died of wounds. Many years after the war, four chaplains were awarded the Medal of Honor.[20]

Union chaplains got a much better deal than their Confederate counterparts. Initially, they were paid $145 a month, plus three daily rations and forage for one horse. Although their pay was later reduced to $100 a month, in 1864 chaplains were officially designated as officers, with the equated rank of captain. In addition, Union chaplains had a prescribed uniform, though many never wore it, preferring civilian clerical garb.

Conscription

By the winter of 1861/62, both sides were beginning to feel a manpower crunch. This was particularly crucial for the Confederacy, since many of the troops who had volunteered in the spring of 1861 had signed up for just one year, which meant that their enlistments would end just as the campaigning season began. So, in April 1862 the Confederate Congress passed the Conscription Act. This made all able-bodied, legally resident white men aged 18 to 35 (later raised to 45, and then 50) liable for three years' service in the Provisional Army, and extended the enlistments for all men who had already volunteered for one year's service to three years, effectively drafting virtually all the men already under arms. The act was viewed by many ardent secessionists as a gross violation of states' rights.

The Union had begun enlisting men for 3 years in 1861, and thus felt less pressure to recruit more manpower, meeting the need with new calls for volunteers, who were offered cash bonuses to join up; this brought in over 500,000 men, mostly for three years' service. But by the spring of 1863, the Union too imposed a draft.

In both North and South the draft was run by the Army. The Confederate Army's Conscription Bureau sent agents into all counties to enroll men, a task the Union assigned to the Army's Provost Marshal's Office. Both South and North conscription met with considerable resistance. Although in colonial times states had often used a draft to fill militia quotas, and during the War for Independence to provide troops for the Continental Army, the idea that the national government could act directly on a person in this way was widely resented, although it was certainly constitutional; in 1814, Congress had enacted a federal draft, though it had not been implemented when the War of 1812 ended.

Both the Confederacy and the Union provided ways to avoid the draft. Most government officials and employees were exempt, as were people in certain occupations, such as clergymen, telegraphers, railroad and river transport workers, miners, blacksmiths, druggists, and teachers. In the South, there was a special exemption for slave-owners, initially one man—presumably to serve as an overseer—for every twenty slaves, which was later changed to one for every fifteen, a matter that caused much resentment in the ranks, with mutterings of "A rich man's war, a poor man's fight."

Both sides permitted men to pay commutation to have their draft postponed, $300 in the North and $500 in the South, well beyond the financial resources of most men of the time. Another way of avoiding the draft was to provide a substitute, that is, to get someone not liable for the draft to enlist in one's place, such as a resident foreigner or a discharged veteran.

Draft resistance

North and South men resisted being drafted. As historian James L. Robertson, Jr., wrote of the Confederate draft, "School teaching jumped overnight in popularity; apothecary shops' opened, selling everything from hair dye to strawberries; many young men became tanners or blacksmiths but had no idea what the work entailed." In addition, physicians were frequently bribed to provide medical testimony as to a draftee's fitness and enrollment officers were not above exempting friends and relatives, or strangers, for financial consideration.[21] One option, open to many, was to move west; after a short stint in the secessionist Missouri State Guard in 1861, Samuel Clemens, better known as "Mark Twain," deserted and headed for Nevada, where he got a job working for the Union governor, while Simon Stover, member of a pacifistic Mennonite sect, fled from Virginia to Ohio to avoid conscription by the Confederate Army, bringing along his infant daughter Ida, who became the mother of Dwight D. Eisenhower.

Dodging the draft wasn't the only form of resistance to conscription. In both the Union and the Confederacy there were disorders, desertions, and in some cases rioting. The most serious outbreak in the North comprised the New York Draft Riots (July 13–16, 1863), which required substantial numbers of special police, militiamen, and troops to put down, and caused some 115–125 deaths—not several thousand as is often claimed—among them about a dozen African Americans, and millions of dollars in property damage. In the South, several areas fell into virtual rebellion in their opposition to conscription, such as Jones County, in Mississippi, subject of the reasonably accurate recent motion picture *The Free State of Jones*, as well as in Appalachia, requiring a military presence to protect conscription officers and pursue draft dodgers. Writing in his diary on March 24, 1863, Confederate War Department clerk John Beauchamp Jones noted: "In Eastern Tennessee, 25,500 conscripts were enrolled, yet only 6,000 were added to the army. The rest were exempted, detailed, or deserted." Desertion and draft evasion in this region was so pervasive that by early 1863, six companies of cavalry had to be detailed to hunt down draft dodgers.[22] In the course of the war, the Confederate Conscription Bureau saw about sixty of its agents killed trying to enroll and draft people, mostly in Appalachia.

How effective was the draft?

On paper, only about a quarter of Confederate troops entered service through the draft, either as conscripts or substitutes. This does include the approximately 400,000 volunteers already in service in April 1862, who had their 1-, 2-, or 3-year enlistments extended for the duration of the war, an action that met with some resistance in the ranks, which was at times rather harshly suppressed.

A Confederate householder fighting with a Union looter.

In the case of the Union, although published figures vary, the four drafts affected 776,000 men. About 160,000 never reported for induction, and some 75,000 more were sent home because the quotas for their districts were already filled. This left about 540,000 men available for service, of whom about 320,000 were let go because they were the sole supporters of a family or had physical, mental, or other disqualifications. Of the remaining 216,000 men, about 87,000 paid commutation and another 75,000 or so hired substitutes. In short, although some 776,000 men were drafted, only about 54,000 of them actually ended up in uniform, so that, including substitutes, conscription added fewer than 130,000 men to the Union ranks, about 6 percent of the 2 million or so men who served. Nevertheless, the draft worked because its primary purpose had been to encourage volunteering; drafted men did not receive an enlistment bonus, while volunteers did, in part paid for by commutation fees, plus additional money contributed by the federal, state, and local governments, which in some cases amounted to more than $1,000 dollars, easily the equivalent today of $100,000.

Soldiers' words

The troops both North and South developed an elaborate vocabulary, a mix of old soldiers' slang, professional jargon, contemporary usage, and new coinages.[23] Some notion of the richness of this vocabulary can be seen in these examples, a few of which are still in use.

Acknowledge the corn or confess the corn	Admit to wrongdoing.
Absquatulate (and variants thereof)	To run away, often implying cowardice or criminality, as in "He absquatulated with the payroll."
Acquire	To steal.
Big bugs	Generals, VIPs.
Boot snake	A loose shoe lace.
Bummer	Men who deliberately lagged behind to loot, while assiduously avoiding performance of any military duties. As the war dragged on large numbers of "bummers"—including deserters from both sides—followed in the train of moving troops, such as during Sherman's March to the Sea, preying on local people.
Chicken guts	Gold braid and such on uniforms.
Coffee cooler	A worthless soldier; also "skulker", "sneak beat," "straggler," "parlor soldier," "Sunday soldier."
Cyprian	Prostitute; also "fallen angel", "fancy girl," "daughter of Eve," "fast trick," "daughter of joy," "public woman," "nymph" or "nymph du pave," "woman of the town," and many more.
Dog tent	The common name for what was later called the "pup tent," in which generations of American soldiers have often spent their nights, which was first issued during the Civil War.
Dose	A venereal disease, sometimes called an "ailment of Venus."

Flag flopper	A signalman.
Flour tile	Double baked bread, also known as "hard tack," "Lincoln loaves," "Lincoln pie," "million-fold cursed crackers," "sheet iron crackers," "teeth dullers," "worm castles," "sea biscuit," and many more.
Grapevine	Rumor.
Hors de Combat	French for "out of combat," which could refer to those killed, wounded, or ill.
Horse and buggy	Having sex, also "riding," "screwing," "horizontal refreshment," etc.
Hospital rat	Someone feigning illness, a malingerer.
Lark, larking, on a lark	A joke or playing a joke, especially on a "rookie."
Parlor wound	An injury neither life threatening nor disfiguring, but sufficiently serious as to secure a soldier a furlough, so that he could recover while sitting in his parlor with his family and friends.
Quick-step	Diarrhea, also "the flux," "the trots," "screamers", etc.
Rookie	An inexperienced new hand, derived from "recruit," which became "reckie," and then "rookie."
Seam squirrels	Lice, also "travelers," or "Tennessee travelers," "body guards" (in the Confederate Army of Tennessee often found as "Bragg's body guards"), "cooties," "crumbs," "gray backs," "pants rabbits," and undoubtedly some more.

Seeing the elephant	Experiencing combat, something which, like an elephant, has to be seen to be understood, probably inspired by the old Indian story of the six blind men who went to "see" the elephant.
Skirmishing	Picking lice, also "fighting under the black flag;" discarding infested clothing was called "paroling the lice."
Take the cars	Go by rail.
Tight	Drunk, also "wallpapered," "loose," etc.

This is but a tiny sample of the rich vocabulary employed by the troops, which could easily fill a book, and in fact there are several works on Civil War soldier slang.

The regimental punch

No, not the punch the regiment delivered on the battlefield, but the one they drank on special occasions. In addition to their often elaborate uniforms and spectacular kit, militia units frequently had a favorite alcoholic beverage. Many of these can be found in *The Bon Vivant's Companion*, subtitled *How to Mix Drinks*, published in New York in 1862. The author, Jeremiah P. Thomas (1830–85), was the master bartender of New York's posh Metropolitan Hotel at Broadway and Prince Street, frequented by the notables of the age, such as the Lincolns, as well as senior Army and Navy officers, politicians, diplomats, businessmen, filibusters, and wealthy tourists. Often called "The Father of the Cocktail," in the 1850s and 1860s Thomas easily earned over $100 a week, rather more than the Vice President of the United States. Below are a few regimental favorites, from both North and South.

The Charleston Light Dragoons[24]

Formed in the eighteenth century, the company attracted the sons of some of the most prominent families of the South Carolina Lowcountry, the dozen or so southeastern counties, and had served in the War for Independence.

The Dragoons spent most of the war on coast defense duty, during which they became Company C of the 4th South Carolina Cavalry. In March 1864, the regiment joined the Cavalry Corps of the Army of Northern Virginia, fighting in the Overland and Petersburg campaigns. In early 1865, it joined the Army of Tennessee and served in the Carolinas Campaign, surrendering with the army in April. During the war, about 160 men served in the company, of whom thirty died and many others were invalided out by injury or disease, or transferred to other commands. Although reformed after the reconstruction, the Dragoons were eventually disbanded.

This drink was obviously something the dragoons prepared for special occasions, as it's a lot of punch, with a high alcohol content, though rather on the sweet side.

Charleston Light Dragoons punch

Ingredients
Rye whiskey, 3 gallons
Rum, 2 quarts
Champagne, 3 gallons
Grenadine syrup, 1 quart
Raspberry syrup, 1 quart
Curaçao syrup, 1 bottle
Water, 2 quarts
Green tea leaves, ¼ pound
Red cherries in syrup, 1 quart
White cherries in syrup, 1 quart
Pineapple pieces, in syrup, 1 quart
Lemons, 6 dozen
Oranges, 6 dozen

Procedure
1. Start with a large tub or vat, of 10-gallon capacity or more.
2. Squeeze the lemons and oranges, and mix in the vat with the grenadine, raspberry, and curaçao.

3. Boil the lemon and orange rinds in 2 quarts of water and use this to make the tea.
4. Cool the tea, then add it to the juice and syrup mixture.
5. Add the cherries and pineapple, with their juice, to the vat and mix thoroughly.
6. Add the rum and whiskey while mixing thoroughly.
7. Decant the mixture into bottles, sealing them, and store them.
8. Wait 5 days.
9. Place a block of ice in a large punch bowl.
10. Pour two parts of the mixture and one of champagne over the ice.
11. Drink.

The National Guard

Organized in New York City in 1806, the later 7th New York Militia adopted the name "National Guard" after the Marquis de Lafayette declared them an outstanding body of men during his tour of the U.S. to commemorate the 50th anniversary of the War for Independence. Later nicknamed the "Silk Stocking Regiment" because it was popular with the city's elite, the regiment performed several tours of active service in the harbor forts during the War of 1812 (1812–15), sent many men into the volunteers during the Mexican-American War, and performed numerous state missions. The regimental punch was rather simple.

The National Guard's punch

Ingredients
Sugar, 1 tablespoon
Lemon juice, ¼ cup
Brandy, 4 ounces
Catawba wine, 4 ounces
Raspberry syrup, dash

Thomas specifies the use of a "large bar glass," presumably 12 ounces, and adds: "Fill the glass with shaved ice. Shake and mix thoroughly, then ornament with slices of orange, pineapple, and berries in season, and dash with Jamaica rum. This delicious beverage should be imbibed through a straw."

During the war, the 7th New York saw several months of active duty, helped suppress the so-called Draft Riots, and served as an officer-training unit for the many volunteer regiments. Although it suffered not a man lost to combat during its 150 days of federal active duty during the war, of the 991 officers and men who marched with the regiment into Washington in April of 1861, 603 (60.9 percent) become officers in other regiments, fifty-eight of whom died in the service, and two were awarded the Medal of Honor (Maj. Gen. Rufus King, Jr., and Col. Robert Gould Shaw, who fell at the head of the 54th Massachusetts at Fort Wagner, as depicted in the film *Glory*, though he had to wait over a century for his.)

The Fighting 69th

Formed by New York City's Irish Catholic citizens in 1851, incorporating several older militia companies, including one formed by veterans of the War for Independence, the 69th New York State Militia initially preferred a rather potent mixture.[25]

Fighting 69th's punch

Irish whiskey, 2 ounces
Scotch whiskey, 2 ounces
Sugar, 1 teaspoon
Lemon, 1 piece
Hot water, 8 ounces

These were combined in a slightly warmed pint-sized earthenware mug, and made what Jerry Thomas called "the capital punch for a cold night."

After serving as a militia unit at Bull Run, the 69th was reformed as a volunteer regiment and became part of the Irish Brigade in the Army of the Potomac, commanded by Irish nationalist hero Thomas Francis Meagher (1823–67). Colonel Meagher (pronounced "Marr") liked a little taste every now and again—or more accurately, a little now, and then a little more again. His favorite drink was Irish whiskey with two parts Vichy

Brigadier General Thomas F. Meagher, of the Irish Brigade. (Wikimedia Commons)

water. On campaign in Virginia one day in 1862, Meagher ran out of Vichy. A search by his orderly only turned up two bottles of champagne. Probably desperate for a drink, Meagher tried the bubbly French wine in lieu of the bubbly French spring water. It went down well, promptly becoming Meagher's favorite drink, and soon became the 69th's regimental punch, which it remains today.

The 69th New York Volunteers campaigned with the Army of the Potomac from the spring of 1862 through Appomattox, fighting with particular distinction in the Seven Days', during which Robert E. Lee is said to have dubbed them "The Fighting 69th," Antietam, Fredericksburg, and Gettysburg, and is listed as one of the 300 "fightingest" Union regiments by William H. Fox.[26]

The Chatham Artillery

Formed at Savannah in 1786 by War for Independence veterans, the Chatham Artillery saw federal service during the War of 1812 and was on state duty numerous times, while undergoing several reorganizations. Like most artillery punch recipes, that for the Chatham Artillery punch was complex.

Chatham Artillery punch

Ingredients

1 pound green tea leaves, steeped overnight in 2 gallons of cold water, then strained and discarded, reserving the water
3 gallons pink Catawba wine, the darker the better
1 gallon rum
1 gallon brandy
1 gallon rye whiskey
5 pounds brown sugar
2 quarts fresh cherries
1 gallon gin
12 quarts champagne

Mix these in a very large punch bowl or firkin, since they run to over 12 gallons, enough for about 100 4-ounce "rations". The ingredients oddly lack two common additives often found in artillery punch: the dash of gunpowder needed to give it "bite," and the mule shoe for the "kick."

The Chatham Artillery spent most of the war on coast defense duty in the environs of Charleston, initially as part of the 1st Georgia Militia, which became the 1st Georgia Volunteers. On September 28, 1861, the company became an independent light battery, and several times engaged Union warships and troops. On the fall of Charleston in late 1864, the company joined the remnants of the Army of Tennessee, and surrendered to Union forces near Greensboro, NC on April 26, 1865.

Signs of the times

On the eve of the Civil War, some 3,165,000 men were officially enrolled as militiamen on paper, about 650,000 of them in the South, but only about 115,000 had any training or equipment, of whom some 35,000 were in the South.

Although only about one-third of Southern families held slaves, nearly two-thirds of the officers in the Army of Northern Virginia in 1862 came from slaveholding households, as did nearly 45 percent of the enlisted men.[27]

When formed many years before the war, Rochester's Pioneer Rifles—later part of the 54th New York—sported "a tall beaver hat, a green, swallowtail coat with large cuffs and a high collar, and white pants," among the most curious uniforms in the militia of the day.[28]

At the start of the war, raising, equipping, and mounting a cavalry regiment of 1,200 men cost the Union about $300,000, after which annual pay and maintenance ran at about $90,000; it was considerably less for the Confederacy, as the troopers were "permitted" to supply their own horses.[29]

Of 753 men who accompanied the 1st Vermont Militia to Washington in the spring of 1861, 250 reportedly went on to serve as officers in various volunteer regiments later in the war, while Pittsburgh's "Duquesne Grays" began the war with about eighty men of whom seventy became officers; one major general (Alexander Hays), nine colonels, four lieutenant colonels, six majors, twenty captains, and twenty-nine lieutenants.[30]

In 1863, the U.S. Congress declared chaplains were non-combatants, and stipulated that Confederate chaplains were not to be held as prisoners of war.

By the time the Confederacy abolished substitution, in 1864, an estimated 50,000 drafted men had provided paid replacements, often laying out as much as $5,000 in hard money to secure a suitable recruit, an enormous sum for the day.[31]

Although the 54th New York was composed overwhelmingly of recently immigrated Christian German-Americans, the men elected Rabbi Fabian Sarner as their chaplain, also a recent German immigrant.[32]

On both sides, officers hardly ever received death sentences by courts martial, and if so, were rarely executed; the Union apparently never executed an officer, though the Confederacy did execute two or three.[33]

A number of veterans of the 1st Mississippi Mounted Rifles, which had fought with distinction at Buena Vista in 1847 during the Mexican-American War, served the Confederacy, most notably the regimental commander Jefferson Davis, who became President, as well as seven men who became brigadier generals, and six colonels or lieutenant colonels.[34]

Irish-born Father Peter Whelan (1802–71), of South Carolina, voluntarily served as a chaplain to the Union prisoners in Andersonville from June through October 1864, even borrowing money to buy bread for them, until taken ill.[35]

To encourage older and exempt men to provide substitutes for military service, in 1864 Lincoln paid $500 to John Summerfield Staples, a veteran of the 176th Pennsylvania, who had been discharged in early 1863 due to an illness from which he had recovered, to enlist in the 2nd District of Columbia Volunteers, which served on garrison duty in the Washington area until the end of the war.[36]

Arguably the highest-ranking officer of African descent in the war was John Wayles Jefferson (1835–92), the grandson of Thomas Jefferson (1743–1826) and his slave mistress Sally Wayles Hemings (c. 1773–1835), who was passing as white, and rose to colonel of the 8th Wisconsin, being twice wounded in action during the war.

Robert E. Lee endorsed nearly 75 percent of court martial death sentences he reviewed, though urging his subordinates to avoid carrying them out on the Sabbath, while Ulysses S. Grant confirmed only about half of those submitted to him; though since both Jefferson Davis and Abraham Lincoln were reluctant to confirm such sentences, only 22 percent of Lee's death warrants and 19 percent of Grant's were actually carried out.[37]

CHAPTER 5

Incidents and Anecdotes of War

The story of a war—any war—is too often told in terms of the political and military leaders and decisions reached in cabinet rooms and of the armies and their movements, clashes, and decisions reached on the battlefield. But wars are more than that, involving ordinary people, including soldiers and sailors, and touch upon all aspects of life.

1861

Mrs. Hancock's dinner party

On June 15, 1861, Capt. and Mrs. Winfield Scott Hancock gave a farewell dinner party at Los Angeles for several officers who had just resigned their commissions in order to join the Confederacy.

The guest of honor was Col. Albert Sidney Johnston, commander of the 2nd Cavalry, a brevet brigadier general widely considered to be one of the most capable officers in the army, who had been acting commander of the Department of the Pacific. Also present were Maj. Lewis A. Armistead, Capt. Richard B. Garnett, and several other officers.

Despite the somewhat awkward circumstances, the evening passed in good spirits and everyone parted on friendly terms, with Maj. Armistead, a close friend of the Hancocks, giving Mrs. Hancock a prayer book as a parting gift.

It had been an unusual dinner in many ways, and the aftermath was to be even more so. Years later, Mrs. Hancock observed that three of the officers present died at Gettysburg during Pickett's Charge, which broke against her husband's Second Army Corps on Cemetery Ridge on July 3, 1863. Two of the officers were Armistead and Garnett, both of whom commanded brigades during the "High Tide of the Confederacy." Alas, she could not recall the name of the third, nor has his identity been established with any degree of satisfaction.

As for the guest of honor, Albert Sidney Johnston, he had perished at the head of a Confederate army at Shiloh on April 6, 1862.

The "Wild Rose" of the Confederacy

The most important Confederate intelligence agent in the war was probably Rose O'Neal Greenhow (*c.* 1814–64). "Wild Rose" Greenhow, a prominent member of Washington society, was a witty, educated, wealthy, and attractive widow with a young daughter. For years, her lavish soirées were attended by such notables as John C. Calhoun, a personal friend, President James Buchanan, and other prominent political, military, business, and social leaders.

Despite being an outspoken secessionist sympathizer, she was so well connected that shortly before Fort Sumter, she was even a guest of the Lincolns at a White House reception. Some time during early 1861, Greenhow was recruited as a Southern agent by Capt. Thomas Jordan, an active duty U.S. Army officer who was certainly indictable as a traitor by any standard. Washington, a slave-holding Southern city, had many secessionist sympathizers, so Greenhow quickly developed a large espionage ring, which was active well before fighting began, including agents or contacts in Congress and in the War, Navy, and State departments.

Greenhow's most important intelligence coup came early. The months following the firing on Fort Sumter saw Union troops—regulars, militiamen, and volunteers—concentrating in the Washington area, so that by mid-July, there were 35,000 around the capital and 18,000 at Harper's Ferry, and an offensive to capture Richmond was imminent. In opposition, the Confederacy had only about 22,000 men in front of Washington and 10,000 more near Harper's Ferry, giving the Union a distinct edge in manpower. Greenhow romanced Massachusetts Senator Henry Wilson (1812–75), chairman of the Military Affairs Committee, who despite being an abolitionist, seems to have let slip details of the Union plans for an offensive to begin on July 16. This information, and information from other sources as well, permitted Confederate commander Gen. Pierre G. T. Beauregard to shift troops from the Harper's Ferry area by rail to reinforce his main army. The resulting hard-fought First Battle of Bull Run on July 21 was a critical Confederate victory; had the battle gone the other way, the war would have ended much sooner.

After the battle, Greenhow continued her work for the Confederacy. But by then, she had attracted the attention of Allan Pinkerton (1819–84), head of Union counterintelligence, who put her under surveillance. It quickly became clear that there was a lot of traffic at her home at all hours, including many men who often spent long periods with Greenhow.

In late August 1861, while conducting nocturnal surveillance of Greenhow's home, Pinkerton saw a young officer admitted by a servant. Peering through a window, Pinkerton saw the officer meet Greenhow in a parlor. The two chatted for a short while, and then the officer drew a document from his coat, and held it up to show Greenhow; it was a map of the defenses of Washington. The two spread the map out on a table and discussed it for a while, Greenhow apparently asking various questions. The pair then left the room. They returned about an hour later, entering arm in arm. Shortly afterwards, following smooches with Greenhow on her doorstep, the officer departed, followed by Pinkerton.

After a short walk, the officer quite suddenly entered a guarded building. The sentries detained Pinkerton, who was locked up overnight until released by order of the Assistant Secretary of War. The evidence gathered by Pinkerton led to the arrest of Greenhow and the disgrace of the officer, 1st Lt. John Elwood of the 5th Infantry, who died under questionable circumstances in 1862, probably a suicide.

Greenhow was placed under house arrest, but proving resourceful, continued to carry on her espionage activities. As a result, she was incarcerated in the Old Capitol Prison, so named because it had temporarily housed Congress after the British had burned Washington in 1814, and later became a hotel owned by her father. She quickly charmed her jailer, who permitted her visitors; this enabled her to continue her espionage work, and she even secured important documents and another military map from a clerk of the Senate Military Affairs Committee, smuggling them out to the Confederacy, with the help of her 12-year-old daughter, known as Little Rose, who was shortly jailed as well. Greenhow's imprisonment was of great propaganda value to the Confederacy. Southern newspapers and tracts harped on "Yankee brutality" toward the refined lady and her "innocent" daughter being held in prison, echoed by Southern-sympathizers in Britain; that Greenhow was trading sex for

Rose O'Neal Greenhow and "Little Rose," apparently taken at the Old Capitol Prison, Washington, DC. (National Archives)

information was then—and for the most part has been since—politely unmentioned, as was the hanging in the Confederacy of several women accused of being Union spies, mostly without benefit of trial. In June 1862, Greenhow and her daughter were sent south in a prisoner exchange.

Dispatched to Europe to help drum up support for the Confederacy, Greenhow toured France, where she was a guest of Emperor Napoleon III, and Great Britain, and wrote a highly fictionalized memoir about her adventures, which sold very well. Returning to the Confederacy in late 1864, her ship ran aground in heavy seas off Cape Fear, NC. Greenhow was carrying a lot of gold in her clothing, and when her lifeboat overturned it dragged her down and she drowned.[1]

The 1st Minnesota on the road to Bull Run

Some veterans of the 1st Minnesota had a curious tale to tell about how they came to acquire their reputation as one of the toughest outfits in the Union Army. According to oral tradition handed down through their descendants, it happened on the morning of July 21, 1861, as the regiment was marching along a road that would shortly take it to what would soon be known as the First Battle of Bull Run or, on the South, Manassas. Trudging along, the troops passed many people by the roadside watching them. For the most part these were Confederate sympathizers, but there were a few Unionists among them.

At one point, while the regiment was taking a break, the troops noticed a very old black man who appeared to be wearing faded bits and pieces of a Revolutionary War uniform, boldly waving "Old Glory."

Some of the troops went over to speak with the old gentleman. Giving his name, he told them that as a boy he had been drummer for "Gen'r'l Washington." Staunch Unionists all, and some abolitionists as well, the troops exchanged pleasantries with the man, questioning him about the earlier war and listening to his advice on soldiering. Then, as they were being called back into ranks, one of the troops asked if the old man would bestow a veteran's blessing upon them. He did so, calling on the Lord to watch over the regiment and give the men strength for the fight. Shortly, the regiment marched off, never to see the old man again.

Later that day, the 1st Minnesota was heavily engaged in the thickest of the fighting for Hull House Hill, helping to beat off three successive attacks. The only Union outfit that had to be ordered to retreat, the 1st Minnesota incurred the heaviest casualties of any regiment in the battle, 180 men killed or wounded. It was a performance that the regiment would repeat, less than two years later, when it incurred the highest percentage of casualties of any regiment in the war in a single action, reportedly 82.4 percent of 262 men engaged at Gettysburg on July 2, 1863, in a counterattack against some 1,600 Confederate troops. When it mustered out of federal service in April 1864, the 1st Minnesota had lost ten officers and 177 enlisted men killed in action or died of wounds out of 1,242 who had served in its ranks, a 15 percent combat death rate, exceeded only by about a score of the approximately 2,000 regiments in the Union Army. The regiment also lost another two officers and ninety-seven enlisted men to disease, for a total of 286 fatalities, and had 609 men wounded, some more than once.

Years after the war, veterans of the 1st Minnesota often attributed the regiment's combativeness in action to the old man's blessing. The lineage of the 1st Minnesota is today preserved by the 2nd Battalion, 135th Infantry Regiment of the Minnesota National Guard.[2]

"No dodging now ... Hold up your heads like men!"

In combat, the "field grade" officers of a regiment—the colonel and his principal subordinates, a lieutenant colonel and a major—were supposed to insure that the troops were properly maneuvered as appropriate to the tactical situation. But their most important role was to lead and inspire the troops in action, insuring that the men held on and did their damnedest. Of course, this exposed the field grade officers to considerable danger, and many made the supreme sacrifice.

But inspiring the troops could have its lighter moments. For example, consider this tale about the 19th Indiana in action at Lewinsville, in what is now McLean, VA, on September 11, 1861. The regiment, commanded by Col. Sol Meredith, was part of a small brigade making a reconnaissance in force toward Lewinsville, when the troops encountered Confederate forces in some strength. Finding his men under heavy fire, the good colonel put them into battle line, and then ordered them to shift position to help cover the brigade's rear and protect a nearby battery. In his official report, Meredith wrote:

> we proceeded for half a mile towards camp under a terrific shower of shell, causing to my own command, however, no casualty, while other regiments were less fortunate. The position of the enemy's guns being ascertained, our guns were placed in battery, and we with the rest of the infantry were formed in line, my command still covering the rear ... After a considerable interval, our batteries having silenced those of the enemy and recalled his cavalry, we quietly returned to camp, still covering the rear, till we met reenforcements.
>
> My men were under fire about two hours, and during the whole of that time behaved with the utmost coolness and gallantry, obeying all orders promptly and with but little confusion.

But Meredith omitted from his report something that endured in the lore of the regiment. It seems that as Confederate artillery shells began exploding in the air over their heads, the good colonel rode along his men, shouting inspiring lines such as, "No dodging now ... Hold up your heads like men!"[3] But quite suddenly, a particularly heavy shell—reportedly an 18-pdr—burst within yards of him, and he too instinctively dodged, as did his horse. Nonplused, Meredith recovered quickly, shouting, "Boys, you may dodge the large ones!"

The 19th Indiana would fight as part of the famed Iron Brigade from Second Bull Run through the early stages of the siege of Petersburg, being mustered out of service in October 1864, having lost 201 officers and men in combat, and over 100 to disease. Colonel Meredith would command the Iron Brigade for a time, and rose to brigadier general.

"Stand just where you are"

On the morning of November 7, 1861, Union Brig. Gen. Ulysses S. Grant began advancing a mixed force of over 3,000 men against Belmont, a small Missouri town on the Mississippi. Trying to determine what Grant was up to, Confederate Brig. Gen. Benjamin Franklin Cheatham decided to make a personal reconnaissance. With only his orderly for an escort, he rode out a little in advance of the Confederate positions. As the area was rather wooded, he tarried too long beyond his lines. Quite suddenly, a small contingent of Union cavalry came upon the general and his orderly standing on a country lane. As the Union troopers quickly spotted the pair, escape was impossible. With great presence of mind, Cheatham casually rode towards the column. As he was not what one would term a natty dresser—a trait he shared with Grant—the Union troopers failed to recognize him as a Confederate.

Coming within a few yards of the Union troopers, Cheatham asked in an authoritative tone, "What cavalry is this?"

Sensing the presence of a senior officer—which indeed Cheatham was—the officer commanding the Union detail replied promptly, "15th Illinois Cavalry, sir."[4]

"Oh, Illinois cavalry. All right, stand just where you are."

With a brief exchange of salutes, Cheatham and his orderly rode casually on, passing the halted troopers, and an infantry regiment which halted behind them, before doubling back through the woods and on to the safety of their own lines.[5]

"The Battle Hymn of the Republic"

Julia Ward Howe (1819–1910), daughter of a wealthy New York banker and mother of six, was noted as an abolitionist, women's rights advocate, writer, poetess, and reformer. Editor, with her husband, Samuel G. Howe, of the abolitionist journal *Commonwealth*, she had several books to her credit before the Civil War. After the war, she wrote more books, became prominent in the international peace movement, and was the first woman elected to the American Academy of Arts and Letters. Despite all of this noteworthy

Julia Ward Howe, in an engraving by Caroline Amelia Powell, made about 1887 from a photograph of an unknown date by J. J. Hawes. (Library of Congress)

activity, Mrs. Howe is best remembered for "The Battle Hymn of the Republic."[6]

In November 1861, Mrs. Howe paid a visit to the Army of the Potomac in the company of Governor John A. Andrew of Massachusetts and several friends. They were present at a military review, during which some Massachusetts troops began singing "The John Brown Song." It was an inspiring scene, but the lyrics seemed wrong.

> John Brown's body lies a-mouldering in the grave; *(repeat three times)*
> His soul's marching on!
>
> *(Chorus)*
>
> Glory, glory, hallelujah! *(repeat three times)*
> His soul's marching on!
>
> He's gone to be a soldier in the army of the Lord! *(repeat three times)*
> His soul's marching on!
>
> *(Repeat chorus)*

John Brown's knapsack is strapped upon his back! *(repeat three times)*
His soul's marching on!

(Repeat chorus)

His pet lambs will meet him on the way; *(repeat three times)*
They go marching on!

(Repeat chorus)

They will hang Jeff Davis to a sour apple tree! *(repeat three times)*
As they march along!

(Repeat chorus)

Now, three rousing cheers for the Union; *(repeat three times)*
As we are marching on!

Mrs. Howe and her companions apparently remarked upon the lyrics and the Rev. James Freeman Clarke (1810–88) suggested she write better ones. Later that night—it was November 18, 1861—as she lay asleep in the Willard Hotel, some words came to Mrs. Howe which somehow seemed more fitting, and she got up and jotted them down in the dark. The next day, she revised them and thus was born "The Battle Hymn of the Republic."

Mine eyes have seen the glory of the coming of the Lord;
He is trampling out the vintage where the grapes of wrath are stored;
He hath loosed the fateful lightning of His terrible swift sword:
His truth is marching on.

(Chorus)

Glory, glory, hallelujah! *(repeat three times)*
His truth is marching on.

I have seen Him in the watch-fires of a hundred circling camps,
They have builded Him an altar in the evening dews and damps;
I can read His righteous sentence by the dim and flaring lamps:
His day is marching on.

(Chorus)

Glory, glory, hallelujah! *(repeat three times)*
His day is marching on.

I have read a fiery gospel writ in burnished rows of steel:
"As ye deal with my contemners, so with you my grace shall deal;"
Let the Hero, born of woman, crush the serpent with his heel,
Since God is marching on.

(Chorus)

Glory, glory, hallelujah! *(repeat three times)*
Since God is marching on.

He has sounded forth the trumpet that shall never call retreat;
He is sifting out the hearts of men before His judgment-seat;
Oh, be swift, my soul, to answer Him! Be jubilant, my feet!
Our God is marching on.

(Chorus)

Glory, glory, hallelujah! *(repeat three times)*
Our God is marching on.

In the beauty of the lilies Christ was born across the sea,
With a glory in His bosom that transfigures you and me.
As He died to make men holy, let us die to make men free,
While God is marching on.

(Chorus)

Glory, glory, hallelujah! *(repeat three times)*
While God is marching on.

The song first appeared in print in the February 1862 issue of *The Atlantic Monthly*, for which Mrs. Howe was paid $4, a goodly sum at the time. It rapidly became one of the most popular, and certainly the most enduring, of all Civil War songs.

The origins of the tune are somewhat vague. It is thought to have originated as a hymn improvised at a religious camp meeting in the South during the early Republic, which spread among African Americans. An early published version was known as "Canaan's Happy Shore," and other versions arose over the years. In the 1850s, William Steffe (1830–90), a South Carolinian working as a bookkeeper in Philadelphia, produced a version as a spiritual entitled "Say, Brothers, Will You Meet Us?" with a melody that was used for several songs over the next few

years. Early in the Civil War, the New England Guards, a battalion of
the Massachusetts Militia (today part of the 50th Air Defense Artillery,
Massachusetts National Guard) was in garrison at Fort Warren in Boston
Harbor. In its ranks was a Scottish soldier who was the butt of friendly
jokes because he bore the same name as the famed radical abolitionist,
John Brown. The battalion bandmaster Patrick Gilmore, and James E.
Greenleaf, a member of the battalion chorus, composed "The John
Brown Song," which became popular with the troops, and in turn
inspired Julia Ward Howe.

Soon after its publication, "The Battle Hymn of the Republic" had
become one of the popular patriotic tunes of the war, a status that it
retains to the present. It's so symbolic of America that by testamen-
tary request it was played at the funeral of Sir Winston S. Churchill in
Westminster Abbey in 1965 to honor his American roots.

1862

"A dozen cigars"

In March 1862, after capturing forts Henry and Donelson, and thereby
unhinging the entire Confederate defense system in Kentucky and
Tennessee, Ulysses S. Grant spent some time calculating his next move.

One evening, while on a steamer, Grant's Chief of Engineers, Lt.
Col. James McPherson, noticed that while the other officers present
were relaxing in the boat's salon with some ladies who were present,
Grant was sitting alone at a table, puffing on a cigar and poring over
some maps. Thinking Grant was working too hard, the young officer
approached him.

"General," he said, "this won't do, you are injuring yourself." Offering
Grant a glass of whiskey, McPherson added, "Join us in a few toasts and
throw this burden off your mind."

Grant looked up, smiled, and replied, "Mac, you know your whiskey won't help me to think; give me a dozen of the best cigars you
can find, and, if the ladies will excuse me for smoking, I think by
the time I have finished them I shall have the job pretty much nearly
planned."[7]

General Jackson deals with conscientious objectors

There were several pacifistic religious groups in the United States in the mid-nineteenth century, such as the Quakers, the Church of the Brethren, and the Mennonites. Since these religious groups were frequently also of an abolitionist bent, some of their Northern members considered abolition a higher moral duty than pacifism and chose to enlist. Similarly, some pacifists in the South thought that securing the Confederacy's independence trumped pacifism and also served. Nevertheless, many pacifists, North and South, chose not to serve.

Neither side offered blanket exemption from military service to members of pacifistic religious communities, nor exemptions for conscientious objectors. Draftees could avoid service by paying a commutation fee, but this was unsavory for most pacifists, since the money was used to further the war effort. Some pacifists who were drafted, by either side were willing to serve in non-combat roles, most notably in hospitals. In the end, the North, with its much greater manpower resources, did issue a blanket exemption, and many pacifists went on to perform important services as civilians in hospitals or providing relief services for soldiers and their families. If a conscientious objector did end up in the ranks and refused combat duty, many commanders treated them as cowards and inflicted severe penalties.

Perhaps due to his own deep faith, Thomas "Stonewall" Jackson was probably the most thoughtful officer in either army on the subject. Although he supposedly once joked that conscientious objectors had to serve, but should aim badly, he more seriously issued orders that conscientious objectors be formed into special details and assigned to non-combat duties, which would relieve men willing to fight for duty at the front.

It was not until the First World War that the United States developed a more comprehensive approach to the problem of conscientious objectors in wartime.[8]

Beauregard decoded

On April 11, 1862, Union troops under Brig. Gen. Ormsby MacKnight Mitchel (1809/1810–62) captured the critical rail nexus at Huntsville,

AL. A graduate of West Point (1829, with Robert E. Lee and Joseph E. Johnston), Mitchel was a very interesting man, not only an excellent soldier, but also an attorney, publisher, engineer, surveyor, mathematician, and the nation's foremost astronomer.

By capturing Huntsville, Mitchel gained control of rail lines and river crossings across a 100-mile swath of northern Alabama, severing Confederate communications between the East and the Mississippi Valley. In addition, some 200 prisoners were taken, along with fifteen locomotives, a large amount of rolling stock, and some military supplies. Best of all, Mitchel bagged an enormous amount of letters, telegrams, and official documents.

Some of the telegrams captured were communiqués between General Pierre G. T. Beauregard, other commanders, and even Confederate President Jefferson F. Davis.

One message read:

Corinth, April 9

To Gen. Samuel Cooper, Richmond, Va.

All present probabilities are that whenever the enemy moves on this position, he will do so with an overwhelming force of not less than yrzole xriy lohkjnap men, by wna ahc vkjlyi hate nqhkl lorite xrmy lohkjnap yx31 wlrmqj mna phia may possibly shrakj ra n xyc pnejcrlo nghkl xr1ly 5a lohkjnap vhmy. Can we not be reenforced xrhm dyvgzilhaj nive. If defeated here cy thjy loy vryq mnt3yc nap dchqn4te hki wnkiy whereas we could even afford to lose for a while wonilyjlha nap inmnu5yl for the purpose of defeating qkyt4j nive which would not only insure us the valley of the Mississippi but also our independence.

P. G. T. Beauregard

In preparing the telegram, Beauregard's staff had used a simple cypher to conceal certain passages. So, Mitchel set to work. Since there are only a few one-letter words in English, and not a lot of two-letter ones in common usage, Mitchel could make educated guesses as to the meaning of "ra," "n," "cy," and "5a," as well as of some of the three-letter words. It also helped that the message mixed plain text with cyphered text, since the plain text suggested possible meanings for the cyphered. Consider the phrase "overwhelming force of not less than yrzole xriy lohkjnap men." The three words "yrzole xriy lohkjnap" could only be some sort of number, and "lohkjnap" appears three times in the message, providing more fodder for analysis, particularly given Mitchel's knowledge of the military situation.

These clues enabled Mitchel to decipher the message in about 20 minutes, which permitted him to read it and many others. The code was so simple, in fact, that the letters were not even distributed randomly, but were linked in pairs. For example, "n" was substituted for "a" and "a" for "n" rather than using a wholly different letter. As a result, after just a few inferences, Mitchel realized he could identify two letters each time he solved one, enabling him to build a key.

Beauregard's cipher

Letter:	a b c d e f g h i j k l m n o p q r s t u v w x y z
Substitute:	n q w p y x z o r s u t v a h d b I j l k m c f e g

Deciphered, the message read:

Corinth, April 9

To Gen. Samuel Cooper, Richmond, Va.

All present probabilities are that whenever the enemy moves on this position, he will do so with an overwhelming force of not less than 85,000 men. We can now muster only about 35,000 effectives. Van Dorn may possibly join us in a few days with 15,000 more. Can we not be reenforced from Pemberton's army. If defeated here we lose the Mississippi Valley and possibly our cause whereas we could even afford to lose for a while Charleston and Savannah for the purpose of defeating Buell's army which would not only insure us the valley of the Mississippi but also our independence.

P. G. T. Beauregard

Now there were some tricky bits in the message that may have given Mitchel a moment's pause. For one thing, perhaps rushing to get the job done, whoever enciphered the message seems to have made a couple of spelling mistakes. For example, "nghkl" for "about" rather than "nqhkl." There are also occasional conjoined words, such as "shrakj" for "join us" or "pnejcrlo" for "days with," which may have been deliberate attempts to further conceal the message, or perhaps merely errors. That some words had numbers in them, such as "mnt3yc" and "inmnu5yl", may have slowed Mitchel down a bit, but he quickly concluded that the digit indicated a repeat of that numbered letter in the word, thus "mnt3yc" reads "valley," the fourth letter being a repeat of the third, and "inmnu5yl" means "Savannah," the sixth a repeat of the fifth. Then there are the split words, notably "xr1ly 5a" which is actually "fifteen" and the very complicated "yx31 wlrmqj" for "effectives". Even the enigmatic "vrjq," which transcribes as "misb" probably didn't offer much trouble, given it is followed by "valley," and thus looks suspiciously like an abbreviation for Mississippi.

By the end of the Civil War, far more sophisticated ciphers were employed by both sides, some of which might have challenged even Mitchel's skills. But that was not to be. Promoted to major general as a result of his work in northern Alabama, in September 1862 this fine officer was assigned command of the Union Tenth Army Corps, on the Carolina coast, and died there of yellow fever on October 30.[9]

"Go to your right"

During the Second Battle of Bull Run (August 30, 1862), William F. Jenkins, a 17-year-old private in the 12th Georgia, was severely wounded and left on the field. Soon after nightfall, two of his comrades came looking for him. By good fortune they located Jenkins, gave him what help they could, and began to carry him to a field hospital. Making their way through the darkness they heard a challenge.

"Who goes there?"

"Two men of the 12th Georgia," they replied, "carrying a wounded comrade."

A Yankee sentry appeared. "Don't you know you're in the Union lines?"

"No," said the startled Rebels.

"Well you are," said the Yankee, adding "Go to your right."

As the bluecoat faded back into the darkness, one of Jenkins' buddies called out, "Man, you've got a heart in you," and they continued on their way.

"Hello, old fellow!"

A fine commander, Israel B. Richardson (1815–62), is one the most overlooked generals of the war. Graduating from West Point 38th in the Class of 1841, which produced thirteen generals in blue and six in gray, Richardson served on the frontier and in Mexico, and then retired to private life. Returning to the Army as a volunteer in 1861, he rose quickly from colonel of the 2nd Michigan to major general, by dint of hard fighting and outstanding tactical skill.

A highly unconventional officer, in terms of uniform Richardson belonged to the "rough and ready" school of generalship, rarely wearing a proper uniform, usually dressing so casually he was once seen in "an old blouse, pantaloons torn on one leg from the knee down, and an old black hat," looking "more like a teamster than a general".

Richardson also had a very fine sense of humor, as can be seen in this lightly edited anecdote from Daniel G. Crotty's war memoir *Four Years Campaigning in the Army of the Potomac.*[10]

> One morning, while walking along the road, the General was accosted by a sprig of a Lieutenant, who looked as though he was fresh from a bandbox, saying: "Hello, old fellow, can you tell me where General Richardson's headquarters are?"
>
> The General looked at him with his peculiar grin, and told him that he could, pointing out the direction to him. The General then strolled on leisurely toward his log hut on the hill, and found the dandy saying all kinds of things, for he was mad that no one waited on him. When the Lieutenant saw the General approaching, he told him to hurry up and hold his horse while he went in to deliver the dispatches he had for the General. The good natured General took the horse, tied him to a stake, went in by another door, and stood before the coxcomb Lieutenant with his stars on his shoulders.
>
> "Now," said he, "what do you want?"
>
> The dandy would gladly have crawled through a knot-hole just then, but he had to face the music, and handed the dispatches to his late groom with trembling hands. He was doubtless relieved of a heavy load when the good natured General told him "that will do," and the sprig of a shoulder-strap was doubtless taught to find out whom he talked to before asking them to hold his horse.

On September 17, 1862, Richardson was commanding the 1st Division of the Second Army Corps at Antietam. Shortly before 1:00 p.m., he put himself at the head of the Irish Brigade, saying, "Men, follow me and where I will not go, I will not ask you to go." He then led them in an attack that gained a position from which they could enfilade the Confederates holding the "Bloody Lane." There Richardson was struck by a shell fragment, and was carried to the rear. Although his wound was not considered life-threatening, infection set in, and the general died on November 3, 1862.

"Have I got a surprise for you"

Late in 1862, Lt. Col. Judson Kilpatrick was on a foraging expedition in Virginia with the 2nd New York Cavalry. Although the troops were supposed to pay for whatever they took, and not take everything so as to leave the local people destitute, these guidelines were most often honored in the breach. In fact, whoever did it, foraging was rough on the local people.

On this particular occasion a farmer complained that the 2nd New York had looted his property so efficiently that, "Everything that I have they have taken; everything except my hope in the hereafter, but that they can't take."

At that, Kilpatrick replied: "Don't be too sure; the 10th New York is coming right behind you."[11]

1863

The signing of the Emancipation Proclamation

Accompanied by his son Frederick, at 11:00 a.m. on January 1, 1863, Secretary of State William H. Seward brought the official text of the Emancipation Proclamation into Abraham Lincoln's office in the White House.

Lincoln took the scroll, unrolled it, and laid it on a table. Picking up a pen, he dipped it in ink and prepared to sign. But then he paused, removed his hand from the paper, and put down the pen. For a moment Lincoln merely sat there. Then he again picked up the pen, re-inked it, and held it once more over the page, only to hesitate yet again. He laid down his pen for a second time.

Looking up, Lincoln saw that Seward was puzzled by his apparent reluctance to sign.

The President smiled and said: "I have been shaking hands since 9 o'clock this morning and my right arm is nearly paralyzed. If my name ever goes down into history it will be for this act, and my whole soul is in it. If my hand trembles when I sign the Proclamation, all who examine the document hereafter will say, 'He hesitated.'"

Then Lincoln turned to the table once more, took up the pen again, re-inked it yet again, and, with a firm hand, slowly signed his name across the bottom. When he finished, he looked up, smiled, and said, "That will do."[12]

The 20th Tennessee receives a new flag

Until the turn of the twentieth century, flags played a critical role in military tactics. Carried into battle, they helped troops know the direction of the advance, provided them with a rallying point in a reverse, and were the symbolic embodiment of a regiment's honor. Hundreds of men died carrying or defending flags from capture, and they were the heart of any regiment. So the awarding of a flag to a regiment was the occasion of great ceremony.

On March 19, 1863, an elaborate ceremony was held near Tullahoma to honor the Confederacy's 20th Tennessee for gallantry in the Battle of Stones River (December 31, 1862– January 2, 1863). Major General John C. Breckinridge presented the regiment with a new flag, made from the dress worn by Ms. Mary Cyrene Burch on December 12, 1843, when she became his wife.

Breckinridge's division formed a hollow square. In its center, accompanied by a pomposity of generals and other dignitaries, Breckinridge's chief of staff Col. Theodore O'Hara made the formal presentation, prefacing it with a flowerily oration of over 600 words, before handing the colors to regimental commander Col. Thomas Benton Smith. Smith made a short, dignified reply, as reported by Capt. Tod Carter of the 20th Tennessee on March 25 in the *Chattanooga Daily Rebel*:

> In behalf of the officers and soldiers of my regiment, I accept this beautiful flag. My language does not permit me to express my feeling on this occasion.

This compliment, unexpected as it is, is doubly pleasing, coming as it does from Kentucky, the land of chivalry and from the noblest of her daughters. A State whose name is linked with the brightest jewels of American history, her women are as lovely as her mountain flowers. For my officers and soldiers, I thank you. When the storm of battle rages fiercest amid the wildest conflict, we will think of the fair donors, and cling to this banner. For the complimentary manner, Sir, in which you have presented it, I thank you.

Soldiers! To you I commit this gift. In its folds rests your honor. Let it never be contaminated by foemen's hand. Let the Confederacy and the world see that in the hour of her darkest trials, Tennessee will stand by the colors of Kentucky, as they would by the standard of their native State. They feel that their honor, their glory, their safety, their people are one!

Like many battle flags, that of the 20th Tennessee took its share of punishment. Although it was not lost in action, the banner didn't survive the war, disappearing during the Atlanta Campaign.

Captain Carter, an attorney and native Tennessean, was mortally wounded during the Battle of Franklin (November 30, 1864) crying, "Follow me boys, I'm almost home!" as he led the regiment in a charge to capture his family home, in which he died two days later.[13]

The Jackson Cotton Works

On May 15, 1863, after capturing Jackson, MS, Ulysses S. Grant and William T. Sherman took a stroll about town. They chanced upon a cotton mill, with everyone busily at work, oblivious of the fact that a battle had been fought for the town and that it was now occupied by Union troops. No one paid the least bit of attention to the pair of Yankee generals as they entered the place and wandered around, watching as a great many women tended various machines, which were turning out tent cloth by the mile, with "C.S.A." woven into each bolt. After they had toured the place for a bit, Grant turned to Sherman, saying, "I think they have done work enough." He then ordered all work to cease. Telling the women that they could take as much cloth as they wished, he ordered them to leave the premises. When the workers had left, he had the place burned down. As an incident of war, it was a minor one and soon forgotten.

Forgotten, that is, until one day many years later.

During Grant's presidency, a Southern gentleman turned up in Washington and requested a meeting. The man stated that he had been the owner of the cotton mill in Jackson that Grant had put to the torch. Claiming that the place was private property, he asked the President to provide him with written confirmation of the fact that it had been burned at Grant's orders, for he wished to lay a claim for recompense on the Congress.

Grant demurred, the laconic "I declined" which appears in his memoirs perhaps concealing somewhat stronger sentiments on the matter.[14]

"Don't fire, Yanks!"

At Gettysburg on the morning of July 3, 1863, as the Army of Northern Virginia and the Army of the Potomac prepared for yet another day of bloodletting, skirmishers from both sides were active in the verdant fields that formed the no man's land between the two armies. By 9:30 a.m., with the heat and humidity already high, elements of the 8th Ohio were already hotly engaged against some Rebels ensconced at the Bliss Farm. Quite suddenly, amidst the pot shots, there came the cry, "Don't fire, Yanks!" Heeding the call, the boys in blue ceased fire, and peered through the standing wheat to see what the Rebs were up to.

A Confederate soldier came from behind the shelter of a large tree not 30 yards in front of the Union skirmish line. Several of the Ohioans thought to take aim at him, but were dissuaded by their comrades, who saw that the man's rifle was slung over his shoulder, and that he carried a canteen in his hand. The man walked to one of the wounded Yankees lying in the wheat and gave him a drink. Then he went from wounded man to wounded man, regardless of uniform, to give what comfort he could, amid cheers of "Bully for you, Johnny!" from the Ohioans.

When he had run out of water, the man stood up and walked back to the Rebel lines. Reaching the safety of his tree again, the man ducked down, calling out, "Down Yanks, we're going to fire." The business of killing began again.[15]

"I have the honor herewith ..."

On July 8, 1863, Maj. Gen. George G. Meade, commanding the Army of the Potomac, dispatched a message to Brig. Gen. Lorenzo Thomas, the Adjutant General of the Union Army, to accompany tangible evidence of the victory at Gettysburg less than a week earlier, during which perhaps 84,000 Union troops and about 70,000 Confederates had been engaged, with casualties respectively of about 23,050 and 28,500:

> Headquarters Army of the Potomac,
> July 8, 1863
>
> Brigadier General L. Thomas,
> Adjutant General, Washington.
>
> General: I have the honor herewith to transmit thirty-one battle-flags, captured from the enemy in the recent battle at Gettysburg. Several other flags were captured on that occasion, but those sent embrace all thus far sent in by corps commanders.
>
> Very respectfully your obedient servant,
> Geo. G. Meade,
> Major General Commanding.
>
> General Barksdale's sword was given in my charge to bring with the above flags.
> Ed. Schriver,
> Inspector General

At least fifty-five Confederate battle flags were captured over the 3 days of Gettysburg, and some estimates place the figure higher. The greatest number were taken on July 3, during Pickett's Charge, when over thirty flags were taken from the forty-one participating regiments, nearly as many as the Union lost over the entire 3 days of the battle.[16]

Charles De Kay and the Draft Riots

Little more than a week after the Battle of Gettysburg, even as the armies were still maneuvering back towards the Rappahannock line, serious disorders occurred in several cities across the North. The introduction of the nation's first federally administered military draft, which provided loopholes for those with money to avoid service, touched off long-standing resentment among urban workers, particularly Irish immigrants, but others as well, who had experienced social discrimination and religious persecution, and who generally opposed abolition, fearing that hosts of freedmen would flood the North, taking their jobs.

The worst disorders were in New York.[17] On July 13, a mob sacked the Provost Marshal's office. Bands of rioters began rampaging across Manhattan, looting and burning, attacking prominent Republicans and African Americans, and forcing bystanders to join them or be beaten. Armories and arms factories were attacked, and while watchmen and police managed to beat the mob off from some, others were overrun, and the rioters obtained arms. With the police greatly outnumbered, troops were called in from the harbor forts and militia units on duty in Pennsylvania and Washington were recalled. The riots lasted four days. A huge mob attempted to attack City Hall, only to be defeated in an open battle by hundreds of truncheon-wielding police officers under Inspector Daniel Carpenter (1816–66), who ambushed them at Broadway and Bleeker Street and sent them flying. The Colored Orphan Asylum at Fifth Avenue and 43rd Street was sacked and burned, though the staff managed to evacuate 237 children, although one died in a fall. Another mob tried to sack the offices of *The New-York Daily Tribune* and lynch editor Horace Greeley, but was smashed by Carpenter and 200 cops assisted by the employees and an armed squad from the rival *The New York Times*. The mayor's house was attacked, but successfully defended by a combination of oratory and conspicuously displayed force. The posh men's shop Lord & Taylor escaped unscathed, defended by its staff, armed by the police, but the rival Brooks Brothers, which had poor labor-management relations, lost over $50,000 when their store was looted and burned.

The 15th was the critical day. By evening, the 7th and 65th New York Militia regiments arrived in the city from Pennsylvania, while the Roman Catholic archbishop, John Hughes, spoke to a large crowd gathered outside his residence, and the mayor announced that the city would pay the $300—a year's pay for most workers—commutation for any drafted man or as an enlistment bonus to those who chose to serve. The next day, the troops and police began to suppress the rioting on a district by district basis, reinforced by several more regiments. On the 17th, no serious outbreaks were reported, though tensions ran high and

An incident during the Draft Riots, when the mob attacked a detail of about fifty recuperating soldiers from the Invalid Corps who had been hastily armed and sent in to help restore order, July 13, 1863.

heavy patrolling was necessary. Things calmed down quickly as more troops arrived.

While the number of deaths in the riots is often claimed to have been over a thousand, the actual figure appears to have much lower; about 110 bodies were recovered and some others may have been incinerated in the fires. Most of the dead were rioters or innocent bystanders, killed by police or troops or other rioters. Eleven of the dead were black men, three were police officers, eight soldiers, and one a civilian police volunteer. At least 268 people (105 policemen, thirty-five soldiers, and 128 citizens, including at least twenty-three African Americans) were seriously injured with a further 600 or so less seriously. Although 443 people were arrested, only about sixty were convicted. John V. Andrews, a Virginian resident in the city, received the heaviest penalty, three years on a charge of treason, having made an inflammatory speech at the onset of the riots.

The financial loss from the riots is estimated to have been as high as $2.5 million, but the city only paid out about $1.5 million in claims.

The city's African American community suffered most in the riots. In addition to the dead, hundreds lost everything when their homes were destroyed, many others saw their jobs go up in smoke. A group of prominent merchants organized a committee to assist blacks in finding jobs and homes, but the blow to the black community was devastating. By 1865, the African American population of the city had fallen by nearly a quarter, from 12,581 to 9,943, as people left town.

Among the eyewitnesses to the riots was a young student, Charles De Kay, who penned a poem on the subject.

The Draft Riot

In the University Tower: New York, July, 1863

Is it the wind, the many-tongued, the weird,
That cries in sharp distress about the eaves?
Is it the wind whose gathering shout is heard
With voice of peoples myriad like the leaves?
Is it the wind? Fly to the casement, quick,
And when the roar comes thick,
Fling wide the sash,
Await the crash!

Nothing. Some various solitary cries, —
Some sauntering woman's short hard laugh,
Or honester, a dog's bark, — these arise
From lamplit street up to this free flagstaff:
Nothing remains of that low threatening sound;
The wind raves not the eaves around.
Clasp casement to, —
You heard not true.

Hark there again! a roar that holds a shriek!
But not without — no, from below it comes:
What pulses up from solid earth to wreck
A vengeful word on towers and lofty domes?
What angry booming doth the trembling ear,
Glued to the stone wall, hear —
So deep, no air
Its weight can bear?

Grieve! 't is the voice of ignorance and vice,—
The rage of slaves who fancy they are free:
Men who would keep men slaves at any price,
Too blind their own black manacles to see.
Grieve! 't is that grisly spectre with a torch,
Riot — that bloodies every porch,
Hurls justice down
And burns the town.

Charles De Kay (1848–1935) was one of four sons of George Coleman
De Kay (1802–49), who had risen to commodore in the Argentine Navy

by the age of 25, rendered services to the Ottoman Navy, and engaged in many other adventures as well. In 1864, Charles entered Yale, and graduated in 1868. He became a noted critic, linguist, fencer, diplomat, and journalist, and was a founder of the National Arts Club.[18] His older brothers all served in the war.

" … and come in to dinner"

Many families found themselves divided by the war. Such was the case of the Ghormley family, of Chilhowee, a small town in the Smoky Mountains of East Tennessee. Mrs. Nancy Ghormley had five sons, two wore Confederate gray and three, along with two grandsons, Union blue. From time to time the boys would drop in for a visit—and a home-cooked meal.[19]

On one occasion, Mrs. Ghormley's two gray-clad boys, one the Provost Marshal of Tennessee and the other a recruiting officer, popped by for a visit. Just as they stabled their horses in the barn, five blue-clad members of the family turned up. For a moment the men glared at each other in their mother's yard. Words passed between them, and became heated.

Then Mrs. Ghormley stepped out of the house, saying "Gentlemen, leave your guns and swords in the yard and come in to dinner. You are all my children."

Whereupon a good meal was had by all.

The Gettysburg Address

"Four score and seven years ago our fathers brought forth, upon this continent, a new nation, conceived in Liberty, and dedicated to the proposition that all men are created equal.

"Now we are engaged in a great civil war, testing whether that nation, or any nation, so conceived, and so dedicated, can long endure. We are met here on a great battlefield of that war. We have come to dedicate a portion of it as a final resting place for those who here gave their lives that that nation might live. It is altogether fitting and proper that we should do this.

"But in a larger sense we can not dedicate—we can not consecrate—we can not hallow—this ground. The brave men, living and dead, who struggled here, have consecrated it, far above our poor power to add or detract. The world will little note, nor long remember, what we say here, but can never forget what they did here. It is for us, the living, rather to be dedicated here to the unfinished work which they have, thus far, so nobly carried on. It is rather for us to be here dedicated to the great task remaining before us—that from these honored dead we take increased devotion to that cause for which they gave the last full measure of devotion—that we here highly resolve that these dead shall not have died in vain; that this nation shall have a new birth of freedom; and that this government of the people, by the people, and for the people, shall not perish from the earth."

Abraham Lincoln
November 19, 1863

1864

Killing Jeff Davis

On February 28, 1864, Col. Ulric Dahlgren, a 21-year-old Union cavalryman, took command of one of several columns of cavalry in a complex series of raids conceived by Maj. Gen. Judson Kilpatrick to liberate Union prisoners of war held in and near Richmond. Confederate forces responded to the raids more quickly than anticipated, and the plan soon collapsed, after several days of hard riding and fighting. While attempting to extricate his troops, on March 2, Dahlgren was killed near Stevensville, VA, about 30 miles northeast of Richmond. In his pocket were found orders in his own hand that ended with the phrase, "once in the city it must be destroyed and Jeff. Davis and Cabinet killed." The apparent attempt to decapitate the Confederacy aroused considerable controversy, many in the North, including government and military officials, branding the documents a forgery, while in the South they were touted as evidence of Yankee barbarism. Today, the scholarly consensus is that the papers are authentic, but their origins remain highly controversial. It's possible that Dahlgren himself modified his original orders to include killing Davis and members of the cabinet. Alternatively the orders may have secretly been issued by Secretary of War Edwin Stanton or General Kilpatrick, the latter in particular would certainly have had no difficulty about murdering Davis had the idea occurred to him. Some historians believe the incident may have inspired John Wilkes Booth to murder Lincoln.[20]

"You got my hog!"

Sam Watkins (1839–1901), a private in Company H of the Confederate 1st Tennessee, saw much of the war, enlisting in the Spring of 1861, and fighting from Shiloh through the Vicksburg, Atlanta, Chattanooga, and Franklin-Nashville campaigns. He surrendered with the remnants of the Army of Tennessee at Bentonville, NC, on April 26, 1865, by which time there were only seven men left in his company.

In the early 1880s, Watkins wrote a series of newspaper articles about his adventures in the war, which were published in 1882 as *"Co. Aytch": Maury Grays, First Tennessee Regiment or, A Side Show of the Big Show*, an amusing work full of often bitterly insightful comments on life and war, such as, "Dying on the field of battle and glory is about the easiest duty a soldier has to undergo."

One tale in the book is about foraging for food during the winter of 1863/64. Having been forced into northern Georgia by the Union victory at Chattanooga in November 1863, the Army of Tennessee had taken up winter quarters south of the Conasauga River. It was a harsh winter, and food supplies ran low, so the troops often foraged from the surrounding area, despite the fact that the local people were fellow Confederates, a matter that troubled some, like Watkins, as seen in this lightly edited excerpt from *"Co. Aytch"*:

> One day, a party of "us privates" concluded we would go across the Conasauga River on a raid. We crossed over in a canoe. After traveling for some time, we saw a neat looking farm house, and sent one of the party forward to reconnoiter. He returned in a few minutes and announced that he had found a fine fat sow in a pen near the house. Now, the plan we formed was for two of us to go into the house and keep the inmates interested and the other was to toll and drive off the hog. I was one of the party which went into the house. There was no one there but an old lady and her sick and widowed daughter. They invited us in very pleasantly and kindly, and soon prepared us a very nice and good dinner.

The old lady told us of all her troubles and trials. Her husband had died before the war, and she had three sons in the army, two of whom had been killed, and the youngest, who had been conscripted, was taken with the camp fever and died in the hospital at Atlanta, and she had nothing to subsist upon, after eating up what they then had. I was much interested, and remained a little while after my comrade had left. I soon went out, having made up my mind to have nothing to do with the hog affair. I did not know how to act. I was in a bad fix. I had heard the gun fire and knew its portent. I knew the hog was dead, and went on up the road, and soon overtook my two comrades with the hog, which had been skinned and cut up, and was being carried on a pole between them.

I did not know what to do. On looking back I saw the old lady coming and screaming at the top of her voice, "You got my hog! You got my hog!" It was too late to back out now. We had the hog, and had to make the most of it, even if we did ruin a needy and destitute family.[21]

"Crazy Bet" Van Lew and her Richmond spy ring

The most successful espionage network of the Civil War was run by Elizabeth Van Lew (1818–1900).[22] The remarkably homely daughter of a prosperous Richmond hardware merchant of Northern origins, she was educated in a Quaker school in Philadelphia, and became a confirmed abolitionist. After her father's death in 1843, Elizabeth, her brother John, who inherited the business, and their mother, Philadelphian Eliza Baker Van Lew, freed the family's nine slaves, many of whom remained with them as hired servants. Over the years, the Van Lews would sometimes buy and free slave families that were about to be split up.

Needless to note, the Van Lews were Unionists. When the war came, brother John managed to get a medical exemption from military service, while Elizabeth and her mother reached out to help Union soldiers who were being held as prisoners of war in Richmond. Most Richmondites thought this was a little odd, and Elizabeth soon decided to become odder, dressing carelessly and even making hostile statements about the Confederacy. Her increasingly unusual ways and outspoken support for the Union made most people think she was merely a rich, eccentric, spinster lady, and she was nicknamed "Crazy Bet," a reputation that gave her excellent "cover" for espionage. Van Lew began spying in small ways. While helping to care for Union prisoners, she realized that they often possessed important information, which could be valuable to the

Union. Van Lew began recruiting agents and couriers from among the many secret Unionist whites in Richmond, as well as among African Americans, both free and slave, and soon developed a complex network that involved dozens of people, male and female, black and white, free and slave, gathering and distributing information.

Van Lew had some innovative ways of getting information to Union forces. She usually encoded messages in a special cypher, often writing in an ink that only became visible when heated. Messages were then sent to her farm outside of the city, where her servants routinely went to bring back milk, eggs, and other products. From there messages would be passed on to other agents, who would ultimately deliver them to Union commanders. The messages were concealed in several ways. A local baker, who visited her daily to buy eggs and milk, would sometimes put messages inside loaves of bread which were smuggled to Union troops, and messages could also be hidden inside eggshells or even in the soles of boots, giving rise to a joke about how information "walked" to the Union Army. None of Van Lew's couriers were ever caught, and it is said that they even delivered fresh flowers from her garden to Union generals such as Benjamin Butler and Ulysses S. Grant during the static fighting around Richmond and Petersburg late in the war.

In addition to managing her espionage ring, Elizabeth often aided Union prisoners of war to escape; in February 1864, she abetted the flight of more than a hundred men from Libby Prison escape by means of a tunnel. She sometimes hid escaped prisoners in a secret room in her house, in which one room was being rented to the commander of one of the Confederate prisons in the city.

Van Lew had dozens of agents, but the most interesting and daring was certainly Mary Jane Bowser, a freedwoman. Born into slavery about 1840, Mary Jane became part of the Van Lew household as an infant, and she was freed in about 1843. Treated as a member of the family by Van Lew, she learned to read and write, among other skills. When Mary Jane was in her teens, Van Lew sent her to a Quaker "Negro School" in Philadelphia. After graduating, Mary Jane may have served as a mission teacher in Liberia, but returned to Richmond shortly before the Civil

War, married a freedman named Wilson Bowser, and after Fort Sumter became involved in Van Lew's espionage work.

In mid-1864, through her many contacts in high Confederate circles (she often took tea with elderly Brig. Gen. John Henry Winder, who acted as Provost Marshal of Richmond), Van Lew learned that Jefferson and Varina Davis were looking to a maid to help with the chores in the Confederate White House and mind their children. Thinking quickly, Van Lew arranged for Mary Bower to pretend to be the illiterate, somewhat dim-witted "Ellen Bond," and recommended her to Mrs. Davis, who hired her.

As Bowser did her chores, which included chasing the Davis children's pet squirrels, she pretty much had the run of the Confederate White House, even the president's office. She frequently read important documents, memorizing them and making copies, and at times overheard conversations between Davis and top political and military leaders. Bowser passed this information on to Van Lew. Bowser worked in the Confederate White House for nearly a year. In early 1865, some Confederate leaders began to wonder about possible "leaks" from the White House. Alerted by Philip Cashmeyer, a detective for the Confederate Provost Marshal who was also one of Van Lew's agents, Bowser took $1,500 of the Davis' money and fled Richmond with Van Lew's help, which made her seem to be just another ordinary fugitive slave, rather than an escaping spy. Alas for history, after her escape from Richmond, Mary Bowser's life becomes murky.

Although Mary Bowser was certainly Van Lew's most impressive agent, "Crazy Bet" had other agents in surprisingly important posts. In addition to Philip Cashmeyer, who was supposed to be catching spies, her agents included the commercial merchant Martin M. Lipscomb, who had contracts to provide supplies for the Confederate Army, and thus was able to learn about military movements; Erasmus Ross, a clerk at Libby Prison, who helped organize several escapes; and Samuel Ruth, Supervisor of the Richmond, Fredericksburg, & Potomac Rail Road, who had access to information about troop movements and a talent for turning 4-hour railroad trips into 40-hour ones; as well as several agents who remain unknown, including one in the Adjutant General's Department at Richmond, with access to the strength reports of Confederate units, and one in the Army's Engineering Department who supplied "beautiful-ly-accurate plans of the rebel defenses around Richmond and Petersburg, which were promptly forwarded to General Grant."[23]

Van Lew did not fare well after the war. Her wartime activities eventually became known, and her unreconstructed rebel neighbors avoided her. Since she had spent virtually all her fortune in the Union cause, she sank slowly into poverty. During Ulysses S. Grant's presidency (1869–77) she was postmistress of Richmond, a profitable job, but after that she was supported largely by donations from many of the soldiers she had helped escape from prison. She died a very lonely woman.

The full story of Elizabeth Van Lew and her network of agents and couriers can never be fully told, because as she lay dying she had all her papers relating to her wartime activities destroyed.

Nathan Bedford Forrest captures Athens

In late September 1864, Confederate Maj. Gen. Nathan Bedford Forrest, a gifted amateur soldier, was leading 4,500 mounted troops on a raid from northern Alabama against Union lines of communication through Tennessee, in an effort to forestall the fall of Atlanta to William Tecumseh Sherman. As always on a raid, time was of the essence. Unfortunately, there were some 575 Union troops at Athens, AL, where Fort Henderson provided a sturdy bastion that would require time to reduce by conventional methods, time which Forrest did not have, given that a column of Union reinforcements was on the march for the post even as his own troops approached it.

Sending a detachment to keep the Union reinforcements entertained, Forrest surrounded the Union post during the night of September 22/23. At 7:00 a.m. the next morning, he began to shell the fort, inflicting several casualties. Naturally, the Union troops replied in kind. Shortly afterwards, Forrest sent a surrender request to the Union commander, Col. Wallace Campbell, of the 110th Colored Infantry. When Campbell rejected the suggestion, Forrest offered to meet to discuss ways of averting unnecessary bloodshed. Campbell agreed, and in his official report wrote:

> I immediately met General Forrest, accompanied by Lieut. Col. J. A. Dewey. General Forrest told me he was determined to take the place; that his force

was sufficiently large, and have it he would, and if he was compelled to storm the works it would result in the massacre of the entire garrison. He told me what his force was, and said myself and one officer could have the privilege of reviewing his force. I returned to the fort, when, after consultation with the commanders of various detachments in the fort, it was decided that [if] after reviewing the force of General Forrest I found he had 8,000 or 10,000 troops, it would be worse than murder to attempt to hold the works. I then took Capt. B. M. Callender, First Missouri Light Artillery, and rode round [Forrest's] entire line, thereby satisfying myself and the captain accompanying me that there were at least 10,000 men and nine pieces of artillery. It was now 11 a.m. I had been "dilly-dallying" with General Forrest since 8 a.m. expecting re-enforcements would be sent from Decatur. Believing they could not reach me, I ordered the surrender of the fort.[24]

Forrest offered very generous surrender terms, on paper, thus securing some 575 prisoners, plus a well-fortified post, with lots of useful supplies, including some 70,000 rounds of rifle ammunition. In addition, he scooped up the relief force, which numbered fewer than 400 men. So it had been a good day for Forrest. In fact, not only very good, but very lucky.

Forrest had pulled the wool over Campbell's eyes. He had divided his command into several contingents. As he leisurely escorted Campbell to each of his positions surrounding the fort, the troops whom they had last visited quickly and quietly moved to another position. In this way, Forrest managed to make his few hundred troops appear to be several times more numerous.

Now Campbell may seem to have been somewhat dim-witted, since arguably he ought to have smelled a rat from the moment Forrest suggested that he inspect the investing troops, but there was, in fact, precedent for just that. Two years earlier, in September 1862, Union Col. John T. Wilder, another talented amateur soldier who later became an excellent cavalrymen, had found himself similarly invested, and requested that he be allowed to inspect Confederate Maj. Gen. Simon Bolivar Buckner's forces in order to assist him in deciding on an honorable and humane course of action. Buckner acceded to the request, and Wilder really was greatly outnumbered, and so surrendered, being satisfied that further resistance would only waste lives. But things were generally a lot more honorable in 1862 than in 1864.

"Marching Through Georgia"

The famous song "Marching Through Georgia" was, of course, about Sherman's March to the Sea in late November and December 1864. Perhaps inspired by a bit of soldier improvisation—as claimed by the same Massachusetts troops who had earlier given us "The John Brown Song"— Henry Clay Work (1832–84), a moderately successful song writer of the day, wrote "Marching Through Georgia," which was published early in 1865. It became popular in the North in the final months of the war and was a commonplace at veterans' reunions ever afterwards, as well as pretty much any time Sherman turned up at a public function, so often that he came to loath it as much as any unreconstructed Rebel.[25]

Marching Through Georgia

Bring the good ol' Bugle boys! We'll sing another song,
Sing it with a spirit that will start the world along,
Sing it like we used to sing it fifty thousand strong,
While we were marching through Georgia.

(Chorus)

Hurrah! Hurrah! We bring the Jubilee.
Hurrah! Hurrah! The flag that makes you free.
So we sang the chorus from Atlanta to the sea,
While we were marching through Georgia.

How the darkeys shouted when they heard the joyful sound,
How the turkeys gobbled which our commissary found,
How the sweet potatoes even started from the ground,
While we were marching through Georgia.

(Repeat chorus)

Yes and there were Union men who wept with joyful tears,
When they saw the honored flag they had not seen for years;
Hardly could they be restrained from breaking forth in cheers,
While we were marching through Georgia.

(Repeat chorus)

"Sherman's dashing Yankee boys will never make the coast!"
So the saucy rebels said and 'twas a handsome boast.

Had they not forgot, alas! to reckon with the Host
While we were marching through Georgia.

(Repeat chorus)

So we made a thoroughfare for freedom and her train,
Sixty miles of latitude, three hundred to the main;
Treason fled before us, for resistance was in vain
While we were marching through Georgia.

(Repeat chorus)

While for obvious reasons the song never caught on in the South, "Marching Through Georgia" gained considerable worldwide popularity: British troops sang it—or variants of it—on the march in India during the height of the Raj in the late nineteenth century and during the Anglo-Boer War, the Japanese played a version of it when they entered Port Arthur in 1905, it was heard in both world wars wherever English-speaking troops were to be found, and the tune has been adapted for many other songs as well.[26]

1865

Jefferson Davis receives a telegram

On Sunday, April 2, 1865, Jefferson Davis attended services at St. Paul's Episcopal Church in Richmond, occupying a pew reserved for his use.

Part way through the service, the church sexton walked quietly up the aisle, leaned over, and handed Davis an envelope.

The Confederate president opened the envelope to find a telegram. Upon reading it, he immediately rose from his pew and left the church, onlookers recalling that his face had turned "deathly pale." The telegram, from Gen. Robert E. Lee, read:

Petersburg
April 2, 1865

I think it is absolutely necessary that we should abandon our position tonight. I have given all necessary orders on the subject to the troops, and the operation, though difficult, I hope will be performed successfully. I have directed General

Stevens to send an officer to your Excellency to explain the route to you by which the troops will be moved to Amelia Court House, and furnish you with a guide and any assistance that you may require for yourself.[27]

"Let us take our stand here"

On April 4, 1865, the Confederate Army of Tennessee, was in dire straits encamped near Selma, NC. Desertions were rising, rations and ammunition in short supply, and William Tecumseh Sherman was closing in, while further north, the Army of Northern Virginia had just been forced from the Richmond–Petersburg lines by Ulysses S. Grant.

Brigadier General Thomas L. Clingman, a politician turned soldier, approached army commander Gen. Joseph E. Johnston. "Sir, much has been said about dying in the last ditch. You have left with you thirty thousand of as brave men as the sun ever shone upon. Let us take our stand here and fight the two armies of Grant and Sherman to the end, and thus show to the world how far we can surpass the Thermopylae of the Greeks."[28]

Fully knowing the Confederacy's war was lost, and mindful of his duty to the men under his command, Johnston replied, "I'm not in the Thermopylae business."

On April 26, Johnston surrendered the Army of Tennessee to Sherman on highly favorable terms near Greensboro, NC.

Mrs. Pickett has a visitor

In 1852, when she was 9, LaSalle "Sallie" Corbell (1843–1931) met the dashing Capt. George Edward Pickett (1825–75), and despite the great difference in their ages, promptly decided to marry him, a goal she achieved in November 1863, by which time the twice-widowed Pickett was a major general in the Confederate Army.

Years after the war, Mrs. Pickett wrote a memoir, *Pickett and his Men*, in which she recounted, with considerable embroidery, her version of the war and her husband's role in it. There are a number of fabrications, including the oft-repeated claim that Pickett received his appointment to West Point in 1842 from Representative Abraham Lincoln, which was patently false, as Abe's one term in Congress was in 1847–49; the appointment was secured by his law partner, Representative John T. Stuart. But Lincoln did know Pickett, who was one of the most popular officers in the "Old Army" and had secured a degree of national fame during the "Pig War," a potential disatrous but peacefully resolved dispute with Britain over ownership of portions of the San Juan Archipelago, between Vancouver Island and what would become Washington State in 1859.

In her book, Sallie recounts a curious incident which *may* have taken place on April 4 or 5, 1865, just a few days after the Confederate Army and government abandoned Richmond.

According to Sallie, a carriage arrived in front of her house in the erstwhile Confederate capital:

> I had seen the carriage and the guard and retinue, but did not know who the visitors were. In those suspicious times of trouble and anxiety we did not wait for formal announcements, and we were following on after the servant who went to answer the bell. When I heard the caller ask for George Pickett's wife, I came forward with my baby in my arms.
>
> "I am George Pickett's wife," I said.
>
> "And I am Abraham Lincoln."
>
> "The President?"
>
> "No; Abraham Lincoln, George's old friend."
>
> Seeing baby's outstretched arms, Mr. Lincoln took him, and little George opened wide his mouth and gave his father's friend a dewy baby kiss, seeming to feel with the prescient infant instinct the tie that binds.
>
> As I took my baby back again, Mr. Lincoln said in that deep and sympathetic voice which was one of his greatest powers over the hearts of men: "Tell your father, the rascal, that I forgive him for the sake of your mother's smile and your bright eyes."
>
> I had sometimes wondered at the General's reverential way of speaking of President Lincoln, but as I looked up at his honest, earnest face, and felt the warm clasp of his great, strong hand, I marveled no more that all who knew him should love him.
>
> When, but a few days later, the wires flashed over the world the tragic message which enveloped our whole nation in mourning, General Pickett said: "My God! My God! The South has lost her best friend and protector, the surest, safest hand to guide and steer her through the breakers ahead. Again must she feel the smart of fanaticism."[29]

Given Sallie's track record, it's hard to say whether this tale is true or not; aside from the fact that there is no corroborating evidence, note that she did not notice her visitor was Lincoln until he identified himself, which is hard to believe. An old Italian adage may apply: *Se non è vero, è ben trovato*—If it's not true, it's well told.

Telegrams

Having withdrawn from the Richmond–Petersburg lines amidst widespread demolitions on the night of April 2/3, 1865, Robert E. Lee and the Army of Northern Virginia attempted to flee west, in the hope of eventually joining Joseph E. Johnston's Army of Tennessee somewhere in North Carolina. The Union armies under Ulysses S. Grant undertook a close pursuit, seeking to trap Lee and his army. A series of often desperate battles resulted—Namozine Church, Beaver Pond Creek, Amelia Court House, Paineville, Amelia Springs, Saylor's Creek, Rice's Station, High Bridge—as the Union troops increasingly encircled Lee's army.

On April 6, Maj. Phil Sheridan, commanding Grant's cavalry corps sent a telegram to Lt. Gen. Ulysses S. Grant:

> Cavalry Headquarters
> April 6, 1865

> Lieut. Gen. U. S. GRANT,
> Commanding Armies of the United States:

> GENERAL: I have the honor to report that the enemy made a stand at the intersection of the Burke's Station road with the road upon which they were retreating. I attacked them with two divisions of the Sixth Army Corps and routed them handsomely, making a connection with the cavalry. I am still pressing on with both cavalry and infantry. Up to the present time we have captured Generals Ewell, Kershaw, Barton, Corse, De Foe [Du Bose], and Custis Lee, several thousand prisoners, 14 pieces of artillery, with caissons, and a large number of wagons. If the thing is pressed I think that Lee will surrender.

> P. H. Sheridan,
> Major General, Commanding.

Grant forewarded the telegram to Lincoln, and on the following day, the President sent a telegram back to the general:[30]

To Ulysses S. Grant
Headquarters Armies of the United States,
City-Point

Lieut. Gen. Grant. April 7. 11 a.m. 1865

Gen. Sheridan says "If the thing is pressed I think that Lee will surrender." Let
the *thing* be pressed.

A. Lincoln

On Apil 9, Lt. Gen. Grant telegrammed Secretary of War Edwin M.
Stanton:[31]

> Headquarters Armies of the United States.
> April 9, 1865—4.30 p.m.

Hon. E. M. Stanton,
Secretary of War:

General Lee surrendered the Army of Northern Virginia this afternoon upon
terms proposed by myself. The accompanying additional correspondence will
show the conditions fully.

U. S. Grant,
Lieutenant General.

Having given Gen. Robert E. Lee and his Confederate troops generous terms and immunity from retaliation, after nearly 4 years of hard
campaigning and hundreds of thousands of deaths, the Civil War was
effectively over.

"Welcome home, Private Alderson!"

Private George H. Alderson, who had been serving in the 14th Virginia
Cavalry in the Shenandoah Valley, was one of the first Confederate
veterans to return home after the surrender at Appomattox. As he made
his way to his hometown, Summersville, in what is now West Virginia,
he passed through nearby Lewisburg, bringing the news of Lee's surrender. But no one believed him. Declaring him a deserter, the local
sheriff promptly threw Alderson in jail. There the unfortunate soldier
languished, despite repeated attempts to convince all and sundry of his

erstwhile neighbors that the war really was over. A day or so later, after several other veterans drifted into town with the sad news, Alderson was released to continue on his way.

George H. Alderson was among the first of over nearly 1.4 million soldiers to go home.

The Confederate Army had actually begun to disband even before the surrender of the Army of Northern Virginia at Appomattox in April 1865. As 1865 dawned, tens of thousands of Confederate troops, seeing the end coming, began demobilizing themselves, simply going home, deserting the cause in its death throes to go to the aid of their families. On paper, Confederate strength was still something like 500,000 men at the beginning of April 1865, but only about 350,000 men appear to have actually been with the armies. The Army of Northern Virginia, which numbered about 60,000 men in March, surrendered barely 28,000 in April, and the condition of the other armies was even worse. Most of the men just walked away. One officer described the dissolution of a Texas outfit as "a widespread and immediate decamping of soldiers with whatever army property they could lay their hands on."

Union demobilization took longer. There were large areas that had to be patrolled, as even before the war ended, some Confederate irregulars

Table 6: Union Army strength

Date	Number
May 1, 1865	1,034,000
Aug 7, 1865	359,710
Aug 22, 1865	281,178
Sep 14, 1865	259,409
Oct 15, 1865	215,311
Nov 15, 1865	199,613
May 1, 1866	80,000
Dec 31, 1866	65,000
Jun 1, 1869	35,000

Note: Figures are for the U.S. Regular Army and Volunteer Army, omitting the Navy and Marine Corps.

and partisan rangers, as well as deserters from both armies, had found banditry more to their taste than war. The occupation of the South had to be taken in hand, and troops were needed to guard the Mexican border, where the French-imposed "Emperor" Maximilian von Hapsburg was engaged in a fierce, conflict with Mexico's republicans under Benito Juarez. Despite this, the Federal armies still melted away almost as rapidly as had the Confederate ones.

Within 18 months of Appomattox, the U.S. Army went from being the largest in the world to one of the smallest of any of the major Western nations.[32]

Lincoln, on Lee

On the morning of April 14, 1865, as Lincoln was having breakfast in the White House, his son Robert came down to join him. Robert, who had been serving as a captain on Grant's staff, was just up from Appomattox, where he had witnessed the surrender of the Army of Northern Virginia.

The young man had a photograph in his hand, which he passed to his father.

It was a picture of Robert E. Lee, taken just a few days earlier, after the surrender at Appomattox.

Lincoln gazed at the image for a few minutes, saying nothing.

Then he spoke, "It is a good face; it is the face of a noble, brave man. I am glad the war is over at last."

That evening the President and Mrs. Lincoln went to Ford's Theatre.[33]

Jefferson Davis comforts a frightened child

On Sunday, April 16, 1865, during his flight south from Richmond in the waning days of the war, Jefferson F. Davis reached Salisbury, NC. The weary Confederate President was made welcome by the rector of St. Luke's Episcopal Church, the Rev. Thomas G. Haughton.

The next morning, while at breakfast, the Rev. Haughton's little daughter, aged about 7 or 8, came in crying, "Oh, Papa, old Lincoln's coming and going to kill us all."

At that, Davis placed his hand on the girl's head and said, "Oh, no, my little lady, you need not fear that. Mr. Lincoln is not such a bad man, and he does not want to kill anybody, and certainly not a little girl like you."

Lincoln, of course, had died very early the previous day, though Davis would not learn of this until somewhat later.

Davis and his party were captured on May 10.[34]

Signs of the times

Graduating early from West Point due to the outbreak of war, in May 1861, several newly commissioned 2nd lieutenants under orders to proceed to Washington made a quick stop in New York to buy uniforms, kit, and side arms, and then took a train to Philadelphia, where they were promptly arrested as suspected secessionist sympathizers.[35]

Campaigning in mid-1861 in what is now West Virginia, some Illinois volunteers were wearily making their way down a road in execrable order when their captain shouted, "Close up, boys! Damn you, close up! If the enemy were to fire on you when you're straggling along that way, they couldn't hit a damn one of you! Close up!", whereupon they closed up.[36]

In 1861, 16-year-old Frank Rockefeller, who had an older brother just beginning to build a fortune, enlisted in the 7th Ohio after putting a note in his shoe with "18" written on it, so that when asked his age he could reply, "I'm over 18, sir," an attempt to avoid an outright lie apparently used by many underage volunteers.[37]

Early in the war, many religious recruits on both sides were shocked to find that services were frequently not held on the Sabbath, nor were training, drilling, campaigning, or even fighting suspended for the Lord's Day.[38]

Hearing an indignant Southern woman complain that her chickens had been stolen by some of his soldiers, Brig. Gen. Eleazer Arthur Paine replied, "Madam, we are going to put down this rebellion if it takes every [expletive deleted] chicken in Tennessee."[39]

While campaigning in Virginia in 1862, Union troops sometimes found plantation owners hiding in slave shanties, apparently on the theory that Yankees were less likely to fire on the "servants' quarters" than on the "Big House."[40]

When a hotelkeeper in the newly captured Jackson, MS, demanded payment for rooms used by Ulysses S. Grant and his entourage on the night of May 14/15, 1862, Assistant Secretary of War Charles A. Dana, a member of the general's party, gladly paid—with a crisp new $100 bill, in Confederate money.[41]

One chilly day late in November 1863, some men of Pegram's Brigade of the Army of Northern Virginia, after concluding an unofficial truce with nearby Union pickets, undertook to baptize some of their comrades in the chilly Rapidan River, and during which they were joined in the hymn singing by their Yankee friends.[42]

Trudging to a village in central Pennsylvania at the head of his division on the road to Gettysburg in June 1863, Confederate Maj. Gen. George Pickett doffed his hat and bowed to a young "Dutch" girl who was defiantly waving the Stars and Stripes. When accused by an aide of saluting the enemy's flag, he replied: "I did not salute the enemy's flag. I saluted the heroic womanhood in the heart of that brave little girl, and the glorious old banner under which I won my first laurels."[43]

On August 21, 1863, which Jefferson Davis had designated as "A day of fasting, humiliation, and prayer," Confederate raiders under the notorious William Quantrill (1837–65) killed between 150 and 200 civilians in Lawrence, KS.[44]

The posh New York Hotel, on Broadway and Waverly Place, "occupying the highest rank among American hotels," was a favorite hangout for Southern sympathizers and spies, which made it rather easy for the police and Provost Marshal to keep track of the comings and goings of some of the less adept Confederate agents.[45]

At one point during the Chattanooga Campaign, a Union officer called out the guard to salute Ulysses S. Grant, who was examining positions along Chickamauga Creek, whereupon

Confederate troops on the opposite bank also turned out to salute the general, who returned their honors.[46]

Shortly after the Battle of Missionary Ridge (November 25, 1863), a Union chaplain supervising burials asked Maj. Gen. George Thomas whether the dead should be sorted and interred by state, to which the general replied, "Mix 'em up. I'm tired of state-rights."[47]

While in winter quarters in 1863/64, twenty-two cobblers serving in the ranks of Maj. Gen. Lafayette McLaw's Confederate division were assigned to ply their civil trade, producing 1,500 pairs of new shoes, and repairing thousands of old ones.[48]

In the spring of 1864, representatives of the Christian Commission asked that Bibles and religious tracts be exempted from a ban on civilian goods being carried on the Nashville & Chattanooga Railroad. Major General William T. Sherman replied, "Tracts and Bibles are very good in their way, gentlemen, but rations and ammunition are much better."[49]

In November 1864 the 3rd Colorado Volunteer Cavalry, under the command of Col. John Milton Chivington, a Methodist minister and elder, massacred an entire village of Cheyenne at Sand Creek, Colorado Territory, who were at the time under the protection of the United States of America.[50]

Some years after the war, a citizen of Augusta, GA is reported to have asked William T. Sherman why he had bypassed the city during his famous March to the Sea, to which the general is said to have replied that if the local people felt slighted, he would be happy to get some of his old boys together and pay a visit.[51]

CHAPTER 6

The Naval War

The Civil War was not just fought on land. It was also fought, as Lincoln put it, "on the deep sea, the broad bay, and the rapid river, but also up the narrow muddy bayou, and wherever the ground was a little damp."[1] In the naval war great battles were few, and casualties relatively low. The principal work of the navies was in supporting the armies, defending or attacking coastal installations and river fortresses, in raiding commerce or pursuing raiders, and in the long days and nights of tedious duty on blockade. In the end, the U.S. Navy—what Lincoln called "Uncle Sam's web-feet"—prevailed, but the Confederate Navy (C.S.N.), despite extraordinary handicaps, turned in an impressive performance.[2]

At the start of the war, the Union did not have much of a fleet, and the Confederacy none at all. Each side made enormous efforts to create a strong, effective navy and ultimately the naval forces of both sides were largely built in the course of the war.

The U.S. Navy began the war with ninety ships, all wooden hulled and many obsolete, with only forty-two actually in commission, manned by some 1,350 officers, including Academy midshipmen, about 20 percent of whom would shortly join the Confederacy, and 7,600 seamen. Under the able leadership of Secretary Gideon Welles (1802–78) and Assistant Secretary Gustavus Fox (1821–83), by war's end the Navy had more than 700 ships, including some sixty ironclads, with more abuilding, manned by more than 6,750 officers and over 50,000 sailors, many of them African American, the enlisted ranks of the service having always been open to black men.

The Confederacy began the war with little more than a dozen useful vessels, mostly former revenue cutters, none of which could be properly termed "warships," and perhaps 100 officers recently resigned or dismissed from Union service. On March 4, 1861, this unpromising force was entrusted to Stephen R. Mallory (1812–73) as Secretary of the Navy. Mallory held the office for the rest of the war, one of only two members of the Confederate cabinet to serve throughout. An admiralty lawyer who had done his bit as a volunteer during the Second Seminole War (1837–39), Mallory had represented Florida in the Senate (1851–61), where he served on the Committee on Naval Affairs. He proved an extremely able and innovative administrator, and under his guidance, the Confederate Navy commissioned nearly 200 warships, among them about two dozen of the fifty or so ironclads on which work was begun, though the maximum number of ships in commission at one time barely approached 100. At maximum strength, in 1864, the C.S.N. had about 500 officers of the line or engineering corps and several thousand seamen; after this date, many personnel began passing into the Army.

Marines

Union naval hero—and shameless self-promoter—David Dixon Porter once stressed the important of marines to the naval service by remarking that, "A ship without marines is like a garment without buttons." On the eve of the war, the U.S. Marine Corps had forty-eight officers and about 1,750 men, most serving afloat or at the various naval bases. But secession and then war caused twenty-seven officers to leave the service; three joined the Union's Volunteer Army, three retired to civil life, and twenty-one joined the Confederacy, eighteen serving as officers in the C.S. Marine Corps and three in the Confederate Army.

Some 5,000 men served as officers or enlisted men in the U.S. Marine Corps during the war, with strength peaking in early 1865 at eighty-seven officers and about 3,775 enlisted men. U.S. Marines served in virtually all actions of the Navy in the war, and 148 marines were killed in action or died of wounds, while another 312 died of other causes.

Formed in part from men already recruited by some state navies, the C.S. Marine Corps had an initial strength of twenty-seven officers and about 350 enlisted men. During the war, fifty-eight men were granted commissions and about 1,200 served as enlisted personnel, but strength peaked at about forty officers and about 550 enlisted men in 1864. Casualties among Confederate marines are not known, aside from one officer who died of disease.

On both sides, marines performed their traditional duties, primarily in providing security for ships and naval installations and serving in boarding, cutting out, and landing parties. Although Union forces carried out several amphibious landings during the war, these were done primarily by army personnel, with marines only peripherally involved, as the Commandant of the Marine Corps, Col. John Harris (1795–1864), believed his primary purpose was to support the fleet, thus missing the opportunity to develop a new mission for the corps.

The fleets

Some idea of the effort put into the naval side of the war can be gained by looking at the strength of the fleets. At the start of the war, the U.S. Navy had just ninety vessels, many of them obsolete, old sailing ships of the line and frigates, such as the USS *Constitution*. Only about 75 percent of the ships were serviceable, and of these only forty-two were in commission, most on distant stations, from the Mediterranean to the coast of Africa and even in the Far East. Worse, only half of the serviceable ships were steamers, and of those fewer than half were in commission. So the U.S. Navy had slender resources with which to commence a major war.

Of course, Confederate naval resources were even slimmer than those of the Union. Although six revenue cutters, three coast survey vessels, about a dozen lighthouse tenders, and a few other miscellaneous government-owned vessels fell into Confederate hands during the Secession Crisis, not a single useful U.S. Navy vessel was captured,

Table 7: Union and Confederate warships in commission

	U.S. Navy			C.S. Navy			Ratio of C.S.N.: U.S.N. (as %)		
Date	Start	Added	Lost	Start	Added	Lost	Start	Added	Lost
1861	42	264	6	0	38	3	—	16.5%	50.0%
1862	300	170	11	35	45	30	13.2%	26.5%	272.7%
1863	459	190	26	50	45	35	11.8%	23.7%	134.6%
1864	623	100	20	60	20	24	10.2%	20.0%	120.0%
1865	703	12	6	56	1	30	7.5%	8.0%	500.0%
Total losses			69			122			176.8%

Notes:

All figures are approximate, and small vessels are omitted.

The column "Start" refers to all vessels in commission at the start of the year, including riverine and local defense vessels.

"Added" covers ships entering service in the course of the year.

"Lost" covers those sunk, captured, scuttled, foundered, transferred, or otherwise lost by the service during the year.

For 1865, "Added" only covers vessels commissioned by the end of May, thus omitting many U.S. ships completed but not yet commissioned.

For 1865, "Lost" includes vessels scuttled in the final days of the war.

The USS New Ironsides, *being struck by a "spar torpedo"—essentially a bomb attached to a pole—driven against her hull by the semi-submersible CSS Davis, October 5, 1863. Both the 4,100-ton ironclad frigate and the 4-ton torpedo boat survived, with some damage.*

as naval officers put ships to the torch rather than see them fall to the Rebels; only one ship was salvable, the steam frigate USS *Merrimac*, the burnt-out hulk of which was rebuilt as the famed ironclad *Virginia*. From these inauspicious beginnings, the Confederacy started to build a Navy. All sorts of miscellaneous vessels were pressed into service, usually with minimal refitting as warships, and in addition an ambitious building program was undertaken. Surprisingly, despite lacking the industrial resources of the North, the Confederacy seems to have converted or built nearly 200 warships of various types, including about two dozen ironclads of the nearly fifty begun or projected. This was a prodigious effort, marked by considerable success, despite the lack of industrial resources.

The single largest cause of loss for U.S. warships was by marine mine—called "torpedoes" at the time—twenty-seven ships being sunk, not quite 40 percent of all vessels lost in the war, including those lost to the hazards of the sea or accidents.

The ironclads

The one thing most people are certainly sure of when the subject of the navies in the Civil War comes up is that it was a clash of armored—"ironclad"—vessels which had made wooden warships totally obsolete. Like many other well-known "facts" about the war, that's not quite true. In fact, most ironclads on both sides were wooden hulled, and many of them were virtually immobile. But ironclads, though surprisingly few in number, played a critical role in the war.

Ironclads had started appearing in navies in the late 1850s, and by the outbreak of the Civil War, France and Britain each had one or two in commission, and along with other countries, many more under construction. But the U.S. Navy had not yet acquired any, nor had plans to do so. So when, on May 10, 1861, Confederate Secretary of the Navy Stephen R. Mallory sent a lengthy letter to the chairman of the Congressional Naval Affairs Committee, reviewing recent trends in naval science, and concluding "I regard the possession of an iron-armored ship as a matter of the first necessity. Such a vessel at this time could traverse the entire coast of the United States, prevent all blockades, and encounter, with a fair prospect of success, their entire Navy," he initiated what might be called an "ironclad race" between the Confederacy and the Union.

The Confederacy got out of the gate first in the ironclad race, taking in hand the sunken hulk of the 1855 steam frigate USS *Merrimack*, which had been torched in a dry dock when Union forces abandoned the navy yard at Norfolk, VA on April 20, 1861. The ship's machinery was ruined, but her hull was sound, and Confederate naval engineers, among them Catesby ap Roger Jones and John M. Brooke, began converting her into a "casemate" ironclad, looking rather like an iron-plated bastion mounted on a ship.

Word of the project to convert the *Merrimack* into an ironclad quickly reached Washington, and on August 3, 1861, Congress appropriated money for the Navy to acquire ironclads. The Navy convened an Ironclad Board, which approved construction of three ships: the wooden-hulled broadside ironclad *Galena*, the wooden-hulled ironclad frigate *New Ironsides*, and the all-iron turret ship *Monitor*. Designed by Swedish-born engineer John Ericsson, *Monitor* was the most innovative of the three, her design reportedly including 208 newly patented inventions.[3] All three were built with surprising speed, most notably the *Monitor*, laid down in Greenpoint, Brooklyn, on October 25, 1861, she was commissioned at the Brooklyn Navy Yard on February 25, 1862, just a few days after the Confederacy commissioned the former *Merrimack* as the CSS *Virginia*.

The two ships were quite different: *Virginia* displaced about 4,000 tons and was armed with ten heavy cannon in fixed casemates, so that only three could bear on the same target, while *Monitor* was just under 1,000 tons, and had only two very heavy 11in. Dahlgren smooth-bore cannon, in a rotating turret. Both vessels were underpowered, the *Virginia* able to make little more than 5 knots, and the *Monitor* just about 6 (*c.* 7 mph), and neither was particularly seaworthy.

On March 8, 1862, Confederate Flag Officer Franklin Buchanan led a small flotilla of gunboats and the *Virginia* from the Gosport Navy Yard, near Norfolk, VA, into Hampton Roads to do battle with blockading Union ships. The result seemed a disaster for the Union. The sail frigate *Congress*, in which Franklin's Unionist brother Cdr. McKean Buchanan was serving, grounded, and was shelled into a burning wreck which later blew up spectacularly. The sail frigate *Cumberland* was rammed and sunk by the *Virginia*, which briefly became entangled in the wreckage and almost sank herself. The steam frigate *Minnesota*, which had grounded on a mudflat, was severely damaged by gunfire, while two other Union ships, a steam frigate and a sail frigate, had grounded before they could get into action. Only the fall of night, and the fact that Fl. Off. Buchanan had been wounded, saved the Union from further destruction, as the *Virginia* returned to her base. Although the *Virginia* had suffered some damage from gunfire and the shock of ramming the *Cumberland*, her officers were confident that she would make quick work of the surviving Union vessels the next day.

But when the *Virginia* steamed into Hampton Roads on the morning of the 9th, under the command of Lt. Catesby ap Roger Jones, the tactical situation had completely changed. Overnight, the Union's new ironclad, the turret ship *Monitor*, commanded by Lt. John L. Worden, and looking literally like a "cheese box on a raft," had steamed into Hampton Roads and taken up a position to cover the *Minnesota*, still aground. In the ensuing fight, the first ever between ironclad warships, the *Monitor*, hardly a greyhound of the sea, was just faster enough and more nimble than her opponent, and having a much shallower draft (10½ft vs 21–22ft), managed to outmaneuver the *Virginia*. Finally, the *Virginia* withdrew. During the approximately 2-hour fight, both ships took some damage, *Virginia* further straining her hull in an unsuccessful attempt to ram her opponent, but neither suffered any permanent harm. Tactically, the fight was a draw, but strategically, the *Virginia* had failed in her mission to break the blockade.

Although the success of the *Virginia* on the 8th is often hailed as a demonstration of the superiority of the ironclad, there are a lot of "what ifs" about the battle. All the Union ships were anchored when the *Virginia* made her sortie into Hampton Roads. Both *Cumberland* and *Congress* were not only wooden hulled, but sailing vessels, and even upon hoisting anchor could not get enough speed to maneuver, while the steam-powered *Minnesota* had to raise steam. Had all the Union vessels been steam powered, and had steam been up, the *Virginia* may well have suffered the fate of the CSS *Tennessee*, a smaller but similar ironclad, which was overwhelmed at Mobile Bay on August 5, 1864, albeit that the presence of the aggressive David Farragut may have been more critical than any material concerns.

As for the battle on the second day, the *Virginia* arguably got off easy. The *Monitor's* two 11in. (XI in the usage of the day) muzzle-loading smooth-bore cannon fired a 166-pound shell. During the battle on the 9th, the powder charge was limited to 15 pounds, which was believed was the maximum the gun tube could tolerate. This was enough to hurt the "soft" parts of the *Virginia*, but was not powerful enough to smash

The battle between the CSS Virginia *and the USS* Monitor, *in Hampton Roads, March 9, 1862, engraved in 1863 by J. Davies from a drawing by C. Parsons. (National Archives)*

her armor. It was later found that the 11in. gun could be safely fired with charges as large as 30 pounds of powder, which would have been more than enough to smash the *Virginia*.

Despite their history-making clash at Hampton Roads, neither the *Virginia* nor the *Monitor* played much of a role in the war. After she emerged from dry dock for repairs in early April, *Virginia* made several sorties into Hampton Roads in company with various gunboats, in an effort to entice the Union blockaders into a fight, but none ever took place. On May 8, 1862, as Union troops were advancing north from the Carolina coast threatening Norfolk, the *Virginia*, which drew too much water to escape up the James River to Richmond, was towed to Craney's Island and set afire on May 10, exploding spectacularly early the next morning.

The *Monitor* remained on blockade duty after her battle with the *Virginia*, none of her damage requiring yard work. She several times raised steam to counter the sorties of her rival in April, but the two never fought again. On May 15, the *Monitor*, the broadside ironclad

Galena, and several gunboats attempted a run up the James River to capture Richmond, but became engaged with Confederate batteries at Drewry's Bluff, and after a short action drew off with some casualties. In September, while still on blockade duty at Hampton Roads, the ship's hastily built engines were condemned, and she was sent to the Washington Navy Yard for a major overhaul. Ordered to Beaufort, NC in December 1862, the *Monitor* foundered in heavy seas southeast of Cape Hatteras on the 31st, with the loss of eighteen men.

In the course of the war, the Union commissioned about sixty ironclads, and at war's end had over twenty more still under construction, many of which were cancelled. For various reasons, figures on Confederate ironclads are harder to determine. Nearly fifty were planned, but many of them were never completed or had very short service lives. For example, the barely completed casemate ironclad *Louisiana*, built at New Orleans, was commissioned on April 20, 1862, only to be blown up to prevent capture on the 28th, while the incomplete *Mississippi*, launched at New Orleans on April 24, 1862, was burnt the next day. Other "ironclads" could only by courtesy be called "warships," such as the floating battery *Georgia*, commissioned in 1863, and scuttled at the end of 1864, which could barely make 2 or 3 knots, or the *Hunstsville*, completed in mid-1863 and captured at Mobile at the end of the war, which could make 4 knots. The best of the Confederate ironclads were five ships ordered in Europe; only one ever entered service under the Confederate flag, the twin-screw *Stonewall*.

The second of two ships ordered in France as the *Cheops* and *Sphynx*, the CSS *Stonewall*, a wooden-hulled armored ram, was built between 1863 and 1864. While under construction, they were sold respectively to Prussia and Denmark (who were at war with each other for a time), but ownership soon reverted to the builders, who sold them to the Confederacy. *Stonewall* was commissioned in the Confederate Navy at Copenhagen, Denmark on January 6, 1865, and despite a leaky hull and some shakedown problems, managed to elude Union cruisers sent after her, making stops for repairs at Quiberon Bay, France, and then at La Coruña in northwestern Spain. From there she sailed for the Americas, arriving in Havana in May. With the war over, the ship's captain sold her to the Spanish government, which sold her to the United States, which sold her to Japan, and she served many yeas as HIJMS *Kotetsu*. The other Confederate European-built ironclads served in the Prussian, Danish, and British navies.

Virtually all of the Civil War ironclads were poor ships, suitable primarily for coastal and riverine operations. Despite this, several monitors actually made ocean crossings, remarkable feats of seamanship given that they were literally almost awash in anything but calm water.

Confederate commerce raiders

Raiding the enemy's commerce is an ancient strategy in naval warfare. During the Civil War, the Confederacy sent two types of raiders to sea: privateers (privately owned vessels licensed to attack enemy shipping), and warships of the Confederate Navy.[4]

Privateers had served the United States well during the first and second Wars for Independence, so on April 17, 1861, President Jefferson Davis began issuing "letters of marque and reprisal" as authorized by the Confederate constitution. By a curious bit of historical irony, in 1854 the principal naval powers, Great Britain and France, had convened a conference in London to promote a ban on privateering. Had the United States ratified the agreement, the states that subsequently formed the Confederacy would have been bound by the agreement under international law, but while the proposal received the unanimous support of all the participating powers, the United States dawdled over ratification. About a week after Davis' proclamation, the U.S. Senate hastily notified the other contracting parties as to its willingness to accede to the convention. The British and the other parties to the agreement rejected this belated effort to ratify the convention, on the grounds that it could not be applicable in an existing state of belligerency.

Confederate privateers took a goodly number of U.S. merchant ships, but privateering never became a significant factor in the war against Northern maritime commerce. The prompt imposition of the increasingly effective blockade of Southern ports reduced the number of ships able to get to sea, and in any case few privateers were capable of outfighting even improvised blockading warships. Moreover, the profits from privateering were not nearly so great as those from blockade running, while the risks were greater. So the burden of the Confederacy's war on Union merchant shipping was largely borne by a handful of raiders sent to sea by the Confederate Navy.

Some of the Confederate naval raiders were built or converted in the South, some procured illegally in Britain, and a few converted from prizes by their captors. Confederate raiders took 263 American flag vessels during the war, most by the eleven commissioned C.S.N. cruisers.

Rear Admiral Raphael Semmes, CSN, the most successful commerce raider of the Civil War, and one of the most successful in all history, in an engraving by Henry Bryan Hall, Jr., published in Semmes' book Memoirs of Services Afloat during the War between the States. *(U.S. Naval History and Heritage Command).*

Confederate Navy cruisers

CSS *Alabama*	Under Capt. Raphael Semmes (1809–77), she took or sank seventy ships, including the small gunboat USS *Hatteras*, between August 1862 and June 1864, when she was sunk off Cherbourg in a duel with the USS *Kearsarge*, by which she was considerably outgunned.
CSS *Archer*	A prize captured by the CSS *Tacony*. She took only one ship, and that a blockader, before being taken in turn by other Union blockaders.
CSS *Chickamauga*	Made one cruise from mid-October to mid-November 1864, accounting for three or four prizes, and was scuttled when Wilmington fell to the Union.

CSS *Clarence*	A sailing ship, and a prize of CSS *Florida*. She accounted for five ships before being burned when her skipper decided to transfer to the much better *Tacony*, which he had just been captured.
CSS *Florida*	Took thirty-seven prizes in two voyages, broken by a 4-month stay in Mobile, to accomplish which she had to run the Union blockade twice. In October 1864, she was illegally taken by the USS *Wachusett* in Brazilian territorial waters. After some international acrimony, the U.S. agreed to return the ship to the Confederacy, but she sank in Hampton Roads after an "accidental" collision.
CSS *Georgia*	Made one voyage in mid-1863, taking nine prizes, and was then relegated to other duties.
CSS *Nashville*	The first Confederate warship to visit Europe, in November 1861. She took two prizes, and upon returning to the Confederacy was relegated to other duties.
CSS *Shenandoah*	Commanded by Capt. James Waddell. Between October 1864 and August 1865, she took thirty-eight ships, most after the collapse of the Confederacy. Then, learning of the war's end, she sailed for Liverpool, and surrendered to the British authorities. *Shenandoah* was the only Confederate ship to circumnavigate the globe.
CSS *Sumter*	Commanded by Raphael Semmes. She took or sank eighteen ships between June 1861 and January 1862, when engine trouble caused her to put in at Gibraltar, where she was sold out of the service.
CSS *Tacony*	A sailing ship. She was a prize taken by *Florida*'s prize *Clarence*, and took or sank nineteen ships. Upon capturing the steamer *Archer*, her crew and armament were transferred to the new ship and she was burned.

CSS *Tallahassee*	Made two voyages, one of 20 days in August 1864, taking thirty-three prizes, and then, after being renamed *Olustee*, she made a short second voyage, during which she took six vessels, before becoming a blockade runner.

The 263 ships taken or destroyed by Confederate commerce raiders totaled about 105,000 gross tons. Although this was only about 2 percent of the U.S. merchant fleet, at 5.5 million tons the second largest in the world, nervous ship owners transferred nearly 1,000 vessels totaling some 800,000 gross tons to foreign flags, a blow from which the U.S. merchant marine was long in recovering.

The blockade and blockade runners

Within days of the firing on Fort Sumter, Lincoln decreed a blockade of Southern ports. This was a delicate bit of business. Declaring a blockade conceded belligerent status—albeit not recognition—to the blockaded, such as had been the case when the British blockaded the rebellious American colonies during the War for Independence. The blockade permitted the United States to intercept suspect foreign-flagged ships beyond the nation's territorial waters. Initially, there were not enough ships available to make the blockade enforceable everywhere, as the Confederacy had some 3,500 miles of coastline, with some 180–190 harbors, bays, inlets, river mouths, and such at which ships might land cargo. But there were enough ships to deter foreign powers from declaring the blockade invalid, and as more were hastily added to the fleet, and Union forces occupied portions of the Southern coastline, the blockade became tighter and tighter.[5]

As the blockade grew increasingly tight, the flow of foreign goods into the Confederacy slowed, and blockade running became increasingly profitable. Blockade runners could experience profits as high as 700 percent for their owners, some of whom were in the North, and even ordinary crewmen could make several hundred dollars a voyage,

"Hauling Down the Flag—Surrender of the Alabama *to the* Kearsarge *off Cherbourg, France, 19 June 1864", from the collection of President Franklin D. Roosevelt, 1936. (U.S. Naval History and Heritage Command)*

more than they might earn in a year of merchant service. These profits were particularly high if the ships were carrying luxury goods, from fine wines to pool tables, silks to chinaware, which blockade runners favored over more important but less profitable cargoes such as arms and munitions. In a major blunder, not until February 1864 did the Confederate government begin acquiring its own blockade runners, and requisitioned half of all cargo space on privately owned blockade runners for government cargo, primarily munitions, a measure that was widely criticized as a violation of property rights, but was long overdue.[6] Despite this, blockade runners still mostly carried luxury goods. For example, on January 19, 1865, Union warships intercepted three ships, the *Stag, Charlotte,* and *Blenheim,* attempting to run the blockade into the Cape Fear River. Rear Admiral David Dixon Porter, commanding the blockaders, examined the cargoes and found, "The main cargo of one vessel was composed of articles for ladies' use, and all three were plentifully stocked with liquors and table luxuries," including several

Sailors and Marines of the USS Mendota, *1864. Converted from an incomplete commercial hull, the 974-ton gunboat armed with ten cannon was typical of the many improvised warships that enforced the blockade. Note the integrated crew. (National Archives)*

crates of Bass ale and cognac addressed to "His Excellency, Jefferson Davis, President of the Confederate States of America."[7]

In addition to high profits from "honest" blockade running, the blockade opened up excellent opportunities for graft. Some Union naval officers were willing to issue "exemptions" to blockade runners for a consideration, while some blockade runners would sabotage their vessels or betray them to the Union and then make claims on their insurers in Britain or France. In November 1862, sometime Confederate Army officer Charles Carroll Hicks (1828–1906), one of America's truly great—if little known—rogues, was entrusted with a goodly sum to deliver to the privateer *Retribution*, fitting out at St. Thomas, but somehow found his way to New York by February 1863, where he began spending freely and getting into trouble with the law.[8]

David Dixon Porter, foster-brother of David Glasgow Farragut. Porter was a shameless self-promoter, impressive humorist, notoroius looter, and tough sea dog, who rose from lieutenant to rear admiral during the war. (National Archives)

Nevertheless, despite their inefficiencies and preference for luxury cargoes, blockade runners played an important role in keeping the Confederacy alive. By one estimate, they supplied the South with about 400,000 infantry rifles, nearly two-thirds of its modern long arms, as well as many artillery pieces, about 3 million pounds of lead, and some 2¼ million pounds of saltpetre, vital for making gunpowder, not to mention uniforms, shoes, and even rations.[9]

The Union blockade was run on numerous occasions, and some observers have argued that it was not terribly effective. But that conclusion is based on several misleading assumptions. In the 4 years prior to the Civil War, about 20,000 ships had entered or cleared ports in states which would become the Confederacy, particularly New Orleans. In the 4 years of the war, only about 8,000 ships entered or cleared Confederate ports, most in the first year; from the end of 1861 to the end of the war, about a third of all ships *trying* to run the blockade were intercepted. The most successful blockade runners were some 300 or so fast steamers, either converted to or built especially as blockade runners. Of these, about three-quarters which tried to run the blockade, either into or out of a Southern port, succeeded, but more than half of them eventually ended up sunk or captured by the end of the war. Overall, some 1,500 ships were intercepted by the blockaders.[10]

So blockade running was risky, and blockade runners tended to be captured, sooner or later. But there were men who savored the risk; as one former officer of a blockade runner later put it: "Nothing I ever experienced can compare with it. Hunting, pig-sticking, steeple-chasing, big-game hunting, polo—I have done a little of each—all have their thrilling moments, but none can approach running a blockade."[11]

The blockade was one of the most critical factors shaping the outcome of the Civil War.

James Sprunt's "The Chase"

Blockade running hardly seems a likely subject for poetry, but James Sprunt (1846–1924), who immigrated from Scotland with his family in 1854, settling in Wilmington, GA, followed his father into blockade running in 1863, when the 17 year old signed on as a purser in blockade runner *North Heath*. He later sailed in the *Lilian*, a very small paddle wheeler that drew only about 7 or 8ft. and with no more than 3 or 4ft. of freeboard, so that she labored mightily in heavy seas. Sprunt had many adventures, including shipwreck, capture, and escape, and postwar went into the shipping business with his father, while becoming active in philanthropy and penning a number books on maritime history, including *Tales of the Cape Fear Blockade* (1902), from which "The Chase" is taken.

The Chase

Freed from the lingering chase, in devious ways
Upon the swelling tides
Swiftly the Lilian glides
Through hostile shells and eager foemen past;
The lynx-eyed pilot gazing through the haze,
And engines straining, "far hope dawns at last."
Now falls in billows deep the welcome night
Upon white sands below;
While signal lamps aglow
Seek out Fort Fisher's distant answering gleams,
The blockade runner's keen, supreme delight, —
Dear Dixie Land, the haven of our dreams!

David Dixon Porter invents the "command ship"

Modern navies have something called a "command ship," essentially a sea-going headquarters with elaborate communications and data processing facilities to enable commanders and their staffs to manage operations.

Arguably, the command ship was invented by David Dixon Porter (1813–91). Porter, who rose from lieutenant to rear admiral during the war, was a big, stubborn, egocentric, hard-fighting fellow whose dour

The USS Malvern, *from a watercolor drawing by R. G. Skerrett, 1900. (Naval History and Heritage Command)*

appearance masked an inventive mind and a notable sense of humor, which enabled him to freely swap jokes with Lincoln.

On October 10, 1864, Porter was assigned to command the North Atlantic Blockading Squadron. His mission was to maintain the blockade and render naval support to the Army along the Virginia and North Carolina coasts, an ocean frontage of about 300 miles, without counting the vast enclosed waters of the Chesapeake Bay and the Carolina Sounds. Naturally, as an admiral commanding a squadron, Porter needed a flagship. On October 12, Porter made the sidewheel steamer *Malvern* his flagship.

A former blockade runner, the *Malvern* measured 1,477 tons, was 240ft long and had a beam of 33ft, with a draft of only 10ft. Her 500 hp engine could propel her at speeds of 15 knots or so. Although *Malvern* was lightly armed (with four 20-pdr Dahlgren rifles and eight 12-pdr smooth-bore cannon, all more or less obsolete muzzle-loading weapons), she was fast and highly maneuverable, and thus ideal for operating in shallow coastal waters, while still able to perform well on the high seas.

Built in 1860 at Wilmington, Delaware, as the *William G. Hewes,* she began regular service between New York City and New Orleans in January 1861. On April 28, while lying at New Orleans, the *Hewes* was seized by the state of Louisiana. Fitted as a blockade runner, she could carry as many as 1,441 bales of cotton at relatively high speed, usually making for Havana. As the Union blockade closed in on New Orleans, the *Hewes* began operating from the Confederate East Coast. Renamed *Ella and Annie*, she began making regular runs from Charleston, SC or Wilmington, NC to Bermuda.

On the morning of November 8, 1863, the *Ella and Annie* was intercepted by the iron-hulled gunboat USS *Niphon* off New Inlet, NC. After a short skirmish, during which she even managed to ram the sturdy gunboat, *Ella and Annie* took several hits, leaving one man dead and her hull damaged, forcing her surrender. According to *The New York Times*, she was carrying "480 sacks of salt, 500 sacks of saltpetre, 281 cases of Austrian rifles, 500 barrels and 42 cases of paper. She had no ship's papers. Of 38 persons on board, only one was a native of the United States." Condemned by an admiralty court in Boston, the ship was bought by the Navy, refitted, rearmed, renamed *Malvern*, and entered service in December 1863. *Malvern* was soon performing routine duties in support of the blockade and commerce protection.

Early in 1864, *Malvern* was assigned to the North Atlantic Blockading Squadron, and, of course, in October became Porter's flagship. Porter's choice of so small a vessel for his flagship surprised many. Traditionally, admirals picked the largest, most powerful vessels. But not Porter, who realized that selecting a major fleet unit as flagship was counterproductive; service as a flagship would often remove the ship from its normal duties. What he wanted was a small, fast ship that could carry him from one part of his command to another without noticeably reducing the strength of the blockading forces lying offshore.

Malvern was directly under Porter's command, and permitted him to go between the various subordinate divisions of his squadron, each of which was responsible for covering the ports and inlets along specific stretches of the Confederate coast. *Malvern* was particularly valuable during the Union attempt to capture Fort Fisher, covering the Confederacy's last open port, Wilmington, NC. During both the unsuccessful attack of December 24–27, 1864, and the successful one of January 12–15, 1865, Porter used *Malvern* to flit about between the divisions of bombarding

Slaves and people fleeing enslavement— "contrabands"—often proved a major source of reliable intelligence for Union troops.

vessels, and occasionally to approach close to the defenses in an effort to evaluate the effectiveness of the shelling.

After the fall of Fort Fisher, *Malvern* continued in service, capturing several blockade runners; supported the attack on Fort Anderson, up the Cape Fear River from Fort Fisher; and hosted President Lincoln during the final days of the war, conveying him up the James River to visit Richmond following the Confederate retreat from the city on April 2, 1865.

Malvern was decommissioned in October 1865, and shortly sold back to her original owners. Refitted to carry passengers and cargo, she reverted to her original name, *William G. Hewes*, and in early 1866 returned to commercial service in the Gulf of Mexico and the West Indies. She was wrecked on a reef off Cuba in 1895.

Porter's use of *Malvern* as a specialized command ship drew no attention from the world's navies. But some 75 years later, the idea was revived, as specialized command ships began to appear in the British and American navies.[12]

Signs of the times

David Glasgow Farragut (1801–70), the most notable naval officer of the war, joined the U.S. Navy as a midshipman in 1810, at the age of 9. In June 1813, during the War of 1812, when he was 12, he commanded the prize crew aboard the captured British brig *Alexander Barclay*, bringing her into port for adjudication by a prize court.[13]

Although abolition was first proposed in 1820, flogging in the U.S. Navy was only ended by Congress on September 28, 1850, passing the Senate 26 to 24, with twelve members abstaining or absent.

Only two members from Slave States voted for abolition; most of the rest—including Jefferson Davis—voted against.[14]

Union Commodore Andrew Foote seems to have been a man of considerable persuasive powers; while commanding the Asiatic Squadron during the mid-1850s, he "converted every officer and man in the fleet to the principles of temperance, and had every one of them sign the pledge."[15]

The very first ironclad to enter service in the war, and the first to see action, was the 387-ton Confederate ram *Manassas*, improvised from an ice-breaking tug at Algiers, LA; on October 12, 1861— during the Battle of the Head of Passes on the Mississippi—she rammed the paddle steam frigate USS *Richmond* inflicting little damage, though suffering much in return before withdrawing.

Of the eighteen former U.S. Marine Corps officers who joined the Confederate Marine Corps, four were shortly dismissed from the service for incompetence or peculation.[16]

The U.S. Navy's casualties in the fight with the ironclad *Virginia* at Hampton Roads on March 8, 1862 (261 killed and 108 wounded) were its heaviest losses in a single day between the explosion of the frigate *Randolph* while in action against several British vessels on March 7, 1778 (311 killed, with only four survivors) and the Japanese attack on Pearl Harbor on December 7, 1941 (2,008 sailors and 109 marines killed, 710 sailors and 69 marines wounded).[17]

Robert L. Meade, son of Maj. Gen. George G. Meade, and George M. Welles, the son of Secretary of the Navy Gideon Welles, were both commissioned in the U.S. Marine Corps during the war.

Fugitive slaves were often a major source of information for naval officers on the location of Confederate "torpedoes" since they were usually the ones who did the work of planting mines in rivers and coastal waters.[18]

In September 1861, Congress abolished the U.S. Navy's twice-daily 4-ounce ration of a grog consisting of 80 percent water and 20 percent whiskey, substituting a 5 cents a day pay boost, which most sailors considered a poor trade.[19]

Of 418 vessels bought for the U.S. Navy during the Civil War, about half were converted into warships at the Brooklyn Navy Yard.[20]

Although some 700,000 bales of Confederate cotton managed to elude the Union naval blockade and reach Europe during the 4 years of war, this represented less than a quarter of the total export volume of 1860, the last prewar year.[21]

The yacht *America*, which had won the Queen's Cup in 1851, initiating yachting's premier race, became a blockade runner in 1861, but was then scuttled to prevent capture. Raised and refitted with three small cannon by the U.S. Navy, she served on blockade duty commanded by Midn. Robley D. Evans, later the admiral who commanded the Great White Fleet, and after the war was owned for a time by former Maj. Gen. Benjamin Butler.

The sixty or so vessels that comprised the Union naval squadron during the attack on Fort Fisher, off Wilmington, on January 13, 1865, was the largest concentration of American warships for a combat operation until the eve of the invasion of North Africa on November 8, 1942.[22]

Naval personnel were awarded "prize" for capturing enemy ships or property, with the lion's share going to the senior officers. Rear Adm. Samuel P. Lee—a cousin of Robert E. Lee—netted nearly $110,000 in prize commanding the North Atlantic Blockading Squadron (September 1862–September 1864), more than any other officer in the war, while Vice Adm. David G. Farragut, who spent a lot of time actually fighting the Rebels, only realized about $56,000, and his foster-brother Rear Adm. David Dixon Porter, notorious for sniffing out loot, some $90,000.[23]

CHAPTER 7

War and Society

Although ordinary people had supported the war effort in various ways during the Wars of Independence and that with Mexico in 1846–48, the self-mobilization of citizens during the Civil War far outstripped these earlier manifestations of popular support. The war permeated all levels of society in both the Union and the Confederacy, and people far from the theaters of war stood up in support of the war effort to a degree unmatched until the World Wars. Ordinary citizens, and particularly women, organized to raise money, establish hospitals, care for the injured, provide amenities to the troops in the field, and promote broader and more ardent popular support for the war.

Sanitary fairs and other events

In order to coordinate the efforts of private citizens to further the war effort by providing the troops with whatever Uncle Sam couldn't deliver—at times seemingly almost everything—on June 18, 1861, Congress chartered the United States Sanitary Commission, inspired by an organization formed by patriotic British women during the Crimean War.[1]

The Sanitary Commission was formally headed by men, the most important of whom was famed landscape architect Frederick Law Olmsted (1822–1903), who served as Executive Director, but he wisely let women take over the actual management of the organization. Almost all the commission's work was done by women. Many women held executive positions, leading local branches of the Sanitary Commission. or serving as treasurers at all levels in the organization; others organized events and fundraising, and still others engaged in everything from making clothing, baking goods, delivering supplies, running canteens, and managing hospitals. Some Sanitary Commission women worked directly with particular army corps, divisions, or brigades, ascertaining their needs and coordinating the movement of supplies. The most famous Sanitary Commission agent was certainly Mary Ann Ball Bickerdyke (1817–1901), known as "Mother Bickerdyke," who had proven so helpful to the troops in the Mississippi Valley that William T. Sherman asked her to serve as the Sanitary Commission agent for his army during the Atlanta Campaign, on the March to the Sea, and during the Carolina Campaign, right through to the surrender of the Confederate Army of the Tennessee. Bickerdyke was then honored by being asked to march at the head of the Fifteenth Army Corps during the second day of the Grand Review of the Union Armies, in Washington on May 24, 1865.

Women were very active in fund raising, ultimately securing over $25 million for the cause, equal to perhaps between $3 and $6 *billion* today. Sanitary fairs were a common way of raising funds. First held in Lowell, MA in 1863, there were ultimately hundreds of sanitary fairs, ranging in size from modest one- or two-day events in small towns to a week or more in major cities such as Boston, Brooklyn, Buffalo, Chicago, Cincinnati, New York, Philadelphia, and St. Louis. These fairs were often attended by prominent politicians and officers; the Lincolns, for example, attended the Philadelphia fair on June 16, 1864, where the President delivered a moving speech.[2]

The biggest of these fundraisers was New York's Great Metropolitan Sanitary Fair, from April 4–23, 1864, held in a specially erected building on 14th Street, between Sixth and Seventh avenues.[3] The fair raised $1,351,275.94, which after expenses left an impressive $1,184,487.72. The money came from admission tickets to the fair itself and to some of the special exhibitions and performances, as well as auctions, contests, and donations.

Souvenir of the Pittsburgh Sanitary Fair (June 1–18, 1864, showing an image of models of the USS Monitor and artillery pieces that were exhibited. Sales of souvenirs such as this, with an image taken by Purviance's Photographers, as well as admission fees, auction proceeds, and donations, helped make the Pittsburgh fair one of the most successful, raising $322,217.98 for servicemen's relief. (Naval History and Heritage Command)

Fundraising at the Great Metropolitan Sanitary Fair

New York City police officers donated $4,031.35.[4]

Visitors could pay one dollar to vote for the best Army and Navy officer, which brought in $100,000, with Lt. Gen. Ulysses S. Grant and Rear Adm. David G. Farragut winning, each receiving a Tiffany presentation sword studded with rubies, diamonds, and sapphires, representing the national colors, and with a gold scabbard. Jealous supporters of presidential candidate Maj. Gen. George B. McClellan, who received only about 14,000 "votes" to Grant's 30,000 or so, charged that the Lincoln Administration had arranged to stuff the ballot box.[5]

Two dozen napkin rings carved by Pvt. Nicholas Pfeiffer of the 19th Illinois, donated by Maj. Gen. George Thomas, brought in $600 at auction, one of many soldier artifacts sold at the fair.[6]

An album with hundreds of autographs of noted Europeans and Americans, such as George Washington, King William IV, Queen Victoria, King Victor Emanuel, Florence Nightingale, Thomas Carlyle, Lord Macaulay, Charles Dickens, Giuseppe Garibaldi, Count Cavour, and opera singer Jenny Lind, donated by Anne Lynch Botta, wife of the prominent New York University Prof. Vincenzo Botta, sold at auction for $500—nearly 2 years' pay at the prevailing "minimum wage."[7]

Several noted art collectors donated over 200 paintings and some sculptures, which sold at auction for $28,300.07.

The New York City men's clothing makers and sellers association, which included such merchants as Brooks Brothers and the Straus Brothers, donated $29,162.

In addition to the Sanitary Commission, many other organizations provided support for the troops, such as the private United States Christian Commission. The Christian Commission, founded at the suggestion of YMCA leaders, supported care for the sick and wounded, and coordinated Protestant religious and social services for the troops. Existing Catholic religious orders and charities provided similar support.

The Confederacy never developed nationwide institutions to raise funds and render aid to the troops such as the Sanitary Commission or the Christian Commission. On the local level, however, there were was much activity, such as the fundraiser depicted in *Gone With the Wind*, in which, just as in the North, women were particularly prominent. Mary Elizabeth Adams Pope Randolph (1830–71), wife to George W. Randolph, a brigadier general and sometime Secretary of War of the Confederacy, helped form the Richmond Ladies Association, which held fairs and the like, and, at her insistence, albeit not without acrimony, allocated some of the proceeds to the care of wounded and sick Union prisoners of war.[7] Mrs. Randolph's friend Phoebe Yates Levy Pember (1823–1913), the widowed daughter of a prosperous Charleston Jewish family, directed the Chimborazo Hospital in Richmond, turning it into one of the best medical facilities in the world despite enormous obstacles. She later penned the memoir *A Southern Woman's Story: Life in Confederate Richmond*, which offers a wealth of information on medical practice of the day and wartime conditions in the Confederate capital.[8]

In many ways, the enormous popular support for welfare of the troops that emerged during the Civil War foreshadowed the experience of the World Wars.

War brides: some notable Civil War weddings

As is often the case in wartime, there was a noticeable increase in the marriage rate during the Civil War. Of course, some of these marriages were—or are now—more interesting than others. Here is a sample of weddings that either made a considerable splash at the time, bringing a little glamor to the otherwise increasingly grim business that was at hand, or had interesting longer-term importance.[9]

April 18, 1861: New York attorney Francis C. Barlow (1834–96) wed Arabella Wharton Griffith (1824–64), and enlisted in the 12th New York Militia the next day. Shortly commissioned, Barlow began an outstanding wartime career, rising to major general of volunteers. Mrs. Barlow served as a volunteer nurse in Army hospitals, twice even nursing her husband back to health, once while he was a prisoner of war, but contracted typhoid fever and died in mid-1864. Postwar,

Barlow had a brilliant career in law and politics and married Ellen Shaw (1845–1936), the sister of Col. Robert Gould Shaw (1837–63) of the 54th Massachusetts; they had two children, the youngest living until 1965.

September 24, 1861: Brig. Gen. Edmund Kirby Smith, C.S.A. (1824–93) wed Cassie Selden (1836–1905), whom he had met at her family home while recuperating from wounds he took at Bull Run. The wedding was a major social event and the new Mrs. Kirby Smith was dubbed "The Bride of the Confederacy." The match was long-lasting and fruitful, the pair having five sons and six daughters.

December 14, 1862: Widower Brig. Gen. John Hunt Morgan (1825–64) wed Martha "Mattie" Ready (1840–87), daughter of a prominent Tennessee family, at her parents' home in Murfreesboro. The match was sanctified by the Episcopal Bishop of Louisiana Leonidas Polk, who was also a lieutenant general, and attended by generals Braxton Bragg, William J. Hardee, Benjamin Cheatham, John C. Breckinridge, and numerous lesser dignitaries; President Jefferson Davis, who had been visiting the Army of Tennessee, had to leave the day before the nuptials, but promoted Morgan to brigadier as a wedding gift. Morgan was killed in action in 1864. Seven months later, on April 7, 1865, Mattie gave birth to their daughter, Johnnie Hunt Morgan. Mattie subsequently remarried, but died in 1887. Johnnie Morgan died the following year, of typhoid.

December 23, 1862: Maj. Gen. John A. McClernand, U.S.A. (1812–1900), a widower since the death of his wife Sarah Dunlap McClernand (1824–61), wed her sister Minerva Dunlap (1836–1931) in Jacksonville, IL, with the governor and many other dignitaries in attendance. The general almost immediately afterwards departed for Mississippi and an acrimonious meeting with Ulysses S. Grant.

January 29, 1863: Maj. Gen. Alexander McDowell McCook, U.S.A. (1831–1903) married Kate Phillips (1837–81), a wealthy Ohioan. The couple had three children. The general was one of fourteen members of the extended McCook family to serve in the war, earning them the nickname "The Fighting McCooks of Ohio", three of whom died in the war.

February 10, 1863: Lavinia Warren (1841–1919) and Charles Sherwood Stratton (1838–83), better known as "General Tom Thumb," America's most famous "Little People," wed in Grace Episcopal Church, Manhattan, and had a grand reception at the posh Metropolitan Hotel attended by some 2,000 of the glitterati of the age. After visiting the Lincolns in the White House, the couple departed on a world tour, visiting Europe, India, and Japan.

March 2, 1863: Col. Alfred M. Scales (1827–92), 13th North Carolina, married Kate Henderson (1846–1930). The couple had several children, among them the grandfather of Robert Scales, the retired general and defense analyst.

May 25, 1863: Lt. Gen. Richard S. Ewell, C.S.A. (1817–72), married the widow Lizinka Campbell Brown (1820–72), his distant cousin and the mother of one of his aides. A formidable woman, even after they were married the general often introduced her as "Mrs. Brown." In January 1872, both contracted pneumonia and died within a few days of each other.

November 12, 1863: William Sprague (1830–1915), the dashing Governor of Rhode Island, who had commanded the state's troops at First Bull Run, married Katherine Jane "Kate" Chase (1840–99), daughter of Secretary of the Treasury Salmon P. Chase, the belle of Washington society. Perhaps the most spectacular nuptials of the war, the wealthy Sprague gave his bride a $50,000 tiara, which easily overshadowed her father's gift, a $3,000 shawl. America's "glamor couple" for some years, they had four children, but the match turned disastrous, ending in alcoholism, adultery, and divorce.

November 13, 1863: Maj. Gen. George Edward Pickett, C.S.A. (1825–75), twice a widower, wed Sallie Corbell (1843–1931) in a gala affair at Richmond. He had first met Sallie when she was a small child; supposedly, at age 9 she had vowed to marry him.

October 27, 1863: Brig. Gen. Stephen Dodson Ramseur, C.S.A. (1837–64) married his long-time fiancé Ellen E. "Nellie" Richmond (1840–1900). Ramseur was mortally wounded on October 20, 1864, shortly after learning that he had become a father.

January 13, 1864: Lt. Gen. William J. Hardee, C.S.A. (1815–73), who had been widowed in 1853, married Mary Foreman Lewis (1838–75), an Alabama plantation owner whom he had met about a year earlier while on campaign.

February 9, 1864: Brig. Gen. George Armstrong Custer, U.S.A. (1839–76) married Elizabeth "Libby" Bacon (1842–1933), whom he had first met when he was 10 and she about 7. They were very close, and Libby became the principal architect of the Custer legend following his death at Little Big Horn.

January 16, 1865: Maj. Gen. John Pegram, C.S.A. (1832–65) married Hetty Cary (1836–92), one of the Confederacy's famous "Cary Girls," called by Henry Kyd Douglas "the most beautiful woman of her day and generation." It was a spectacular affair, with President and Mrs. Davis in attendance. On February 6, 21 days later, Pegram was killed at Hatcher's Run. Nearly 15 years later, Hetty married the noted physiologist Newell Martin, and become so involved in his work that they co-authored a book.

August 21, 1865: Maj. Gen. George Crook (1830–90) wed Miss Mary Dailey (1842–95) of Cumberland, MD, despite the fact that on the previous February 21, the general had been captured while visiting her home by a band of Confederate partisan rangers led by her brother, a tale the general would at times recount with great relish in the years after the war, when he had become a noted Indian fighter, respected by his foes for his honesty, integrity, and knowledge of their culture. The Crooks had no children.

August 23, 1865: Miss Eleanor Swain (*c.* 1843–81), the daughter of Dr. David Swain, President of the University of North Carolina, married Union Col. Smith D. Atkins (1835–1913) who had serenaded her with the band from a regiment in his brigade. The most controversial marriage to come out of the war, Eleanor's mother refused to dine with Atkins, while her father lost his job at the university, and she was never afterwards welcome in her home town. The couple settled in Freeport, IL, where Atkins was editor of the local newspaper. Although three of their six children died in childhood, they have living descendants.[10]

A considerable disparity in age between the groom and the bride will be noted in several of these marriages. At the time, it was by no means uncommon for the groom to be 10 or even 20 years older than his bride, especially in the case of second marriages. The national average for marriage was the early 20s for women and late 20s for men, though in the South it was a bit younger for both.

There were, of course, many other marriages during the war, as getting hitched is often something people do in haste when war comes, such as Scarlett O'Hara's marriage to Charles Hamilton in *Gone With the Wind*.

In addition to Ms. Swain and Col. Atkins, there were a surprising number of romances and marriages between Union soldiers and Southern belles, so many that they were the subject of several novels after the war, the best of which is probably John W. De Forest's *Miss Ravenel's Conversion from Secession to Loyalty.*[11] Unfortunately, there are no statistics on the number of Union soldiers who brought home a Southern war bride, among whom there are known to have been a number of African American women wed to white veterans.

Of course, since many wartime marriages were, like that of Scarlett and Charles, rather spur of the moment, it's not surprising that the two decades following the war saw the divorce rate rise precipitously, from about 3–4 percent of marriages in 1860 to some 5–6 percent by 1880. And of course, many wartime marriages ended on the battlefield, as did Ramseur's and Pegram's; in Virginia alone, an estimated 4,000–6,000 women became widows as a result of the war.

How many people died in the Civil War?

Now that would seem to be an odd question. After all, for a century and a half the number "about 620,000" has been generally accepted as the death toll in the Civil War, both sides taken together, mostly from disease, with "only" 175,000 or so killed in battle or died of wounds.

But how accurate are these figures?

The answer is, probably not very accurate at all.

To begin with, the "about 620,000" figure is for deaths among military personnel. And that number has recently come into question. A rigorous analysis of census records suggests that the number of military deaths has been underestimated by about 15 percent, more or less, and that the actual number is probably closer to 720,000, again mostly from disease.[12] But that still doesn't give us even an approximation of the number of war-related deaths, as it leaves out *civilian* deaths.

The number of civilians who died in the war has never been systematically calculated. Yet civilians certainly did die, in the tens of thousands. Some, a handful, died unintentionally, caught by what Franklin D. Roosevelt would later call "the violences of war," such as Mrs. Judith Carter Henry, an 85-year-old invalid who was mortally wounded on July 21, 1861, when her house, on Henry House Hill at Bull Run was shelled by Union artillery, or Jennie Wade (1843–63), killed by a stray Confederate round while kneading dough in her sister's house at Gettysburg on July 3, 1863. Many people died in atrocities perpetrated by ill-controlled partisan bands of both sides, while a great many more succumbed to disease and privation engendered by the war.

Consider some examples:

- Secessionist–Unionist rioting in St. Louis on May 10, 1861 left some thirty dead, the first of an estimated 10,000 civilians to die during partisan fighting in Missouri.
- In East Tennessee during the opening months of the war, scores of people—women as well as men—were lynched as suspected "bridge burners" or Union spies by Confederate irregulars and vigilantes.
- Hundreds of civilians died during a scarlet fever epidemic at Richmond during the winter of 1861/62, among them three children of Confederate general James Longstreet.
- A smallpox epidemic that swept through the South beginning in 1862 may have killed as many as 60,000 people, many of them African Americans.[13]
- On August 10, 1862, thirty-four German Texans, who were fleeing to Mexico to avoid the draft, were murdered by Texas Rangers and Confederate troops, an incident grandiloquently called "The Battle of the Nueces River."

- An outbreak of yellow fever in Wilmington, NC in 1862 may have killed as many as 1,200 people.
- About 1,700 Delaware Indians died from war-related causes in Kansas.[14]
- Over fifty people—including some women—were lynched in the "Great Hanging" of suspected Unionists at Gainesville, TX in October 1862.[15]
- On July 4, 1863, Confederates troops preparing to attack Helena, AR paused to sack two shanty towns inhabited by "contrabands," killing scores of fugitives from slavery.[16]
- About 120 people died in the so-called Draft Riots in New York in July 1863.[17]
- A yellow fever outbreak at Galveston in 1864 resulted in hundreds of deaths.
- Over 250 "contrabands" fleeing slavery were killed on December 9, 1864, when the Ebenezer's Creek bridge was blown up during Sherman's March to the Sea.
- Some 1,500 newly freed African Americans, mostly women and children, died of disease and hardship during the winter of 1864/65 in a shanty town near Camp Nelson, at Louisville, KY, a training camp for black recruits.
- Scores—perhaps hundreds—of people (deserters, family members, innocent bystanders) died in the mini-civil war that occurred in Mississippi's "Free State of Jones," an episode depicted in the recent motion picture of the same name.[18]
- An estimated 7,000 Cherokee died in the Indian Territory from war-related privation and violence, about a third of the tribe.[19]
- At least 200 workers on both sides—mostly women and girls—died in several munitions factory explosions.[20]

That's nearly 80,000 dead. And there certainly were more, a recent estimate putting the number at 100,000, which itself may be too low.

How many died in the irregular warfare in West Virginia, East Tennessee, and other parts of Appalachia? How many died in war-related industrial and rail accidents? How many died from hunger and privation due to the disruption of commerce or the destruction of crops and homes? How many died in atrocities? How many died in riots? How many died of hunger, disease, exposure, or murder while fleeing slavery? How many died years, even decades later, from the lingering effects or wartime privation or wounds?

How many died?

Signs of the times

Of some 630 students enrolled at the University of Virginia for the 1860–61 academic year, 515 joined the Confederate Army, of whom eighty-six died in action.[21]

On October 10, 1861, the Richmond *Daily Dispatch* solemnly reported that the Lincoln administration was considering declaring all marriages between loyal Unionists and their Confederate spouses dissolved.[22]

L. M. Johnson's *Elementary Arithmetic: Designed for Beginners*, published in South Carolina in 1864, included such problems as, "If one Confederate soldier can whip 7 Yankees, how many Confederate Soldiers can whip 49 Yankees?" and, "A Confederate Soldier captured 8 Yankees each day for 9 days; how many did he capture in all?"[23]

Many states and municipalities in the North provided payments to help the wives and children of servicemen; Wisconsin granted wives $5 a month plus $2 for each child, while Philadelphia granted families an average of $6.75 a month, more than a week's pay for a common laborer.[24]

Reportedly, early in the war, a fashionable young woman visited a hospital in Richmond and offered to wash a wounded soldier's face, to which he replied fatalistically, "Well, if you want to right bad, I reckon you must; but that will make seven times that my face has been washed this evening."[25]

A curious consequence of the war was that the number of patents awarded for new inventions nearly doubled, while those given to women, which had averaged about 1 percent of all patents since 1790, rose to somewhat over 11 percent, or about twenty annually.[26]

Having lost a bet on a local election in 1864, Reuel C. Gridley (1829–70), a shopkeeper in Austin, NV, toted a 20-pound sack of flour a mile through the town and then sold it at auction, donating the proceeds to the United States Sanitary Commission. The buyer gave the sack back, and Gridley began selling, and then reselling the sack in cities across the west and as far east as St. Louis, eventually raising about $275,000.[27]

Both First Families had lost a child before the war, and both lost one during it as well; 11-year-old William Wallace "Willie" Lincoln died of typhoid in the White House in 1862, and 5-year-old Joseph Evan Davis died in 1864 in a fall while playing in the Confederate White House, the dangers of infancy and childhood being enormous in their times.

The United States Christian Commission distributed approximately 1.5 million Bibles to the troops, including some to men in gray.[28]

Confederate general James Longstreet married Maria Louise Garland, who also bore the name Messaw-wakut, as her maternal grandfather Jacob Smith had been adopted into the Ojibwa Nation, which has led some careless people to claim she was of Native American ancestry.[29]

Perhaps no place in America felt the war more than Winchester, in the Shenandoah Valley, which changed hands more often than any other town in the country, going back and forth between Yanks and Rebs as many as ninety-eight times, six of them just in the 60 days from July 21 to September 19, 1864.[30]

On July 1, 1863, during the opening round of the Battle of Gettysburg, Pvt. Asa Hardman of the 3rd Indiana Cavalry took refuge in the Shead house, used as a school for young ladies, and although hidden, was taken prisoner when the Rebels captured the place. After the war, Hardman returned to pay his respects, and on February 28, 1866, married 31-year-old Louisa Shead, who, alas, died only a few weeks later.[31]

Operated entirely by volunteers and supported by public donations, the Cooper Shop and the associated Union Volunteer Refreshment Saloon in Philadelphia provided free meals to some 1.3 million troops by the end of the war.[32]

During the final days of the war, some Richmond citizens were wont to throw "Starvation Parties," at which elegantly attired guests would gather at soirées where the finest silver and crystal tableware was used, though there were usually no refreshments save water.[33]

Mrs. Lincoln's family, the Todds of Kentucky, were wealthy slave-owners, and all of her brothers served the Confederacy during the war, three of them being killed in action, as was her sister's husband.[34]

Although women comprised fewer than 1 percent of the approximately 2,000 professional telegraphers in the United States on the eve of the war, by its end they appear to have numbered in the hundreds, serving on both sides.[35]

An 1861 lithograph by W. Boell, of the Cooper Shop and the Volunteer Refreshment Saloon in Philadelphia. (National Archives)

CHAPTER 8

The Generals

On the eve of the war, there were not a lot of men in the United States who had experience commanding large bodies of troops. The four generals of the line in the Regular Army were all experienced commanders, but getting on. Three, brevet Lt. Gen. Winfield Scott (1786–1866), Brig. Gen. David E. Twiggs (1790–1862), and Brig. Gen. John E. Wool (1784–1869) were veterans of the War of 1812 (1812–14), and along with Brig. Gen. William S. Harney (1800–89) had seen extensive service in the three Seminole Wars (1816–19, 1835–42, 1855–58) and other conflicts with Native Americans, as well as in the Mexican-American War (1846–48), in which the Quartermaster General of the Army, Brig. Gen. Joseph E. Johnston (1807–91) had served. Only two other men in the country had ever commanded substantial numbers. George Washington Morgan (1820–93), a West Point dropout who had soldiered for the Republic of Texas, had earned a brigadier generalcy by brevet in the Mexican-American War, but had long been out of the Army, and in 1860–61 was serving as Minister to Portugal, while Albert Sidney Johnston (1803–62), a West Pointer who had soldiered for the Republic of Texas and then returned to U.S. service, and in 1860 was colonel of the 2nd Cavalry, had a brevet as brigadier general for commanding the Utah Expedition of 1857–58, which had required more tact than military prowess.

Although some of these men would perform valuable duties during the war (the two Johnstons in Confederate service, and Scott, Wool, and

Morgan for the Union), they were certainly not enough to command the hosts that were soon under arms.[1]

Finding the generals

As both the Union and Confederacy mobilized in 1861, both sides had to find new generals quickly.

It is sometimes said that the armies in the Civil War were largely led by amateurs, but that isn't precisely true. Even at First Bull Run, although the troops were largely green, thirty-one of fifty-one Union and thirty-four of forty-six Confederate regimental and battalion commanders who fought in the battle had trained at a military academy or seen active service as a soldier, including some in foreign armies, or as volunteers in an earlier war, or had long service in the militia; thirty-nine of these ninety-seven men eventually rose to generalships, twenty-two in blue and seventeen in gray. Many generals emerged from among the lower ranking officers of the Regular Army, some 300 of whom rose quickly during the war, and more were found among the abler volunteers who proved themselves on the battlefield. Of course, it did take some time, and on both sides some men were made generals who proved inept, but in the end, some excellent commanders emerged.

The "canonical" list of generals was compiled by Ezra Warner, in two monumental biographical references, *Generals in Blue* and *Generals in Gray*, with 584 in blue and 425 in gray, for a total of 1,009 generals. Their military backgrounds, shown in Table 8, are of some interest.

On each side, about two-thirds of the men who became generals can be shown to have had some sort of military training or experience before the Civil War: 396 of the 584 Union generals, and 291 of the 425 Confederate ones. Of course, the nature of their military background varied considerably.

It's worth keeping in mind that an officer might have had several different types of military experience, so a West Pointer might also have done some time with the militia or the volunteers, or even had a turn as a filibuster.

Table 8: Military backgrounds of the generals

Background	U.S. (%)	C.S. (%)
U.S. military academy	**238 (40.8)**	**175 (41.2)**
Annapolis Graduate	1 (0.2)	1 (0.2)
West Point	228 (39.1)	151 (35.5)
Graduate	*217 (36.7)*	*139 (32.7)*
Dropout	*11 (2.4)*	*12 (2.8)*
Other U.S. academy	9 (1.5)	23 (5.4)
U.S. non-academy officers	**36 (13.1)**	**18 (4.2)**
U.S. Army	34 (5.9)	14 (3.3)
U.S. Navy	2 (0.3)	3 (0.7)
U.S. Marine Corps	—	1 (0.2)
Other U.S. service	**102 (17.5)**	**95 (22.4)**
Militia	40 (6.8)	20 (4.7)
Volunteers and others	62 (10.6)	75 (17.6)
Foreign military service	**20 (3.4)**	**4 (0.9)**
Unknown military experience	**188 (32.2)**	**133 (31.3)**

Notes:

"U.S. military academy" includes West Point and Annapolis, with "Other" covering private or state schools such as Norwich University or the Virginia Military Institute. The West Point figure "Dropout" refers to men who resigned or were expelled before graduation. Both academy graduates and non-graduates would often also have had service as officers in the Army, Navy, or Marine Corps.

"U.S. non-academy officers" covers those who had served as regular officers at some time before the war but lacked academy training, which includes all four generals of the line on active duty in the old army at the start of the war.

"Other U.S. service" covers men with experience solely derived from the Militia, including university militia corps as well as in the prewar state militias, or as volunteers during the Mexican-American War, the Seminole Wars, the Army of the Republic of Texas, or as American filibusters and mercenaries.

"Foreign military service" includes officers with European or Latin American military experience who volunteered for the war.

"Unknown military experience" includes all others, some of whom may have been militiamen, as the records from some states are quite poor.

It's interesting that eleven naval officers or former naval officers became generals. Eight of these men served the Union, resigning from the Navy or coming out of retirement, to join the Volunteer Army, the most notable of whom were Lt. Samuel Powhatan Carter, who rose to brigadier general of volunteers and later returned to the Navy to become a rear admiral, the only man ever to have attained flag rank in both the U.S. Army and U.S. Navy; and Lt. William "Bull" Nelson, who rose to major general of volunteers before he was murdered in a personal quarrel. In gray, Cdr. Richard L. Page rose to captain, and Cdr. Raphael Semmes to rear admiral in Confederate service, before being appointed brigadier generals near the end of the war, while U.S. Marine Corps 1st Lt. William Whedbee Kirkland joined the Confederate Army and rose to brigadier.

How many generals were there? Warner lists 584 generals in blue and 425 in gray, the later group including David Twiggs, who began the war in Union service, and thus arguably served on both sides. Their distribution by highest rank attained is shown in Table 9.

In both armies, the proportion of brigadier generals to other generals was the same, as was the proportion of men ranking higher than brigadier, the Union being rather stingy with rank in this regard, having only one man above major general.

Warner's list is generally considered canonical. But there are some curious angles to the question of how many generals there were. For example, the eight men indicated as full generals in the Confederate Army were, in order of seniority, Samuel Cooper, Albert Sidney Johnston, Robert E. Lee, Joseph E. Johnston (who argued incessantly that he should rank first, because of the old U.S. Army rank), Pierre G. T. Beauregard, and Braxton Bragg, who held permanent rank as generals, plus Edmund Kirby Smith, who held provisional rank, and John Bell

Table 9: General officer distribution by rank

	Union (%)	Confederate (%)
Brig. Gen.	450 (77.2%)	328 (77.2%)
Maj. Gen.	132 (22.6%)	72 (16.9%)
Lt. Gen.	1 (0.2%)	17 (4.0%)
Gen.	—	8 (1.9%)
Total	**583**	**425**

Hood, who was a temporary general and reverted to his permanent rank of lieutenant general after his disastrous invasion of Tennessee in 1864.

In addition, in an appendix to his list of Confederate generals, Warner briefly mentions a hundred or so officers, usually colonels, "assigned as generals" in the Confederate Army, that is, men who were given the authority but not the rank of a general. Similarly, Warner's list of Union generals usually does not include men who were promoted to general, and served as such, but were then not approved by Congress, or colonels acting as brigade commanders. Nor does he include the Union's brevet generals, of whom there were nearly two regiments' worth; ignoring the difference between brevets in the Volunteer Army and those in the Regular Army, there were 1,400 brevet brigadier generals and some 300 brevet major generals. Warner also excludes militia generals on each side, some of whom actually took the field, mostly in Confederate service; several states were quite generous in awarding high rank in the militia, especially to politicians, so that, for example, on the eve of the war, the Virginia militia, with 14,000 more or less reliable troops, had over fifty generals.[2]

Although during the war there were 584 generals in blue and 425 in gray, the number on active duty peaked at the end of the war at 419 Union generals and 309 Confederate ones, not all of whom were actually employed. Combat deaths totaled forty-seven Union and seventy-seven Confederate generals, while ninety Union generals and thirty-nine Confederates left the service during the war for other reasons, such as wounds.

"Foreign" generals

It may seem odd that some foreign soldiers, even men who were not immigrants, became generals, but we have to keep in mind that aside from Winfield Scott, John E. Wool, and Albert Sidney Johnston, no one in the United States had ever commanded as many as 5,000 men, and few had even maneuvered a full regiment, 1,100 or so men. This was one reason why the Union made generals of Louis Blenker (1812–63), Franz Sigel (1824–1902), and August von Willich (1810–75), trained officers who had commanded substantial forces—5,000 men or more—during the German revolutions of 1848–49.[3] While none of them were brilliant commanders, they had managed to lead their hastily organized troops with some success for a time, and usually averted annihilation at the hands of Prussian regulars. Similarly, the Confederacy's Camille Armand Jules Marie de Polignac (1832–1913) was a veteran of the Crimean War, while Augustus Carl Buchel (1813–64), who died just before his promotion to brigadier was to be approved, was a soldier of fortune who had served with the French Foreign Legion and later became a colonel in the Turkish Army, before settling in Texas.

How many generals died in the war?

We tend to think that generals don't get killed very often in wars, but that certainly wasn't the case during the Civil War. In both armies, an officer's chance of being killed in action was about 15 percent higher than an enlisted man's, while a general's was about 50 percent greater. On paper, the combat death rate of Confederate generals was about 60 percent higher than that for Union generals (77:47), but the figures are deceptive. Confederate brigades were usually led by brigadier generals, but the Union was rather stingy with rank, and brigades were often commanded by colonels; on both sides, brigade commanders, who were supposed to lead their men into action sword in hand, had very high casualties. We can see this if we look at the fate of the generals who fought at Gettysburg.

During the 3 days of Gettysburg (July 1–3, 1863), five Confederate and four Union generals were killed or mortally wounded and a dozen Confederate and thirteen Union generals were less seriously wounded, making for a Confederate

An artist's rather fanciful impression of a general leading the troops into action at Fredericksburg. While most generals took their troops into action on foot, whether afoot or mounted, leading the troops was dangerous, which is why proportionately so many generals were killed in action.

general officer casualty rate of 32 percent and a Union one of 26 percent. Of colonels leading brigades, the Union lost four killed and seven wounded, the Confederacy six wounded. So, 30 percent of the Union officers holding brigade or higher commands became casualties, as did 38 percent of their Confederate counterparts, exclusive of men taken prisoner.

"The best school"—West Point

Most of the men who attained the highest ranks during the Civil War, whether in Union or Confederate service, were graduates of the Military Academy at West Point, and academy alumni commanded on both sides in nearly all of the major battles in the war.

The academy, established 1802 at West Point, about 50 miles north of New York City, where an old War for Independence fortress housed a school for artillerymen and engineers, took a while to develop as both an academic and military institution. During its early years, there was no prescribed course of study, and cadets sometimes graduated in only one or two years. Despite this, graduates performed well during the War or 1812. In 1817, Sylvanus Thayer (1785–1872), who had attended in 1807–08, was appointed Superintendent, and over the next 16 years turned the struggling institution into one of the premier officer-training schools in the world, instituting strict admissions requirements, a four-year curriculum, the Honor Code, the demerit system, and annual summer encampments, while requiring high physical, mental, and academic standards. By the time Thayer resigned as superintendent in 1833, after repeated clashes with anti-academy President Andrew Jackson, academy graduates comprised half of the officers in the Army.

Although he left the academy in 1833, Thayer's regime at West Point continued virtually unchanged for decades. It was a tough one. Entrance requirements were so daunting that in some years as many as 20 percent of the young men who were notified of their tentative acceptance never showed up for the admissions exams, and of those who did, about 60 percent failed the academic tests and about 7.5 percent failed the physical examination, with some overlap between the two groups.[4] Of those admitted, 26.2 percent failed to graduate due to academic deficiencies, primarily in mathematics, science, or engineering; only 6.3 percent were expelled due to conduct, and just two cadets in the entire period were dropped by reason of failure in tactics.[5] As some men resigned for personal reasons, on average during the 1840s and 1850s, only 51–52 percent of cadets admitted graduated.[6]

The curriculum

Modeled by Thayer on that of France's École Polytechnique, 71 percent of the curriculum was devoted to engineering, mathematics, and natural science, the heavy doses of mathematics in particular being the bane of most cadets.[7] As Cdt. George Cushing wrote to his father: "I can't write as good a letter as I used to—as I am always thinking of Math.—I have a nightmare every night almost of it.—Gigantic X's and Y's, +'s and –'s squat on me—and amuse themselves in sticking me with equations and pounding me on the head."[8]

Cushing, who entered the academy in 1854, was one of many who succumbed to mathematics, and never graduated. Deficiencies in mathematics and science were apparently the main reason the graduation rate for Southern cadets was lower than that for those of Northern or Western origins, only about 36.9 percent compared to about 48.6 percent. About 40 percent of Northern graduates of West Point ranked in the top quarter of their class, as against only about 25 percent of their Southern brethren, while about 23 percent of Southern graduates ranked in the bottom quarter of their class, as against only 6 percent of Northerners. This appears to have been due to a lack of educational opportunity in the South, where, in contrast to the North, most states lacked a public school system. Even the sons of prosperous Southern families often lacked adequate preparation in mathematics and science, since they were frequently educated by tutors, who usually provided a heavy dose of the arts and humanities but not much in the sciences.

West Point was a pioneering institution in American education. It was the first engineering school in the United States, and its alumni took part in the founding of virtually every other engineering school in the nation during the nineteenth century. The academy was also quick to adopt innovative techniques and technologies. It was one of the first American schools to install blackboards, then considered a major innovation, and in contrast to a purely lecture mode of instruction, it pioneered the "recitation" method, that is, students were assigned readings and problems—i.e. homework—and then had to demonstrate their skills before, and be critiqued by, their classmates and instructors.

Since West Point was a *military* academy, military training figured large in the lives of the cadets. There was a lot of "good old fashioned drill," by 1850 totaling over 1,000 hours over 4 years; 540 of infantry drill and evolutions, 268 of cavalry practice and maneuvers, and 204 of artillery service and tactics.[9] The curriculum included many practical military subjects, including fortification theory (a subject heavy with mathematics), weaponry, and even the manufacture of rockets, priming tubes, canister shot, quick and slow match, and various types of cartridges, including blanks, ball, buckshot, and buck and ball.[10] There was also instruction in drawing, a necessary skill for the military engineer, which was also useful in helping cadets develop an eye for terrain, invaluable for battlefield tactics.

Oddly, the curriculum was weakest in military history, theory, and strategy. During a cadet's entire time at the academy, there was just a single 9-hour seminar devoted to "The Science of War," usually conducted by Dennis Hart Mahan (1802–71), who had begun teaching at the academy while still a cadet, before graduating first in the Class of 1824.[11] From then until 1871, when he committed suicide upon being told he should retire, Mahan was continuously associated with the academy as an instructor, with occasional tours of military institutions in Europe to keep up with current trends. He was a devoted student of Baron Antoine-Henri Jomini (1779–1869), a Swiss officer who had for some time served Napoleon, before defecting to the Russians, afterwards producing a prodigious body of work on military history and theory. Jomini's work was rather formulaic, even mathematical, involving complex relationships between bases, lines of operation, strategic points, and such. And although he did clearly stress the need to concentrate superior power at decisive points, Jomini thought the primary objective of a military campaign was to secure critical territory, and particularly the enemy's capital, while believing that wars could be won in a single great hammer-blow battle. The influence of Jomini, as filtered through Mahan's instruction, on Academy graduates and on the Civil War in particular, is difficult to assess. There was much theory, but not a lot of history in the course, and perhaps too much stress on Napoleon, and, oddly, not much at all about American campaigns, such as those of George Washington or General-in-Chief Winfield Scott.

This limited coverage of history, theory, and strategy could be supplemented by participation in the "Napoleon Club," an extra-curricular seminar conducted by Mahan (and thus with still more Jomini), and the academy library had an extensive collection of military literature; Cdt. Robert E. Lee was so inveterate a reader that between January 26 and May 24, 1828, during his third year at the academy, he borrowed fifty-two books from the library.[12] In addition, since all students had to take French, their coursework included reading, in the original, a number of works that touched upon military history, such as Voltaire's *Histoire de Charles XII*, the "Swedish Thunderbolt," who conducted a series of brilliant, if ultimately unsuccessful, campaigns against Russia and Denmark.

The Academy and the war

By 1860, some 1,760 men had graduated from West Point. Of course, by then, some of these men were either dead or too old for active service, while many others were no longer in the Army, having found work as civil engineers, in the railroad industry, or other civil pursuits, among them such later famous commanders such as Ulysses S. Grant (working as a clerk in a leather goods store), or William T. Sherman and Thomas J. Jackson (both of whom had assumed academic posts). When the Civil War broke out, many of these men re-entered the service. In addition, some men who had attended the Academy but failed to graduate received commissions—after, all they did have some military training—and sixteen of them became generals as well, eleven in blue and five in gray, including Lewis A. Armistead (1817–63), who rose to Confederate brigadier general and died leading a brigade at Gettysburg during Pickett's Charge; Armistead had been expelled in

1836 for breaking a dinner plate over the head of fellow cadet and future Confederate lieutenant general Jubal Early (1816–94) during a mess-hall quarrel.

Academy graduates and dropouts accounted for about a third of Confederate generals and some 40 percent of Union generals.

"Wet" generals and "dry" generals

A Rebel trooper who had taken part in the abortive Confederate invasion of New Mexico in 1862 wrote that the expedition's commander, Brig.

Gen. Henry Hopkins Sibley had a "love for liquor [which] exceeded that for home, country, or God." Sibley was by no means the only heavy toper to attain high rank in the war. On both sides, there were some officers who indulged rather too much, but there were also some who never touched the stuff.[13]

So, here's a look at the drinking habits—or lack of same—of some of the senior political and military leaders of the day. This list is hardly complete.

Thirsty troops buying drink, probably whiskey.

Some Confederate abstainers

- Gen. Braxton Bragg, who characteristically was rather intolerant of those who did imbibe.
- Adm. Franklin Buchanan, a strong temperance man who was very "intolerant of drunkenness" and would lecture his crews on the evils of drink and punished it sternly, particularly among officers.
- Gen. Edmund Kirby Smith, a lifelong dry; tried to impose prohibition in his Trans-Mississippi theater, with only moderate success.

- Lt. Gen. Nathan Bedford Forrest reportedly was very abstemious, only taking alcohol on a couple of occasions when he was wounded.
- Lt. Gen. Thomas "Stonewall" Jackson, was apparently very easily affected by alcohol, and thus rarely ever touched the stuff, very occasionally taking a glass of wine on extremely cold days.
- Lt. Gen. Leonidas Polk; although he drank as a young man, having taken part in the Christmas "Egg Nog" at West Point in 1826, apparently he gave up liquor when he took holy orders.
- Maj. Gen. Thomas Hindman was an active member of the "Sons of Temperance" in Mississippi.
- Maj. Gen. Patrick Cleburne, reputedly a big drinker back home in Ireland, apparently took "The Pledge" upon reaching America in 1849.
- Maj. Gen. James L. Kemper became a member of the Temperance Society when he was about 19, and remained a lifelong dry.
- Maj. Gen. James Ewell Brown Stuart, may have had his first and only sip of booze as he lay dying. He also did not smoke.
- Brig. Gen. Micah Jenkins; as a very young child, he promised his mother never to use alcohol, and seems to have kept his word for the rest of his life.

Some Union abstainers

- Secretary of the Navy Gideon Welles.[14]
- Maj. Gen. Francis C. Barlow, a Unitarian, seems to have been a lifelong abstainer.
- Maj. Gen. George R. Crook was described by his sometime aide John Bourke as "a man who never indulged in stimulant of any kind—not so much as tea or coffee—never used tobacco ... never heard to employ a profane or obscene word."[15]
- Maj. Gen. George Armstrong Custer; reportedly, as a teenager he once became so drunk that he thoroughly disgraced himself and told his mother he would never touch a drop again, a promise he appears to have kept.
- Maj. Gen. Oliver O. Howard, nicknamed "The Christian General," was an extremely religious man (he once frightened some Indians

when, during a peace conference, he suddenly dropped to his knees to call for divine guidance). He abstained from drinking and swearing, though not from proselytizing. A heavy smoker, he several times tried to give it up, but never succeeded.[16]

- Maj. Gen. Judson Kilpatrick, was reported by one officer as having "one redeeming quality—he rarely drinks spirituous liquors, and never to excess", women and spite being his principal vices.
- Maj. Gen. Irwin McDowell, was so firmly anti-drink that once, having been rendered unconscious by a fall from a horse, he resisted the efforts of a doctor to revive him with a little brandy. He also seem to have been rather sanctimonious about it. Another non-smoker.[17]
- Maj. Gen. Emory Upton, a brilliant tactician, did not drink and after the war worked to bar alcohol from Army posts.
- Brig. Gen. Neal S. Dow, a Maine politician and major Temperance advocate, entered the war as commander of the 13th Maine, the "Maine Temperance Regiment," and emerged as a brigadier general. Nicknamed the "Napoleon of Temperance" and the "Father of Prohibition," he was the Prohibition Party candidate for President in 1880, garnering only 10,305 votes.
- Brig. Gen. Clinton B. Fisk, another Temperance leader, ran for President on the Prohibition line in 1888, doing much better than Dow, coming in third with an impressive 249,506 votes. Fisk University in Nashville, founded in 1866 as a free school for African Americans, is named after him.
- Brig. Gen Rutherford B. Hayes, a lifelong Temperance man, as President banned alcohol from the White House, as well as dancing, smoking, and card playing.
- Brig. Gen. Nelson A. Miles was an ardent prohibitionist, which caused some problems after the war as he tried to bar booze from military posts.

Some Confederate boozers

- Lt. Gen. Benjamin Franklin Cheatham, quite fond of whiskey, was reportedly so drunk at Murfreesboro/Stones River (December 31, 1862) that he fell out of the saddle.[18]

- Lt. Gen. Jubal Early, although not reputed to be an imbiber, was fond of whiskey to the point of sometimes filling his canteen with it, and particularly enjoyed a 12-ounce glass filled with cracked ice, a tablespoon of sugar, two shots of bourbon, and equal parts of hard cider and Virginia Concord red wine, called a "stone wall" because its effect was like hitting one.[19]
- Maj. Gen. John C. Breckinridge, formerly James Buchanan's Vice President, drank prodigiously. Although he had the reputation of being able to hold his liquor well, Braxton Bragg accused him of being drunk during the battles of Stones River, Chattanooga, and Missionary Ridge.[20]
- Maj. Gen. George B. Crittenden, brother of the Yankee general Thomas Crittenden, also a boozer, was once arrested for drunkenness along with Brig. Gen. William H. Carroll.[21]
- Maj. Gen. Fitzhugh Lee, Robert E. Lee's nephew, had a reputation as a hard drinker from his days at West Point.
- Maj. Gen. George Pickett, in the "Old Army," had a reputation as a drinker from his West Point days, but he apparently went on the wagon in 1863, when he became engaged to the much younger LaSalle Corbell.
- Maj. Gen. Earl Van Dorn's heavy drinking had forced him to resign from the Army after the Mexican-American War, and his habits hadn't changed much by the Civil War.[22]
- Brig. Gen. John Dunovant was dismissed from the service for drunkenness in November 1862, while commanding the 1st South Carolina Infantry, but returned to active duty in mid-1863, and rose to brigadier general.
- Brig. Gen. Arnold Elzey, Brig. Gen. Louis T. Wigfall, and Brig. Gen. Nathan G. "Shanks" Evans were named by Maj. Thomas J. Goree, of James Longstreet's staff, as "always more or less under the influence of liquor, and very often real drunk," though he added that Evans, who went into battle with an orderly carrying a "barrelita" of whiskey, in case he felt the need for a drop in the midst of battle, was also "one of the bravest men I ever saw and … a good officer when sober."[23]

- Brig. Gen. John B. Magruder was so widely known for his heavy drinking that stories circulated about his adventures while drunk, though his fondness for liquor doesn't seem to have notably affected his military performance.[24]
- Brig. Gen. Henry Hopkins Sibley, already mentioned above, was said by one officer to have been "a walking whiskey keg," and managed to be "sick" for virtually all of the engagements during his New Mexico expedition (February–April 1862).
- Brig. Gen. John Tyler Morgan, was once arrested for "drunkenness in the face of the enemy."[25]
- Brig. Gen. Robert Toombs, who had aspired be the first President of the Confederacy, and did serve as its first Secretary of State, was several times reported drunk while on duty, and eventually died from alcoholism, though his drinking does not seem to have hampered his battlefield performance.

Some Union boozers

- President James Buchanan, though he apparently held his liquor well.
- Vice President, and then President, Andrew Johnson drank heavily, and was apparently inebriated during his inauguration as Vice President.
- Senator Stephen A. Douglas; one historian commented that "his excesses at parties and enjoyment of alcohol became small legends in Illinois," and while campaigning for President, and then later in support of the Union war effort, he drank heavily to cope with stress, which probably contributed to his death from typhoid.[26]
- Maj. Gen. Thomas L. Crittenden, and his brother the Rebel general George Crittenden, were both boozers.[27]
- Maj. Gen. Gordon Granger drank heavily, though it does not seem to have affected his battlefield performance.[28]
- Maj. Gen. Joseph Hooker was so well known as a drinker that when it was learned he had been on the wagon during the disastrous Chancellorsville Campaign (a matter confirmed by no less a teetotaler than Henry Ward Beecher), one general remarked that he

had lost because he was *not* drunk. According to teetotaler Union Provost Marshal Marsena Patrick, Hooker was particular fond of a concoction of whiskey, water, sugar, and nutmeg. A well-known gambler and womanizer, he was also the most senior Union Army officer to lack facial hair.[29]

- Maj Gen Stephen Hurlbut, a notoriously heavy drinker, called by John Pope "a common drunkard," was also a heavy and usually unlucky gambler, but postwar went on the wagon and became a Temperance advocate.[30]
- Maj. Gen. Andrew Jackson Smith was so widely known to be a drinker that his nickname was "Whiskey."
- Maj. Gen. David S. Stanley, considered a "worthless drunk" by Maj. Gen. George Thomas, and called by one historian "a bitter alcoholic," nevertheless put in an outstanding performance on the battlefield with considerable regularity, and was eventually award-ed the Medal of Honor. Postwar, his drinking increased, and he displayed characteristics of alcoholism.[31]
- Brig. Gen. William Dwight, called by one historian "an inept and lazy alcoholic," was certainly drunk on May 27, 1863, while commanding a brigade of African American troops during a futile assault on Port Hudson.[32]
- Brig. Gen. Edward Ferrero, often drunk on duty, during the Battle of the Crater (July 30, 1864) was found sharing a bottle with Brig. Gen. James Ledlie, even as their troops were being cut down in droves.[33]
- Brig. Gen. Henry M. Judah was reputedly fond of drink even as a junior officer before the war, which did not seem to affect his performance, most of the time.[34]
- Brig. Gen. James H. Ledlie was often drunk on duty, notably during the Battle of North Anna (May 24, 1864) and the Battle of the Cra-ter (July 30, 1864), when he shared a bottle with Ferrero.[35]
- Brig. Gen. Thomas Meagher, a heavy drinker who usually held it well, though at Gaines' Mill (June 27, 1862) eye witnesses reported the he was too drunk to control his horse.
- Brig. Gen. Edwin Stoughton indulged heavily in booze and women.[36]

- Brig. Gen. Lorenzo Thomas, the Adjutant General of the Army, and later Chief of the Bureau of Colored Troops, had a long history of heavy drinking, once being charged with a "fondness for medicinal whiskey," which never seems to have affected his work.[37]

Readers may wonder at the absence of several people from one or the other list. For example, such reputedly heavy drinkers as Ulysses S. Grant, Alexander Hays, and John Newton are not among the boozers, nor Lincoln and Lee among the abstainers.

It's important to understand that whether an officer was a "boozer" or a "teetotaler" is in many cases largely anecdotal. In some cases the reputation was probably unmerited. A social drinker, for example, might be viewed as a boozer by a committed temperance type. Grant, Hays, and Newton certainly drank, but their fondness for drink appears to be very overstated. Moreover, it's worth keeping in mind that on both sides it was not unusual for an officer who had done poorly in action to be accused of having been drunk on duty, often accompanied by a charge of "treason."

The effects of illness were sometimes taken for drunkenness. Rufus King, the Union brigadier who had formed the "Iron Brigade," behaved erratically during the Battle of Groveton (August 29, 1862), and was rumored to have been drunk, but in fact had a history of epileptic seizures, and was shortly dispatched to represent the U.S. at the Vatican. Similarly, the Confederacy's Maj. Gen. William H. C. Whiting, a quarrelsome officer at best, was widely believed to have been drunk while commanding a division during the Second Battle of Drewry's Bluff, in May, 1864, but may have been under medication.[38]

Several of those listed as boozers, such as President Buchanan, Lorenzo Thomas, and Fitzhugh Lee, were not widely known as such because they held their liquor well. This was in contrast to Grant or the Confederacy's John Dunovant, and probably many other officers who reputedly had a "problem" with booze, but were mostly social drinkers with an occasional incident of overindulgence.

As to why some men were heavy drinkers and some never touched a drop, the reasons vary. The abstainers often had a religious or moral aversion to alcohol, or in some cases had some particularly unpleasant experience with drink. In Stonewall Jackson's case, abstention was probably a manifestation of his remarkable self-discipline, for he seems to have had a low tolerance for alcohol and had resolved never to touch the stuff; on the very few occasions when he is known to have had even a small drink, eye-witnesses remarked that he became very animated and spoke uncharacteristically loudly and freely. Some of the boozers were probably more or less addicted to hard liquor, such as Hurlbut, Henry Hopkins Sibley, Evans, Carroll, and Meagher, who drowned after falling off a riverboat while drunk. Then too, there were some officers who perhaps used drink to help work up the courage necessary to face battle, such as Ledlie and Ferrero, and, of course, there were probably some men who drank heavily to cope with combat stress.

Although both Lincoln and Robert E. Lee were widely considered abstainers, both were known to take a glass of wine or champagne at dinner or on other occasions, and Lee, who was a non-smoker, occasionally gave bottles of wine to distinguished visitors.[39] As a young man, Jefferson Davis drank heavily, while at West Point taking part in the "Egg Nog" riot, but later became a social drinker.

How did drink—or lack of same—affect the performance of these men? Well, there were good commanders and poor commanders on both lists. Certainly, some hard drinking officers were utterly incompetent, such as Henry Hopkins Sibley, Carroll, Ledlie, or Morgan. But others—Fitz Lee, Granger, David Stanley, Hurlbut—proved quite able. And while such outstanding commanders as Jackson and Cleburne are numbered among the teetotalers, so too are Bragg, Pillow, Howard, and Polk, who tasted victory about as infrequently as they appear to have tasted booze.

Fat boys—some overweight generals

Although we like to think that generals must look the part, historically there have been a surprising number of whom were seriously overweight, and there were several such on both sides during the Civil War.

Some of them proved good in the field and some did not, pretty much the pattern for any of the men who commanded during the war.[40]

Confederate

- Brig. Gen. William Barksdale (1821–63), was "a large, portly man," which did not seem to affect his battlefield performance; it was his brigade that spearheaded the devastating Confederate assault on the Union Third Army Corps at Gettysburg on July 2, 1863, during which he was mortally wounded.[41]
- Brig. Gen. Abraham Buford (1820–84), "an extremely large man for the times, weighing over 300 pounds and standing over six feet tall," was, surprisingly, a very able cavalryman.[42]
- Maj. Gen. Howell Cobb (1815–69), generously described as "portly" when he commanded Georgia's Confederate Reserve Force, was a lifelong politician, and President of the Confederacy's Provisional Congress; he performed fairly well in the field.[43]
- Brig. Gen. Adley Gladden (1810–62), described as "portly," nevertheless performed well at Shiloh, where he was mortally wounded on the first day while leading his troops, having had, according to Gen. Pierre G. T. Beauregard, a "marked influence" on the fighting.[44]
- Brig. Gen. Roger Weightman Hanson (1827–63), described by Brig. Gen. St. John Richardson Liddel as "a large fat man," was mortally wounded at Murfreesboro leading the Kentucky "Orphan Brigade."[45]
- Brig. Gen. Humphrey Marshall (1812–72), a West Pointer (1832) and Kentucky politician, did well as colonel of volunteers in Mexico when he weighed close to 200 pounds, but when commissioned a brigadier in 1861 was about 300 pounds. He had some success in Kentucky early in the war, but suffered from pains in his joints and fatigue, falling asleep during conversations. He resigned from the Army in mid-1863 and entered the Confederate Congress.[46]
- Brig. Gen. Albert Pike (1809–91), an Arkansas attorney and Mexican-American War veteran, weighed between 275 and 300 pounds by 1861. He carried out diplomatic missions to various Indian nations, getting about in a buggy, usually accompanied by

his black manservant and cook, who weighed about the same; surprisingly, he died at 81.

- Maj. Gen. Sterling Price (1809–67), rather generously described by one historian as "portly," was just fat. When he was wounded during the Battle of Wilson's Creek (August 10, 1861), he said, "That isn't fair; if I were as slim as Lyon that fellow would have missed me entirely," referring to his notably thinner opponent Union Brig. Gen. Nathaniel Lyon, who was killed that day.[47]
- Lt. Gen. Leonidas Polk (1806–64), the "Fighting Bishop," was frequently described by contemporaries as "portly" and pictures certainly endorse that assessment, though he was quite tall as well.[48]
- Brig. Gen. John S. Williams (1818–98), an attorney, politican, and former Mexican-American War volunteer, entered Confederate service as colonel of the 5th Kentucky in 1861, weighing in at some 300 pounds, and oddly served in Humphrey Marshall's command in Appalachia. Promoted to brigadier in April 1862, he led a brigade of cavalry in Joseph Wheeler's division, performing well, though on one occasion may have suffered from hallucinations due to heat prostration.[49]

Union

- Brig. Gen. Romeyn Ayres (1825–88), although only 38 when he fought at Gettysburg, was described as "portly and balding."[50]
- Maj. Gen. Ben Butler (1813–93) certainly merited the frequent description "fat," though he was by no means as obese as hostile engravings often suggest.[51]
- Rear Adm. Louis M. Goldsborough (1805–77) was nicknamed "Old Guts," not so much for his combativeness as for his heft, weighing about 300 pounds; he was described by Navy Paymaster William F. Keeler as "a huge mass of inert matter."[52]
- Maj. Gen. Irvin McDowell (1818–85) was described by Brig. Gen. Henry Haupt, the Army's principal railroader, as "a fat boy," and by Army Quartermaster General Montgomery Meigs as a "fat man."[53]
- Maj. Gen. Winfield Scott Hancock (1824–86), a fine figure of a man early in the war, at 6ft. 1½in. and some 200 pounds, gained

considerable weight while recovering from his Gettysburg wounds, and returned to duty so fat that one soldier remarked, "If, as has been asserted, 'all flesh is grass,' General Hancock may be said to be a load of hay."[54]

- Brig. Gen. Michael K. Lawler (1814–82), an Irish immigrant and veteran of the Black Hawk and Mexican-American Wars, was "five feet, nine inches tall and weighed 300 pounds" when he reentered the Army in 1861, which did not impede his battlefield skills, as he commanded brigades and then a division in the Army of the Tennessee; Grant supposedly said, "When it comes to just plain hard fighting, I would rather trust Old Mike Lawler than any of them."[55]

- Maj. Gen. Alexander McDowell McCook (1831–1903), sometimes described as "portly," was rather more than that, given his troops nicknamed him "Gut" for his impressive figure, though only in his early 30s.[56]

- Maj. Gen. William "Bull" Nelson (1824–62), the naval officer who became a major general, and was then bumped off by Brig Gen. Jefferson C. Davis, was described as "portly," weighing in at about 300 pounds, though it was well distributed over his 6ft. 4in. frame.[57]

- Maj. Gen. Lovell Harrison Rousseau (1818–69) was described variously as "a little too bulky" and "portly."[58]

- Maj. Gen. John M. Schofield (1831–1906) was described by one historian as a "portly Achilles."[59]

- Brevet Lt. Gen. Winfield Scott (1786–1866), the General-in-Chief until late in 1861, was not only overaged, but ill and quite overweight, tipping the scales at about 300 pounds. But he was an important mainstay of the Union war effort until he left the service, perhaps his greatest contribution being the so-called "Anaconda Plan," which, although ridiculed at first, was effectively the winning strategy in the war.

- Brig. Gen. Edwin H. Stoughton (1838–68) was described as "over-weight … far too obsessed with fine foods, wine, and women," which probably helps explain his death at age 30.[60]

- Brig. Gen. Regis de Trobriand (1861–97) was described as "a fat jolly Frenchman."[61]

- Brig Gen. John Basil Turchin (1822–1901) was called "a dumpy fat Russian with short legs," which made him a poor horseman; in any case, although very energetic, he was hardly a superior commander, nor even a mediocre one.[62]

It's worth noting that although overweight, some of these men—Price, Buford, Hancock, Schofield—were able commanders, each having, as one historian wrote of a heavy general in a later war, "no fat above his collar."[63]

Some notably skinny generals

There were several thin generals in the war, arguably as unsoldierly looking as their fat counterparts. Although the Union's Maj. Gen. James Blunt (1826–81) was nicknamed "Fat Boy," which would certainly imply that he was carrying a little weight, his principal biographer has found *that* nickname derives from a letter written by the general himself, which was a joke, and certainly wartime pictures of Blunt show him to have been rather slender.[64] Major General Philip H. Sheridan (1831–88) certainly merited his nickname "Little Phil," weighing in at only about 115 pounds, on a 5ft. 6in. frame.

But the skinniest general in the war was undoubtedly the Confederacy's William Mahone (1826–95). A railroad executive, he began the war as colonel of the 6th Virginia, and rose to major general, despite a constitution so delicate that he weighed no more than about 100 pounds on a 5ft. 6in. frame. Subsisting on tea, crackers, eggs, and fresh milk, provided by a cow that he always kept around his headquarters, the general had a cadaverous appearance. Wounded on August 30, 1862 at Second Bull Run, one of his aides went to inform Mrs. Mahone of the matter, saying, "It's only a flesh wound," to which she reportedly replied "Now I know it is serious, for William has no flesh whatever!"[65]

Some masters of "Army Latin"

Fighting men tend to be a tad profane, and especially in the heat of battle; even men as self-controlled as George Washington were known to cut loose with an oath or three on particularly stressful occasions.

Major General Philip H. Sheridan, U.S.A.
(National Archives)

Major General William Mahone, C.S.A.
(National Archives)

Known during the Civil War as "Army Latin," in the mid-nineteenth century profanity was frowned upon far more than it is today. In fact, though it seems improbable, the U.S. Army actually had a regulation mandating a fine of 1 dollar for swearing, a rule which if rigorously applied might have helped finance the war.

Several Civil War generals were noted for the richness of their vocabularies. Alas, given the reticence of the times, while everyone knew the various swear words common to the English language, it is rare to find a direct quote of a general uttering curses or oaths; so, much of our evidence as to someone's command of profanity is rather indirect, often turned up by historians dredging through obscure documents, diaries, letters, and the like.[66]

Some swearers in blue

- Maj. Gen. Thomas L. Crittenden, described variously as "showy, free with his use of booze and profanity" and "notorious for his profanity."[67]
- Brig. Gen. Jefferson C. Davis cursed rather freely, often swearing at his subordinates, which many of the enlisted men resented.[68]

- Maj. Gen. (Acting) Charles C. Gilbert could unleash "a tirade of profanity and abuse" when angry.[69]
- Rear Adm. Louis M. Goldsborough was described by Navy Paymaster William F. Keeler as "coarse, rough, vulgar, & profane in his speech."[70]
- Maj. Gen. Winfield Scott Hancock, had "a well-deserved reputation for sulfurous language," with "a ferocity and profanity on the drill field and in battle that became legendary." He was a man who, in the words of one soldier, was unable to give an order "without taking God's name in vain," and at Gettysburg was observed standing in his stirrups dressing down a regimental commander "in the most choice and forcible language."[71]
- Maj. Gen. Joseph Hooker swore so freely that Secretary of the Navy Gideon Welles actually called him "blasphemous."[72]
- Maj. Gen. Andrew A. Humphreys was well known as a "profane swearer," though he reminded his critics that he never swore at the Almighty.[73]
- Maj. Gen. Judson Kilpatrick was known to be "salty with his words," and Libby Custer wrote that "he used an oath with every sentence that he uttered," while Col. William Douglas Hamilton of the 9th Ohio Cavalry wrote that he had "a vocabulary which he did not learn in Sunday School."[74]
- Brig. Gen. Nathaniel Lyon "swore at his men as if they were mules."[75]
- Rear Adm. James Lardner: according to Robley D. Evans, a passed midshipman (ensign) during the war, who decades later would command the Great White Fleet, "To a naturally fluent tongue, the Admiral added a vocabulary of oaths so fine that it was musical, and when aroused he did not hesitate to speak his mind in the language all seamen understand."[76]
- Maj. Gen. George G. Meade was widely known for a fiery temper and "extreme use of profanity," which earned him the nickname the "Old Snapping Turtle."[77]
- Maj. Gen. William "Bull" Nelson was, according to Charles Francis of the 85th Illinois, "The best, finest, and most elegant and original

cusser and swearer in the whole United States Army." He once got into a cursing match with Maj. Gen. John Pope over whose troops had arrived at a particular objective first, "to the horror and scandal of everybody," and later with Brig. Gen. Jefferson C. Davis, which got him murdered.[78]

- Maj. Gen. John Pope, apparently normally rather tame in his language, as noted above once became involved in a mutual swearing match with William Nelson.[79]
- Maj. Gen. Israel B. Richardson had the habit of "swearing most vehemently on the most trifling of occasions," and in battle was often seen and heard "swearing like a trooper."[80]
- Maj. Gen. William S Rosecrans was "a devout Catholic, but a man who could also erupt into profanity and impatient outbursts," though in battle he was calm.[81]
- Maj. Gen. Philip Sheridan: "his picturesque profanity was legendary," and during a battle he might be seen "hat in one hand and sword in the other, fighting as if he were the devil incarnate, and swearing as if he had a fresh indulgence from Father Tracy every five minutes." Once admonished to watch his language, he replied "I can't help it. Unless I swear like hell the men won't take me seriously."[82]
- Maj. Gen. Gouverneur K. Warren swore so mightily when he was angry that one colonel "was convinced that Warren could outswear anyone in the army," including George G. Meade.[83]
- Brig. Gen. Thomas J. Wood, noted for his "free use of profanity," once unleashed "an avalanche of oaths" on an unfortunate officer that was "a masterpiece of profanity, faultlessly rendered."[84]

Some swearers in gray

- Lt. Gen. Richard H. Anderson was a normally affable man, but during at least one battle, when his men were falling back in confusion, went among them "cursing and whacking them with the flat of his sword."[85]
- Gen. Braxton Bragg was often heard "cursing like a sailor" on stressful occasions, such as during the Battle of Missionary Ridge.[86]

- Lt. Gen. Benjamin Franklin Cheatham was described by one historian as "an unsavory Tennessean widely known for his drinking [and] outbursts of profanity."[87]
- Lt. Gen. Jubal Early, a seriously "hard-swearing" man, "habitually spiced his conversation with language which made sailors cringe," and was even known to use profanity in the presence of Robert E. Lee.[88]
- Lt. Gen. Richard S. Ewell was known as a "hard swearing man," "famous among his fellow generals for his hot temper and rich use of profanity," who could unleash a "terrible volley of oaths" in the midst of battle.[89]
- Lt. Gen. Nathan Bedford Forrest swore often, using "damn" frequently, and at times could be heard "cursing a blue streak" during charges or battles, but once became very upset with one of his comrades, who let slip some profanity while they were entertaining a Methodist bishop.[90]
- Brig. Gen. John D. Imboden swore so outrageously at one point in the Battle of Bull Run that Thomas "Stonewall" Jackson demanded he apologize, adding "Nothing can justify profanity," which the then captain of artillery took to heart thereafter.[91]
- Maj. Gen. William W. Loring was reputed to have so rich a vocabulary that one of the men once remarked he could "curse a cannon up hill without horses."[92]
- Maj. Gen. Lafayette McLaws, a historian wrote, "developed a mastery of profanity, and could appear blunt and coarse" but was in fact "a sensitive soul," which seems rather contradictory.[93]
- Lt. Gen. Richard Taylor "could swear in Spanish, French, and English."[94]

Of course some officers didn't swear. Ulysses S. Grant was reputed to have never been heard uttering even the mildest oath, to the point that once, during the Battle of the Wilderness, his staff officers were surprised when he several times said "Confound it!" or "Doggone it!" Similarly, the worst ever heard from Maj. Gen. George Thomas seems to have been a "Dang it!" when he believed Grant, Maj. Gen. Henry Halleck, and Secretary of War Stanton were conspiring against him.[95] Among

Confederates, Robert E. Lee and Thomas "Stonewall" Jackson appear to have been even less inclined than Grant to swear, Lee at times even publicly rebuking officers for using "improper and uncalled for" language.[96] And of course Leonidas Polk, perhaps by virtue of his normal occupation as Episcopal Bishop of Louisiana, never uttered profanity, though at one point during the Battle of Murfreesboro he was heard to shout "Give 'em what General Cheatham says, boys! Give 'em what General Cheatham says!" as Maj. Gen. Benjamin Cheatham was shouting "Forward, boys, and give 'em hell, boys."[97]

A fanciful engraving showing Gen. Joseph E. Johnston and Lt. Gen. William Hardee reaching the body of Lt. Gen. Leonidas Polk, killed by cannon fire, June 14, 1864, while on a reconnaissance near Marietta, GA.

So what did they say?

Civil War soldiers used pretty much the same hoary Anglo-Saxon swear words, curses, and blasphemies that we still use today, though it was rare to find them written in letters or diaries, and almost unheard of for them to appear in print.[98] Even words or phrases that would be considered very mild today were often rendered using dashes, such as "H--l!" or "d--n!" or masked by the use of substitutes, such as "H" for "Hell" or "dang" and "darn" for "damn." Stronger curses were sometimes rendered by using similarly spelled or sounding words, a practice which can cause the modern reader confusion. Take, for example, "puppy."

Three violent personal encounters during the war occurred because one "gentleman" called another "puppy," which seems rather curious.

Lieutenant Colonel Robert B. Rhett, 1st South Carolina Artillery, used the word with reference to his commander, Col. William Ransom Calhoun, leading to a duel on September 5, 1862, in which the latter was killed, an event that also led to Rhett's promotion to command of the regiment.

Union Maj. Gen. William "Bull" Nelson used it while slapping Brig. Gen. Jefferson C. Davis during an argument on September 29, 1862, which precipitated his murder by Davis a few minutes later.

Confederate Maj. Gen. Earl Van Dorn used it when his lover's husband, Dr. James Bodie Peters, confronted him over their affair on May 7, 1863, and the good doctor promptly shot him.

To the modern reader, "puppy" hardly seems particularly offensive. In the mid-nineteenth century, however, it was the polite usage when quoting someone who had used a more common derogatory term for female genitalia.

Walt Whitman's "I Saw an Old General at Bay"

During the early part of the war, Walt Whitman continued to work as a journalist in Brooklyn, writing articles on various subjects and an occasional poem about the conflict. Although he didn't see war up close, he knew something about it from carefully following news reports and other accounts of the fighting, and his steady correspondence with his brother, George Washington Whitman, an officer in the 55th New York.[99]

Walt Whitman. (National Archives)

In late 1862, a newspaper appeared to list brother George among the casualties of the Battle of Fredericksburg (December 13). Whitman headed for Virginia in search of him. As it turned out, George had only been lightly injured. But Whitman was deeply moved after witnessing the great numbers and enormous suffering of the wounded in the many hospitals around Washington, and decided to remain and lend a hand. For about 2 years, he worked tirelessly as a volunteer nurse in various hospitals, while supporting himself with a part-time job in the Army Paymaster's Office.

It was apparently during this time that Walt wrote a number of poems about the war and the wounded, which he said were, "put together by fits and starts, on the field, in the hospitals as I worked with the soldier boys." Among these was "I Saw an Old General at Bay."

I Saw an Old General at Bay

> I saw old General at bay,
> (Old as he was, his gray eyes yet shone out in battle like stars,)
> His small force was now completely hemm'd in, in his works,
> He call'd for volunteers to run the enemy's lines, a desperate emergency,
> I saw a hundred and more step forth from the ranks, but two or three were selected,
> I saw them receive their orders aside, they listen'd with care, the adjutant was very grave,
> I saw them depart with cheerfulness, freely risking their lives.

While it's unlikely that Whitman actually witnessed an episode such as he depicted in the poem, it certainly describes a commonplace of warfare at the time, as the commander of a hard-pressed force calls for volunteers for the dangerous mission of carrying a desperate plea for support.

In 1864, physically exhausted, Whitman returned to Brooklyn to recuperate, and began putting his war poems together for publication. They appeared as *Drum Taps* in 1865, a collection of forty-three poems, which were later revised and expanded, and still later incorporated in the final edition of his *Leaves of Grass*.

Signs of the times

According to Edgar Allan Poe, who dropped out of West Point in his second year, "the sole congenial soul in that God-forsaken place" was First Classman Jefferson F. Davis.[100]

Tradition has it that while a cadet in the West Point Class of 1842, John Pope (1822–92), later one of the less-able Union generals, invented the buttoned "fly" for trousers, in place of the buttoned flap such as was until recently still worn by sailors.[101]

Learning that his uncle, General-in-Chief of the Army Winfield Scott, refused to join the South, Col. Joseph W. Harper ordered his slaves to take the portrait of the old soldier that had for years hung prominently in the family home and throw it in the Nottoway River.[102]

After a newspaper mentioned that he was holding a cigar during the Confederate breakout attempt at Fort Donelson on February 15, 1862, patriotic citizens in the North sent Ulysses S. Grant 10,000 stogies in all their infinite variety, and his consumption eventually rose to about two dozen a day.[103]

Fully 129 (30.6 percent) of the 425 Confederate generals, but only 126 (21.6 percent) of the 583 Union generals, had been lawyers before the war.

On Sunday, September 7, 1862, even as the Army of Northern Virginia was marching through Maryland on the road that would lead to Antietam, Lt. Gen. Thomas J. Jackson—the "Gallant Stonewall"—carefully wrote out a pass for himself, so that he could be absent from duty for a time to attend to some more important business: divine services.[104]

More than a dozen veterans of the "Red '48" revolutionary outbreak in Europe in 1848–49 became Union generals, the most notable among them being Maj. Gen. Carl Schurz—later a successful politician and reformer—and Brig. Gen. August von Willich, a sometime colleague of Karl Marx, whom he once challenged to a duel.[105]

Reportedly, in March 1863, having been informed that Rebel raider John S. Mosby had captured Brig. Gen. Edwin Henry Stoughton and 110 horses, Lincoln expressed concern about the loss of horseflesh, observing, "I can make a brigadier general in five minutes, but it's not easy to replace 110 horses."

Confederate Brig. Gen. Gideon Pillow—arguably the second most inept general in the war after John B. Floyd—had served as a major general of volunteers during the Mexican-American War courtesy of his friend President James K. Polk, a post in which he was so unsuited that he built some fortifications that faced the wrong way.[106]

In January 1864, Union Brig. Gen. John Beatty resigned his commission in order to go home and relieve his brother of the burden of running the family business, so that the latter could join up and get a taste of military life.[107]

Union Maj. Gen. William S. Rosecrans was a fine commander, if a mite meticulous, and bombarded the War Department with so many telegrams that, at one point, an exasperated Henry Halleck wired back to complain about "the enormous expense to the Government of your telegrams, more than that of all the other generals in the field."[108]

Although officially ranked as a brigadier general, Herman Haupt apparently never officially accepted a commission nor received pay from the Federal government, so that he could continue to pursue private business interests while organizing and operating the Union's military railroading system, at which he did a brilliant job.[109]

Touring the trenches before Petersburg one day in early 1865, Gen. Robert E. Lee found that Brig. Gen. Archibald Gracie, Jr., appeared to be obscuring his view as he observed points of interest in the Yankee lines, and so remarked, "General, you should not expose yourself so much," to which Gracie—who was trying to shield Lee from Union marksmen—replied, "If *I* should not, General Lee, why should you?" at which Lee smiled and retired to a less exposed position.[110]

On April 6, 1865, during a skirmish at High Bridge, VA just days before Lee's surrender, Union Brig. Gen. Theodore Read was slain in an exchange of pistol shots with Confederate Brig. Gen. James Dearing, whom he mortally wounded; the latter died on April 23.

On April 26, 1865, 4 years to the day after resigning his commission as Quartermaster General of the United States Army to go South, Joseph E. Johnston, a full general in the Confederate Army, surrendered his Army of Tennessee to William T. Sherman.

The last Civil War general to cross the river was the Union's Adalbert Ames (1835–1933), who graduated from West Point in May 1861 and by war's end had risen to brigadier general in the Regular Army, with a brevet for major general.

CHAPTER 9

Money, Graft, and Corruption

The Roman statesman Marcus Tullius Cicero (106–43 BC) once said: "The sinews of war are endless money." Finding and managing that money is a major factor in winning wars. Of course, when governments begin hastily throwing money around with great enthusiasm, there are plenty of people willing to dip their fingers—or even their fists—into the pie. As the late novelist and Civil War historian Fletcher Pratt is reputed to have said, "No one ever went broke supplying an army," and the Civil War was much like any other when it came to some people finding ways to exploit opportunities for graft, crooked deals, nepotism, and other forms of corruption.

Paying for the war

In practical terms, there are only three ways a country at war can find money; taxation, borrowing, and running the printing presses, i.e. inflation. The key to success in financing a war is to find the right balance among these three options. The "Founding Fathers" had spent about £165 million achieving American independence, about $868 million at the time, and perhaps $400 billion or so today, in a nation of only about 3 million, a per capita liability approaching $135,000, well over twice the current US per capita debt. About two-thirds of this money was in the form of printed paper with no backing other than the word of Congress or the issuing state that it was worth something, which is sometimes known as "fiat money." Borrowing brought in most of the remaining third, primarily from domestic sources, but some from French, Dutch, and other foreign investors. Taxation and the sale of confiscated Loyalist and Crown properties brought in a tiny sum. Running the printing presses led to enormous inflation; by the end of the war, a dollar in Continental currency was down to about a quarter of a cent of its original value.[1]

With the outbreak of the Civil War, both the Union and the Confederate governments had to start finding the money to fight. Each developed a different balance among taxes, loans, and inflation.

In August 1861, the United States introduced a graduated income tax, starting at 3 percent on incomes exceeding $800 a year (later dropped to $600) and rising to 5 percent on those over $10,000, with the uppermost rate being doubled in 1864. In August 1862, the Confederacy also introduced an emergency war tax based on property worth more than $500, including slaves, and various luxury items, and in April 1863 imposed a "tax in kind," which took a tenth of all agricultural product by state for government use, primarily to feed the Army. As the Confederate

Table 10: Comparison of war finance sources

Source	C.S.	U.S.
Loans	30%	62%
Paper	60%	13%
Fees and revenues	5%	4%
Taxes	5%	21%

Notes:

All states also incurred some expenses, but these have apparently never been systematically calculated.

Figures are approximations, as estimates vary.

"Loans" include those made by Confederate citizens, who often paid in Confederate money, and bankers and people abroad, primarily in Britain and France, who usually paid in more substantial money.

"Paper" includes only issues by the two national governments; some states in the South also issued paper money.

"Fees and revenues" include such items as import tariffs, port duties, and license fees.

"Taxes" include excises on alcohol and some other luxury items; both sides also introduced some direct taxation.

Table 11: Value of the dollar, 1861–65

Date	U.S. $	C.S. $
Apr 1861	1.00	1.00
Jun 1861	1.00	0.90
Nov 1861	1.00	0.80
Dec 1861	1.00	0.75
Feb 1862	1.00	0.60
Mar 1862	0.97	0.58
Aug 1862	0.83	0.50
Dec 1862	0.80	0.25
Feb 1862	0.75	0.20
Jun 1863	0.58	0.08
Mar 1864	0.40	0.05
May 1864	0.35	0.05
Oct 1864	0.48	0.045
Jan 1865	0.53	0.025
Mar 1865	0.60	0.015

government lacked an effective administrative infrastructure, neither tax was ever properly collected, and the tax in kind was bitterly resented as confiscation.

During the war, both sides suffered from inflation. But the Union's greater reliance on taxes and bonds to bring in revenue helped soak up a lot of the fiat money, which kept inflation from becoming a serious problem, while the Confederacy's heavy reliance on printing unsupported money led to serious inflation.

The war began with the Confederate dollar pegged at the U.S. gold dollar. But the Confederacy only issued a very small amount of coinage, mostly just running off U.S. coins at mints captured during Secession until the dies wore out. So the Confederacy began printing money early, without imposing taxes, and serious inflation followed. By the spring of 1862, inflation was beginning to have a devastating impact on the ordinary people of the Confederacy, and there were "bread riots" in Richmond and several other cities.

The U.S. began issuing fiat money—the famous "greenbacks"— in February 1862, and it too began experiencing a decline in the value of the dollar. By war's end, the U.S. government had issued about $450 million in paper money, while the Confederacy may have issued as much as $1.5 billion.[2] On July 1, 1865, the U.S. national debt, which stood at $65 million on July 1, 1860, had increased by over 412 percent to $2.678 billion, today arguably equivalent to $10.4 trillion in relative economic value.[3]

The Richmond bread riot of April 2, 1862, from a newspaper illustration. (Library of Congress)

J. P. Morgan turns a tidy profit[4]

In 1857, the U.S. Army's New York quartermaster depot condemned a lot of about 5,000 carbines. The weapons languished in storage until 1861. Shortly after the outbreak of the Civil War, rising young financier J. P. Morgan learned of their existence. Through an agent, Morgan offered the St. Louis quartermaster depot "5,000 new carbines in perfect condition" for $109,912, about $22 apiece. The St. Louis depot decided it was a good deal, and telegraphed acceptance of the offer. Morgan took the telegram to a bank, where he used it to secure a loan. He then purchased the condemned carbines from the New York depot, paying $17,486 for the lot, about $3.50 apiece. As soon as he received title to the weapons, Morgan had them shipped directly from the New York depot to the one at St. Louis, without ever actually taking possession and at government expense.

Shortly after the St. Louis depot received the "new carbines in perfect condition," it became clear that the weapons were faulty, indeed, so faulty that several test firers were injured. The Army therefore tried to cancel the deal and refused to pay Morgan the money owed him.

Morgan insisted on being paid, and threatened to take the Army to court. Seeking to avoid a court battle, the Army then offered to pay $65,600 for the lot, about $13.30 apiece, still much more than they were worth. However, Morgan insisted on payment of the full contracted sum and the matter ended up in court. Amazingly, the court ruled in Morgan's favor. He shortly thereafter received his money from the government, making a profit of about $92,500, roughly 500 percent over his cost, leaving him with a tidy sum after repayment of his bank loan.

Morgan's profitable hustle was hardly the only instance of corruption during the Civil War.

For example, on March 2, 1865, a *The New York Times* account of an investigation of the procurement of supplies by navy yards reported: "The expenses of these examinations at the navy-yards were $14,894. Restitution to the amount of $47,661 has been made by persons arrested in consequence of these inquiries who have confessed their guilt. Parties have also been fined to the amount of $75,000." These were enormous sums for the day, considering that the ironclad USS *Monitor* only cost $275,000 to build.

It's worth nothing, however, that at times, charges of corruption were ill founded. For example, early in the war, many Union troops were issued uniforms that were brown, black, and even gray, rather than in Uncle Sam's customary blue, which caused some to see graft at work. But Quartermaster General Montgomery G. Meigs replied that there was a shortage of cloth in the appropriate color, and issuing uniforms in non-standard colors was better than seeing "sentinels walking post about the capitol of the United States in freezing weather in their drawers, without trousers or overcoats."[5]

Charges of crooked practice were sometimes prompted by a contractor's political or business rivals, such the case of Franklin W. Smith, a hardware dealer in Boston who had helped reveal the corruption at navy yards. A cabal of corrupt businessmen, Navy Department officials, and even some naval officers, several of substantial rank, apparently including the Chief of the Bureau of Ordnance, conspired to frame Smith, who was arrested and held at $500,000 bail in a case that became a cause célèbre. Personally intervening, President Lincoln reviewed the evidence and on March 18, 1865, wrote that Smith "had transactions with the United States Navy Department to a million and a quarter of dollars, and had the chance to steal a quarter of a million; and *whereas*, he was charged with stealing only ten thousand dollars, and from the final version of the testimony it is only claimed that he stole one hundred dollars, I don't believe he stole anything at all."[6]

The improbable John B. Floyd

John B. Floyd (1806–63) was the son of Virginia politician John Floyd (1783–1837), who, in 1831, while governor of the state in the aftermath of the Nat Turner Slave Rebellion, attempted to make a case for abolition.[7] As a young man, he read law and practiced in Virginia, before relocating to Arkansas, where he spent nearly 10 years trying to get rich planting cotton, at which he proved singularly unsuccessful, losing a substantial sum inherited from his father. Back in Virginia, Floyd entered politics, served several terms in the House of Delegates, and became governor (1849–52). Although he supported expansion of the franchise to all adult white men, he was a staunch slavery man, even proposing a decidedly unconstitutional import tax on goods entering the state from states that refused to surrender fugitive slaves; but he was not a secessionist.

In March 1857, President James Buchanan appointed Floyd Secretary of War, in succession to the able Jefferson F. Davis. Floyd proved a singularly poor secretary. His mismanagement greatly hampered the operations of the so-called Utah Expedition of 1857–58, led by the Army's rising star Albert Sidney Johnston, and, reflecting the remarkable disorder of his own financial affairs, he was careless about record-keeping, so that large sums went unaccounted for. Although never proven in court, he was widely believed to have helped enrich his cronies by well-placed contracts or insider information. For example, in 1858, "without consulting with, without the advice, and without the knowledge of any officer in the service of any rank," Floyd sold 8,000-acre Fort Snelling, MN for $90,000, a deal in which War Department agent John C. Mather, who supervised the condemnation and sale of the post, was also a partner on the purchasing end—a clear conflict of interest, prompting a member of Congress to declare on the floor, "this action on the part of the Secretary of War was a grave official fault."[8] Later that year, in an impressive bit of graft that certainly outstrips anything seen in recent decades, after approving construction of coastal fortifications on a tract near Line Point, on the north side of the Golden Gate in California, near Fort Baker, Floyd alerted one of his cronies of the plan, who purchased the land for $500, and then sold it to the Army for $200,000, yielding 4000 percent profit.[9]

In addition, following the lead of his predecessor Jefferson F. Davis, Floyd favored Southerners in officer appointments. Of thirty-four officers in the new 2nd Cavalry Regiment appointed by Davis or Floyd, nineteen (56 percent) were from the Slave States, at a time when white residents of those states amounted to only about a third of the country's free population, and an approximate third of the officer corps. Twelve of these men defected to the Confederacy, nine of them becoming generals, including Albert Sidney Johnston, Robert E. Lee, Earl Van Dorn, E. Kirby Smith, and John Bell Hood. Floyd was also not above a bit of nepotism, in June 1860 appointing his kinsman Joseph E. Johnston Quartermaster General of the Army with the rank of brigadier general, despite the fact that several men, including Robert E. Lee and Albert Sidney Johnston were senior to him. In 1859, in the aftermath of John Brown's raid, Floyd began shipping some 115,000–135,000 stand of older muskets (i.e., a musket plus bayonet, ammunition pouch, and belt) to arsenals in several Southern states, and some officers believed he deliberately reduced the size of garrisons at some critical posts in the Slave States.[10]

And then there was the matter of Messrs. Russell, Majors, and Waddell, who held the contract to deliver supplies to army posts on the frontier. In 1858, company president William H. Russell approached Floyd and confessed that the firm was having financial problems. Floyd decided to lend a hand. He later claimed he thought the company was having what we would now call a "cashflow" problem but was otherwise sound, and argued that they were the only people capable of delivering supplies across the vast distances on the frontier. Floyd issued drafts to

Russell in anticipation of future work. Russell used these as collateral to borrow from banks, which believed the notes were proper government securities. Russell came back for more several times, and each time Floyd issued additional drafts, despite warnings from friends, political associates, and even President Buchanan that he was on shaky ground. In mid-1860, Russell was out of credit; if he could not pay the loans he had secured on the basis of the War Department drafts, his company would go under, sparking a major scandal.

Now, in a little bit of nepotism, Floyd had secured a post in the Interior Department for his kinsman Godard Bailey, as manager of the Indian Trust, bonds held by the government for various tribes, some $2.5 million in negotiable paper. In July 1860, Bailey gave Russell $150,000 in bonds in return for a note in that amount and a promise that the bonds would be returned in 3 months. Three months later, Russell was back, having speculated away the money, asking for more "help," and then again 3 months after that. Altogether, Bailey handed Russel $870,000 in Indian Trust bonds, and the money then vanished. The matter soon erupted in the press. Although the case of the "abstracted Indian Trust bonds" never made it into a court of justice, the court of public opinion was firmly convinced that Floyd was guilty.

Meanwhile, the country had gone through the election of 1860 and in December, South Carolina declared itself in secession. Just after Christmas, Maj. Robert Anderson withdrew his troops from Fort Moultrie to Fort Sumter, and Floyd ordered him back to Moultrie, an absurd idea that would have led to their capture, which President Buchanan vetoed. Meanwhile, Floyd ordered heavy artillery shipped to several coast defense forts still under construction in the South. By then, Buchanan had asked for Floyd's resignation, which was accepted on December 29.

Floyd became a brigadier general in the Confederate Army in May 1861. His military career was primarily noted for ineptitude, climaxing at the siege of Fort Donelson (February 11–16, 1862), where, in the final hours, he fled the scene after turning over command to the some-what less inept Brig. Gen. Gideon Pillow, who decided to flee with him, and passed command to Brig. Gen. Simon Bolivar Buckner, who surrendered the post to Ulysses S. Grant.

For his pusillanimous performance at Donelson, Floyd was relieved of command by Jefferson Davis and never employed again.

Judgements on Floyd have been harsh, including being labelled "the most worthless officer in the Confederate camp" (Col. Charles Whittlesey, 20th Ohio)[11], "a scoundrel beyond redemption" (Maj. Gen. Stephen Dodson Ramseur, C.S.A.)[12], and "a man of no principle" (Qm. Gen. Montgomery C. Meigs, U.S.A.)[13]

It should be noted, however, that while Secretary of War, Floyd actually had done something right. He had the wit to see that despite the drawbacks, the experiment in the use of camels to help supply garrisons in the West, initiated by his predecessor Jefferson Davis, had proven their effectiveness, and in late 1858 Floyd asked Congress for funds to import a thousand more camels. But Congress demurred.[14]

Signs of the times

Early in the war, the Confederacy contracted in New York with the American Bank Note Company, which still exists, and the National Bank Company, which doesn't, to print paper money, until the Federal government noticed the arrangement, whereupon one of the firms opened a branch office in New Orleans.[15]

When U.S. Secretary of War Simon Cameron complained that Thaddeus Stevens had accused him of graft, Lincoln asked the Senator, "You don't mean to say you think Cameron would steal?", who replied, "I don't think he would steal a red-hot stove."[16]

In late 1863, 18-year-old Capt. James R. Hagood of the 1st South Carolina was promoted to colonel over several more senior officers, becoming the youngest regimental commander in the Confederacy, for "distinguished skill and valor," according to the officer who promoted him, Brig. Gen. Johnson Hagood, his brother.[17]

Audited in late 1863, Maj. Alfred M. Barbour, Chief Quartermaster to Confederate forces in western Virginia in 1862–63, was found to have "shortages" in his accounts amounting to "at least $854,971," today perhaps equal to about $156 million.[18]

Between December 1, 1863 and January 1, 1864, Robert Murray, the federal marshal for the Southern District of New York, conducted a series of raids to bust a network that was secretly printing bonds and money for the Confederate government, seizing $7 million in securities and currency intended for use in Europe to purchase war materiel, while taking into custody dozens of people and impounding presses, plates, and other equipment.[19]

Between September 1861 and April 1865, an estimated 780,000 bales of Confederate cotton were shipped into the North, many of them by smugglers, so that an estimated 60 percent of the Union's cotton goods were made from Rebel raw materials.[20]

In March 1862, as Union forces closed in on Winchester in Virginia's Shenandoah Valley, Edwin S. Brent, bookkeeper of the Bank of the Valley, headquartered there, collected the bank's records and took them for safekeeping to Baltimore, which was firmly behind Federal lines.[21]

While looting the camp of the 55th Illinois at Shiloh on April 6, 1861, men from the 2nd Texas came upon a box filled with several thousand dollars in newly printed greenbacks, which they are said to have discarded, not having heard that Uncle Sam had gone into the paper money business.[22]

On May 29, 1863, Col. George Frederick d'Utassy of the 39th New York (the "Garibaldi Guard") was dismissed from Union service for, among other things, selling officer appointments and promotions, soliciting bribes from his officers and soldiers in return for favors, and falsely billing the government for $3,645.40; he was shortly a guest of New York's famous Sing Sing prison.[23]

Union Col. James A. Tait, the Provost Marshal General for the Washington defenses on the south side of the Potomac, was dismissed from the service in September 1863 for having engaged in smuggling goods into the Confederacy, including 4,000 decks of playing cards.[24]

Counterfeiting of Confederate currency was so common that when, in July 1864, during Sherman's Atlanta Campaign, Maj. Gen.

Lovell Harrison Rousseau and some of his officers were each given several thousand dollars as souvenirs, *New-York Herald* correspondent William F. G. Shanks commented that the stuff was "the genuine article, which is said to be nearly as valuable as the imitation, though not equaling it in engraving and printing."[25]

On October 3, 1864, Confederate partisan rangers under Lt. Col. John S. Mosby conducted what has come to been known as the "Greenback Raid," capturing a Baltimore & Ohio train carrying about $170,000 from a Union Army payroll, today perhaps $300 million on the "economic power" scale. None of this went to the Confederate treasury, all disappearing into pockets of the troops.[26]

So meticulous was the management of the U.S. Army Pay Department during the war that less than 0.05 percent of the funds entrusted to it failed to reach the personnel for whom it was intended.

Commanding in Alaska in 1870, Brig. Gen. John C. Tidball, an able horse artilleryman, was informed by the War Department that his accounts from the war were short one axe haft, and threatened dire consequences should he fail to come up with sixteen cents.[27]

Lawsuits arising out of contractual disputes between the Navy Department and shipbuilders over "cost overruns" resulting from construction delays due to changes in the design of warships built during the Civil War dragged on into the twentieth century, until March 31, 1919, when the U.S. Court of Claims settled the last three, brought by the successors of Secors & Company of New York, by dismissing them.[28]

An 1863 Confederate $500 bond, worth nearly 2 years' income for a day laborer in New York at the time, can be bought today for $330.[29]

CHAPTER 10

The Naughty Bits

Despite our firm belief that Americans had higher moral standards back in the nineteenth century, the men and women of the times were not all that different from those of later ages. Rich and powerful men had mistresses, and those with less money could resort to bawdy houses, which were quite common in cities and most small towns. Husbands were unfaithful to their wives, wives cheated on their husbands, and so forth.

Perhaps the most notable difference between our modern attitude about sex and that of our nineteenth-century predecessors is that folks back then talked about the subject much less openly, and disapproved much more vehemently, despite their actual behavior. It may come as a surprise to many, but premarital sex was not uncommon, even in supposedly staid New England, where at mid-century about 10 percent of "native born" white brides were pregnant at marriage, and the illegitimacy rate was about 8 or 9 percent of all live births for whites, about what it would be a century later on the eve of the "Sexual Revolution."[1] There was a thriving, if covert, business in naughty books, racy photographs (nicknamed "actress cards"), sexy undergarments, contraceptives, sex toys, and, for those unlucky enough to catch a "dose," medicines that would supposedly cure them, and abortions were widely available.

As Thomas P. Lowry so aptly put it in the title of his book on the subject, sex was "The story the soldiers wouldn't tell."[2]

"A vast horde of loose women"

Prostitution flourished in America's cities and towns well before the Civil War, so much so that there were guidebooks to the bawdy houses of New York, New Orleans, and other major cities, where streetwalkers were also common. The coming of the war signaled a significant increase in the trade. As Bell Irvin Wiley, the distinguished pioneering social historian of the Civil War, wrote over 60 years ago, the raising of the armies "was paralleled by informal mobilization for active service of a vast horde of loose women."[3] Statistics are necessarily spotty, but it's interesting to note the following:

- Alexandria, VA: In 1860 there were officially seven "soiled doves" working in two bawdy houses, figures likely much too low for a port town of 12,000 inhabitants. During the war, the number was estimated at about 2,500 women in seventy-five brothels, causing the town to be called "a perfect Sodom."[4]
- Chicago, IL: *c.* 2,000 women were working as prostitutes during the war.
- Memphis, TN: While the number of prostitutes is unknown, they were sufficiently numerous for the city to be nicknamed "The Gomorrah of the West," and the Union Army instituted a program to register them and require periodic medical examinations.[5]
- Nashville, TN: In 1860, the city had about 17,000 inhabitants, and about 200 prostitutes, a rather high ratio. By early 1863, there were about 1,500, of whom 352 were "registered" with the Union Army and subject to periodic medical examinations. In an attempt to reduce their number, the Provost Marshal loaded some scores or hundreds on a steamboat and shipped them to Louisville, which refused his thoughtful gesture, as did several other cities, and the ladies all returned to Nashville.[6]
- New Orleans, LA: No reliable estimates can be found as to the number of prostitutes in the city, but the war certainty did not interfere with its already thriving sex industry, which involved both white, mixed race, and black women, the latter sometimes free but including many enslaved.

- New York, NY: Before the war, it was estimated that there were some 7,500–8,000 prostitutes in the city, roughly one for every fifty-seven men, which probably doubled by mid-1863.[7]
- Richmond–Petersburg, VA: On the eve of the war, there were more than 300 prostitutes in Richmond proper, proportionately about the same as in New York, adjusted for population. During the war, about 7,500 prostitutes were working in Richmond, Petersburg, and adjoining suburbs, eliciting protests from "respectable women" about their lewd and rude behavior, their threat to soldiers' health, and their unpatriotic displays of luxury, complaints common in other cities as well.[8]
- Washington, DC: Seeking to confirm a rumor that there were 15,000 prostitutes active in the District of Columbia, in late 1861, an investigation by *The Evening Star* concluded that there were *only* about 5,000.[9]

The background of the women who went into prostitution varied. While most resorted to prostitution out of financial desperation, some saw it as a viable career path, with the potential to earn far more than women in more legitimate occupations, and even more than most men; on the eve of the Civil War an estimated 40 percent of women across the nation who were property owners in their own right were prostitutes. Most prostitutes were from poor families, of course, but some middle class and even upper class women resorted to prostitution to escape abusive family situations or after having been seduced and then abandoned by predatory lovers and rejected by their families. In New York and other major ports, many prostitutes had immigrant backgrounds; one estimate is that 1 in 250 immigrant women became prostitutes. In other areas, native-born women predominated, including African Americans, whether slave or free. Many women were prostitutes for short periods only, or worked in the trade part time, and a surprising number ultimately married and became "respectable."

Some generals with special "friends"

Even before the war, many officers in the old army out on the frontier kept mistresses, often Native American women, in some cases even going through a traditional Indian wedding ceremony. These relationships often produced offspring, and while some officers, such as Phil Sheridan, August V. Kautz, and George Pickett, looked after their mixed-race children, others did not.[10]

During the war, opportunities for hanky-pankey increased, as the habits of the several particularly notorious womanizers noted here will demonstrate.

- Lt. Gen. Jubal Early, C.S.A.: Although a confirmed bachelor and notorious misogynist, from about 1850 into the early 1870s, he had a relationship with Ms. Julia McNealy (c. 1833–1905), a Virginia belle of good family, which produced four children who bore his name and for whom he provided generously; he also had several children by another white mistress, as well as one or more with an African American woman.[11]

- Maj. Gen. Joseph Hooker, U.S.A.: While it's not true that prostitutes are nicknamed "Hookers" after "Fighting Joe," presidential grandson and great-grandson Charles Francis Adams, Jr., wrote of him: "During the winter (1862/63), I can say from personal knowledge and experience, that the Headquarters of the Army of the Potomac was a place to which no self-respecting man liked to go, and no decent woman could go. It was a combination of bar room and brothel."[12]

- Maj. Gen. Judson Kilpatrick, U.S.A.: A "boy wonder" cavalryman who became a brigadier general within 2 years of graduating from West Point, he was probably the most notorious womanizer of the war. Even before he became a widower, in mid-1863, he almost always had at least one mistress or prostitute around, of all races. Campaigning in Georgia and the Carolinas late in the war, he was accompanied by a white woman known as "Charley," who wore a uniform, as well as by an Asian woman named "Molly," a laundress who was pregnant with his child. Early on the morning of March 10, 1865, Kilpatrick was roused from his bed by a sudden Confederate raid, and fled in his nightshirt, leaving behind South Carolina belle Mary Boozer, another of his girlfriends. In addition to disguising his mistresses as soldiers (on one occasion as a major), Kilpatrick reportedly once passed a girlfriend off as his wife.[13]

- Brig. Gen. Edwin H. Stoughton, U.S.A.: Described as "far too obsessed with fine foods, wine, and women," he was once captured in flagrante with a lady love in a room littered with empty champagne bottles, by the redoubtable partisan ranger Col. John S. Mosby.[14]
- Maj. Gen. Earl Van Dorn, C.S.A.: While married with two children, he also had a long-term mistress named Martha Goodbread, with whom he had several children. He reportedly had so many affairs with married women that one journalist dubbed him "the terror of ugly husbands," at least until May 7, 1862, when Dr. James Bodie Peters shot him through the back of his head for "violating the sanctity of his home" by dallying with his wife Jessie McKissack Peters, who perhaps not coincidentally, delivered a baby girl in January 1863.[15]

Honorable mention: Annie E. Jones

While several generals accumulated a string of mistresses during the war, one young woman managed to accumulate a string of generals. Early in the war, Massachusetts gal Annie E. Jones (*c.* 1840–?), having decided to do her bit for the Union, became the special "friend" to an officer on the staff of the Union's Maj. Gen. Franz Sigel. She then spent some time as the "guest" of Brig. Gen. Julius Stahel, after whom she graduated to Maj. Gen. Judson Kilpatrick, but then left him for his handsome young subordinate Brig. Gen. George A. Custer. That led the irate Kilpatrick to have her arrested for espionage, and it required the intervention of Lincoln himself before she was cleared. She later apparently became a teacher for the Freedman's Bureau for a few years, after which she disappears from recorded history.[16]

Mary Ann Hall, "hostess" to Washington's elite

On January 31, 1886, *The Evening Star*, the capital's principal afternoon newspaper, ran a short obituary:

> Mary Ann Hall, long a resident of Washington. With integrity unquestioned, a heart ever open to appeals of distress, a charity that was boundless, she is gone; but her memory will be kept green by many who knew her sterling worth.

Born and raised in the District of Columbia, Mary Ann Hall (1815–86) was one of six children of working class parents. Although her father died in 1820, Mary Ann would ultimately become one of the wealthiest businesswomen in America, by engaging in what is often called "the oldest profession."[17]

We do not know how Hall got her start in prostitution, but by 1840 she was running a bawdy house in Washington in which her sisters Elizabeth and Frances and two other women were working, and she owned two slaves, apparently a housekeeper and a handyman. Three years later, she built a large, three-story brick house at 349 Maryland Avenue, lavishly furnished, with an excellent wine cellar and elaborate kitchen, and opened for business. The location was ideal, well situated to attract a high-class trade: it was just a tad over a third of a mile from the front of the Capitol building. Hall's establishment quickly became the best and most popular "parlor house" in Washington.

In the complex hierarchy of prostitution, a "parlor house" was a high-class operation, with a posh front parlor, usually some small private dinning rooms, in which potential clients could meet the ladies of the house for a drink and conversation, perhaps with musical accompaniment, and have some drinks and snacks or even a sumptuous meal, after which they could repair to a well-appointed boudoir, all for a price, of course, a high price.

Hall ran a class operation. Her girls were generally young, attractive, and relatively educated, and didn't steal from the customers, as was common in lower-class houses. There seem to have never been any incidents involving disorderly clients, nor was her establishment ever mentioned in the press in connection with some scandal. Business was good, and by 1860, Hall's house was worth $14,600 and her personal property $3,700 more, today easily $500,000, and arguably as much as $7.3 million.

The war caused business to boom, and by mid-war, the Army Provost Marshal reported that her house, with eighteen working women, was the largest in Washington, and *The Evening Star* rated the "old and well-established house" in the "upper ten" of the eighty-five parlor houses in the city (out of about 450 "houses" of all categories), noting that it had "a national reputation for the last quarter century."

Hall never married nor had any children, It's not known what happened to her sisters, who may have married out of the business, as was by no means unusual. In 1871, she passed management of the business to her brother Basil's daughter Lavinia. Basil was a prosperous sea captain and businessman, with an extensive plantation in Arlington, VA, but Lavinia had followed her aunt into prostitution, suggesting it was a relatively good career choice. When Hall died, she left the business to Lavinia. This touched off a complex court battle over her estate, since Hall's two other brothers tried to grab a piece of the pie.

As a result of the litigation, we know a great deal about Mary Ann Hall's financial situation. Despite considerable charity work, she was a very wealthy woman. In addition to the bawdy house on Maryland Avenue, she had a summer home on the Potomac in what is now Arlington, which with her household goods were valued between $87,000 and $100,000, an impressive sum for the day.

There are a couple of ironic footnotes to the story of Mary Ann Hall. The site of her country place in Arlington is now occupied by Marymount University, a coeducational Catholic institution, while that of her bawdy house on Maryland Avenue is under the National Museum of the American Indian; an archaeological dig during construction of the museum yielded a wealth of artifacts, such as expensive women's combs, corset fasteners, buttons, and the like, corks from Piper-Heidsieck and other costly wines, bits of fine crockery and porcelain, and beef, pork, and poultry bones, oyster shells, seeds, and other kitchen scraps that suggest a well-laden table.

Mary Ann Hall is buried under an elaborate monument in the Congressional Cemetery in Washington. Unlike more recent purveyors of sex to the rich and powerful in New York, Washington, Hollywood, and elsewhere, Mary Ann Hall never named names, so although her clients included politicians, officers, businessmen, and other prominent men of the times, not a single name has come down to us, a great loss to historians.

Signs of the times

While Governor of South Carolina in the 1840s, pro-slavery firebrand James Henry Hammond (1807–64)—who coined the phrase "Cotton is King"—had, in his own words, sexual "dalliances" with four nieces aged 13 through 17, daughters of his sister-in-law Ann Fitzsimmons Hampton. The incestuous affairs caused a scandal, which briefly ruined Hammond's political career, but amazingly he was elected to the U.S. Senate in 1857. During the war he virtually broke the family fortune by investing in Confederate bonds, but was an inveterate critic of Jefferson Davis. The young women never married, being considered "tainted" by the standards of the day; why their father, Wade Hampton II, or brother, Wade Hampton III, later a famous cavalryman, didn't shoot Hammond in proper Southern fashion is unknown.[18]

Early in the Civil War, women who gave photographs of themselves to soldiers who were not kinsmen were often criticized for being very forward.

Apprehended in uniform near an army camp in Virginia, two women plying their trade told military authorities that they were merely doing their bit for the cause, and that if all the women of the Confederacy were as patriotic as they, the war would have been long over.[19]

In late 1861, learning that some ladies in St. Louis were wearing red and white rosettes to express their secession sentiments, the Union's Maj. Gen. Henry Halleck distributed large numbers of the very same rosette to the city's prostitutes, thus rather quickly ending this expression of Rebel sympathies.[20]

The Confederacy's Gen. Braxton Bragg periodically took a "mercury preparation" due to "liver problems," suggesting he suffered from syphilis, commonly treated by various mercury-based concoctions, which may also help explain his acerbic and erratic character.[21]

In the mid-nineteenth century, the age of consent in most states ranged between 10 and 12, though in Delaware it was only 7.[22]

Capt. Jerome B. Taft, 59th New York, was unusually close to Pvt. Charles Johnson, who turned out to be his girlfriend, Harriet Merrill.[23]

The appointment of former Regular Army Lt. Powell T. Wyman (1828–62) as colonel of the 16th Massachusetts in 1861 caused some controversy, due to his long affair with Eliza Crane Brannan (1829–92), wife to Brig. Gen. John M. Brannan (1819–92), and mother of an 8-year-old girl, with whom he eloped to Europe in 1859. The stir ended abruptly when Wyman was shot through the heart during the Battle of Glendale (June 20, 1862).[24]

Colonel Richard W. Carter (1837–88) of the 1st Virginia Cavalry, a notorious coward, Capt. James Keith Boswell (1838–63), an engineer on Stonewall Jackson's staff, and an unnamed clergyman, were all sexually involved with the same woman, a love quadrangle that ended when Boswell was killed during the incident that cost Jackson his life, and the preacher committed suicide.[25]

In April 1863, the Episcopal chaplain of the 2nd Wisconsin, James Cook Richmond, developed a "crush" on Ms. Rosa Bielaski, a Treasury Department clerk. Although she spurned his advances, he began sending her increasingly obscene mash notes. An investigation by the Army recommended his dismissal and relegation to an insane asylum, but he was merely banished from the nation's capital, and later claimed that during the war he had been "driving the devil out of Washington."[26]

Samuel Perkins Spear (1815–75), who commanded the 11th Pennsylvania Cavalry and emerged from war as a brevet for brigadier general, had three wives, none of whom were aware of the others until his death, when they all filed for widow's benefits, one of several similar cases encountered by the Pension Bureau.[27]

CHAPTER 11

The Troops

Over the course of the war there were somewhat more than 2 million enlistments in the Union armed forces, and slightly more than 1 million in the Confederate ranks. Although many boys—and some girls—as young as 10 served, and some volunteers were well into their 70s, most of the troops were in their early 20s, and their officers were aged only about 28.

While there are no figures for the "average" Confederate soldier, there are some for Union troops, and it's likely there wasn't much difference. Considering white troops only, it appears that the "average" Union soldier was 5ft. 8¼in. tall and weighed 143½ pounds. About 38 percent of the men had black or dark hair, 30 percent brown, and a similar number light or sandy, with redheads at about 3 percent. Blue eyes were commonest, at 45 percent, followed by gray at 24 percent, hazel 13 percent, dark at 10 percent, and black at 8 percent.

They came from all walks of life, although most were farmers, reflecting societies that were both heavily agricultural.

Since the men of both sides were Americans—"A band of brothers fighting," in the words of Union general John Gibbon, who had three brothers in gray—there was a lot of fraternization throughout the war. For example, one chilly day shortly before Fredericksburg, some Yankees chanced upon some Rebels helping to baptize a comrade in the Rapidan River, and promptly joined in the hymn singing. Men often met between the lines to swap sundries (coffee was scarce in the South,

Table 12: Occupational patterns and recruiting in the Civil War[1]

	Union		Confederacy	
	Pop.	Troops	Pop.	Troops
Agriculture	42.9%	47.5%	57.5%	61.5%
Skilled workers	24.9%	25.1%	15.7%	14.1%
Unskilled workers	16.7%	15.9%	12.7%	8.5%
White-collar workers	10%	5.1%	8.3%	7%
Professionals	3.5%	3.2%	5%	5.2%
Others	2%	3.2%	0.8%	3.7%

Notes:

Figures are approximations based on fragmentary evidence.

"Pop." is the percentage of the population engaged in the indicated occupation.

"Troops" is the percentage of recruits reported as having that occupation.

"Agriculture" includes plantation owners and managers, as well as farmers and farm hands.

"White-collar workers" includes government employees, office workers, commercial agents, sales clerks, and so on.

"Professionals" covers physicians, academics, clergy, attorneys, and the like.

tobacco in the North), newspapers, and gossip. Sometimes, the troops assisted each other in burying the dead, suspending the war to tend to this grim duty, and there were even occasions on which the men of one side invited those of the other to a party or a card game or even to attend divine services or a Masonic lodge meeting.

Native Americans in the war

In 1860, there were about 340,000 Indians in the United States, of whom some 45,000 were living "as a part of the ordinary population of the country," rather than as part of a tribal community. The number of Native Americans who served in the war has been estimated at about 20,000.[12] Although there were some Indian personnel in all theaters, they were most prominent in the Trans-Mississippi, where both the Union and Confederacy recruited heavily in the "Indian Territory," which is now Oklahoma, and adjacent areas, where some 75,000 Indians lived, many belonging to the so-called "Civilized Tribes" that had been forcibly resettled from the southeastern states in the three decades before the war.

An impressive 8,500 men from the Indian Territory served, over a seventh of the population, nearly a maximal turnout. About 5,000 fought for the Confederacy, mostly men from traditionally slaveholding tribes: Cherokee, Chickasaw, Choctaw, Creek, Osage, and Seminole. Forming seven regiments and a battalion of infantry, three regiments and two battalions of cavalry, and three regiments of mounted rifles, they fought in numerous small actions, and also in the battles of Wilson's Creek (August 10, 1861), Pea Ridge (March 6–8, 1862), and Newtonia (September 30, 1862), where they were engaged with Union Indian troops. In Federal service, there were three regiments of about 3,500 men from the Indian Territory, mostly Cherokees, Creeks, and Seminoles, who saw active service in the Indian Territory, Kansas, Missouri, and Arkansas, fighting mostly in small actions, but also in the Battle of Newtonia (September 30, 1862) and at Prairie Grove (December 7, 1862), as well as several units of militia and home guards.

But if men from the Indian Territory were the most numerous in the war, they were not the only Native Americans who served. Nearly the entire male population of the Catawba of South Carolina served the Confederacy, while the Eastern Band of the Cherokee contributed about 400 men to the Confederacy, serving alongside whites in the 69th North Carolina, known as Thomas' Legion, a special combined-arms regiment composed of infantry, cavalry, and artillery. The Union numbered in its ranks Iroquois from New York, Pequots and Mohegans from Connecticut, and others, who often served integrated in the same companies as whites, such as the Seneca who served in the 132nd New York, while the 1st Michigan Sharpshooters included a company of Hurons, Oneidas, Potawatomi, Ojibwas, and Ottawas. Powhatans of Virginia often served as river pilots, guides, and spies for Union forces, and many Lumbee from the Appalachian parts of the Carolinas escaped Confederate conscription as forced laborers by fleeing into swamps and mountains, where they were joined by Unionist Southerners and Yankee soldiers who had escaped from prisoner of war camps to form several guerrilla bands that raided in the area and later supported Sherman during his Carolinas Campaign in 1865.

It's also worth keeping in mind that many people, both "white" and "colored," were in part Indian. Descendants of Pocahontas and John Rolfe, for example, were numerous among the "First Families of Virginia," such as the Confederacy's Commodore William C. Whittle (1805–78) and his brother Lt. Col. Powhatan Bolling Whittle (1829–1903), who was captured in the "Angle" at Gettysburg during Pickett's Charge, and both Robert E. Lee and his wife, Mary Anna Custis Lee.

The most notable Union Indian soldier was undoubtedly the New York Seneca sachem (leader) Donehogawa, known to the whites as Ely S. Parker (1828–95), who although educated as a lawyer, was denied the right to practice, and became an engineer. He attempted to form an Iroquois regiment on the outbreak of the war, which was nixed by the State of New York, and was also rebuffed in his efforts to join as an engineer. But in 1863, his friend Ulysses S. Grant secured him a commission as a staff engineer during the siege of Vicksburg, and Parker later served as Grant's adjutant and then became his military secretary. In that capacity, on April 9, 1865, Parker, by then a lieutenant colonel, arrived at Wilmer McLean's house in Appomattox, to draw up the surrender terms for Robert E. Lee and the Army of Northern Virginia.

On the Confederate side, the most notable Native American soldier was Degataga, known among the whites as Stand Watie (1806–71). A leader of the secessionist faction of the Cherokee of Oklahoma, he rose to brigadier general while commanding Indian troops in several actions. Watie was the last Confederate general in the field, not surrendering his 1st Indian Brigade until June 23, 1865.

African Americans in Union service

One of the very first Union casualties in the war was an African American, a former slave, Nicholas Biddle (*c.* 1796–1876) of Pottsville, PA.[3] At the start of the war, although technically a civilian, he had long been a member of the town's militia company, the Washington Artillery, and was serving as a uniformed orderly to Capt. James Wren (1825–1901) in the 27th Pennsylvania Militia. On April 18, 1861, the regiment arrived in Baltimore to change trains for Washington. The troops, uniformed but not armed, marched across the city, and a secessionist mob some

2,000 strong began harassing them, making threats, spitting, and throwing trash. When someone spotted Biddle, the cry "Nigger in uniform!" went up. Biddle was struck in the head by a brickbat, and knocked to the ground. The men around him helped him to his feet, and hurried on, as the hostile barrage continued, inflicting injuries to some of the others. Reaching Washington by train that evening—the first troops to arrive in the city since Sumter had fallen—the wounded men received treatment, and Biddle, the most seriously injured, was visited the next day by President Lincoln, even as the men of the 6th Massachusetts were being subjected to even more serious harassment, including gunshots, to which they replied with deadly effect.

Black men answer the call

It's well known that Lincoln's call for volunteers on April 15, 1861 sparked enthusiastic volunteering across the North. Less well known is that black men as well as whites stepped forward to serve. Black volunteer companies were organized in New York, Boston, and Cleveland, and a battalion even began forming in Washington. But Lincoln understood that arming black men to fight whites was politically explosive, and would have pushed the still-loyal Slave States—at the time including Arkansas, North Carolina, and Tennessee, as well as Delaware, Maryland, Kentucky, and Missouri—into the Confederate camp. So African Americans who offered to serve were rejected.

Through the first 18 months of the war, Frederick Douglass, other African American leaders, and many abolitionists kept the issue of service by black men alive, though making little progress, most failing to understand Lincoln's dilemma. Despite this, African Americans began serving in the Army in numerous ways.

As the number of people fleeing slavery grew, "contrabands" became a commonplace feature of military life. Black men began working as camp servants paid by individual soldiers or their units, as well as teamsters and laborers, often on the Army's payroll. In mid-1862, for example, on garrison duty in Louisiana, the 12th Connecticut had about sixty "contrabands" working as nurses, hospital attendants, cooks, and officers' servants, while the 13th Connecticut had about forty African

American laundresses.[4] Gradually, as casualties mounted and as the issue of emancipation came to the fore, the hostility toward black men serving in the ranks eased.

Organizing "the Sable Arm"

On May 7, 1862, Brig. Gen. David Hunter (1802–86), a Regular Army officer and committed abolitionist, commanding Union forces on the Carolina coast, organized the 1st South Carolina Volunteers, entirely on his own authority. While African American leaders and abolitionists praised the action, the political outcry was immediate. In the North, many people, including political and military leaders, were either openly hostile to arming blacks or held reservations about their military prowess. The reaction in the Confederacy was worse; Jefferson Davis declared that the men in the ranks would be treated as fugitive slaves and sold if captured, while their officers would be hanged for inciting servile rebellion. The regiment was promptly disbanded, but Hunter quietly kept Company A in existence.

Despite the outcry against the 1st South Carolina, in July 1862, 2 months *before* the preliminary Emancipation Proclamation, Congress authorized the President to raise black troops, and on August 25 the War Department issued instructions on organizing "colored" regiments. Soon afterwards, on September 22, Lincoln issued the preliminary Emancipation Proclamation, and recruiting of African Americans for military service began in earnest.

The question of which African American unit was the first to enter service is a tricky one. Naturally, the 1st South Carolina Volunteers can put in a claim, but it was not formally reestablished until late in 1862, around the covertly maintained Company A, and not accepted for Federal service until January 1863. The first officially recognized black regiment was the 1st Kansas Colored Volunteers (later the 79th U.S. Colored Troops), which was granted authority to organize in July 1862, but recruiting problems delayed its acceptance for service until January 1863, by which time it had already seen combat.

Then there's the 1st Louisiana Native Guards, a regiment with a unique lineage. It was originally formed as a unit of the Louisiana militia, composed of free black men. The regiment turned out and was accepted for state service when Louisiana seceded from the Union, even parading to cheers through New Orleans. But the regiment was never accepted for Confederate service. By April of '62, when David Farragut brought the Union fleet up the Mississippi to capture New Orleans, a change in the state's militia law had caused the regiment to be disbanded. Months later, after the War Department authorized the formation of black regiments, Maj. Gen. Benjamin Butler, commanding at New Orleans, who was already in contact with the regiment's former officers, reformed the regiment, and it was mustered into Federal service on September 27, 1862.

The implementation of the Emancipation Proclamation on January 1, 1863 removed all formal obstacles to black recruitment, though the

The 26th U.S. Colored Volunteer Infantry on parade, at Camp William Penn, PA, in 1865. Raised in New York in early 1864, the regiment took part in the battles of John's Island, Honey Hill, and Tulifinny, losing 145 dead from all causes. (National Archives)

racism of individual commanders and political leaders often impeded efforts to raise troops in particular areas. Meanwhile, African American troops had already seen action under "Old Glory".

Black men in blue

The first black military organization to see combat was the 1st Kansas Colored Volunteers, composed of African Americans and mixed race "Cherokee Negroes." While only partially organized, the regiment and the white 5th Kansas Cavalry beat off an attack by Confederate forces at Island Mound, MO, on October 28–29, 1862; a correspondent from *The New York Times* who was present wrote of the "Desperate Bravery of the Negroes."[5] Over the next 8 months, black troops took part in an increasing number of actions, serving with particular distinction in the Siege of Port Hudson (May 27–July 9, 1863) and the Battle of Milliken's Bend (June 6–8, 1863), where 600 black recruits from Louisiana and Mississippi, mostly men with less than a month's training, supported by about 100 white Iowa veterans and two navy gunboats, took heavy losses beating off some 2,500 Texas troops, an action about which Ulysses S. Grant would later write: "This was the first important engagement of the war in which colored troops were under fire. These men were very raw ... but they behaved well."[6] However, the public did not begin to take notice of the martial abilities of black troops until the 54th Massachusetts' unsuccessful attempt to storm Fort Wagner, on Morris Island, near Charleston, SC on July 18, 1863, losing a quarter of its men, including white Col. Robert Gould Shaw (1837–63), an action portrayed in the 1989 motion picture *Glory*.

African American troops served well, despite considerable discrimination and mistreatment. Until nearly the end of the war, the pay for black enlisted men was $10 a month, regardless of rank, from which $3 were deducted as a clothing allowance, leaving but $7, little more than half what white privates earned; the 54th Massachusetts refused to accept any pay until the inequity was rectified. In addition, African American troops often found themselves doing more than their fair share of fatigue duties. Black troops took part in about 4 percent of the combat actions of the war, nearly 450 engagements, including some of the most sanguinary, such as Port Hudson (June 14, 1863), Olustee (February 20, 1864—where casualties exceeded 25 percent of the forces engaged, and one black regiment, either the 54th Massachusetts or the 35th U.S. Colored Troops, actually formed a square to help cover the Union retreat), and the Battle of the Crater (July 30, 1864).

Statistically, African American combat casualties were 35 percent higher than white casualties, partially due to the Confederate penchant for slaughtering blacks captured in arms, most notably at Fort Pillow (April 12, 1864), where 80 percent of the black troops engaged were killed, many while trying to surrender; Sgt. Achilles V. Clark of the Confederate 20th Tennessee Cavalry wrote: "the poor, deluded negroes would run up to our men, fall upon their knees, and with uplifted hand

Company E, 4th U.S. Colored Infantry, at Fort Lincoln, in the defenses of Washington, an image taken by William Morris Smith. After occupation duty in eastern Virginia, the regiment campaigned with the Army of the James, the Army of the Potomac, helped capture Fort Fisher, and then supported Sherman in the Carolinas until the end of the war, despite which it lost only 104 men in combat, though nearly 200 from other causes. (Library of Congress)

scream for mercy, but were ordered to their feet and then shot down."[7]
During the last 2 years of the war, African American troops served in
every theater, and were particularly important in the Mississippi Valley
and along the Gulf Coast, where they constituted a significant proportion of Federal forces, which was one reason black troops suffered
heavily from disease, as those regions were subject to malaria, yellow
fever, and other afflictions.

Although figures as high as 230,000 have been cited for African
American enlistments in the Union armies, the actual number of men
enrolled appears to have been around 180,000. The disparity between
the two figures is the result of multiple-counting of the troops, as
"colored" units were often redesignated, creating some confusion as to
how many regiments there actually were. For example, the 1st Louisiana
Native Guards became the 1st Regiment, Corps d'Afrique, and then
the 73rd Infantry, U.S. Colored Infantry, while the other twenty-one
regiments in the corps were similarly redesignated. Likewise, the 1st
Kansas Colored Volunteers became the 79th U.S. Colored Infantry, the
1st South Carolina Volunteers the 33rd U.S. Colored Infantry, and the
30th Connecticut Volunteers (African Descent) never recruited enough
men to be mustered into service, so that its troops were absorbed into
the 31st U.S. Colored Infantry.

Overall, African Americans amounted to about 8 percent of total
manpower recruited for the Union. But since most black troops served
later in the war, they comprised about 12 percent of Union forces on
active duty in the spring of 1865. Most black troops, about 57 percent,
were recruited in the Confederate States, with about 24 percent in the
Border States, and 19 percent in the Northern or Western States.[8]

Many African American soldiers credited to the Northern or Western
states were actually recruited in the erstwhile Confederacy. For example, Kansas, which had only about 700 African American residents,
was credited with providing 2,080 black troops for the Army, while
Colorado, with just forty-six black residents in 1860, was credited with
providing ninety-five African American men for the Army. Only about
half of the 4,125 African American troops credited to New York, which
furnished the 20th, 26th, and 31st U.S. Colored Infantry, were actually

"YOU MUST THROW AWAY THAT CIGAR, SIR!"

A Phalanx guard refusing to allow General U. S. Grant to pass by the commissary store-house till he had thrown away his cigar.

Spotting Ulysses S. Grant walking along a dock, an African American sentry said, "No smoking on the dock, sir." Receiving an affirmative reply to his question "Are these your orders?" Grant said, "Good orders," threw away his cigar, and appointed the soldier his orderly. Image from Joseph T. Wilson, The Black Phalanx (Hartford, CT: American Publishing, 1890).

Table 13: The U.S. Colored Troops, 1865

Arm	Regiments	Batteries
Infantry	137	
Heavy Artillery	13	10
Cavalry	6	

residents of the state; most of the rest came from the Carolinas, plus small numbers from almost every other state, as well as several foreign nations, including Britain, France, Portugal, various Latin American countries, Canada, the British West Indies, and some other places.

Most African American troops were only recently freed from slavery, either having taken advantage of the chaos of war to escape or having found themselves behind Union lines as the war progressed. The 54th Massachusetts Infantry, one of only a handful of regiments that was composed largely of free men, many rather prosperous, probably had men from more states than any other, and was also one of the most literate units in the war, black or white.

Altogether, about 180,000 black men served in the Union Army, and perhaps 35,000 more in the Navy, virtually all of them as enlisted men. Only about 100 or so black men were commissioned as officers, almost all of them as lieutenants, with a few as captains, and a handful as majors.

African American soldiers and sailors earned twenty-six awards of the Medal of Honor, several posthumously; the last award was in 2001.[9]

Women in the ranks

Some women, North and South, found their desire to serve went beyond urging men to enlist or becoming nurses or running canteens for the troops: they wanted to do their bit under fire. Very early in the war, some young women, both North and South, attempted to enlist, only to be turned down, sometimes earning praise for their zeal, but frequently ridiculed for overstepping their ascribed gender roles.[10]

But women began entering military service anyway. Regiments largely composed of European volunteers or which had adopted French *chasseur* or Zouave uniforms and drill, such as the 39th New York "Garibaldi

Guard" or "Avegno's Zouaves" of the 13th Louisiana, often went to war with a *vivandière* or two on their rolls. A *vivandière* was a uniformed woman, often a daughter or wife of one of the men, who acted as a combination of sutler, den mother, nurse, and mascot to the troops, tending the wounded under fire, and at times even taking up the colors to lead the men in action.

Some *vivandières* became famous. Kady Brownell (1842–1915), an expert with pistol and saber, enlisted at age 19 with her husband Robert S. Brownell in the 1st and later the 5th Rhode Island, and carried the colors—and a rifle and sword—under fire at First Bull Run, reputedly saving the regiment from a "friendly fire" incident by running between the two units with the colors in hand. Anna Etheridge (1839–1913) served in the 2nd, 3rd, and 5th Michigan, often under fire, from First Bull Run to Petersburg, was lightly wounded at Gettysburg, and was awarded the Third Army Corps' Kearny Cross, as was Mary Tippee (1834–1901), nicknamed "French Mary," of the 114th Pennsylvania.

But beyond service as *vivandières*, some women wanted to fight in the ranks, and an unknown number managed to do so. This was possible

Mary Tippee or Marie Tepe, vivandière *of the 114th Pennsylvania (Collis' Zouaves). (National Archives)*

because, especially early in the war, the physical examination given recruits was at best cursory; Sara Emma Edmonds (1841–98) recalled that only her hands were examined. A woman who cut her hair, put on men's garments, bound her breasts, padded her clothing to disguise her figure, and adopted male mannerisms— smoking, spitting, drinking, and cursing, for example—could easily pass for a man, particularly in a culture in which women were supposed to be passive and demure. Some women were aided in their efforts to join by lovers, brothers, or husbands, and sometimes even male comrades. The number of women who served is unknown, but over 500 have been identified, and estimates range up from there to 750, which may still be too low. Of the women known to have served disguised as men, about a third were Confederates and the rest Unionists, roughly proportional to the ratio of troops between the two armies.[11]

In most cases, a female soldier's sex was only discovered when wounds or illness forced a hospital stay. The identity of most women soldiers was probably never revealed: Albert Cashier (1843–1915), born in Ireland as Jennie Hodges, was passing as a man even before the war, and managed to continue to do so while serving in the 95th Illinois during the war, and for decades after it; her sex was only discovered after an automobile accident in 1911.

The number of women killed in action is unknown. Occasionally a burial party would find a woman among the dead; one was found among the Confederate dead in front of Cemetery Ridge at Gettysburg, after Pickett's Charge on July 3, 1863, one of five women known to have taken part in the battle. Most who died in the war, Union and Confederate, were buried in mass graves on the field, often days after they had fallen, circumstances unlikely to favor the discovery that a particular "soldier boy" was actually a "soldier girl."

Black men in gray

On the eve of the war, there were around 650,000 black men of military age in the Slave States, of whom fewer than 3 percent were free, potentially an extraordinarily valuable pool of manpower.[12] Since the 1970s, Confederate apologists, claiming to be "setting the record straight," have asserted that the Confederacy dipped into this pool of manpower, in an attempt to make a case that slavery was not the primary cause of the war. Claims have been made that large numbers of African Americans—figures in excess of 65,000 are often found—served in the Confederate Army. There is no denying that many black men were present with the Confederate forces, but there's a difference between being a servant accompanying his master or a slave hired or impressed for labor service, and a soldier.[13] The Confederate Army Regulations of 1861 limited enlistment to "Any free white male person above the age of eighteen and under thirty-five years," which was repeated in the regulations of 1863.[14]

Hearing rumors that some in the North thought there were black men serving the Confederacy, on March 22, 1863 Confederate War Department clerk J. B. Jones noted in his diary, "This is utterly untrue. We have no armed slaves to fight for us, nor do we fear a servile insurrection. We are at a loss, however, to interpret the meaning of such demonic misrepresentations."[15]

The beginning

Oddly, at the start of the war, some free black men, especially those who had attained a measure of success in Southern society, did volunteer for Confederate service. After all, their state was their home, and they were doing well within the system, particularly since they were quite aware that white Northerners were no more committed to an egalitarian society than were white Southerners. There was a tradition of black military service in some Slave States, such as Alabama, Tennessee, and particularly Louisiana, with its legal system rooted in the *Code Napoléon* and its large, relatively prosperous, and influential free black community that supplied companies of "Free Men of Color" in the defense of New Orleans in January 1815. On the outbreak of the war, free black men volunteered at Nashville, Memphis, Mobile, and New Orleans, but were rejected, save for those in New Orleans. The free black people of New Orleans raised, organized, and equipped the 1,400-strong Louisiana Native Guards, with its thirty-three black officers. The regiment was accepted by the state militia and received a friendly reception from the white populace when it paraded with the rest of the militia on November 23, 1861. But the regiment was never accepted into the Provisional Army of the Confederate States. The troops provided security for the city, guarded prisoners of war, and performed similar military duties until January 1862, when the state legislature amended the militia laws to limit service to free white men.[16] The regiment was disbanded, though some of its men later formed the cadre of the Union's 1st Louisiana Native Guards, raised in New Orleans at the behest of Maj. Gen. Benjamin Butler, and eventually became the 73rd U.S. Colored Infantry.

Despite the experience of the Louisiana Native Guards, a few Confederate regiments did include black or mixed-race men. The 6th Louisiana Cavalry, for example, which performed garrison, internal security, and courier duties in the northern part of the state, seems to have included about a half-dozen free men of mixed race, as initially did the 8th and 16th Louisiana Infantry. But when these units were sent to other states, such as Virginia, the mixed race men were declared "colored" and dismissed. In several states, from the start of the war, black men—even slaves serving under the command of their masters—were sometimes found in militia and local defense units, pursuing deserters, draft dodgers, Union raiders, and even fugitive slaves. There were also some African Americans who served as scouts for Confederate forces, or in guerrilla, partisan ranger, or similar irregular units, some of which were indistinguishable from bandit gangs.[17] The able Confederate irregular cavalryman Nathan Bedford Forrest had a number of slaves and former slaves in his entourage, among them his "honorary" chaplain Louis Napoleon Nelson, a slave who had accompanied his master James Oldham's sons when they went to war in 1861.[18] At most, however, we're talking about some scores of men.

Servants, cooks, and musicians

An unknown number of the African Americans who accompanied the Confederate armies were camp servants. Many prosperous Confederate soldiers, particularly officers, went to war accompanied by personal servants, often a man who had been their companion since childhood, and Confederate soldiers often hired African Americans, even fugitive slaves, as camp servants.[19] During the Gettysburg Campaign, Maj. Gen. William D. Pender had two African American camp servants, Joe and Columbus, though Gen. Robert E. Lee managed to make do with just one, William Mack Lee. The 3rd Alabama went to war with about a thousand white troops, plus a hundred or so black servants, similarly uniformed. The bonds of loyalty forged over a lifetime could be strong, and stronger still were bonds of blood that often linked master and slave.

For example, Dr. John Luther Vertrees, the surgeon of the Confederate 6th Kentucky Infantry, was accompanied by his slave half-nephew Peter Vertrees, who acted as an aide, servant, and bodyguard, often under fire. Enslaved camp servants often insisted on taking a deceased master's remains home. Taken by Confederate commentators as proving the devotion of slaves to their masters, the servant's real purpose was often primarily to get himself home.

In addition to camp servants, many Confederate regiments unofficially employed black musicians, who performed important duties in combat, conveying orders by flute or drum. Probably the most famous black field musician in the war, on either side, was Dick Slate, nicknamed "Old Dick," who had accompanied his master during the Mexican-American War as a drummer in South Carolina's Palmetto Regiment. Slate served in the 18th Virginia in 1861, and during a hot moment at First Bull Run, took part in the pursuit of the retiring Union troops, capturing several, including Col. Alfred M. Wood of the 14th New York Militia, who was later mayor of Brooklyn. Although well regarded by his comrades, when away from his regiment, Slate—described in the press as a "venerable darky in uniform"—was subject to some abuse by other Confederate soldiers, and was once even arrested and jailed for being armed. His freedom was eventually bought by the town of Danville in 1863, for $750.[20]

Beginning in 1885, various of the erstwhile Confederate States provided pensions for men who served as camp servants, the last in 1921. Demonstrating that these men were not *soldiers*, pension applications included the name of the man's master, and often required affidavits from white Confederate veterans to confirm their status, while their pensions were lower than that for white veterans, underscoring their inferior status.[21]

Black laborers

The most important contribution of slaves to the Confederate war effort was through their labor. From the start of the fighting, the Confederate war effort was dependent on slave labor.[22] Without slaves, the Confederacy would not have been able to put a seventh of its white population under arms, a maximal effort matched in Western history only by Rome during the Second Punic War and Germany during the Second World War, both also slave-based economies.[23]

From the outbreak of the war, tens of thousands of slaves were engaged in constructing defenses for the Confederacy. Slave owners were compensated for the work of their "servants." In early 1862, the Quartermaster General of the Confederate forces on the Virginia Peninsula offered slave owners "$15 per month" per slave if hired for 6 months, "with rations, comfortable quarters, and medical attendance free, and usual allowance of clothing," with higher rates for teamsters and mechanics, adding: "The Government will be responsible for the value of these negroes if captured by the enemy or allowed to escape to them or killed in action."[24] At the time, the pay for a Confederate private was $11 a month; so the Confederacy was paying its white privates *less* than it was paying white masters for the hire of their slaves. Free black men could enroll as well, receiving the pay directly, and were thus earning more than Confederate privates. In February 1864, the Confederate Congress authorized the army to impress free black men, and conscript up to 20,000 slaves for permanent service as laborers, using terminology very specifically intended to distinguish them from soldiers, such as forming them into "gangs" rather than "companies" commanded by "overseers" rather than "officers" and so forth.[25]

This extensive use of slave labor for military construction soon led the Union to a major policy decision. On May 23, 1861, three black laborers working on fortifications on the Virginia Peninsula near Fort Monroe—Frank Baker, Shepard Mallory, and James Townsend—turned up at the fort seeking freedom. The very next day, Maj. Gen. Benjamin Butler arrived to assume command of the post.

Described by one officer as "Short, fat, shapeless; no neck, squinting, and very

Major General Benjamin F. Butler, the Union general the Confederacy loved to hate, in an image taken by the Brady Studio at an unknown date during the war. (Library of Congress)

bald headed," Butler was probably the ugliest general on either side, and would certainly become the most unpopular in the South. While a poor a field commander, he understood the nature of the war better than most.[26] When Col. Charles Mallory of the 115th Virginia Militia, the "owner" of the three men, demanded the return of his "property," Butler declared the trio "contraband of war." As he explained to General-in-Chief Winfield Scott, "I am credibly informed that the negroes in this neighborhood are now being employed in the erection of batteries and other works by the rebels, which it would be nearly or quite impossible to construct without their labor. Shall they be allowed the use of this property against the United States, and we not be allowed its use in aid of the United States?"[27] Butler's action, confirmed by the Army and the President, sent a powerful signal to those in slavery, touching off a flood of "contrabands" to the Union lines, while drawing attention to the extensive use of slaves in the Confederate war effort, a point underscored during the Peninsula Campaign in the spring and summer of 1862, and was an important step on the road to the Emancipation Proclamation.

The use of impressed or conscripted African American labor in fortification work by the Confederacy continued to the end of the war. The total number of black men who worked as laborers for the Confederacy is not known, but at any given time it was certainly in the tens of thousands. None of these men were, however, formally enrolled in the Confederate Army, and they certainly weren't armed and trained to fight.

Toward black recruiting

The idea of raising a black army for the Confederacy eventually began to surface. Proposals to recruit African Americans appear to have first been aired in Alabama, where in some parts free blacks had more legal status than in most of the country due to an old treaty with France, including the right to military service. A few newspapers in the state began raising the question publicly, provoking considerable furor, and the matter died. But over the next year or so, the idea of a more systematic use of military-age male slaves as labor troops, to relieve white men for combat, became more or less acceptable, and there were even calls to recruit black men for combat.

The first African Americans formally enlisted in the Confederate Army were musicians. As noted, many regiments had gone to war with black musicians. On April 15, 1862, making a virtue of necessity, the Confederate Congress amended military regulations to read: "whenever colored persons are employed as musicians in any regiment or company, they shall be entitled to the same pay now allowed by law to musicians regularly enlisted." So, the first genuine "Black Confederates" were musicians.[28]

Meanwhile, the idea of black men in arms was taken up by several politicians and began circulating in the Army. Some "Southrons" who hated Yankees more than they loved slavery had long privately discussed abolishing slavery to secure independence, since the "peculiar institution" was a major obstacle to securing foreign recognition. In January 1864, Irish-born Maj. Gen. Patrick R. Cleburne (1828–64), considering the idea had merit, publicly circulated a detailed discussion of the subject, expressing a willingness to raise, train, and command a division of blacks, a sentiment that appears to have been shared by many of the officers in his division.[29] But the implications of using slaves as soldiers were too complex: after all, the principal Southern war aim was the protection of property in slaves, and the conscription of slaves would clearly run counter to that objective. In the end, Cleburne's enthusiasm for the proposal probably prevented his promotion to lieutenant general, for which he was highly qualified. Nevertheless, as the war continued, and the Confederacy's white manpower dwindled, the question persisted, despite opposition.

On November 3, 1864, Confederate Secretary of War James A. Seddon submitted a long memorandum to Jefferson Davis reviewing recent events, analyzing the manpower resources remaining to the Confederacy, and addressing the question of arming African Americans. He concluded: "It will not do, in my opinion, to risk our liberties and safety on the negro, while the white man may be called to the sacred duty of defense. For the present, it seems best to leave the subordinate labors of society to the negro, and to impose the highest, as now existing, on the superior class."[30]

Seddon's memorandum did not deter the *Richmond Enquirer* from coming out in favor of recruiting 250,000 black men for combat service, the first Richmond paper to do so. By then, the manpower situation was so bad, the Confederate Congress strengthened the black labor conscription bill, while Jefferson Davis proposed the purchase of 40,000 slaves for labor service, with the promise of freedom at the end of the war. Many other Confederate political and military leaders, including Robert E. Lee, began to support the idea of arming blacks for combat. Opposition remained strong, however. On January 8, 1865, Maj. Gen. Howell Cobb (1815–68), former governor of Georgia and in 1861 President of the Provisional Congress of the Confederate States, wrote the Secretary of War:

> You cannot make soldiers of slaves, nor slaves of soldiers. The moment you resort to negro soldiers, your white soldiers will be lost to you; and one secret of the favor with which the proposition is received in portions of the army is the hope that when negroes go into the Army they will be permitted to retire. It is simply a proposition to fight the balance of the war with negro troops. You can't keep white and black troops together, and you can't trust negroes by themselves. It is difficult to get negroes enough for the purpose indicated in the President's message, much less enough for an Army. Use all the negroes you can get, for all the purposes for which you need them, but don't arm them. The day you make soldiers of them is the beginning of the end of the revolution. If slaves make good soldiers our whole theory of slavery is wrong.[31]

Just weeks later, in February, a bill to enlist African Americans as soldiers was defeated in the Confederate Congress, despite strong sentiment from the ranks: Maj. Gen. John B. Gordon (1832–1904), of Lee's Second Army Corps, hardly a champion of racial equality, observed that his men were "decidedly in favor of the voluntary enlistment of negroes." The proponents of enlisting black troops tried again the following month with the backing of Robert E. Lee, who added that such men should be given their freedom. Finally, on March 13, 1865, with Union troops under Grant camped just miles from Richmond, and more under Sherman marching their way through the Carolinas, the Confederate Congress authorized President Davis to enlist as many as 300,000 slaves for general service in the Confederate Army, with the permission of their owners if possible, but by conscription if necessary.

Recruiting of black men began almost immediately. Two battalions of four companies each were authorized to be raised in Virginia and another in South Carolina, while separate companies were authorized in Florida and Alabama. The first two companies of black troops—fewer than 100 men together—were mustered into the Confederate Army in Capitol Square in Richmond on March 23, 1865, and according to the *Daily Dispatch* were cheered as they drilled with "aptness and proficiency," but were also jeered by some. Little more than a week later, the Army of Northern Virginia evacuated the city. So, although in the end the Confederacy had come around to recruiting black men, the measure was far too late to be of help in averting defeat, and was effectively an admission of defeat.

As for the claim by some Neo-Confederates that thousands of black men were fighting in Southern ranks from the start of the war, why weren't Jefferson Davis, Robert E. Lee, James A. Seddon, or Howell Cobb aware of their existence, since until virtually the end of the war they opposed arming slaves? And why did there have to be a heated public debate about the subject, before the reluctant decision to conscript African Americans in March 1865, when the question had became a matter of too little, too late?

Signs of the times

Fully 41 percent of Northern white men born between 1822 and 1845 served in the war, and an impressive 81 percent of those born in 1843, though these figures were exceeded by some Southern states.[32]

An estimated 5 percent of Confederate soldiers appear to have been born in the North.[33]

Some estimates suggest that about 70 percent of soldiers in blue were unmarried, a figure that is probably lower for men in gray, because the Confederacy dipped much more deeply into its manpower pool than did the Union.[34]

On October 24, 1861, the *Citizen and Gazette* of Urbana, OH, reported that a batch of thirty-two recruits for the 66th Ohio had an aggregate weight of 4,172 pounds and a collective height of just over 182ft., or 130.4 pounds and 5ft. 8½in. a head, surprisingly close to the overall "average" for Union troops during the war.

On average during the Civil War, 710 of every 1,000 regulars in the Union Army were present for duty at any given time, in contrast to 646 of every 1,000 white volunteers and 769 of every 1,000 black volunteers.[35]

On both sides, the troops often had mascots, from dogs and cats to bears and camels, but the most famous of them was Old Abe, the eagle of Company C, 8th Wisconsin Volunteers, who took part in forty-two combats over 4 years, often soaring over the battlefield and screeching through the fighting. Old Abe later lived in honorable retirement in the state capitol until he died in a fire in 1881, and is today commemorated by the "Screaming Eagle" insignia of the 101st Airborne Division.[36]

David Bailey Freeman, born in Georgia on May 1, 1850 or 1851, is generally cited as the youngest Confederate soldier, enlisting on May 16, 1862, and serving 3 years as a regular private in Company D of the 6th Georgia Cavalry. He survived the war and lived on until 1929.[37]

No one knows whether it was a Yank or a Reb who made one of the most monumental discoveries of the war, but the troops of both sides quickly learned that with a little ingenuity, the barrel of a musket could hold nearly a pint of whiskey.

The first of some scores of Chinese Americans in Union service to fall in the war was apparently Pvt. John Tommy, of the 70th New York, mortally wounded at Gettysburg on 2 July 1863.[38]

Many Irishmen who volunteered for service, whether for North or South, were members of the Fenian Movement, and are rumored to have held clandestine meetings between the lines during the war in order to lay plans for postwar operations against Britain.[39]

The Union's black volunteers were a surprisingly sober bunch: only one in 4,500 required medical attention for alcohol-related problems, in contrast to one in 220 for their white comrades.[40]

William H. "Willie" Johnston (1850–99), of St. Johnsbury, VT, a drummer boy in Company D, 3rd Vermont, greatly distinguished himself during the Seven Days' retreat in the Peninsular Campaign. He was the only drummer in his division to come away with his instrument, for which he was awarded the Medal of Honor, becoming, at 13, the youngest person to have ever received the decoration.

Analysis of available data on Confederate deserters suggests that married men were about 30 percent more likely to desert than single men, while the desertion rate for men with children rose to about 55 percent; the latter figure rose as the war dragged on.[41]

Private Bill Redman of the 62nd U.S. Colored Infantry may have been the last Union soldier to die in the war; mortally wounded during the Battle of Palmito Ranch, TX (May 12–13, 1865), he died on June 4, 1865.[42]

Michael Moore (c. 1801–97) joined the Army as a field musician at the age of 11 in 1812, and remained continuously on active duty through the Civil War, after which he was promoted to second lieutenant in the 9th Infantry in 1869, and retired from the service in 1870.

CHAPTER 12

Civil War Medicine

The state of medicine in the mid-nineteenth century hardly rose to the level of a science. To be sure, surgery was reasonably well grounded in a detailed knowledge of anatomy, and had become considerably safer since the introduction of anesthesia shortly before the war with Mexico, though many surgeons thought pain necessary for proper healing. But there was no scientific explanation for the causes of infection and disease; the idea that microorganisms might be responsible—"the germ theory of disease"—was just beginning to suggest itself to some medical researchers in Europe, and would take many years to become firmly established. Nevertheless, there was a general understanding that an adequate balanced diet and clean water had something to do with health, as did cleanliness. And while the pharmacopeia included valuable drugs such as quinine, iodine, and opium, there were also a lot of other things—calomel, arrowroot, acacia, camphor, belladonna, mustard, asafetida—with limited usefulness, and some—mercury, strychnine, ammonia, potassium arsenate, lead acetate, turpentine—literally dangerous.

In the U.S., medical education was rather poor, even by the standards of the time. Most physicians and surgeons learned their craft through apprenticeships, and the few medical schools in the country were only somewhat better at training doctors; Harvard, probably the best in the country, seems to have owned neither a microscope nor a stethoscope until after the war. There was also little state supervision over the profession and only the beginnings of professional organization.

Disease

The biggest killer was disease, not combat, causing more than twice as many deaths as battle. Union records show that only 67,058 men were killed in action (18.65 percent of deaths among the troops) and a further 43,012 died of wounds (11.96 percent), for 110,070 battle-related deaths (30.6 percent) of the total 359,528 men officially recorded as having died. Disease accounted for 224,586 deaths (62.57 percent), with all other causes totaling 24,972 (6.9 percent), including homicides (520), executions (267), drownings (4,944), other accidents (4,114), and so forth, plus a large number of unknowns (12,121).

The greatest losses from disease came early in the war, particularly in the first year. With literally hundreds of thousands of men flocking to the colors, training camps were hastily improvised, often with inadequate sanitary arrangements, poor food, and scarce or shoddy clothing and poor shelter. Since most Union troops and nearly all Confederate troops were of rural origins, many had not been subject to various illnesses which, though rather mild in childhood, could create serious problems for adults, such as measles and chickenpox. This lack of immunity, combined with the crowded, poor conditions and inadequate food in the camps led to widespread illness and death. As one Union officer observed during the Peninsular Campaign of 1862: "big stalwart men from the rural districts ... suffered more from bad water and food and the exposure incident to service in the Chickahominy swamps than the men from the cities, who, although not possessing their physique, were accustomed to a more irregular life."[1]

In time, the armies learned, though only the Union had the resources to fully cope with the problem. During the Mexican-American War, the average annual death rate from disease in the U.S. Army had been about 10.2 percent of strength, which during the Civil War, little more than a dozen years later, fell to 6.2 percent. However, even at the end of the war, a soldier in either army was still more likely to succumb to disease than to bullets, the odds had just changed somewhat in favor of the latter.[2]

Physicians for the fight

At the beginning of the war, physicians volunteered along with everyone else. While a surprising number signed up to fight rather than to heal, most physicians became surgeons, serving either as commissioned officers or under contract. The shortage of trained physicians often meant that half-trained medical students were quickly commissioned as surgeons, particularly in the South; of about 3,000 surgeons in the Confederate Army, only a handful appear to have had experience performing surgery prior to being commissioned.[3] Surgeons usually ranked as majors or captains, while contract surgeons held the temporary rank of lieutenant. Some of these surgeons were inept, some were unsuited to the military persuasion, and some could not take the pressure—nurses frequently observed that doctors were often drunk on duty—but most did their jobs as best they could. In the field, they worked under appalling conditions, often in barns and hayricks, and at times under fire. The firearms of the period fired low-velocity, relatively heavy bullets which smashed bone with great effectiveness, making any surgical procedure difficult. Nevertheless, the surgeons tried, with varying degrees of success.

Many military surgeons showed great courage and devotion. At Gettysburg, for example, two Union surgeons, Lt. Col. Theodore Heard (1836–1906) and Maj. Thomas H. Bache (1826–1912), remained behind as the First Army Corps fell back through the town on July 1, to tend the wounded, Union and Confederate alike, until the end of the battle. Maj. Augustus M. Clark (1835–1915), Acting Chief Surgeon of the Union Fifth Army Corps, was wounded on July 2 whilst directing the corps field hospital. Three Confederate surgeons stayed with 225 seriously wounded soldiers when the Army of Northern Virginia retreated from the field on July 4, among them Dr. Simon Baruch (1840–1921) of the 13th Mississippi Infantry Regiment, the father of the famous Bernard Baruch, the twentieth-century financier and statesman.[4]

Reorganizing the medical services

In both armies, medical services were initially organized on a regimental basis. On paper, a Union regiment had a surgeon, two assistant surgeons, and a hospital steward, while Confederate regiments made do with only a surgeon and an assistant surgeon. These men would set up a regimental hospital as needed to treat the sick and wounded. This proved inadequate. During a battle, some regiments might have more wounded than others and did not have sufficient medical personnel to take care of everyone. Things began to change rapidly. As early as Shiloh (April 6–7, 1862), a tent field hospital was established by pooling regimental resources so that the wounded could be treated as close to the battle line as possible. But it was the Union's Dr. Jonathan Letterman (1824–72) who probably made the most important innovations.

Letterman, a surgeon major in the Regular Army, was appointed Medical Director of the Army of the Potomac in June 1862, shortly before the Seven Days' Battles, and began instituting significant changes. While each regiment continued to have a medical detachment, regimental aid stations were no longer organized. Instead, all medical personnel in each brigade established a single field hospital. This worked better, but was still not satisfactory, so Letterman instituted divisional field hospitals. Functioning under the chief surgeon of the division, each hospital had a surgeon, two assistant surgeons, three medical officers with three assistants, plus various stewards and nurses, who would be supplemented by regimental medical personnel at need. Each divisional hospital had four medical wagons and fourteen transport wagons, permitting the establishment of a twenty-two-tent complex, complete with cooking and laundry facilities. This worked well, insuring that all available medical personnel would actually be tending the wounded, regardless of the regiment to which they officially belonged. In addition, the new arrangement greatly facilitated the complex supply arrangements needed by medical units; each medicine wagon had various amounts of seventy-six different medicines, eighteen different types of dressings, various numbers of seventeen different medical instruments, and dozens of other items, from bedpans to razors and matches to pill boxes, plus a supply of food staples and the utensils for their preparation.

Letterman also organized the collection of the wounded. Early in the war, a wounded man who could not get himself to the rear would remain on the field until someone took pity on him. This often led some men to leave the firing line and carry wounded friends to safety, either a comradely deed or an excuse for the faint-hearted to get out of danger. Letterman organized the Ambulance Corps, a disciplined body of men tasked with recovering the wounded and bringing them to the field hospitals. Each regiment, brigade, and division had its Ambulance Corps detachment, all under the control of the Medical Director of the corps. In an infantry regiment, the ambulance detachment comprised a sergeant, nine privates, and three ambulance wagons with drivers, supplemented by the bandsmen in those regiments which had a band.

Letterman also decided that rather than moving the wounded to hospitals, hospitals should be established as close to the front as possible, to treat the worst of cases in place. Largely as a result of these arrangements, a wounded man had a fair chance of survival; of the wounded who received medical assistance, only 13.3 percent died, despite the inadequacies of the medical science of the day. Of about 29,980 amputations performed by U.S. Army surgeons, "only" 24 percent resulted in the death of the patient; in contrast, during the Franco-Prussian War (1870–71), about 77 percent of the approximately 13,000 amputations performed by French surgeons resulted in death.

Letterman's system worked so well that it was soon extended to all the Union forces, though it took an Act of Congress to overcome the resistance from arch-conservatives in the Medical Department.

The public steps up

The scandalous health crisis in the mustering grounds and training camps at the start of the war sparked public interest in fixing the problem, particularly among women. In both North and South, women joined volunteer nursing organizations, and many thousands were formally enrolled as army nurses. A number of women, such as Clara Barton (1821–1912), Mary Ann Bickerdyke (1817–1901), and Anna Etheridge (1839–1913), even went into the field to succor the troops, often under fire. In addition, women were prominent in setting up new hospitals all over the country, and in the volunteer organizations that sprang up to render aid to the troops. In the North, the Sanitary Commission and the Christian Commission began to wield considerable political clout. Using it unashamedly, and with the enthusiastic support of the men in the field, they virtually took over the direction of medical affairs from the Medical Department.

The War Department also began to implement changes, the most notable of which was the appointment of Dr. Joseph K. Barnes (1817–83), a career army surgeon, as Acting

Clara Barton, wartime nurse and humanitarian relief worker, and later a founder of the American Red Cross.

Surgeon General and Medical Inspector in early 1863. Barnes began a thorough reform of the Medical Department, greatly improving services to the sick and wounded. By the end of the war, the Medical Corps had evolved to the point where military hospitals had a capacity of 136,894 beds, or roughly one for every eight men in the Army. It was, however, the common people of America, both North and South, who, with help from some particularly devoted surgeons, were largely responsible for the many changes which affected the practice of medicine in the field, and the health and safety of the troops.

The Medical Department of the Confederacy, under Dr. Samuel Preston Moore (1813–89), a former U.S. Army medical major, did its best, but despite some success at improvisation, it could not really cope with a persistent shortage of resources, including surgeons, medicines, and other supplies. Although severely criticized by the public and the Confederate Congress, the Medical Department was a victim of the military and economic situation of the South. Despite the often great efficiency of privately run medical facilities, Confederate deaths from disease and wounds were relatively higher than Union ones.

Getting a dose: VD in the Civil War

Venereal diseases were pretty common in nineteenth-century America. Many troops, from both North and South, were infected, from common soldiers up to generals, such as the Union's Maj. Gen. George Armstrong Custer and the Confederacy's Lt. Gen. Ambrose P. Hill, both of whom contracted gonorrhea while cadets at West Point and from which they apparently suffered throughout their lives. Venereal Disease (VD) was a major cause of non-battle related casualties in both armies. Medical records indicate 182,779 reported cases and 136 deaths from VD among white volunteer troops just in the Union Army.[5]

The VD rate for men in the Union Army ran at about 82 cases per 1,000 on strength per year. Although these figures seem high (in the Second World War, the rate was 49 per 1,000 on strength per year), it's worth noting that in the same period, the rate in the British Army was about 200 per 1,000 men per year.

Because Confederate record-keeping was poor, and many documents were lost or destroyed at the end of the war, it's hard to determine the infection rate for Confederate troops. Some accounts put the number of syphilis cases at 73,000 and gonorrhea cases at 31,000, the first disproportionately high and the second disproportionately low when compared with the more reliable Union medical figures. There are some figures available for particular divisions or brigades in the Army of Northern Virginia (see Table 15).

Naturally it's hard to generalize from such spotty data, particularly as these figures are for *new* infections, but the adjusted rate per thousand men on strength is roughly about the same as that for the Union.

Table 14: Reported cases of VD: Union volunteer troops

Disease	Cases	Deaths
Gonorrhea	102,893	7
Orchitis★	14,554	10
Syphilis	75,599	151★★
Total	193,046	178

Notes:
★ Testicular inflammation caused by chlamydia, gonorrhea, or other agents.
★★ In addition 1,865 troops (1,779 white and 86 black) were discharged during the war due to advanced syphilis.

Table 15: Periodic reporting of new VD infections, Army of Northern Virginia

Month	Regiments (troops)	Syphilis	Gonorrhea	Rate
Jul 1861	12 (11,452)	44	204	1 in 46 men
Aug 1861	29 (27,042)	102	152	1 in 106 men
Sep 1861	38 (33,248)	70	148	1 in 145 men
Dec 1861	43 (34,865)	36	40	1 in 458 men
Mar 1862	28 (19,942)	10	14	1 in 860 men
Dec 1862	12 (6,253)	10	36	1 in 135 men

Note:

"Regiments" indicates the number of regiments surveyed, with the number of troops in parentheses.

For those who were unfortunate enough to get VD, treatment options were limited. While there were palliatives for chlamydia, gonorrhea, or other minor afflictions, these were usually not life-threatening. Those who acquired syphilis had a grimmer prognosis. While mercury and arsenic preparations could ease some of the symptoms, both were almost as dangerous to the patient as the disease itself.

Augustus M. Clark, Medical Inspector of Prisoners of War

On September 11, 1862, Augustus M. Clark (1835–1915), a graduate of the College of Physicians and Surgeons in New York, was appointed an Assistant Surgeon, U.S. Volunteers. By the end of the year he had been promoted to surgeon and attached to the Regular Army's 4th Infantry Regiment, serving in the Fifth Army Corps. At Gettysburg, Clark was acting chief surgeon of the corps. Wounded on July 2, he remained on duty, and commanded the corps hospital on the field over the next few weeks. In September 1863, Clark was appointed acting Medical Inspector of Prisoners of War.[6]

Until late in the nineteenth century, the treatment of prisoners of war was largely an afterthought in military planning. With facilities improvised, usually overcrowded, and always poorly staffed and funded, prisoners usually endured great privation. During the Civil War, prisoners were usually exchanged fairly promptly during the first 2 years, but in 1863, the exchange cartel—the formal agreement on how troops were to be exchanged—broke down largely over the status of African American

Prisoners lined up in preparation for formal exchange.

troops, whom the Confederacy refused to treat as soldiers. Thereafter, perhaps 200,000 Union soldiers and at least as many Confederates ended up enduring long periods in prison camps.

Prisoner of war camps were often established in old forts or army camps, or requisitioned buildings, which although austere, provided shelter from the weather. Some Confederate camps, most notably Andersonville, were merely enclosures, with no structures nor shelter from the elements, nor provision for clean water, kitchens, or latrines, called "sinks" in contemporary usage. Over 30,000 Union men held as prisoner by the Confederacy died (about 15½ percent), as did nearly 26,000 Confederates held by the Union (about 12 percent). The death rate among Confederate prisoners of war was about the same as that for non-combat deaths in the armies, while the higher rate for Union prisoners of war was largely due to deaths at Andersonville, where 13,000 of the 45,000 prisoners died.[7]

Dr. Clark spent 8 months travelling the country inspecting and reporting on the condition of prisoners of war. Many of his reports are in the *Official Records of the Union and Confederate Armies* and *The Medical and Surgical History of the War of the Rebellion*, and are often cited in books and articles about the Union prisoner of war system during the war.

Following a visit to the prisoner of war camp at Alton, IL on October 15, 1863, Clark reported to the Commissary General of Prisoners:

> the prison is overcrowded; there is only sufficient accommodation for about 900 prisoners; many of the cells are occupied by two men; the cells are well ventilated by means of shafts opening into the cells, and communicating with a main shaft opening on the outside of the building; they are well warmed by means of stoves in the corridors. Such quarters as were formerly used as workshops are tolerably

The interior of Andersonville Prison, with Union prisoners of war lined up awaiting ration distribution, in an image taken on August 17, 1864, by A. J. Riddle. Note the improvised shelters. (National Archives)

well ventilated by means of side windows, and are warmed by stoves and open fireplaces. Cooking—the kitchen is well arranged and is well kept; the food and cooking for the prisoners is frequently inspected by the surgeon in charge. Cleanliness of men and clothing is better observed than in the other prisons which I have visited, but is still not as strictly enforced as it should be; the laundry facilities are entirely insufficient. Clothing—sufficient and good, obtained on requisition from quartermaster's department. Prison fund—over $7,000 now on hand. Articles purchased from this fund are registered, ready to be accounted for when necessary. In this prison more than any other which I have yet visited, regard seems to be paid to the comfort as well as security of the prisoners. The military discipline maintained is not as strict as it should be, yet every precaution seems to be taken to prevent escapes.[8]

A few weeks later, Clark visited Camp Morton, at Indianapolis, and issued a scathing report:

This camp is a disgrace to the name of military prison. It is filthy in every respect. The vicinity of the sinks [latrines] is obvious for many yards around, they being perfectly open; no attempt made to disinfect them. They are, moreover, insufficient in number. The seven rebel officers confined here are crowded into a small room about ten by twelve and eight feet high. In this they sleep, live, and cook. There are good natural facilities for drainage, but the drains are choked with rubbish, and the large central ditch is a grand receptacle for the refuse of the whole camp. The main hospital ward is in so dilapidated a condition that the patients are obliged to fasten their blankets along the wall for partial protection from wind and weather, and are thus deprived of the necessary covering. In fact, every patient whom I examined had more or less of pulmonary trouble accompanying his disease, whatever it might be. The hospital cook-house was in filthy condition, and the food which had just been prepared for dinner at the time of my visit was most miserably cooked. I found the bath and wash house used for storing straw for bedding. The hospital fund is not expended with sufficient freedom in procuring comforts for the sick, nor could I ascertain that any account of the less perishable articles, as table furniture, &c., purchased from the fund is kept. The commanding officer states that he has been directed to erect two additional hospital barracks, but they are not as yet commenced.[9]

Later that year, he inspected conditions aboard the "truce ship" *New York*, which transported prisoners of war being exchanged, and reported:

Acting Assistant Surgeon Carey is the medical officer in charge, assisted by an acting hospital steward, two nurses, and two negroes for police duty, &c. These, Doctor Carey states, are sufficient, for in every load of prisoners there are many who are able and willing to act as nurses. Through Doctor Carey I ascertained that there are on board 600 blankets, 40 cots, 160 bed sacks, all filled with straw except 15, a sufficient supply of urinals and chamber utensils, and a sufficiency of table furniture. These are all in tolerably good order, except that, as I am informed, the blankets are not, as they should be, washed after each trip. There is no difficulty in obtaining abundant supplies of medicines and materials for dressing, as well as prepared coffee and beef tea from the medical purveyor. The coffee and beef tea are prepared for the use of the sick by means of a steam apparatus. In cases of necessity, the doctor says, the captain's wife is very kind in preparing cornstarch and other delicacies. The cooking-stove on the forward deck is also used for the hospital when necessary. The hospital is clean, though not in very good order. Chloride of lime is plentifully used as a disinfectant. I would suggest that a supply of the Ridgewood disinfectant powder be ordered for use on board the boat.[10]

There's considerable evidence that Dr. Clark's work bore fruit. A report critical of conditions at the Rock Island prison camp recommended extensive changes, including new construction, which was subsequently taken in hand.[11]

In May 1864, Dr. Clark returned to duty with the troops, and rose to Medical Director of the Tenth Army Corps, in the Army of the James later that year. In the course of the war, Clark served in nineteen battles from Second Bull Run through Appomattox, and was present at the surrender of Robert E. Lee. He ended the war with a brevet for lieutenant colonel.

After the war, Dr. Clark returned to private practice in New York, married, and had a family. Like many old soldiers, he joined various veterans' groups, and commanded the honor guard at Ulysses S. Grant's catafalque when it lay in state in New York's City Hall.

Augustus M. Clark's "escutcheon" of service. Many veterans commissioned these plaques to commemorate their service. (Courtesy Clark Family Collection)

Signs of the times

Among the thousands of young Southern men studying in Northern schools and colleges who headed home when war began were several hundred medical students, most of whom shortly therafter served as surgeons in the Confederate Army, often despite having only the most rudimentary training.[12]

The blockade dried up the supply of surgical silk to the Confederacy, forcing Southern medical officers to improvise, using horse hair for suturing, boiling it first to soften it, which unbeknownst to them also greatly reduced the chance of infection.[13]

At least nine physicians became generals in the war by commanding troops rather than healing them: the Confederacy's Maj. Gen. James P. Anderson and brigadiers John Bratton, Lucius B. Northrop, and Jerome Bonaparte Robertson; and the Union's Maj. Gen. Samuel Crawford, who began the war as the post surgeon at Fort Sumter, as well as brigadiers James L. Kiernan, Nathan Kimball, Robert K. Scott, and Edward A. Wild.

An unknown number of soldiers became addicted to opiates as a result of the lavish use of drugs by surgeons during the war; Union surgeons distributed over 2.8 million ounces of opiates in tincture or powdered form, and almost 10 million opium pills, while their Confederate counterparts used them less generously, as the blockade greatly affected their supply.[14]

According to the U.S. Army's Medical Department, during the war, 32,080 troops suffered from a condition known as "Army Itch," though none of them died of it.

More than 12,000 physicians served in the Union Army, either as commissioned or contract surgeons, of whom more than 300 died from combat, disease, or accidents, compared with about 3,000 working in Confederate service, for whom casualty figures appear to be unknown.

The shortage of cotton cloth for bandages at times led Confederate medical personnel to use raw cotton when dressing wounds, which seems to have reduced infection, since the normal custom of the times was to wash and reuse bandages, which increased the risk of infection, while the raw cotton had to be discarded after use.

Of the estimated 5,600 women nurses who worked in Union medical facilities, over 600 were members of Roman Catholic orders such as the Daughters of Charity and the Sisters of Mercy, who were probably the most well-trained nurses in the country, though Superintendent of Army Nurses Dorothea Dix, an outspoken anti-Catholic, was opposed to their presence.[15]

Governor Zebulon Vance of North Carolina refused to allow the Confederate Army Medical Department to produce medicinal whiskey in his state because it violated the liquor laws.[16]

The Union's Brig. Gen. Henry Lawrence Eustis (1819–85), who had ranked first in the West Point Class of 1842, was relieved of duty on June 12, 1864, after the Battle of Cold Harbor, having been found to be addicted to opium.[17]

At its peak population, in August 1864, when it held approximately 33,000 Union prisoners, Andersonville was the fifth largest "city" in the Confederacy.

Sally Louisa Tompkins (1833–1916) opened the Robertson Hospital in Richmond in the aftermath of Bull Run and treated 1,334 wounded by the end of the war, with only 73 deaths, the best survival rate of any medical facility, North or South. She became one of just two women commissioned as officers in the Confederate Army.[18]

Despite having tuberculosis, Marcellus M. Crocker volunteered to fight for the Union in 1861, became a brigadier general in November 1862, and although several times too ill to perform administrative duties, never missed a battle due to illness, fighting at Shiloh, Corinth, Vicksburg, and Nashville, only succumbing to the disease in August 1865.

By the end of the war, the Confederate Medical Department had opened 154 major military hospitals all across the South, but mostly in Georgia, which had fifty, and Virginia, thirty-nine, not to mention many smaller temporary facilities.[19]

Statistically, during the war, an average of one man was killed or mortally wounded for every 4.8 who suffered non-mortal wounds.

Although Dorothea Dix made many important contributions to the Union cause, she did less well when the lifelong spinster designed a new type of underwear for the troops, which proved so uncomfortable the men reportedly discarded them at the first opportunity.[20]

The 65th U.S. Colored Infantry, which served from March 11, 1864, until January 1867, mostly in marshy regions of Louisiana, had the dubious distinction of having more deaths from disease than any other Union regiment, losing 750 officers and men out of a total of nearly 1,770 enrolled, over 42 percent, though not a single man died in combat.[21]

The Civil War since the Civil War

The Civil War ended more than 150 years ago, but is perhaps the best proof of William Faulkner's often quoted phrase, "The past is never dead. It's not even past."

Although conventional wisdom has it that "the winners write the history," that's not necessarily true. The Civil War is one of several events in which historical memory has been formed largely by the losers; consider, for example, the romantic associations of Bonnie Prince Charlie and the Jacobite cause, or the continuing adulation of Napoleon. In the case of the Civil War, historical memory was for a very long time largely set by Confederate sympathizers, who created what is generally known as the myth of the "Lost Cause," of which the *Encyclopedia Virginia* provides one of the best definitions:[1]

> an interpretation of the American Civil War (1861–1865) that seeks to present the war, from the perspective of Confederates, in the best possible terms. Developed by white Southerners, many of them former Confederate generals, in a postwar climate of economic, racial, and social uncertainty, the Lost Cause created and romanticized the "Old South" and the Confederate war effort, often distorting history in the process. For this reason, many historians have labeled the Lost Cause a myth or a legend. It is certainly an important example of public memory, one in which nostalgia for the Confederate past is accompanied by a collective forgetting of the horrors of slavery. Providing a sense of relief to white Southerners who feared being dishonored by defeat, the Lost Cause was largely accepted in the years following the war by white Americans who found it to be a useful tool in reconciling North and South. The Lost Cause has lost

much of its academic support but continues to be an important part of how the Civil War is commemorated in the South and remembered in American popular culture.

The fabrication of the Lost Cause began early. Consider Robert E. Lee's General Order No. 9, issued on April 10, 1865, the day after the surrender at Appomattox, which arguably laid the foundation with the opening line: "After four years of arduous service, marked by unsurpassed courage and fortitude, the Army of Northern Virginia has been compelled to yield to overwhelming numbers and resources" Within a year, books on the theme of the Lost Cause began to appear, most notably Edward A. Pollard's *The Lost Cause: A New Southern History of the War of the Confederates* (1866), and the concept permeated American society, attaining almost doctrinal status even in academic circles until well into the twentieth century, when it began to be challenged with the rise of the Civil Rights Movement and newer generations of historians inspired by the centennial observances of 1959–65.

Nevertheless, the "principles" which sparked secession, the formation of the Confederacy, and the resultant Civil War are still alive in the hearts of a surprising number of Americans, who cling to the myths of the "Gallant South" and the Lost Cause; consider the ongoing dispute over the so-called "Confederate Flag." Although less common than in the past, some politicians still run on their ties to the Confederacy, public funds support commemoration of secession and secessionists, holidays in some states celebrate Confederate leaders, and schoolbooks regularly gloss over the horrors of slavery. And of course, there remains the pernicious persistence of the racism sparked by slavery in American society.

On the plus side of the great interest in the war is that it has helped those working to preserve historic sites and artifacts, such as buildings, ships, battlefields, and more, many of which are still threatened by neglect or aggressive development, while re-enactors, in pursuing their interest in the war, help preserve the commonplaces of military life, thus demonstrating the nature of soldiering in the times, which can often throw fresh light on various events.

The "swift-boating" of James Longstreet

The deliberate slighting or denigration of a person's military reputation for political gain is an extraordinarily ancient practice, found even among the Greeks and Romans, and is hardly unknown in American history. For example, after being wounded during the Battle of Churubusco (August 19, 1847), in the Mexican-American War, Brig. Gen. Franklin Pierce passed out from loss of blood, and during his bid for the presidency in 1852, found his political enemies calling him "The Fainting General," which Ulysses S. Grant later wrote was "exceedingly unjust and unfair," calling Pierce "a man of courage."[2] Similarly, in 1853–57, Secretary of War Jefferson Davis, a Democrat, feuded viciously with General-in-Chief Winfield Scott, a Whig, even charging that, "The only wound [Scott] had ever received came from falling off a horse in New York," absolutely insulting given that the general had been wounded on several occasions, at Lundy's Lane (July 25, 1814) so seriously that he was unable to return to duty for 6 months.

In the aftermath of the Civil War, a number of soldiers on both sides ended up being the victims of what has come to be known as "swift-boating" from a recent manifestation of the phenomenon.

In the aftermath of Robert E. Lee's death, the advocates of the Lost Cause elevated him to almost divine status, and so anyone who criticized Lee, or who could be blamed for "causing" the defeat of Confederacy, was fair game to those who idolized the general. And, of course, anyone who cooperated with reconstruction or Republicans was also likely to find himself unfairly criticized. Perhaps the most egregious case was that of the Confederacy's Lt. Gen. James Longstreet.[3]

During the war, Longstreet's reputation would have seemed unshakable. On four occasions—at Second Bull Run (August 30, 1862), Gettysburg (July 2, 1863), Chickamauga (September 19, 1863), and in the Wilderness (May 6, 1864)—Longstreet had delivered blows that came close to shattering entire Union armies. Lee several times called him "My old war horse," and they had a tearful parting in the aftermath of Appomattox.[4] But after Lee's death in 1870, by which time Longstreet had become a Republican, and made some comments deemed critical to his former commander, he became the target of a vicious campaign to smear his reputation and loyalty to the "Cause." Two of the key players in this movement were Jubal Early, the only general Lee ever relieved of duty for ineptitude,[5] and Lee's own former chief of artillery William Nelson Pendleton, of whom the general had once written, "I do not say he is not competent, but from what I have seen of him I do not know what he is."[6] Early, the first President of the Southern Historical Society, Pendleton, and others, including J. William Jones, a former military chaplain who was the first editor of *The Southern Historical Society Papers*, were particularly well positioned to disseminate what was increasingly the "party line" among the adherents of the Lost Cause. To put it bluntly, these men were abject liars, often citing conversations that were not remembered the same way by participants or that could not be proven to have actually taken place, and in one instance "quoted" a conversation that literally could not have taken place, as the officers said to have been overheard were miles apart at the time it supposedly occurred. They thoroughly enjoyed their work, even exchanging little notes gleefully chortling over Longstreet's distress, such as one to Jones on August 14, 1878, in which Pendleton wrote: "I suspect Longstreet is very sick of Gettysburg before this. Certainly there has not been left 'a grease spot' of him."[7] Their manipulation of the record and outright fabrications ultimately led to Longstreet being held principally responsible for the defeat at Gettysburg, and thus by extension, the disastrous outcome of the war. This effort, which gained the support of members of the Lee family[8] and Jefferson Davis,[9] was so successful that by the onset of the twentieth century, Longstreet's reputation was abysmal. In his 1934 biography of Lee, Douglas Southall Freeman actually wrote that during the Gettysburg campaign, Longstreet "was eating his heart out in sullen resentment that Lee had rejected his long-cherished plan of a strategic offensive and a tactical defensive" and displayed "temper and antagonism" toward his commander, behaviors that one would think Lee would have found intolerable.[10]

The principal "charge" against Longstreet was that his attack on the Union lines at Gettysburg on the afternoon of July 2, 1863 had been intended by Lee to take place at dawn, but that in "culpable disobedience" to his orders, Longstreet had "treacherously" delayed until about 4:00 p.m., and thus the attack, which in fact shredded two Union army corps, had not been as decisive as a dawn one would have been, thereby costing Lee the battle, and, by implication, the Confederacy the war. This was arrant nonsense. There is no documentary evidence that Lee ordered a dawn attack, and in any case Longstreet's troops, who had been scattered from the suburbs of Harrisburg to Chambersburg when the battle erupted, did not begin arriving on the field after some hard marching until about 1:00 a.m. on the 2nd, and his artillery did not arrive until 8:00 a.m., well after dawn. Lee himself clearly did not intend a dawn attack, as he didn't order a reconnaissance until after dawn, which found no Union troops in the area between Seminary Ridge and Cemetery Ridge. It was only after that reconnaissance that the Union's Maj. Gen. Daniel Sickles decided to push his Third Army Corps into the region, setting it up for destruction when Longstreet's attack came in the late afternoon.

Longstreet's reputation has been long in recovering, though the meticulous work of a number of scholars now places him among the ablest corps commanders of the war.

Longstreet was not the only Confederate general who suffered at the hands of the Lost Cause pseudo-historians.

Lieutenant General Richard S. Ewell (1817–72) was told by Lee on the evening of July 1, 1863 to capture Culp's Hill, just north of Gettysburg, if he "found it practicable." Ewell decided not to attack for three reasons: (1) his troops had spent the entire day marching in temperatures rising over 90°F to arrive on the field, and then drove Union troops from their positions north and west of Gettysburg through the streets of the town to Culp's Hill, where fighting continued into the evening; (2) after personally reconnoitering the hill, he concluded it to be strongly held; (3) he was informed that strong Union forces were approaching on his left. Ewell was later criticized by some for this decision, with the claim that it contributed to the Confederate defeat at Gettysburg, though even his subordinate Jubal Early concurred with the decision and stuck by him afterwards. Most historians now conclude Ewell's decision was sound.[11]

General Joseph E. Johnston was widely criticized for favoring delaying actions and retreating to avoid combat, especially during the campaigns for Atlanta in 1864 and in the Carolinas in 1865, his detractors arguing that a more aggressive stance might have saved the South. In contrast, in his memoirs, Ulysses S. Grant wrote: "Johnston's tactics were right. Anything that could have prolonged the war a year beyond the time that it did finally close, would probably have exhausted the North to such an extent that they might then have abandoned the contest."[12]

Major General William Mahone (1826–95), an able division commander, arguably turned in his finest performance on July 30, 1864 during the Battle of the Crater, at Petersburg. A mine blew an enormous breach in the Confederate defenses, into which Union infantry began to pour. Mahone promptly ordered Brig. Gen. David Weisiger's Virginia brigade into action, stabilizing the situation, and ultimately leading to a Confederate victory, for which he received great credit at the time. In the early 1880s, however, Mahone, by then active in politics, concluded a tactical alliance with Republicans, and immediately came under attack. Weisiger and other political opponents charged that Mahone had not been present at the critical moment and that Weisiger had ordered his Virginia brigade into action on his own, both outright lies that were widely believed.[13]

Major General George E. Pickett, following Pickett's Charge at Gettysburg, was accused by some of failing to put himself at the head of the troops in the attack, pusillanimously staying in the rear, and thus was responsible for the failure of Lee's grand assault, and for helping to lose the war. But army doctrine dictated that leading the troops forward was the job of the brigade commanders, a task Pickett's subordinates performed admirably. A division commander's post was in the rear of his troops, directing the advance and shifting brigades about as needed, which Pickett did well, keeping the men moving forward, issuing orders for dressing the lines, and even changing the direction of the advance, while maintaining contact with the other division commanders and his subordinates through messengers. Moreover, he certainly wasn't out of danger, being well within rifle shot of Cemetery Ridge. And of course, although Lee's grand attack has traditionally been named after him,

Pickett was neither in command of the assault, nor even of the majority of the troops involved.

The Lost Cause crew also extended their efforts to attacking Ulysses S. Grant. After all, how could the tanner's son have defeated the godlike Lee in a fair fight? Grant became a major victim of the Lee idolaters, who managed to pin the nickname "Butcher Grant" on him, arguing that his victories, especially those over Lee, were won by the free expenditure of manpower. Supposedly, during the Battle of Cold Harbor (June 3, 1864), anywhere from 7,500 to over 12,000 Yankees were killed, wounded, or missing in a futile frontal attack that lasted just a few minutes; this quickly became a standard criticism of Grant, widely repeated even to the present. This was a massive distortion of the events, though it took more than a century to sort it out. In his *Cold Harbor: Grant and Lee, May 26–June 3, 1864*, historian Gordon Rhea offered a detailed analysis of the battle using contemporary documents from both sides. Union casualties in the hour-long fight at Cold Harbor on June 3 did not exceed about 3,500, dead, wounded, or missing—bad enough, but compare Lee's losses at Gettysburg during Pickett's Charge, some 5,300–5,700 in less than an hour. The oft-cited "7,500" or "over 12,000" killed demonstrates the ways in which the record could be manipulated; 7,500 was the total number of *casualties*—killed, wounded, and missing—incurred by the Union forces under Grant's command on the 3rd, including troops fighting nowhere near Cold Harbor, while the "over 12,000" was the number of casualties—actually 12,788—Grant's troops incurred during the *entire* Cold Harbor campaign, from the start of his attempt to outflank Lee at Cold Harbor on May 31 to the crossing of the James River on June 14.[14]

The manipulation of the record of these officers should remind us that the side which gets into print first is the one that has the greatest influence on historical memory.

Memory, monuments, and memorialization

On the evening of June 17, 2015, a dozen members of Charleston's historic Emanuel African Methodist Episcopal Church, founded in 1816 and known as "Mother Emanuel," sat down for a regularly scheduled prayer meeting and Bible study. Among them was a guest, Dylann Roof, a 21-year-old white man who had expressed an interest in taking part. Soon after the meeting began, Roof started shouting racist statements and then opened fire with a Glock 41 .45-caliber handgun, killing nine of the participants and wounding one other before escaping. Apprehended the following morning, Root was found to have maintained a white supremacist website and written a long, rambling manifesto full of hatred for African Americans, Jews, Hispanics, South Asians, and others, and possessed racist tracts, emblems, and banners, among which was what is commonly known as the "Confederate Flag."

Root's action reignited the never quite dampened national "discussion" of the meaning, memory, and memorialization of the Confederacy, and in particular the display of the so-called Confederate flag. One immediate consequence was that Governor Nikki Haley of South Carolina called for the removal of the flag from the State House grounds, which was endorsed by the State Legislature with remarkable promptitude. That in turn touched off major arguments about the display of the flag and about the many memorials to the Confederacy.

The Confederate flag

The square banner with a red field charged with a blue St. Andrew's Cross studded with white stars that has come to be known as the Confederate flag was in fact not that at all. That flag is a variant of the battle flag introduced into what became the Army of Northern Virginia in late 1861, a version of which was also adopted as a jack by the Confederate Navy, but it was not universally used by the Confederacy's other armies. The St. Andrew's Cross battle flag was designed because of problems with the Confederate *national* flag.[15]

On March 4, 1861, the Confederate Congress adopted a national flag, after which the design was altered twice.

- March 4, 1861: A rectangular flag in the ratio of 2:1, with three stripes, of red, white, and red, and a blue canton on which were arranged a circle of white stars, one for each Confederate state, which promptly became known as the "Stars and Bars." This was too similar to the "Start and Stripes" in dim light or on windless days, and caused some confusion on the battlefield, including "friendly fire incidents," which prompted numerous proposals for its replacement, and the design of the St. Andrew's Cross flag for battlefield use by the Army of Northern Virginia.

- May 1, 1863: A rectangular flag in the ratio of 2:1 with a white field, and the Confederate naval jack in the upper left corner. Nick-named the "Stainless Banner," this too proved unsatisfactory, as it could easily be mistaken for a flag of truce, and was remarkably difficult to keep clean.

- March 8, 1865: A vertical red stripe of about one-quarter the flag's width was added on the fly—outer—edge of the Stainless Banner.

In the immediate postwar period, the Stainless Banner was quite commonly displayed by unreconstructed Confederates to demonstrate where their sympathies lay. This created a problem when Union and Confederate veterans began holding joint reunions in the late 1870s. Union vets objected to its use as a "symbol of secession." As a result, Confederate veterans began using a variant of the Army of Northern Virginia battle flag, to which Union veterans found no objection, since it symbolized the honor and courage of a gallant foe rather than the politics of the Confederacy. During the early stages of the Civil Rights Movement in the 1950s, however, the "battle flag" came to be used by the Ku Klux Klan and other racist groups as a symbol to rally white opposition to a more egalitarian society.

There exists a simple solution to the question of honoring Confederate "heritage," which is to remove the "battle flag" from government and other public facilities and replace it with the first national flag, the Stars and Bars, which served longest as the Confederate flag. This has in fact long been the flag displayed on public buildings in so staunch a bastion of Confederate heritage as Texas without objection.

Monuments and memorials

While there are Civil War memorials and monuments all across the country, they are most common in the South. As historian William Garrett Piston once observed, "The American South is rich in bronze, particularly Confederate bronze."[16] Consider North Carolina, which furnished 127,000 troops to the Confederacy, and has more public monuments commemorating the Civil War than any other event, 187, in contrast to 124 for the War for Independence, eighty-two for the First World War, and only sixty-five for the Second World War.[17] Perhaps even more impressive is Kentucky, which had about 75,760 men in Union service, and perhaps 25,000 (though some claim double that) in Confederate service, a ratio of about 3:1 (or perhaps 3:2); but of seventy-five Civil War memorials in the state, only eleven commemorate the boys in blue, and sixty-four those in gray, a ratio of roughly 1:6.[18] In contrast, New York City, which sent something like 180,000 men into the Army and Navy during the war, has about three dozen public Civil War monuments, out of about 350 public war memorials.[19]

While these monuments recognize service and sacrifice, some of them are more than that, particularly those erected in the immediate aftermath of reconstruction or since the Civil Rights Movement, as they implicitly legitimatize the secessionist cause, and often offer a one-sided, racist, or blatantly fabricated narrative.

For example, the Confederate Memorial at Arlington, the largest monument at the National Cemetery, which was dedicated by the notoriously racist Woodrow Wilson, includes an image of a tearful "mammy" holding a white child up to his father departing for the war and a faithful Negro body-servant "following his young master" to war. Similarly, a marker at the Grant Parish courthouse in Colfax, LA commemorates "the end of carpetbagger misrule in the South," where on Easter Sunday, April 13, 1873, about 300 armed whites attacked a group of black citizens and state militiamen, killing at least sixty and perhaps as many as 200.

In the aftermath of the attack at Mother Emanuel church, there have been calls to move or demolish many of these monuments. A more nuanced response would be better, because by their very existence these monuments remind us that "causes" which they commemorate, legitimate or not, are an important part of our history; out of sight can easily lead to out of mind.

There are several ways to respond to the narrative which such monuments offer. Certainly some should be removed, and relegated to museums, particularly if they have no relevance to their locale, a particular characteristic of monuments erected during and since the Civil Rights era. Others, such as that at Colfax, should be left, but matched by one offering a historical perspective on the event. In fact, erecting new monuments is perhaps the best way to correct the narrative. There are, for example, few monuments commemorating citizens of the secessionist states who refused to support the Confederacy, many of whom suffered persecution and even death at the hands of their erstwhile neighbors. More than 100,000 white men from the seceded states served the Union, and generally lack commemoration, as do the hundreds of thousands of African Americans who served the "Old Flag." There are now movements in states like North Carolina to memorialize the state's Union troops, an effort in Virginia to commemorate Maj. Gen. George Thomas, and similar measures can be expected elsewhere as well

President Barack Obama made a major contribution to resolving this conundrum. During his first year in office, he had to confront the practice by most previous incumbents of sending a wreath on Confederate Memorial Day to the Confederate Memorial at Arlington National Cemetery, with its notorious pro-slavery imagery; rather than discontinue the custom, he instituted a new tradition, sending a wreath to the African American Civil War Memorial in Washington.

Signs of the times

Of some 4,500 people, mostly women, hired by the Freedmen's Bureau as teachers, half were Southern whites, some former plantation mistresses, a third were blacks, mostly from the South, and a sixth Northern whites, who served in nearly 3,000 schools.[20]

Lincoln University of Missouri was founded by a donation of $6,400 from the men of the 62nd and 65th U.S. Colored Infantry, who mustered out of service at St. Louis in 1866.

At a public meeting in New York City on March 3, 1868, Henry Ward Beecher, one of the premier abolitionists of the prewar period and a staunch Unionist, urged Northerners to donate money to the impoverished Washington College, in Lexington, VA, arguing that the college would provide an excellent education to the young men of the South under the leadership of its president, Robert E. Lee.[21]

By March 1868, the Freedman's Bureau had distributed some 18,319,522 rations, to both white and black Southerners.[22]

Learning that a proposed monument to Robert E. Lee was to be made from granite quarried in Maine, former Confederate Lt. Gen. Jubal Early promptly founded a rival memorial committee, to insure that proper "Confederate" stone was used.

During the Great Chicago Fire of 1871, former Confederate Brig. Gen. Robert Toombs, an irreconcilable secessionist, was asked if he'd heard any news, to which he replied, "Every effort is being made to put it out, but the wind is in our favor."[23]

Having just had one of his tall tales of the war debunked by an erstwhile comrade, an old Confederate veteran is said to have remarked, "Another good story ruined by an eyewitness."[24]

By June 30, 1879, the Civil War, plus attendant pensions and the occupation of parts of the South until 1877, had cost the federal government $6,187,243,385 and some cents, a figure which has continued to rise due to over 120 years' worth of additional pensions to veterans—after 1936 from both sides—their wives, and their offspring, not to mention the cost of maintaining monuments, memorials, and museums, or what the Confederacy had spent, or what the erstwhile Confederate states had already laid out in pensions and memorials.

Hearing yet another of his veteran sire's tales of derring-do during the late war, a young child growing up in the 7th Cavalry after the Civil War reportedly once asked, "Father, couldn't you get anyone to help you put down the Rebellion?"[25]

Perhaps the most curious of the many thousands of Civil War monuments is that of the 42nd New York at Gettysburg, which depicts an Indian chief in front of a teepee, commemorating Chief Tammany, the eponym of the famously corrupt Tammany Hall political machine, which raised the regiment.

From 1882, the first year for which statistics are available, through 1952, the first year in which no incidents were recorded, 4,730 persons are known to have been lynched in the United States, of whom 3,438 were African Americans (72.7 percent), and many hundreds more were killed in anti-black rioting.[26]

Sitting for the entrance examination at the Royal Military Academy at Sandhurst in 1893, Winston S. Churchill chose from a list of optional essay topics, "The American Civil War."[27]

Given a brigadier generalship for the Spanish-American War, William C. Oates (1835–1910), who had commanded the 15th Alabama at Little Round Top, the incident which forms the centerpiece of the 1993 film *Gettysburg*, was dismayed to discover that his brigade included the African American 9th Ohio Battalion, and acted so boorishly towards these troops that he was shortly transferred to a less-melanin endowed brigade.

Early in the twentieth century, South Carolina published an official roll of the troops it had provided for Confederate service, noting particularly those who gave their all for the cause, but curiously listing not a single man as having deserted, though many are shown as having gone absent without leave, often with no indication of having ever returned to the ranks.[28]

An old tradition has it that during a visit to New York, a Southern belle, upon seeing the Augustus Saint-Gaudens statue of "Victory Leading General Sherman," at the southeastern corner of Central Park near the Plaza Hotel, supposedly remarked, "Just like a Yankee, to let a Lady walk."

During the First World War, George Bolling Lee, the son of William Fitzhugh "Rooney" Lee, and thus the grandson of Robert E. Lee, served as the chief surgeon of the 369th Infantry, New York

City's black National Guard regiment, which saw more days in the trenches than any other American unit.

Published in 1937, *Gone With the Wind* remains the bestselling Civil War novel of all time, with sales above 30 million copies in scores of languages, and is one of the fifty best selling books in history. The 1939 motion picture based on the book is generally considered the most successful film ever made, grossing an estimated $3.4 billion in ticket sales globally, adjusted for inflation.

Kentucky did not ratify the Civil War Amendments (XIII, XIV, and XV), which abolished slavery, defined citizenship and mandated equal protection of the law to all citizens, and protected the voting rights of former slaves, until March 18, 1976, which may seem a bit slow were it not for the fact that Mississippi didn't ratify the XIII Amendment, abolishing slavery, until March 16, 1995.

The former New Orleans home of the brilliant Confederate cabinet member Judah P. Benjamin today houses a strip joint billing itself as "The Gentlemens' Club in a Class By Itself," which would probably offend its former resident for several reasons, not least the misplaced apostrophe.[29]

In June 2012, a lock of Robert E. Lee's hair was sold at auction for $12,500, considerably more than one from Ulysses S. Grant's head that fetched $5,975, but a lot less than Abraham Lincoln's tresses, which brought $38,837, both of the latter in December 2012.[30]

On May 25, 2015, an unexploded 3.80in. James rifled shell that was presumably fired on December 7, 1862, during the Battle of Prairie Grove, AK, was found and destroyed by a police explosives disposal squad; cannon shells and other explosive munitions from the war turn up regularly, often with fatal results, which prompted the Naval Ordnance School to issue *A Field Guide for Civil War Explosive Ordnance* in 1972, to help explosives disposal personnel identify and disarm them.[31]

President Coolidge's wife Grace claimed to have spotted Lincoln's ghost one night in the Oval Office, which wasn't built until nearly

50 years after his death, while several other people, supposedly including Winston Churchill, are said to have seen him while staying in what was called the "Lincoln bedroom," in which Lincoln never slept, though the spirits of two people who *did* die in that room, President William Henry Harrison (April 4, 1841) and young William Wallace Lincoln (February 20, 1862), have apparently never put in an appearance.[32]

The Civil War and the Presidency

Lincoln and Jefferson Davis weren't the only presidents with a Civil War connection. One way or another the war involved more presidents than any of America's other conflicts. There were several former presidents still living when the war broke out, and the war yielded a bumper crop of veterans who came to serve in the White House, a number matched only by veterans of the Second World War, plus one man old enough to have served, who did not. In addition, three future presidents were children during the war, and felt its influence.

Former Presidents: There were five living former presidents when the Confederacy fired on Fort Sumter: Martin Van Burn (1782–1862), John Tyler (1790–1862), Millard Fillmore (1800–74), Franklin Pierce (1804–69), and James Buchanan (1791–1868).

Veteran Presidents: Seven men who served in the Civil War eventually rose to the presidency: Andrew Johnson (1808–75), Ulysses S. Grant (1822–85), Rutherford B. Hayes (1822–93), James A. Garfield (1831–81), Chester A. Arthur (1829–86), Benjamin Harrison VIII (1833–1901), and William McKinley (1843–1901).

A draft dodger: Grover Cleveland (1837–1908) was drafted in mid-1863, but instead hired a substitute.

Presidential war babies: Theodore Roosevelt, Jr. (1858–1919), William Howard Taft (1857–1930), and Woodrow Wilson (1856–1924).

Notes

Introduction

1   D. J. Eicher, *The Longest Night: A Military History of the Civil War* (New York: Simon & Schuster, 2001), p. 17.

2   U. S. Grant, *The Personal Memoirs of Ulysses S. Grant* (New York, NY: C. L. Webster & Co., 1885-86), Chapter 67. Grant's *Memoirs* were originally published shortly after the President's death under the aegis of Mark Twain in a two-volume set. They have been reissued several times and are also available in several electronic versions. As a result, references to the *Memoirs* will be by chapter, rather than page number.

3   Veit, Chuck, "Accurate Terminology," *The Military Collector and Historian*, 69/1 (2017); A. A. Nofi, *A Civil War Treasury* (Conshohocken, PA: Combined Books, 1992), pp. 98–100.

Chapter 1

1   See, for example, Rachel L. Swarms, "Reckoning with a Legacy of Insuring Slaves' Lives," *The New York Times*, December 19, 2016, p. 1.

2   For an example of an instance of possible food poisoning taken as deliberate, and one of deliberate poisoning, see G. McNair, *Criminal Injustice: Slaves and Free Blacks in Georgia's Criminal Justice System* (Charlottesville, VA: University of Virginia Press, 2009), pp. 63–64.

3   D. C. Downing, *A South Divided: Portraits of Dissent in the Confederacy* (Nashville, TN: Cumberland House, 2007), p. 79.

4   I. Berlin and L. Harris, *Slavery in New York* (New York, NY: New Press, 2005); P. C. Hoffer, *Cry Liberty: The Great Stono River Slave Rebellion of 1739* (New York, NY: Oxford University Press 2010); D. R. Egerton, *Gabriel's Rebellion: The Virginia Slave Conspiracies of 1800 and 1802* (Chapel Hill, NC: University of North Carolina Press, 1993); M. L. Nicholls, *Whispers of Rebellion: Narrating Gabriel's Conspiracy* (Charlottesville, VA: University of Virginia Press, 2012); S. B. Oates, *The Fires of Jubilee: Nat Turner's Fierce Rebellion* (New York, NY: Harper, 2014); K. S. Greenberg, *Nat Turner: A Slave Rebellion in History and Memory* (New York, NY: Oxford University Press, 2004).

5   P. Linebaugh and M. Rediker, "The Many-Headed Hydra: Sailors, Slaves, and the Atlantic Working Class in the Eighteenth Century," *Journal of Historical Sociology*, 3 (1990),

pp. 225–52; I. Hopkins McClain, *A History of Stewart County, Tennessee* (Columbia, TN: privately published, 1965), p. 7; D. E. Reynolds, *Texas Terror: The Slave Insurrection Panic of 1860 and the Secession of the Lower South* (Baton Rouge, LA: Louisiana State University Press, 2007); M. Phillips, "White Violence, Hegemony, and Slave Rebellion in Dallas, Texas, before the Civil War," *East Texas Historical Journal*, 37/2 (1999), *East Texas Historical Journal* [website] <http://scholarworks.sfasu.edu/ethj/vol37/iss2/7>, accessed November 2015; *Texas Troubles* [website] <https://tshaonline.org/handbook/online/articles/vetbr> accessed November 2015; W. D. Jordan, *Tumult and Silence at Second Creek: An Inquiry Into a Civil War Slave Conspiracy* (Baton Rouge, LA: Louisiana State University Press, 1993); M. E. Danforth, *A Quaker Pioneer: Laura Haviland* (New York, NY: Exposition, 1961), pp. 174–75.

6   R. C. Wade, "The Vesey Plot: A Reconsideration," *The Journal of Southern History*, 30/2 (May, 1964), pp. 143–61; T. W. Higginson, "Denmark Vesey," *The Atlantic Monthly*, June 1861.

7   R. P. Forbes, *The Missouri Compromise and its Aftermath: Slavery and the Meaning of America* (Chapel Hill, NC: University of North Carolina Press, 2007); P. Finkelman and D. R. Kennon (eds.), *From the Missouri Compromise to the Age of Jackson* (Athens, OH: Ohio University Press, 2008).

8   S. E. Woodworth, *Manifest Destinies: America's Westward Expansion and the Road to the Civil War* (New York, NY: Vintage Books, 2011); S. Mountjoy, *Manifest Destiny: Westward Expansion* (New York, NY: Chelsea House, 2009).

9   A. A. Nofi, *The Alamo and the Texas War for Independence, 1835–1836* (Conshohocken, PA: Combined Publishing, 1992).

10   J. Eisenhower, *So Far From God: The U.S. War with Mexico* (New York, NY: Random House, 1989); P. Foos, *A Short, Offhand, Killing Affair: Soldiers and Social Conflict during the Mexican-War* (Chapel Hill, NC: University of North Carolina Press, 2002); R. P. Winders, *Mr. Polk's Army: The American Military Experience in the Mexican War* (College Station, TX: A&M Press, 1997); A. S. Greenberg, *A Wicked War: Polk, Clay, Lincoln, and the 1846 U.S. Invasion of Mexico* (New York, NY: Knopf, 2012).

11   F. M. Bordewich, *America's Great Debate: Henry Clay, Stephen A. Douglas, and the Compromise that Preserved the Union* (New York, NY: Simon & Schuster, 2013); J. C. Waugh, *On the Brink of Civil War: The Compromise of 1850 and How it Changed the Course of American History* (Lanham, MD: Rowman & Littlefield, 2003).

12   *Eric Foner on the Fugitive Slave Act* [website] <http://www.pbs.org/wgbh/aia/part4/4i3094.html> accessed January 2016; *Mr. Lincoln and the Runaways: The Case of the Matson Slaves, 1847* [wesbite] <http://www.academia.edu/205654/Mr._Lincoln_and_the_Runaways_The_Case_of_the_Matson_Slaves_1847> accessed January 2016.

13   *Eric Foner on the Fugitive Slave Act* [website].

14   Ibid.

15   R. E. May, *Manifest Destiny's Underworld: Filibustering in Antebellum America* (Chapel Hill, NC: The University of North Carolina Press, 2004), *passim*, but especially p. 35; R. E. May, *The Southern Dream of a Caribbean Empire, 1854–1861* (Gainesville, FL: University Press of Florida, 2002); T. Chaffin, *Fatal Glory: Narciso López and the First Clandestine U.S. War Against Cuba* (Baton Rouge, LA: Louisiana State University Press, 2003); C. H. Brown, *Agents of Manifest Destiny: The Lives and Times of the Filibusters* (Chapel Hill, NC: University of North Carolina Press, 2012); D. Ball, *Army Regulars on the Western Frontier* (Norman, OK: University of Oklahoma Press, 2001), pp. 89–126.

16 W. C. Davis, "Lee and Jefferson Davis," in G. W. Gallagher (ed.), *Lee the Soldier* (Lincoln, NB: University of Nebraska Press, 1996), p. 292; E. Thomas, *Robert E. Lee* (New York, NY: Norton, 1995), p. 148; T. H. Williams, *P.G.T. Beauregard: Napoleon in Gray* (Baton Rouge, LA: Louisiana State University Press, 1995), pp. 42–43.

17 *The New York Times*, January 2, 1860; S. McCurry, *Confederate Reckoning, Power and Politics in the Civil War South* (Cambridge, MA: Harvard, 2010), p. 60.

18 On April 5, 1861, just a week before the firing on Fort Sumter, an amateur astronomer discovered what is now known as Comet C/1861 G1 (Thatcher). This was taken by many people as a sign heralding the coming of the war.

19 W. R. Smith, *South Carolina as a Royal Province, 1710–1776* (New York, NY: Macmillan, 1903), pp. 175–77.

20 D. W. Howe, *What Hath God Wrought: The Transformation of America, 1815–1848* (New York, NY: Oxford University Press, 2007), p. 325.

21 J. Campbell, *Tariff, or Rates of Duties, Payable after the 30th of June, 1828* (New York, NY: Edward B. Gould, 1828); *Niles' Weekly Register*, Volume 41 (September. 1831–March 1832), p. 50; R. Mayo, *A Synopsis of the Commercial and Revenue System of the United States*, Vol. III (Washington, DC: J. and G.S. Gideon, 1847), p. 271; F. Hunt, *The Merchants' Magazine and Commercial Review*, Vol. 27 (July–December 1852), p. 550.

22 *Debt of the Republic of Texas* [website] <https://tshaonline.org/handbook/online/articles/mpdrh> accessed January 2016; S. Lebergott, "Wage Trends, 1800–1900," in *Trends in the American Economy in the Nineteenth Century*, edited by The Conference on Research in Income and Wealth (Princeton, NJ: Princeton University Press, 1960), p. 457.

23 W. S. McFeely, *Frederick Douglass* (New York, NY: W.W. Norton, 1991), p. 71.

24 H. Hattaway and R. F. Beringer, *Jefferson Davis, Confederate President* (Lawrence, KS: University Press of Kansas, 2002), pp. 331–32.

25 S. Northup, *Twelve Years a Slave: Narrative of Solomon Northup, a Citizen of New-York, Kidnapped in Washington City in 1841, and Rescued in 1853 from a Plantation Near the Red River in Louisiana* (New York, NY: Miller, Orton, & Mulligan, 1855).

26 N. Ricketts, *Mormon Battalion: United States Army of the West, 1846–1848* (Boulder, CO: Utah State University Press, 1997).

27 *Winfield Scott Loses a Match* [website] <http://cwbn.blogspot.com/2007/03/winfield-scott-loses-match.html> accessed May 2016.

28 On Tubman, see particularly C. Clinton, *Harriet Tubman: The Road to Freedom* (New York, NY: Little, Brown, 2004); M. C. Sernett, *Harriet Tubman: Myth, Memory, and History* (Durham, NC: Duke University Press, 2007).

29 *New-York Daily Tribune*, February 8, 1856.

30 M. M. Horowitz, "Ethnicity and Command: The Civil War Experience," *Military Affairs*, 42/4 (December 1978), p. 182; W. C. Harris, *Lincoln and the Border States: Preserving the Union* (Lawrence, KS: University Press of Kansas, 2011), p. 123; M. D. Pierson, *Lt. Spalding in Civil War Louisiana: A Union Officer's Humor, Privilege, and Ambition* (Baton Rouge, LA: Louisiana State University Press, 2016), p. 157, note 1.

31 Overviews can be found in B. Schecter, *The Devil's Own Work: The Civil War Draft Riots and the Fight to Reconstruct America* (New York, NY: Walker Books, 2005); J. Tager, *Boston Riots: Three Centuries of Social Violence* (Boston, MA: Northeastern University, 2000).

32 G. Waro, *Warfare and Society in Europe* (New York, NY: Routledge, 2000), p. 36; D. F. Ericson, *Slavery in the American Republic* (Lawrence, KS: University Press of Kansas, 2011), pp. 187–88.

33 D. C. Downing, *A South Divided: Portraits of Dissent in the Confederacy* (Nashville, TN: Cumberland House, 2007), p. 79.

34 S. H. Williamson and L. P. Cain, *Measuring Slavery in 2016 Dollars* [website] <https://www.measuringworth.com/slavery.php>, accessed July 2017.

35 *Selected Statistics on Slavery in the United States* [wesbite] <http://www.civilwarcauses.org/stat.htm> accessed January 2016.

Chapter 2

1 P. F. Boller, *The Congressional Anecdote Book* (New York, NY: Oxford University Press, 1991), p. 233.

2 L. D. Mansch, *Abraham Lincoln, President-Elect: The Four Critical Months from Election to Inauguration* (Jefferson, NC: McFarland, 2005), p. 61. The 1860 turnout has to date only been exceeded once, in 1876, when it reached 81.8 percent.

3 *The Declaration of Causes of Seceding States* [website] <http://www.civilwar.org/education/history/primarysources/declarationofcauses.html> accessed January 2016.

4 W. J. Cooper, *Jefferson Davis, American* (New York, NY: Random House, 2000), p. 301.

5 Alexander H. Stevens, "Cornerstone Address," March 21, 1861, see *George Washington on the abolition of slavery* [website] <https://www.gilderlehrman.org/history-by-era/creating-new-government/resources/george-washington-abolition-slavery-1786> accessed January 2016.

6 M. L. Lause, *The Collapse of Price's Raid: The Beginning of the End in Civil War Missouri* (Columbia, MO: University of Missouri Press, 2016), p. 2.

7 J. M. Matthews (ed.), *The Statutes at Large of the Provisional Government of the Confederate States of America, from the Institution of the Government, February 8, 1861, to its Termination, February 18, 1862, Inclusive*, (Richmond, VA: R. M. Smith, Printer to Congress, 1864), pp. 45–46; W. L. Shaw, "The Confederate Conscription and Exemption Acts," *The American Journal of Legal History*, 6/4 (October 1962), pp. 370–71.

8 A. Castel, *Articles of War: Winners, Losers, and Some Who Were Both in the Civil War* (Mechanicsburg, PA: Stackpole, 2001), p. 2.

9 P. F. Mottelay (ed.), *The Soldier in Our Civil War* (New York, NY: J. H. Brown Publishing, 1884), Vol. I, pp. 22–23; "The Glorious Flag of Ft. Sumter," *Weekly Courier* (Ft. Collins, Co.), January 26, 1899, p. 7; J. G. Foster, "Engineer Journal of the Bombardment of Fort Sumter," *O.R.*, Series I, Vol. I, p. 19.

10 W. C. Davis, *The Union That Shaped the Confederacy: Robert Toombs and Alexander H. Stevens* (Lawrence, KS: University Press of Kansas, 2001), p. 123.

11 A. R. Chisolm, "Notes on the Surrender of Fort Sumter," *Battles & Leaders of the Civil War* (New York, NY: The Century Co., 1887), Vol. I, p. 82.

12 J. K. Mahon, *The American Militia Decade of Decision, 1789–1800* (Gainesville, FL: University of Florida, 1960); J. K. Mahon, *History of the Militia and the National Guard* (New York, NY: Macmillan, 1983); *Thomas Jefferson—Message to the Senate and House of January 16, 1804* [website] <http://avalon.law.yale.edu/19th_century/tj006.asp>, accessed January 2016.

13 *New-York Daily Tribune*, December 17, 1860.

14 M. Dix (ed.), *Memoirs of John Adams Dix* (New York, NY: Harper & Brothers, 1883), Vol. I, p. 345.

15 Millard Fillmore to Daniel Webster, October 23, 1850 in F. H. Severance (ed.), *Millard Fillmore Papers* (Buffalo, NY: Buffalo Historical Society, 1907), Vol. I, p. 335.

16 B. F. Butler, *Autobiography and Personal Reminiscences of Major-General Benj. F. Butler* (Boston, MA: A.M. Thayer & Co., 1892), p. 142.

17 *The Statutes at Large of the Provisional Government of the Confederate States of America, from the Institution of the Government, February 8, 1861, to its Termination, February 18, 1862, Inclusive,* (Richmond, VA: R. M. Smith, Printer to Congress, 1864), p. 151; F. Moore (ed.), *The Rebellion Record: A Diary of American Events* (New York, NY: Putnam's, 1861–68), Vol. I, p. 43; J. C. Schwab, *The Confederate States of America: A Financial and Industrial History of the South During the Civil War* (New York, NY: Charles Scribner's, 1901), pp. 110–11; W. C. Mitchell, *A History of the Greenbacks* (Chicago, IL: University of Chicago Press, 1903), p. 21, note 5; Mansch, *Abraham Lincoln*, p. 159; "Swindling Secessionists in Grief," *The New York Times*, October 26, 1861; E. K. Spann, *Gotham at War: New York City, 1860–1865* (Wilmington, DE: SR Books, 2002), p. 25.

18 Harris, *Lincoln and the Border States*.

19 R. A. Wooster, *The Secession Conventions of the South* (Princeton, NJ: Princeton University Press, 1962), pp. 197–98; G. P. Downs, "The Death Knell of Slavery", *The New York Times*, May 19, 2011.

20 K. T. Dollar, L. H. Whitaker, and W. C. Dickinson (eds.), *Sister States, Enemy States* (Lexington, KY: University Press of Kentucky, 2009), pp. 61, 70, note 30.

21 F. B. Heitman, *Historical Register and Dictionary of the United States Army* (Washington, DC: Government Printing Office, 1903); G. W. Cullum, *Biographical Register of the Officers and Graduates of the United States Military Academy at West Point, New York* (New York, NY: J. Miller, 1879); W. S. Dudley, *Going South: U.S. Naval Officer Resignations and Dismissed on the Eve of the Civil War* (Washington, DC: Naval Historical Foundation, 1981); F. Kern, *The United States Revenue Cutter Service in the Civil War* (Bethesda, MD: Alised Enterprises, n.d.)

22 J. A. Leikert *Racial Borders: Black Soldiers along the Rio Grande* (College Station, TX: Texas A&M Press, 2002), p. 31.

23 F. W. Williams, *Anson Burlingame and the First Chinese Mission to Foreign Powers* (New York, NY: Russell & Russell, 1972), p. 13.

24 E. J. Engstrom and S. Kernell, *Party Ballots, Reform, and the Transformation of America's Electoral System* (San Diego, CA: University of California, San Diego, 2014).

25 D. H. Donald, *Lincoln's Herndon: A Biography* (New York, NY: Da Capo, 1989), p. 144.

26 Mansch, *Abraham Lincoln*, p. 15.

27 Ibid.

28 M. A. Weitz, *A Higher Duty: Desertion among Georgia Troops during the Civil War* (Lincoln, NE: University of Nebraska Press, 2005), p. 14.

29 M. B. Field, *Memories of Many Men and Some Women* (New York, NY: Harper's, 1875), p. 257; value calculated by "comparable economic power."

30 R. J. Tofel, *Eight Weeks in Washington, 1861: Abraham Lincoln and the Hazards of Transition* (New York, NY: St. Martin's, 2011), p. 9.

31 M. B. Bonner, *Confederate Political Economy: Creating and Managing a Southern Corporatist Nation* (Baton Rouge, LA: Louisiana State University Press, 2016), p. 22.

32 F. Hatch, *Protecting President Lincoln* (Jefferson, NC: McFarland, Press, 2011), p. 11.

33 Maury Klein, *Days of Defiance: Sumter, Secession, and the Coming of the Civil War* (New York: Vintage, 1999), p. 165

34 E. S. Bradley, *Simon Cameron: Lincoln's Secretary of War* (Philadelphia, PA: University of Pennsylvania Press, 1966), p. 183.

35 B. I. Wiley, *The Life of Billy Yank* (Indianapolis, IN: Bobbs-Merrill, 1951), p. 18.
36 *The American Annual Cyclopedia and Register of Important Events of the Year 1861* (New York, NY: D. Appleton, 1864), p. 23.
37 Bradley, *Simon Cameron*, p. 198.

Chapter 3

1   W. T. Sherman, *The Memoirs of General W. T. Sherman*, Vol. I, (New York, NY: D. Appleton & Co., 1889), Chapter IX.
2   D. H. Hill, "The Battle of Gaines' Mill," *The Century*, VIII/2 (June 1885), p. 298.
3   D. D. Porter, *The Naval History of the Civil War* (New York, NY: Sherman Publishing, 1886), p. 184.
4   G. Linderman, *Embattled Courage: The Experience of Combat in the Civil War* (New York, NY: The Free Press, 1987), p. 10.
5   *Richmond, Embattled Capital, 1861–1865* [website] https://www.nps.gov/rich/learn/historyculture/richmond-story.htm, accessed July 2017.
6   H. Hattaway, *General Stephen D. Lee* (Jackson, MS: University Press of Mississippi, 1976), p. 55.
7   G. Meade (ed.), *The Life and Letters of George Gordon Meade* (New York, NY: Charles Scribner's, 1913), Vol. I, p. 248.
8   D. G. Martin, *The Vicksburg Campaign: April 1862–July 1863* (New York, NY: Da Capo, 1994), p. 139.
9   F. A. O'Reilly, "Chancellorsville, Action from May 3–6, 1863," *Blue & Gray*, XXIX/5 (2013).
10 J. D. Wert, *General James Longstreet: The Confederacy's Most Controversial Soldier—A Biography* (New York, NY: Simon & Schuster, 1993), p. 278.
11 W. F. Perry, "The Devil's Den," *Confederate Veteran*, Vol. 9 (1901), p. 161.
12 F. A. Haskell, *The Battle of Gettysburg* (Boston, MA: MOLLUS Commandery of the State of Massachusetts, 1908), p. 57.
13 J. R. Carnahan, *Personal Recollections of Chickamauga* (Cincinnati, OH: H. C. Sherrick & Co.,1886), p. 9.
14 C. A. Dana, "Reminiscences of Men and Events of the Civil War," Part IV, *McLure's Magazine*, X/4 (February 1898), p. 352.
15 R. C. Conner, *General Gordon Granger: The Savior of Chickamauga and the Man Behind "Juneteenth"* (Philadelphia, PA: Casemate, 2013), p. 125.
16 H. Porter, "Campaigning With Grant," *The Century Illustrated Monthly Magazine*, 53/1 (November 1896), p. 220.
17 H. Hattaway and A. Jones, *How the North Won: A Military History of the Civil War* (Champaign, IL: University of Illinois Press, reprint 1991), p. 525.
18 H. S. Melchor, "An Experience in the Battle of the Wilderness," *War Papers Read before the Commandery of the State of Maine, Military Order of the Loyal Legion of the United States* (Portland, ME: The Thurston Print, 1898), Vol. I, p. 77.
19 Porter, "Campaigning With Grant," p. 221.
20 W. Garrison, *Curiosities of the Civil War: Strange Stories, Infamous Characters and Bizarre Events* (Nashville, TN: Thomas Nelson, 1995), p. 105; N. A. Miles, *Serving the Republic: Memoirs*

of the Civil and Military Life of Nelson A. Miles, Lieutenant-General, United States Army (New York, NY: Harper and Brothers, 1911), p. 86.

21 "Report of Capt. James Fleming," *Official Records of the Union and Confederate Armies*, Series I, Vol. XXVI, Part 1, p. 390.

22 Estimates of the number of casualties vary greatly, and are difficult to pin down as both armies received reinforcements during the 6 weeks of operations, while statistics often include casualties from engagements in Virginia not directly related to the Overland Campaign.

23 "The Great Contest," *New-York Daily Tribune*, May 13, 1864, p. 1.

24 C. W. Wills (ed. M. E. Kellogg), *Army Life of an Illinois Soldier: Including a Day-by-day Record of Sherman's March to the Sea* (Carbondale, IL: Southern Illinois University Press, 1996), p. 287.

25 R. W. Banks, *The Battle of Franklin, November 30, 1864: The Bloodiest Engagement of the War Between the States* (New York, NY: The Neale Publishing Company, 1908), p. 77.

26 W. Davis, *Camp-fire Chats of the Civil War* (Chicago, IL: A. B. Gehman, 1888), p. 211.

27 *Official Records of the Union and Confederate Armies*, Series I, Vol. XLIV, p. 783.

28 C. L. Harrell, *When the Bells Tolled for Lincoln: Southern Reaction to the Assassination* (Macon, GA: Mercer University Press, 1997), p. 42.

29 Ibid. p. 39; T. Goodrich, *The Darkest Dawn: Lincoln, Booth, and the Great American Tragedy* (Bloomington, IN: Indiana University Press, 2005), p. 160.

30 "For Action on Race Riot Peril," *The New York Times*, October 5, 1919, p. 10.

31 M. Songini, *The Lost Fleet: A Yankee Whaler's Struggle Against the Confederate Navy and Arctic Disaster* (New York, NY: St. Martin's, 2007), p. 101.

32 S. Powers, *A Buff Looks at the American Civil War: A Look at the United States Greatest Conflict from the Point of View of a Civil War Buff* (Bloomington, IN: Author House, 2011), p. 506.

33 O. E. Cunningham (G. D. Joiner and T. B. Smith, eds.), *Shiloh and the Western Campaign of 1862* (El Dorado Hills, CA: Savas Beattie, 2007), p. 61.

34 T. Jordan, "Notes of a Confederate Staff Officer at Shiloh," in R. U. Johnson and C. C. Buel (eds.), *Battles & Leaders of the Civil War* (New York, NY: The Century Company, 1887), Vol. I, p. 595, note.

35 N. A. Miles (ed.), *Tales from McClure's War: Being True Stories of Camp and Battlefield* (New York, NY: Doubleday and McClure, 1898), Preface.

36 D. M. Callaghan, *Thomas Francis Meagher and the Irish Brigade in the Civil War* (Jefferson, NC: McFarlan, 2006), p. 127.

37 D. W. Belcher, *The 11th Missouri Volunteer Infantry in the Civil War: A History and Roster* (Jefferson, NC: McFarland & Co, 2011), p. 118.

38 J. E. Cashin (ed.), *The War Was You and Me: Civilians in the American Civil War* (Princeton, NJ: Princeton University Press, 2002), pp. 215–16; P. C. Vermilyea, "The Effect of the Confederate Invasion of Pennsylvania on Gettysburg's African American Community," *Gettysburg Magazine*, 24 (January 2001).

39 N. Polk and A. J. Abadie (eds.), *Faulkner and War* (Jackson, MI: University Press of Mississippi, 2004), p. 13.

40 S. R. Watkins, *"Co. Aytch," Maury Grays, First Tennessee Regiment: or A Side Show of the Big Show* (Chattanooga: Times Printing Co., 1900), p. 87.

41 E. M. Essen, *Shavetails and Bell Sharps* (Lincoln, NE: University of Nebraska Press, 1997).

42 W. D. Matter, *If it Takes All Summer: The Battle of Spotsylvania* (Chapel Hill, NC: University of North Carolina Press, 1988), p. 155.

43 D. W. Lowe (ed.), *Meade's Army: The Private Notebooks of Lt. Col. Theodore Lyman* (Kent, OH: Kent State University Press, 2007), p. 229.

44 R. P. Broadwater, *The Battle of Olustee, 1864* (Jefferson, NC: McFarland & Co, 2006), p. 2.

45 P. R. DeMontravel, *A Hero to His Fighting Men: Nelson A. Miles, 1839–1925* (Kent, OH: Kent State University Press, 1998).

46 W. C. Davis, *Fighting Men of the Civil War* (Norman, OK: University of Oklahoma Press, 1998), p. 154.

47 R. M. Dunkerly, *To the Bitter End: Appomattox, Bennett Place, and the Surrenders of the Confederacy* (El Dorado Hills, CA: Savas Beatie, 2015), p. 94.

48 A. C. A. Jampolar, *The Last Lincoln Conspirator: John Surrat's Flight from the Gallows* (Annapolis, MD: Naval Institute Press, 2008), p. 11.

49 J. M. Coski, *The Confederate Battle Flag: America's Most Embattled Emblem* (Cambridge, MA: Harvard University Press, 2005), p. 41.

Chapter 4

1 C. G. Hearn, *Lincoln, the Cabinet, and the Generals* (Baton Rouge, LA: Louisiana State University Press, 2010), p. 63.

2 R. Andrew, Jr., *Long Gray Lines: The Southern Military School Tradition, 1839–1915* (Chapel Hill, NC: University of North Carolina Press, 2001), p. 27.

3 J. N. Opie, *A Rebel Cavalryman with Lee, Stuart, and Jackson* (Chicago, IL: W. B. Conkey, 1899), p. 14.

4 W. Watson, *Life in the Confederate Army: Being the Observations and Experiences of an Alien in the South During the American Civil War* (Baton Rouge. LA: Louisiana State University Press, 1995), p. 171.

5 "The Tone of a Bullet," in F. Moore, *Anecdotes, Poetry, and Incidents of the War: North and South: 1860–1865* (New York, NY: privately printed, 1866), pp. 82–83.

6 F. Phisterer, *Statistical Record*, (New York, NY: Charles Scribner's, 1883); F. A. Shannon, "The Mercenary Factor in the Creation of the Union Army," *Mississippi Valley Historical Review*, 12/4 (March 1926), pp. 523–49.

7 D. L. Collin, *Major General Robert E. Rodes of the Army of Northern Virginia: A Biography* (El Dorado Hills, CA: Savas Beattie, 2008), pp. 47–48, 62ff., 72; G. Ward Hubbs, *Guarding Greensboro: A Confederate Company in the Making of a Southern Community* (Athens, GA: University of Georgia Press, 2003), esp. p.100ff.; G. Ward Hubbs (ed.), *Voices from Company D: Diaries by the Greensboro Guards, Fifth Alabama* (Athens, GA: University of Georgia Press, 2003); *5th Alabama Infantry* [website] <http://civilwarintheeast.com/confederate-regiments/alabama/5th-alabama-infantry/>, accessed February 2016; *Fifth Alabama Infantry Regiment* [website] <http://www.archives.alabama.gov/referenc/alamilor/5thinf.html>, accessed February 2016.

8 J. T. Glatthaar, *General Lee's Army: From Victory to Collapse* (New York, NY: The Free Press, 2008), p. 25.

9 Essen, *Shavetails and Bell Sharps*.

10 S. Jones, "The Influence of Horse Supply upon Field Artillery in the American Civil War," *Journal of Military History*, 74/2 (April 2010), p. 360.

11 J. J. Pershing (ed. J. T. Greenwood), *My Life Before the World War, 1860–1917: A Memoir* (Lexington, KY: The University Press of Kentucky, 2012), p. 225.

12 Jones, "The Influence of Horse Supply upon Field Artillery in the American Civil War," p. 362.

13 J. D. Welsh, *Medical Histories of Confederate Generals* (Kent, OH: Kent State University Press, 1995); J. D. Welsh, *Medical Histories of Union Generals* (Kent, OH: Kent State University Press, 1996); G. A. Armistead, *Horses and Mules in the Civil War* (Jefferson, NC: McFarland & Co., 2013), p. 35; J. Robertson, *Stonewall Jackson* (New York, NY: Macmillan, 1997), pp. 584ff., especially note 16.

14 D. S. Freeman, *R. E. Lee: A Biography* (New York, NY: Charles Scribner's, 1934–35), Vol. II, Chapter 24.

15 *Statutes at large of the Provisional Government of the Confederate States of America*, pp. 99, 116, 210, 221, 229, available at <http://www.archive.org/details/statutesatlargeo15conf>, accessed July 2017; Hattaway and Beringer, *Jefferson Davis*, pp. 58ff.; R. J. Miller, *Both Prayed to the Same God: Religion and Faith in the American Civil War* (Lanham, MD: Lexington Books, 2007), pp. 99, 104; A. I. Slomovitz, *The Fighting Rabbis* (New York, NY: New York University Press, 1999); J. W. Brinsfield, *The Spirit Divided: Memoirs of Civil War Chaplains: The Confederacy* (Macon, GA: Mercer University Press, 2005); J. W. Jones, *Christ in Camp: Or Religion in Lee's Army* (Richmond, VA: B. F. Johnson, 1887).

16 Miller, *Both Prayed to the Same God*, p. 104.

17 Brinsfield, *The Spirit Divided*, p. 10.

18 Jones, *Christ in Camp*, p. 36.

19 Miller, *Both Prayed to the Same God*, p. 100.

20 Ibid.

21 J. B. Jones (ed. J. I. Robertson, Jr.), *A Rebel War Clerk's Diary: At the Confederate States Capital*, Vol. I, *April 1861–July 1863* (Lawrence, KS: University Press of Kansas, 2015), p. 410, note 48.

22 Ibid. pp. 248, 419, note 48.

23 J. D. Wright, *The Language of the Civil War* (Westport, CT: Greenwood Publishing, 2001); Wiley, *The Life of Billy Yank*, p. 258; C. R. Knight, *Valley Thunder: The Battle of New Market & the Opening of the Shenandoah Valley Campaign, May 1854* (El Dorado Hills, CA: Savas Beatie, 2010), p. 220.

24 W. E. Emerson, *Sons of Privilege: The Charleston Light Dragoons in the Civil War* (Columbia, SC: University of South Carolina Press, 2005); E. L. Welles, "A note on the 1793 Charleston Light Dragoons' Punch," in *A Sketch of the Charleston Light Dragoons, from the Earliest Formation of the Corps* (Charleston, SC: Lucas, Richardson & Co., 1888); B. S. Allardice, *Confederate Colonels: A Biographical Register* (Columbia, MO: University of Missouri Press, 2008), p. 331.

25 D. M. Callaghan, *Thomas Francis Meagher and the Irish Brigade in the Civil War* (Jefferson, NC: McFarlan, 2006).

26 W. H. Fox, *Regimental Losses of the American Civil War 1861–1865* (Albany, NY: Albany Publishing Co., 1889).

27 Glatthaar, *General Lee's Army*, p. 188; J. T. Glatthaar, "A Tale of Two Armies: The Confederate Army of Northern Virginia and the Union Army of the Potomac and their Cultures," *Journal of the Civil War Era*, 6/3 (September 2016), pp. 325ff.

28 M. D. Doubler, *Civilian in Peace, Soldier in War: The Army National Guard, 1636–2000* (Lawrence, KS: University Press of Kansas, 2003), p. 93; P. Eagan, *Rochester, NY's 54th*

Infantry Regiment [website] <http://padraicmacaodhagain.blogspot.com/2008/01/roches-ter-nys-54th-infantry-regiment.html>, accessed May 2016.

29 E. G. Longacre, *Lincoln's Cavalrymen: A History of the Mounted Forces of the Army of the Potomac* (Mechanicsburg, PA: Stackpole Books, 2000).

30 R. H. Beattie, *Army of the Potomac: McClellan Takes Command* (New York, NY: DaCapo, 2004), pp. 94, 193–94.

31 Downing, *A South Divided*, p. 114.

32 Miller, *Both Prayed to the Same God*, p. 107.

33 T. P. Lowry and L. Laska, *Confederate Death Sentences: A Reference Guide* (n.p.: BookSurge Publishing, 2009), p. 4.

34 J. Giambrone, "The Mexican War Alumni of the 1st Mississippi Rifles," *North & South*, X/3 (October 2007), pp. 11–13.

35 W. Marvel, *Andersonville: The Last Depot* (Chapel Hill, NC: The University of North Carolina Press, 1994), pp. 140–44.

36 J. M. Taylor, *While Cannons Roared: The Civil War Behind the* Lines (Washington, DC: Brassey's, 1997).

37 Lowry and Laska, *Confederate Death Sentences*, p. 4; W. C. Davis, *Crucible of Command: Ulysses S. Grant and Robert E. Lee—The War They Fought, the Peace They Forged* (New York, NY: Da Capo, 2015), pp. 416, 419.

Chapter 5

1 R. O'Neal Greenhow, *My Imprisonment and the First Year of Abolition Rule at Washington* (London, UK: Richard Bentley, 1863); A. Blackman, *Wild Rose: The True Story of a Civil War Spy* (New York, NY: Random House, 2006); A. A. Nofi, *Spies in the Civil War* (New York, NY: Chelsea House, 2000), pp. 36–46; P. Van Doren Stern, *Secret Missions of the Civil War* (New York, NY: Bonanza Books, 1959), pp. 54–64.

2 A. A. Nofi, "An Incident on the Road to Bull Run," *North & South*, III/3 (August 2000), p. 9; Fox, *Regimental Losses in the American Civil War, 1861–1865.*

3 Colonel Sol Meredith to Col. Isaac L. Stevens, September 12, 1861, *Official Records of the Union and Confederate Armies*, Series I, Vol. V, pp. 172–73; C. L. Dunn, *Iron Men, Iron Will: The Nineteenth Indiana Regiment of the Iron Brigade* (Indianapolis, IN: Guild Press of Indiana, 1995), pp. 47ff.; Moore, *Anecdotes, Poetry, and Incidents of the* War, p. 57; *North & South*, X/5, pp. 10–11.

4 The 15th Illinois Cavalry had not yet been formed at the time of this incident, and the troopers were probably from the 2nd Illinois Cavalry. Recounting the tale years later, Gen. Cheatham had probably forgotten the designation and just made one up.

5 E. A. Pollar, *Lee and his Lieutenants: Comprising the Early Life, Public Services, and Campaigns of Gen. Robert E. Lee and His Companions in Arms, with a Record of their Campaigns and Heroic Deeds* (New York, NY: E. B. Trat, 1868), pp. 719–20; A. A. Nofi, "Stand Just Where You Are," *North & South*, I/7 (September 1998), p. 8.

6 J. Stauffer and B. Soskis, *The Battle Hymn of the Republic: A Biography of the Song That Marches On* (New York, NY: Oxford University Press, 2013); F. M. Cutler, *The Old First Massachusetts Coast Artillery in War and Peace* (Boston, MA: Pilgrim Press, 1917), pp. 105–06.

7 B. D. Simpson, *Ulysses S. Grant* (Boston, MA: Houghton Mifflin, 2000), pp. 175–76.

8   Glatthaar, *General Lee's Army*, p. 399 *et passim*.

9   Moore, *The Rebellion Record*, Vol. V (1862), p. 10.

10   D. G. Crotty, *Four Years Campaigning in the Army of the Potomac* (Grand Rapids, MI: Dygert Brothers, 1874), pp. 34–35; Callaghan, *Thomas Francis Meagher and the Irish Brigade in the Civil War*, p. 108.

11   Longacre, *Lincoln's Cavalrymen*, p. 58; A. A. Nofi, "Have I got a Surprise for You," *North & South*, V/5 (July 2002), p. 9.

12   P. Selby, *Lincoln's Life, Stories, and Speeches* (Chicago, IL: J. R. Stanton, 1902), pp. 188–89; F. B. Carpenter, *Six Months at the White House with Abraham Lincoln: The Story of a Picture* (New York, NY: Hurd and Houghton, 1866), pp. 80–81.

13   S. D. Elliott, *Soldier of Tennessee: General Alexander P. Stewart and the Civil War in the West* (Baton Rouge, LA: Louisiana State University Press, 1999), p. 92.

14   Grant, *Memoirs*, Chapter XXXV; A. A. Nofi, "The Jackson Cotton Works," *North & South*, I/7 (September 1998), p. 8.

15   J. M. Priest, *Into the Fight: Pickett's Charge at Gettysburg* (Shippensburg, PA: White Mane, 1998), p. 34; R. Gragg, *Covered with Glory: The 26th North Carolina Infantry at the Battle of Gettysburg* (Chapel Hill, NC: University of North Carolina Press, 2000), p. 165; A. A. Nofi, "'Don't Fire, Yanks!'," *North & South*, III/2 (January 2000), p. 12.

16   Meade to Thomas, July 8, 1863, *Official Records*, Series I, Vol. XXV, Part 1, p. 85; Reports of Col. Norman J. Hall, 7th Michigan Infantry, commanding 3rd Brigade, July 17, 1863, *Official Records*, Series I, Vol. XXV, Part 1, p. 439; "Rebel Battle Flags Captured At Gettysburg," *The Michigan Argus*, August 21, 1863.

17   The most useful works on the riots are I. Bernstein, *The Draft Riots* (New York, NY: Oxford University Press, 1989); T. Anbinder, *Five Points: The 19th-Century New York City Neighborhood that Invented Tap Dance, Stole Elections, and Became the World's Most Notorious Slum* (New York, NY: The Free Press, 2001); A. Cook, *The Armies of the Streets* (Lexington, KY: University Press of Kentucky, 1972), and B. Schecter, *The Devil's Own Work: The Civil War Draft Riots and the Fight to Reconstruct America* (New York, NY: Walker Books, 2005). Two often cited, but much less reliable works are H. Asbury's *The Gangs of New York: An Informal History of the Underworld* (New York, NY: Knopf, 1928), which inspired the 2002 motion picture (it is highly creative and inaccurate), and J. T. Headly's *The Great Riots of New York, 1712–1873* (New York, NY: E. B. Treat, 1873); Headly was a sometime member of the Know Nothing Party and fierce anti-Catholic.

18   *The National Cyclopaedia of American Biography* (New York, NY: James T. White & Co., 1907), Vol. IX, pp. 205–06; de Kay Family Background [website] <http://helenadekaygilder.org/dekayfam/>, accessed September, 2016.

19   J. C. Inscoe and R. C. Kenzer (eds.), *Enemies of the Country: New Perspectives on Unionists in the Civil War South* (Athens, GA: University of Georgia Press, 2001), p. 62; *North & South*, X/5 (March 2008), p. 10.

20   B. M. Venter, *Kill Jeff Davis: The Union Raid on Richmond, 1864* (Norman, OK: University of Oklahoma Press, 2016).

21   Watkins, *"Co. Aytch"*,, pp. 97, 118–19.

22   E. R. Varon, *Southern Lady, Yankee Spy: The True Story of Elizabeth Van Lew, a Union Agent in the Heart of the Confederacy* (New York, NY: Oxford University Press, 2003); Nofi, *Spies in the Civil War*, pp. 12, 24–28, 47–51; W. B. Hoberton, *Homeward Bound: The Demobilization*

of the Union and Confederate Armies, 1865–1866 (Mechanicsburg, PA: Stackpole, 2001), p. 46; "The Richmond Spy," *Daily Dispatch* (Richmond), July 17, 1883.

23 "The Richmond Spy," *Daily Dispatch* (Richmond), July 17, 1883.

24 *Official Records*, Series I, Vol. XXXIX, p. 522.

25 B. R. Todd, *The Music of Henry Clay Work* [website] <http://www.pdmusic.org/work. html>, accessed August 2016; Cutler, *The Old First Massachusetts Coast Artillery in War and Peace*, pp. 105–06.

26 With thanks to the online denizens of *American Civil War Society*.

27 W. C. Davis and J. I. Robertson, Jr. (eds.), *Virginia at War, 1865* (Lexington, KY: University Press of Kentucky, 2012), p. 105.

28 R. M. Dunkerly, *The Confederate Surrender at Greensboro* (Jefferson, NC: McFarland & Co., 2013), p. 15.

29 L. C. Pickett, *Pickett and his Men* (Atlanta, GA: Foote & Davies, 1900), pp. 126–27.

30 R. P. Basler, M. D. Pratt, and L. A. Dunlap (eds.), *Collected Works of Abraham Lincoln* (New Brunswick, NJ: Rutgers University Press, 1953), Vol. 8, p. 393.

31 *Official Records*, Series I, Vol. XLVI, Part 3, p. 663.

32 Hoberton, *Homeward Bound*; *Official Records*, Series III, Vol. V, p. 1,047.

33 E. Keckley, *Behind the Scene* (New York, NY: 1868), p. 135; A. A. Nofi, "Lincoln, On Lee," *North & South*, III/4 (April 2000), p. 8.

34 J. C. Clark, *Last Train South* (Jefferson, NC: McFarland, 1984), p. 102–03.

35 B. R. McEnany, *For Brotherhood and Duty: The Civil War History of the West Point Class of 1862* (Lexington, KY: University Press of Kentucky, 2015), p. 88.

36 *St. Louis Post-Dispatch*, June 28, 1912, p. 14.

37 D. D. Van Tassel, *"Behind Bayonets": The Civil War in Northern Ohio* (Kent, OH: Kent State University Press, 2006), p. 39.

38 T. B. Smith, *Corinth 1862: Siege, Battle, Occupation* (Lawrence, KS: University Press of Kansas, 2012), p. 4.

39 W. P. Lyon, *Reminiscences of the Civil War* (San Jose, CA: Muirson & Wright, 1907), p. 31, note.

40 G. D. Brasher, *The Peninsular Campaign & the Necessity of Emancipation: African-Americans & the Fight for Freedom* (Chapel Hill, NC: University of North Carolina Press, 2012), p. 106.

41 Simpson, *Ulysses S. Grant*, p. 198.

42 J. M. Beadles, "A Unique Incident," *Confederate Veteran*, XXV/10 (October 1917,) p. 471.

43 Pickett, *Pickett and his Men*, p. 409.

44 General Orders No. 43, *O.R.*, Ser. I, Vol. XXX pt. 4, p. 503

45 "The New York Hotel," *The National Quarterly Review*, 20 (1872), p. 29.

46 Grant, *Memoirs*, Chapter XL.

47 C. J. Einolf, *George Thomas: Virginian for the Union* (Norman OK: University of Oklahoma Press, 2007), p. 224.

48 Glatthaar, *General Lee's Army*, p. 355.

49 D. Conyngham, *Sherman's March through the South: With Sketches and Incidents of the Campaign* (New York, NY: Sheldon, 1865), p. 76.

50 A. Kelman, *A Misplaced Massacre: Struggling over the Memory of Sand Creek* (Cambridge, MA: Harvard University Press, 2013).

51 J. F. Marszalek, *Sherman's March to the Sea* (Abilene, TX: State House Press, 2005), p. 61.

Chapter 6

1   Porter, *Naval History of the Civil War*; D. Amen, *The Atlantic Coast* (New York, NY: Chas. Scribner's, 1883); A. T. Mahan, *The Gulf and Inland Waters* (New York, NY: Chas. Scribner's, 1883); J. R. Soley, *The Blockade and the Cruisers* (New York, NY: Chas. Scribner's, 1883); W. H. Roberts, *Now for the Contest: Coastal and Oceanic Naval Operations in the Civil War* (Lincoln, NE: University of Nebraska Press, 2004); J. M. McPherson, *War on the Waters: The Union & Confederate Navies, 1861–1865* (Chapel Hill, NC: University of North Carolina Press, 2012); S. R. Taafe, *Commanding Lincoln's Navy* (Annapolis, MD: Naval Institute Press, 2009); C. Symonds, *The Civil War at Sea* (New York, NY: Oxford University Press, 2012).

2   Lincoln to James C. Conkling, August 26, 1863 in Basler et al. *The Collected Works of Abraham Lincoln*, Vol. VI, p. 409.

3   "Piece by Piece, the Civil War's *Monitor* Is Pulled From the Atlantic's Depths", *The New York Times*, July 18, 2002.

4   Soley, *The Blockade and the Cruisers*; McPherson, *War on the Waters*.

5   L. E. Davis and S. L. Engerman, *Naval Blockades in Peace and War: An Economic History Since 1750* (New York, NY: Cambridge University Press, 2006), pp. 32–33, 127, 129; L. Owsley, Sr., *King Cotton Diplomacy* (Tuscaloosa, AL: University of Alabama Press, 2008); Soley, *The Blockade and the Cruisers*; R. B. Ekelund, Jr., and M. Thornton, *Tariffs, Blockades, and Inflation: The Economics of the Civil War* (Wilmington, DE: Scholarly Resources, 2004).

6   Symonds, *The Civil War at Sea*, pp. 61, 66.

7   D. D. Porter, *Incidents and Anecdotes of the Civil War* (New York, NY: D. Appleton, 1885), p. 174.

8   Moore, *The Rebellion Record*, Vol. 2 (1862), "Rumors & Incidents," p. 31; Vol. 2 (1863), February 20, 1863; "A Former Citizen Turned Traitor," *Daily Dispatch* (Richmond), February 17, 1863; *New York Evening Journal*, February 21, 1863; "Arrivals in the City," *The New York Times*, February 21, 1863; "Arrest of Col. Charles Carroll Hicks," *The New York Times*, February 21, 1863.

9   Symonds, *The Civil War at Sea*, p. 68.

10 J. Black, *Western Warfare, 1775–1882* (Bloomington, IN: Indiana University Press, 2001), p. 78.

11 R. Carse, *Blockade: The Civil War at Sea* (New York, NY: Rinehart and Company, 1958), p. 41.

12 Porter, *Incidents and Anecdotes of the Civil War*; C. M. Robinson III, *Hurricane of Fire: The Union Assault on Fort Fishery* (Annapolis, MD: Naval Institute Press, 1998); C. G. Hearn, *Admiral David Dixon Porter: The Civil War Years* (Annapolis, MD: Naval Institute Press, 1996); "The Blockade Service," *The New York Times*, November 14, 1863; "Dodging the Blockaders," *The New York Times*, September 18, 1892; *Dictionary of American Naval Fighting Ships* [website] <https://www.history.navy.mil/research/histories/ship-histories/danfs.html>, accessed July 2017; D. J. Ringle, *Life in Mr. Lincoln's Navy* (Annapolis, MD: Naval Institute Press, 1998).

13 On Farragut's early life and naval career, see C. L. Lewis, *David Glasgow Farragut: Admiral in the Making* (Annapolis, MD: Naval Institute Press, 2014).

14 L. Fink, *Sweatshops at Sea* (Chapel Hill, NC: University of North Carolina Press, 2011), p. 49.

15   D. W. Miller, *Second Only to Grant: Quartermaster General Montgomery C. Meigs* (Shippensburg, PA: White Mane, 2001), p. 84.

16   R. W. Donnelly, *Biographical Sketches of the Commissioned Officers of the Confederate States Marine Corps* (Shippensburg, PA: White Mane, 2001).

17   McPherson, *War on the Waters*, p. 101.

18   See, for example, K. B. Jeffrey (ed.), *Two Civil Wars: The Curious Shared Journal of a Baton Rouge Schoolgirl and a Union Sailor on the USS* Essex (Baton Rouge, LA: Louisiana State University Press, 2016), pp. 124, 127.

19   Ringle, *Life in Mr. Lincoln's Navy*, pp. 5, 70–71.

20   W. Whyte, "The Brooklyn Navy Yard," *Northern Mariner*, XXII/4 (2012), p. 394.

21   D. G. Surdam, "The Union Navy's Blockade Reconsidered," *Newport Papers*, Autumn 1998, p. 1.

22   Taafe, *Commanding Lincoln's Navy*, p. xi.

23   Roberts, *Now for the Contest*, p. 103.

24   Surdam, "The Union Navy's Blockade Reconsidered," p. 1.

Chapter 7

1   W. Rybczynski, *A Clearing in the Distance: Frederick Law Olmsted and America in the 19th Century* (New York, NY: Scribner's, 2000); E. B. Furgurson, *Freedom Rising: Washington in the Civil War* (New York, NY: Alfred A. Knopf, 2004), p. 305.

2   H. Kyriakodis, *Logan Square, Lincoln & The Great Sanitary Fair of 1864* [website] <http://hiddencityphila.org/2014/06/logan-square-president-lincoln-the-great-sanitary-fair-of-1864/>, accessed March, 2016.

3   *Report of the Treasurer of the Metropolitan Fair: In Aid of the United States Sanitary Commission, Held in New York City, April, 1864, to August 1st, 1864* (New York, NY: J. F. Trow, 1864); "Metropolitan Fair; The Grand Opening Yesterday," *The New York Times*, April 5, 1864; "The Metropolitan Fair; A Week of Great Success," *The New York Times*, April 11, 1864; "The Metropolitan Fair; Closing of the Great Exhibition," *The New York Times*, April 24, 1864; "Art Department of the Metropolitan Fair in aid of the United States Sanitary Commission," *The New York Times*, August 12, 1864.

4   "Munificence of the Police," *The New York Times*, April 1, 1864.

5   M. E. Neely, Jr., *The Boundaries of American Political Culture in the Civil War Era* (Chapel Hill, NC: University of North Carolina Press, 2005), pp. 71–73.

6   Einolf, *George Thomas*, p. 223; E. Clark, *History of the Seventh Regiment of New York, 1806–1889*, Vol. 2, pp. 121–22.

7   M. B. Chestnut (I. D. Martin and M Lockett, eds.), *A Diary from Dixie*, (New York, NY: D. Appleton and Company, 1905), entries for August 18, 22, 1861, and January 8, 1862.

8   P. Y. Pember, *A Southern Woman's Story: Life in Confederate Richmond* (New York, NY: G. W. Carleton/London, UK: Sampson Low, 1879); M. Greenberg, *Phoebe Yates Levy Pember* [website] <http://jwa.org/encyclopedia/article/pember-phoebe-yates-levy>, accessed May 2016.

9   L. J. Daniel, *Battle of Stones River: The Forgotten Conflict between the Confederate Army of Tennessee and the Union Army of the Cumberland* (Baton Rouge, LA: Louisiana State University Press, 2012), pp. 6, 8, 12, 26; G. W. Gallagher, *Becoming Confederates: Paths to a New National*

Loyalty (Athens, GA: University of Georgia Press, 2013), p. 37; D. G. Moore, *William S. Rosecrans and the Union Victory* (Jefferson, NC: McFarland, 2013), pp. 58ff.; P. Magid, *George Crook: From the Redwoods to Appomattox* (Norman, OK: University of Oklahoma Press, 2011), pp. 6, 290–97, 335; R. Kenzer, *Civil War Widows* [website] <http://www.encyclopediavirginia.org/Civil_War_Widows>, accessed July 2017.

10   S. Barile, *Undaunted Heart: The True Story of a Southern Belle & a Yankee General* (Hillsborough, NC: Eno Publishers, 2009); J. G. Barrett, *The Civil War in North Carolina* (Chapel Hill, NC: University of North Carolina Press, 1963), p. 385, note.

11   New York, NY: Harper & Brothers, 1867.

12   J. D. Hacker, "A Census-Based Count of the Civil War Dead," *Civil War History*, 57/4 (December 2011), pp. 306–34.

13   D. R. Petriello, *Bacteria and Bayonets: The Impact of Disease in American Military History* (Philadelphia, PA: Casemate, 2016), p. 155.

14   L. M. Hauptman, *Between Two Fires: American Indians in the Civil War* (New York, NY: The Free Press, 1995), p.36.

15   R. B. McCaslin, *Tainted Breeze: The Great Hanging at Gainesville, Texas 1862* (Baton Rouge, LA: Louisiana State University Press, 1994); J. L. Clark (ed. L. D. Clark), *Civil War Recollections of James Lemuel Clark and the Great Hanging at Gainesville, Texas in October 1862* (College Station, TX: Texas A&M University Press, 1984).

16   Email, Gregory Urwin, December 30, 2003.

17   Bernstein, *The Draft Riots*; Cook, *The Armies of the Streets*; P. Quinn, *Banished Children of Eve* (New York, NY: Penguin, 1995).

18   V. E. Bynum, *The Free State of Jones: Mississippi's Longest Civil War* (Chapel Hill, NC: University of North Carolina, 2001).

19   Hauptman, *Between Two Fires*, p. 92; M. M. Stith, *Extreme Civil War: Guerrilla Warfare, Environment, and Race on the Trans-Mississippi Frontier* (Baton Rouge, LA: Louisiana State University Press, 2016), p. 160.

20   A. A. Nofi, "Some Unsung Casualties of the War," *North & South*, VIII/7 (January 2006), pp. 8–9.

21   C. B. Kelly and I. S. Kelly, *Best Little Stories of the Blue and Gray* (Nashville, TN: Cumberland House, 2006), p. 65.

22   Moore, *The Rebellion Record*, Vol. III, p. 25.

23   B. I. Wiley, *The Life of Johnny Reb* (Indianapolis, IN: Bobbs Merrill, 1943), p. 123, citing L. M. Johnson, *Elementary Arithmetic: Designed for Beginners* (Raleigh, SC: Branson & Farrar, 1864).

24   N. Silber, *Daughters of the Union: Northern Women Fight the Civil War* (Cambridge, MA: Harvard University Press, 2005), pp. 17, 49, 82, *et passim*.

25   F. W. Dawson (ed. B. I. Wiley), *Reminiscences of Confederate Service, 1861–1865* (Baton Rouge, LA: Louisiana State University Press, 1980), p. 52.

26   J. M. Schmidt and G. R. Hasegawa, *Years of Change and Suffering: Modern Perspectives on Civil War Medicine* (Roseville, MN: Edinborough Press, 2009), p. 47.

27   M. Twain, *Roughing It* (Hartford, CT: The American Publishing Co., 1873), pp. 314–20.

28   K. Canavan, *Lincoln's Final Hours: Conspiracy, Terrors, and the Assassination of America's Greatest President* (Lexington, KY: University Press of Kentucky, 2015), p. 12.

29   M. Dugard, *The Training Ground: Grant, Lee, Sherman, and Davis in the Mexican War, 1846–1848* (Lincoln, NE: University of Nebraska Press, 2009), p. 53.

30 R. U. Delauter, Jr., *Winchester in the Civil War* (Lynchburg, VA, 1992), pp. 108–18; R. R. Duncan, *Beleaguered Winchester: A Virginia Community at War, 1861–1865* (Baton Rouge, LA: Louisiana State University Press, 2007), p. 196.

31 T. H. Smith, "A Tour of Gettysburg's Visual Damage," *Adams County History*, Vol. II (1996), pp. 66, 71, notes 72–74, available at [website] <http://cupola.gettysburg.edu/cgi/viewcontent.cgi?article=1007&context=ach>.

32 A. A. Nofi, "The Cooper Shop," *North & South*, IV/5 (June 2001), p. 9.

33 Clark, *Last Train South*, p. 9.

34 Furgurson, *Freedom Rising*, p. 245.

35 T. C. Jepsen, *Women Telegraph Operators in the Civil War* [website] <http://www.mindspring.com/~tjepsen/civilwar.htm>, accessed December 2015.

Chapter 8

1 E. J. Warner, *Generals in Gray: Lives of the Confederate Commanders* (Baton Rouge, LA: Louisiana State University Press, 1959), and *Generals in Blue: Lives of the Union Commanders* (Baton Rouge, LA: Louisiana State University Press, 1964); Cullum, *Biographical Register of the Officers and Graduates of the United States Military Academy at West Point, New York*; Heitman, *Historical Register and Dictionary of the United States Army*.

2 A. A. Nofi, "The Decapitation of the Virginia Militia," *North & South*, XII/3 (September 2010), pp. 6–8.

3 C. Wittke, *Refugees of Revolution: The German Forty-Eighters in America* (Philadelphia, PA: University of Pennsylvania Press, 1952), pp. 233–35.

4 McEnany. *For Brotherhood and Duty*, p. 341; L. Betros, *Carved From Granite: West Point Since 1902* (College Station, TX: Texas A&M University Press, 2012), pp. 14, 332, note 48.

5 J. L. Morrison, "Educating the Civil War Generals," *Military Affairs*, 38 (September 1974), pp. 108ff.; M. Moten, *The Delafield Commission and the American Military Profession* (College Station, TX: Texas A&M, 2000), p. 35.

6 W. L. Ostrander and E. S. Holden, *The Centennial of the United States Military Academy at West Point*, 2 vols. (Washington, DC: Government Printing Office, 1904), Vol. 2 p. 55.

7 W. J. Wood, *Civil War Generalship: The Art of Command* (New York, NY: DaCapo Press, 2001), p. 96.

8 S. E. Ambrose, *Duty, Honor Country: A History of West Point* (Baltimore, MD: Johns Hopkins University Press, 1999), pp. 132–33.

9 Einolf, *George Thomas*, p. 62.

10 J. C. Mason, *Until Antietam: The Life and Letters of Major General Israel B. Richardson, U.S. Army* (Carbondale, IL: Southern Illinois University Press, 2009), p. 8.

11 T. J. Goss, *The War within the Union High Command* (Lawrence, KS: University Press of Kansas, 2003), p.10.

12 E. F. Puryear, Jr., *American Generalship, Character is Everything: The Art of Command* (Novato, CA: Presidio Press, 2000), p. 152.

13 Lowe, *Meade's Army, passim*; J. D. Welsh, *Medical Histories of the Union Generals* (Kent, OH: Kent State University Press, 1996), and *Medical Histories of the Confederate Generals* (Kent, OH: Kent State University Press, 1995), *passim*; R. H. Beattie, *Army of the Potomac: Birth of Command, November 1860–September 1861* (New York, NY: DaCapo, 2002), pp. xxxiii,

331, 344, 303, 352; Polk and Abadie, *Faulkner and War*, p. 14; Elliott, *Soldier of Tennessee*, p. 177; L. J. Daniel, *Days of Glory: The Army of the Cumberland, 1861–1865* (Baton Rouge, LA: Louisiana State University Press, 2004), p. 6; Furgurson, *Freedom Rising*, p. 22; D. L. Gibboney, *Scandals of the Civil War* (Shippensburg, PA: Burd Street Press, 2005), *passim*; W. Mahood, *Alexander "Fighting Elleck" Hays: The Life of a Civil War General, From West Point to the Wilderness* (Jefferson, NC: McFarland & Co., 2005), pp. 179–81; Kelly and Kelly, *Best Little Stories of the Blue and Gray*, p. 99; Glatthaar, *General Lee's Army*, p. 352; B. S. Allardice and L. L. Hewitt (eds.), *Kentuckians in Gray: Confederate Generals and Field Officers of the Bluegrass State* (Lexington, KY: University Press of Kentucky, 2008), pp. 6, 63; Einolf, *George Thomas*, p. 119; T. J. Goree, *Longstreet's Aide: The Civil War Letters of Major Thomas J. Goree* (Charlottesville, VA: University Press of Virginia, 1995), p. 53; C. Symonds, *Confederate Admiral: The Life of Franklin Buchanan* (Annapolis, MD: Naval Institute Press, 1999), p. 55ff.; M. E. Neely, Jr., *Southern Rights: Political Prisoners and the Myth of Confederate Constitutionalism* (Charlottesville, VA: University Press of Virginia, 1995), pp. 17–18.

14 G. Welles (W. E. Gienapp and E. L. Gienapp, eds.), *The Civil War Diary of Gideon Welles, Lincoln's Secretary of the Navy: The Original Manuscript Edition* (Urbana, IL: University of Illinois Press, 2015), p. xviii.

15 P. Magid, *The Gray Fox: George Crook and the Indian Wars* (Norman, OK: University of Oklahoma, 2015), p. 66.

16 Ibid., especially pp. 94–95.

17 Wayne Fanebust, *Major General Alexander M. McCook, U.S.A.* (Jefferson, N.C.: McFarland, 2012), p. 33

18 Daniel, *Battle of Stones River*, p. 17; Dunkerly, *The Confederate Surrender at Greensboro*, p. 7.

19 A. A. Nofi, "General Early's 'Stone Wall' Punch," *North & South*, XIV/3 (September 2012), pp. 7–8.

20 L. H. Harrison, "John C. Breckinridge: Nationalist, Confederate, Kentuckian," *The Filson Club History Quarterly*, 47 (April 1973), p. 134; Daniel, *Battle of Stones River*, p. 17.

21 J. B. Jones, Jr., *Tennessee in the Civil War* (Jefferson, NC: McFarland, 2011), p. 35, citing *Official Records I*, Vol. 10, ii, p. 379, March 31, 1862; J. N. Lash, *A Politician Turned General: The Civil War Career of Stephen Augustus Hurlbut* (Kent, OH: Kent State University Press, 2003), pp. viii.

22 Lash, *A Politician Turned General*, pp. viii.

23 Goree, *Longstreet's Aide*, p. 53.

24 G. W. Gallagher, *Lee and his Generals in War and Memory* (Baton Rouge, LA: Louisiana State University Press, 2004), p. 120–21.

25 D. Evans, *Sherman's Horsemen: Union Cavalry Operations in the Atlanta Campaign* (Bloomington, IN: Indiana University Press, 1996), p. 211.

26 J. L. Huston, *Stephen A. Douglas and the Dilemmas of Democratic Equality* (New York, NY: Rowman and Littlefield, 2007), p. 15.

27 D. Lee, *Thomas J. Wood: A Biography of the Union General in the Civil War* (Jefferson, NC: McFarland, 2012), pp. 81–82.

28 Conner, *General Gordon Granger*, pp. 2, 221; Lash, *A Politician Turned General*, pp. viii.

29 Lash, *A Politician Turned General*, pp. viii; *Was Hooker Drunk at Chancellorsville?* [website] <http://battlecryfreedom.blogspot.com/2009/03/was-hooker-drunk-at-chancellorsville.html>, accessed July 2017.

30 Lash, *A Politician Turned General*, pp. viii, 27, etc.

31 Daniel, *Days of Glory*, p. 161; D. W. Belcher, *General David S. Stanley, U.S.A.: A Civil War Biography* (Jefferson, NC: McFarland, 2014), pp. 162, 229, *et passim*.

32 D. J. Sheffer, *The Buffalo Soldiers: Their Epic Story and Major Campaigns* (Santa Barbara, CA: ABC Clio, 2015), p. 18.

33 J. Anderson, *The Fifty-Seventh Regiment of Massachusetts Volunteers in the War of the Rebellion* (Boston, MA: Stillings & Co., 1896), p. 140.

34 B. B. Smith and N. B. Baker (eds.), *Burning Rails as We Pleased: The Civil War Letters of William Garrigues Bentley, 104th Ohio Volunteer Infantry* (Jefferson, NC: McFarland & Co, 2011), p. 19.

35 Anderson, *The Fifty-seventh Regiment of Massachusetts Volunteers in the War of the Rebellion*, p. 140.

36 C. B. Kelly and I. S. Kelly, *Best Little Ironies, Oddities, and Mysteries of the Civil War* (Nashville, TN: Cumberland House, 2000), p. 184.

37 M. A. Eggleston, *President Lincoln's Recruiter: General Lorenzo Thomas and the United States Colored Troops in the Civil War* (Jefferson, NC: McFarland, 2013), pp. 17, 58, 95; Lash, *A Politician Turned General*, pp. viii.

38 S. M. Chick, *The Battle of Petersburg, June 15–18, 1864* (Lincoln, NE: Potomac Books, 2015), p. 45; R. B. Williams (ed.), *Stonewall's Prussian Mapmaker: The Journals of Captain Oscar Hinrichs* (Chapel Hill, NC: University of North Carolina Press, 2014), p. 133 (June 7, 1864).

39 G. A. Patterson, *From Blue to Gray: The Life of Confederate General Cadmus M. Wilcox* (Mechanicsburg, PA: Stackpole, 2001), p. 86.

40 Welsh, *Medical Histories of the Confederate Generals* and *Medical Histories of the Union Generals*; R. I. Girard, *The Civil War Generals: Comrades, Peers, Rivals—In their Own Words* (Minneapolis, MN: Zenith Press, 2013), pp. 8, 44, 101, 181, 214; M. Dugard, *The Training Ground: Grant, Lee, Sherman, and Davis in the Mexican War, 1846–1848* (Lincoln, NE: University of Nebraska Press, 2009), p. 63.

41 W. C. Davis and J. Hoffman, *The Confederate General* (n.p.: National Historical Society, 1991), Vol. I, p. 59.

42 Allardice and Hewitt, *Kentuckians in Gray*, p. 50.

43 W. H. Bragg, *Griswoldville* (Macon, GA: Mercer University Press, 2000), p. 40.

44 K. Getchell, *Scapegoat of Shiloh: The Distortion of Lew Wallace's Record by U.S. Grant* (Jefferson, NC: McFarland, 2013), p. 121.

45 St. J. Richardson Liddel (N. C. Hughes, Jr., ed.), *Liddell's Record: St. John Richardson Liddell, Brigadier General, CSA Staff Officer and Brigade Command, Army of Tennessee* (Baton Rouge, LA: Louisiana State University Press, 1985), p. 105.

46 Allardice and Hewitt, *Kentuckians in Gray*, p 190; Welsh, *Medical Histories of the Confederate Generals*, pp. 154–55.

47 Smith, *Corinth 1862*, p. xiii.

48 *Leonidas Polk: Southern Civil War General* [website] <http://www.historynet.com/leonidas-polk-southern-civil-war-general.htm>, accessed June 2015.

49 Walsh, *Medical Histories of the Confederate Generals*, p. 236.

50 L. Tagg, *Generals of Gettysburg: The Leaders of America's Greatest Battle* (New York, NY: Da Capo, 1998), p. 91.

51 R. A. Reis, *African Americans and the Civil War* (New York, NY: Chelsea House, 2009), p. 65; T. Lyman (ed. D. W. Lowe), *Meade's Army: The Private Notebooks of Lt. Col. Theodore Lyman* (Kent, OH: Kent State University Press, 2007), p. 227.

52 McPherson, *War on the Waters*, p. 110.

53 M. Burlingame (ed.), *Abraham Lincoln: The Observations of John G. Nicolay and John Hay* (Carbondale, IL: Southern Illinois University, 2007), p. 75; H. Haupt, *Moving the Union Army: Reminiscences of General Herman Haupt* (Milwaukee, WI: Wright and Joys Co., 1901).

54 D. M. Jordan, *Winfield Scott Hancock: A Soldier's Life* (Bloomington, IN: Indiana University Press, 1996), p. 103.

55 C. A. Dana, *Recollections of the Civil War: With the Leader at Washington and in the Field* (New York, NY: D. Appleton, 1902), p. 66; Walsh, *Medical Histories of the Union Generals*, p. 200.

56 Daniel, *Battle of Stones River*, p. 12.

57 R. I. Girardi, "Leonidas Polk and the Fate of Kentucky in 1861," in L. L. Hewitt and A. W. Bergeron (eds.), *Confederate Generals in the Western Theater: Essays on America's Civil War*, Vol. III (Knoxville, TN: University of Tennessee Press, 2011), p. 8.

58 Lee, *Thomas J. Wood*, p. 47; Daniel, *Battle of Stones River*, p. 20.

59 D. B. Connelly, *John M. Schofield and the Politics of Generalship* (Chapel Hill, NC: The University of North Carolina Press, 2006), p. 129.

60 W. C. Jameson, *Lost Treasures of American History* (London & New York: Taylor Trade, 2006), p. 117.

61 H. Newsome, *Richmond Must Fall: The Richmond–Petersburg Campaign, October 1864* (Kent, OH: Kent State University Press, 2013), p. 263.

62 Belcher, *General David S. Stanley*, p. 144.

63 L. Stallings, *The Doughboys: The Story of the AEF, 1917–1918* (New York, NY: Harper & Row, 1963), p. 341.

64 R. Collins, *General James G. Blunt: Tarnished Glory* (New York, NY: Pelican, 2005), p. 13.

65 C. L. Dufour, *Nine Men In Gray* (Garden City, NY: Doubleday, 1963), p. 231.

66 Beattie, *Army of the Potomac: McClellan Takes Command*, p. 473; Daniel, *Days of Glory*, pp. 19, 40; G. Rhea, *Cold Harbor: Grant and Lee, May 26–June 3, 1864* (Baton Rouge, LA: Louisiana State University Press, 2007), p. 12; Einolf, *George Thomas*, p. 134; N. C. Hughes, Jr., and G. D. Whitney, *Jefferson Davis in Blue: The Life of Sherman's Relentless Warrior* (Baton Rouge, LA: Louisiana State University Press, 2002), pp. 103-104; Duncan, *Beleaguered Winchester*, p. 193; G. Ecelbarger, *Three Days in the Shenandoah Valley: Stonewall Jackson at Front Royal and Winchester* (Norman, OK: University of Oklahoma Press, 2008), p 198; M. K. Christ, *Civil War Arkansas, 1863: The Battle for a State* (Norman, OK: University of Oklahoma Press, 2010), p. 100; Mason, *Until Antietam*, p.115.

67 W. Fanebust, *Major General Alexander M. McCook, U.S.A.* (Jefferson, NC: McFarland, 2012), p. 138; C. J. Manvillen *The Limits Of Obedience: Brigadier General Thomas J. Wood's Performance during the Battle of Chickamauga* (n.p.: CreateSpace Independent Publishing Platform, 2014).

68 J. T. Glatthaar, *The March to the Sea and Beyond: Sherman's Troops in the Savannah and Carolinas Campaign* (Baton Rouge, LA: Louisiana State University, 1985), p. 24.

69 Einolf, *George Thomas*, p. 134.

70 McPherson, *War on the Waters*, p. 110.

71 G. C. Rable, *God's Almost Chosen Peoples: A Religious History of the American Civil War* (Chapel Hill, NC: University of North Carolina Press, 2010), p. 98; U. W. Ent, *The

Pennsylvania Reserves in the Civil War: A Comprehensive History (Jefferson, NC: McFarland, 2014), p. 239.

72 Welles, *The Civil War Diary of Gideon Welles*, p. 218.

73 Rable, *God's Almost Chosen Peoples*, pp. 98–99.

74 Venter, *Kill Jeff Davis*, p. 289; W. D. Hamilton, *Recollections of a Cavalryman* (Columbus, OH: F. J. Heer, 1915), p. 152.

75 K. Poulter, "Some Thoughts on Confederate Strategy," *North & South*, XIV/5 (2013), p. 20.

76 R. D. Evans, *A Sailor's Log: Recollections of Forty Years of Naval Life* (New York, NY: D. Appleton, 1908), p. 61.

77 A. R. Trulock, *In the Hands of Providence: Joshua L. Chamberlain and the American Civil War* (Chapel Hill, NC: University of North Carolina Press, 1992), p. 177.

78 Hughes and Whitney, *Jefferson Davis in Blue*, pp. 103–04; J. Pope (P. Cozzens and R. I. Girardi, eds.), *The Military Memoirs of General John Pope* (Chapel Hill, NC: University of North Carolina Press, 1998), p. 259, note 31.

79 Pope, *Military Memoirs*, p. 259, note 31.

80 Mason, *Until Antietam*, pp. 43, 158.

81 W. M. Lamers, *The Edge of Glory: A Biography of General William S. Rosecrans, U.S.A.* (Baton Rouge, LA: Louisiana State University, 2009), pp. xi, 127.

82 *The Civil War: A Visual History* (New York, NY: Penguin Random House, 2011), p. 271; P. A. Hutton, *Phil Sheridan and his Army* (Norman, OK: University of Oklahoma Press, 1999), p. 13; Lamers, *The Edge of Glory*, p. 127.

83 Trulock, *In the Hands of Providence*, p. 177.

84 Lee, *Thomas J. Wood*, pp. 60, 107.

85 G. Rhea, *To the North Anna River: Grant and Lee, May 13–25, 1864* (Baton Rouge, LA: Louisiana State University Press, 2005), p. 20.

86 J. L. Hallock, *Braxton Bragg and Confederate Defeat* (Tuscaloosa, AL: University of Alabama Press, 1991), Vol. II, p. 141.

87 Daniel, *Battle of Stones River*, p. 17.

88 B. F. Cooling III, *Jubal Early: Robert E. Lee's Bad Old Man* (Lanham, MD: Rowman & Littlefield, 2014), p. xiii; G. Walsh, *Damage Them All You Can: Robert E. Lee's Army of Northern Virginia* (New York, NY: Tom Doherty, 2002), p. 273; T. R. Moss, "Jubal Anderson Early: Glory to Ignominy, His Shenandoah Valley Campaign," Master's thesis, University of North Carolina at Chapel Hill (1981), p. 3.

89 B. Farwell, *Stonewall: A Biography of General Thomas J. Jackson* (New York, NY: W. W. Norton, 1993), p. 255; J. C. Griffin, *A Pictorial History of the Confederacy* (Jefferson, NC: McFarland, 2004), p. 56; C. K. Bleser and L. J. Gordon (eds.), *Intimate Strategies of the Civil War: Military Commanders and their Wives* (New York, NY: Oxford University Press, 2001), p. 98.

90 M. R. Bradley, *Nathan Bedford Forrest's Escort and Staff* (Gretna, LA: Pelican Publishing, 2006), p. 72; B. H. Beck, *Streight's Foiled Raid on the Western & Atlantic Railroad: Emma Sansom's Courage and Bedford Forrest's Pursuit* (Charleston, SC: The History Press, 2016), p. 36; "Book Notices," *Methodist Review*, 81 (November 1899), p. 1,012.

91 Farwell, *Stonewall*, p. 200.

92 *William Wing Loring* [website] <https://tshaonline.org/handbook/online/articles/flo77>, accessed March 2016.

93 Tagg, *Generals of Gettysburg*, p. 209.

94   T. Ayres, *A Military Miscellany: From Bunker Hill to Baghdad: Important, Uncommon, and Sometimes Forgotten Facts, Lists, and Stories from America's Rich Military History* (New York, NY: Bantam, 2008).

95   Einolf, *George Thomas*, p. 134.

96   E. B. Pryor, *Reading the Man: A Portrait of Robert E. Lee through his Private Letters* (New York, NY: Viking, 2007), p. 333.

97   J. L. McDonough, *Stones River: Bloody Winter in Tennessee* (Knoxville, TN: University of Tennessee Press, 1980), p. 168.

98   Allardice, *Confederate Colonels*; W. C. Davis, *Rhett: The Turbulent Life and Times of a Fire-Eater* (Columbia, SC: University of South Carolina Press, 2001), especially pp. 507ff.; *Official Records*, Series I, Vol. I, p. 51; *Official Records*, Series I, Vol. XIV, p. 15; C. R. Horres, Jr., "An Affair of Honor at Fort Sumter," *South Carolina Historical Magazine*, 102/1 (January 2001), pp. 6–26.

99   M. Murray, "Walt Whitman on Brother George and His Fifty-First New York Volunteers: An Uncollected New York Times Article," *Walt Whitman Quarterly Review*, 18/1 (2000), pp. 65–70; K. M. Price, "A Newly Discovered Photograph of George Washington Whitman," *Walt Whitman Quarterly Review*, 26 (spring 2009), pp. 216–17; R. Roper, "Jesse Whitman, Seafarer," *Walt Whitman Quarterly Review*, 26/1 (summer 2008), pp. 35–41.

100 Hattaway and Beringer, *Jefferson Davis*, p. 3.

101 Beattie, *Army of the Potomac: McClellan Takes Command*, p. 155.

102 D. Ball, *Army Regulars* (Norman, OK: University of Oklahoma, 2001), p. 191.

103 F. Grant, cited in *The National Magazine*, 29, p. 464; J. E. Smith, *Grant* (New York, NY: Simon & Schuster, 2001), p. 302.

104 J. L. Harsh, *Taken at the Flood: Robert E. Lee and Confederate Strategy in the Maryland Campaign of 1862* (Kent, OH: Kent State University Press, 1999), p. 154.

105 M. Gabriel, *Love and Capital: Karl and Jenny Marx and the Birth of a Revolution* (Londond, UK: Little, Brown & Co., 2011) pp. 139–40.

106 S. E. Woodworth, *No Band of Brothers: Problems of the Rebel High Command* (Columbia, MO: University of Missouri Press, 1999), p. 138.

107 Warner, *Generals in Blue*, p. 28.

108 S. E. Woodworth, *Six Armies in Tennessee: The Chickamauga and Chattanooga Campaigns* (Lincoln, NE: University of Nebraska Press, 1998), p. 4.

109 G. A. Patterson, *Debris of Battle* (Mechanicsburg, PA: Stackpole, 2003), p. 32.

110 W. M. Owen, *In Camp and Battle with the Washington Artillery of New Orleans* (Boston, MA: Boston, Ticknor & Co., 1885), p. 356.

Chapter 9

1   J. L. Smith, Jr., *How was the Revolutionary War Paid For?* [wesbite] <https://allthingsliberty.com/2015/02/how-was-the-revolutionary-war-paid-for/>, accessed April 2016.

2   *Tax History Museum 1861–1865: The Civil War* [website] <http://www.taxhistory.org/www/website.nsf/web/THM1861?OpenDocument>, accessed July 2017.

3   A. A. Nofi, "Money and Inflation," *North & South*, III/2 (January 2000), pp. 14–15; F. Noll, "Repudiation! The Crisis of United States Civil War Debt, 1865–1870," Graduate Institute

of International and Development Studies, Geneva, Pierre du Bois Foundation, available at <http://webdocs.stern.nyu.edu/old_web/economics/docs/Financial%20History/Spring%20 2013/Noll%20Civil%20War%20Debt%202013.pdf> [website], accessed April 2016.

4   A. A. Nofi, "J.P. Morgan Turns a Tidy Profit," *North & South*, I/2 (January 1998), pp. 10–11.

5   Miller, *Second Only to Grant*, p. 117.

6   Baslet et al., *The Collected Works of Abraham Lincoln*, Vol. VIII, pp. 240, 364; Welles, *The Civil War Diary of Gideon Welles*, pp. 352, note 29, 387, 426–27, 460, 575, 605–11; F. W. Smith, *The United States against Franklin W. Smith: Review of the Argument of the Judge Advocate* (Boston, MA: Alfred Mudge & Son, 1865); F. W. Smith, *The Conspiracy in the U.S. Navy Department* (New York, NY: Press of the American Publishing Company, 1890); *The New York Times*: "Thirty-eighth Congress, Second Session, Senate," January 29, 1865; "General News," February 16, 1865; "New From Washington," March 2, 1865; *The United States Army and Navy Journal and Gazette of the Regular and Volunteer Force* (New York, NY), January 27, 1866, p. 368.

7   "Political Affairs," *The New York Herald*, August 13, 1859, p. 2; A. G. Freehling, *Drift Toward Dissolution: The Virginia Slavery Debate of 1831–1832* (Baton Rouge. LA: University of Louisiana Press, 1982), pp. 124–25, citing C. H. Ambler (ed.), *The Life and Diary of John Floyd* (Richmond, VA: Richmond Press, 1918), p. 172

8   *The Washington Union*, June 2, 1858, p. 3.

9   G. S. Henig and E. Niderost, *Civil War Firsts: The Legacies of America's Bloodiest Conflict* (Mechanicsburg, PA: Stackpole, 2001), p. 4.

10   Grant, *Memoirs*, chapters XVI, XXII.

11   Cunningham, *Shiloh and the Western Campaign of 1862*, p. 57, note 40.

12   Gallagher, *Becoming Confederates*, p. 51.

13   Miller, *Second Only to Grant*, p. 58.

14   Castel, *Articles of War*, p. 8; A. H. Meneelen, *The War Department, 1861* (New York, NY: Columbia, 1928), p. 37.

15   Hattaway and Beringer, *Jefferson Davis*, p. 137

16   Furgurson, *Freedom Rising*, p. 110.

17   Glatthaar, *General Lee's Army*, p. 191.

18   H. S. Wilson, *Confederate Industry: Manufacturers and Quartermasters in the Civil War* (Columbia, MO: University of Missouri Press, 2002), pp. 70–74.

19   "Important Seizure and Arrest; Six Million of Confederate Bonds—One Million of Confederate Money," *The New York Times*, January 3, 1864; "Seizure of Confederate Bonds," *The New York Times*, January 4, 1864.

20   Robinson, *Hurricane of Fire*, p 26.

21   Duncan, *Beleaguered Winchester*, p. 44.

22   Cunningham, *Shiloh and the Western Campaign*, p. 210.

23   R. D. Hunt, *Colonels in Blue: New York* (Altglen, PA: Schiffer Military History, 2003), p. 95.

24   R. D. Hunt, *Colonels in Blue: The Mid-Atlantic States* (Mechanicsburg, PA: Stackpole, 2009), p. 243.

25   Evans, *Sherman's Horsemen*, p. 40.

26   Duncan, *Beleaguered Winchester*, p. 174.

27   E. C. Tidball, *No Disgrace to My Country: The Life of John C. Tidball* (Kent, OH: Kent State University Press, 2002), pp. 173–74.

28   W. H. Roberts, *Civil War Ironclads: The U.S. Navy and Industrial Mobilization* (Baltimore, OH: Johns Hopkins University Press, 2002), p. 197.

29   *The New York Times*, October 2, 2011, p. 13.

Chapter 10

1   T. K. Rabb and R. I. Rotberg (eds.), *Marriage and Fertility: Studies in Interdisciplinary History* (Princeton, NJ: Princeton University Press, 2014), p. 363.

2   T. P. Lowry, *The Story the Soldiers Wouldn't Tell: Sex in the Civil War* (Mechanicsburg, PA: Stackpole Books, 1994); E. S. Barber and C. F. Ritter, "Dangerous Liaisons: Working Women and Sexual Justice in the American Civil War," *European Journal of American Studies*, 10/1 (2015).

3   Wiley, *The Life of Billy Yank*, pp. 257–62; A. Winkworth, "Sex and the Civil War: A Medical Perspective," New South Wales Chapter, American Civil War Round Table of Australia (August 2005), available at [website] <http://www.americancivilwar.asn.au/meet/2005_08_mtg_sex_and_the_civil_war.pdf>, accessed June 2015; S. Thompson, "Prostitution in the Civil War," lecture, Gettysburg College, April 13, 2011, available at [website] <http://www.c-span.org/video/?299007-1/prostitution-civil-war>, accessed June 2015.

4   *Sex and the Civil War* [website] https://oldtowncrier.com/2014/12/01/sex-and-the-civil-war, accessed July 2017; Furgurson, *Freedom Rising*, p. 207.

5   D. E. Sutherland, *Expansion of Everyday Life, 1860–1876* (Fayetteville, AR: University of Arkansas Press, 2000), p. 11; D. J. Cole, "Public Women in Public Spaces: Prostitution and Union Military Experience, 1861–1865, Master's Thesis, University of Tennessee, 2007. http://trace.tennessee.edu/utk_gradthes/273, accessed Aug. 10, 2016

6   C. Clinton, "Public Women and Sexual Politics during the American Civil War," in C. Clinton and N. Silber (eds.), *Battle Scars: Gender and Sexuality in the American Civil War* (Oxford and New York: Oxford University Press, 2006), pp. 63ff.; C. E. Swedberg (ed.), *Three Years with the 92nd Illinois: The Civil War Diary of John M. King*, (Mechanicsburg, PA: Stackpole, 1999), pp. 52–53; Cole, "Public Women in Public Spaces."

7   W. J. Fraser, Jr., *Savannah in the Old South* (Athens, GA: University of Georgia Press, 2005), p. 289; Winkworth, "Sex and the Civil War."

8   Clinton, "Public Women and Sexual Politics during the American Civil War," p. 70; *Sex and the City of Richmond: Prostitution on Second Street* [website] <https://urmappingamericanhistory.wordpress.com/2011/02/21/390/>, accessed July 2017.

9   Furgurson, *Freedom Rising*, p. 207.

10   L. G. Kautz, *August Valentine Kautz, USA: Biography of a Civil War General* (Jefferson, NC: McFarland, 2008), pp. 51–52.

11   *Jubal Early's Children* [website] <http://civilwartalk.com/threads/jubal-earlys-children.84586/>, accessed August, 2015; *Alexander and Sally Turner* [website] <http://brattleborohistory.com/slavery/alexander-turner.html>, accessed August 2015; T. P. Lowry, *Sexual Misbehavior in the Civil War: A Compendium* (n.p.: Xlibris, 2006), p. 264.

12   C. F. Adams, Jr., *Charles Francis Adams, 1835–1915: An Autobiography* (Boston, MA and New York, NY: Houghton Mifflin, 1916), p. 161.

13   Lowry, *The Story the Soldiers Wouldn't Tell*, pp. 143–45.

14 Jameson, *Lost Treasures of American History*, p. 117.

15 R. G. Hartje, *Van Dorn: The Life and Times of a Confederate General* (Nashville, TN: Vanderbilt University Press, 1994); A. B. Carter, *The Tarnished Cavalier: Major General Earl Van Dorn, C.S.A.* (Nashville, TN: University of Tennessee Press, 1999).

16 Nofi, *A Civil War Treasury*, pp. 232–33.

17 M. Blitz, *Meet the Madam on the Mall* [website] <http://www.smithsonianmag.com/history/meet-madam-mall-180954371/>, accessed October 2016; F. X. Clines, "Archeology Find: Capital's Best Little Brothel," *The New York Times*, April 18, 1999; D. J. Seiferet, B. B. O'Brien, and J. Balicki, "Mary Ann Hall's First-Class House: The Archaeology of a Capital Brothel," in R. A. Schmidt and B. L. Voss (eds.), *Archaeologies of Sexuality* (New York, NY: Routledge, 2000), pp. 117–28; E. J. Himelfarb, "Capitol Sex," *Archeology* (July/August 1999); D. J. Seifert and J. Balicki, "Mary Ann Hall's House," *Historical Archeology* (2005), pp. 59–73; R. S. Pohl, *Wicked Capitol Hill: An Unruly History of Behaving Badly* (Stroud, UK: History Press, 2012), pp. 97–99; H. D. Winkler, *Lincoln's Ladies: The Women in the Life of the Sixteenth President* (Nashville, TN: Cumberland House, 2004), pp. 123–24.

18 C. K. Bleser (ed.), *Secret and Sacred: The Diaries of James Henry Hammond, a Southern Slaveholder* (New York, NY: Oxford University Press, 1988), pp. 171, 175 *et passim*; C. K. Bleser, *The Hammonds of Redcliffe* (Oxford, UK: Oxford University Press, 1981), pp. 9–18.

19 Glatthaar, *General Lee's Army*, p. 229.

20 E. C. Macartney, *Grant and his Generals* (New York, NY: McBride: 1953), p. 153; J. F. Marszalek, *Commander of All Lincoln's Armies: A Life of General Henry W. Halleck* (Cambridge, MA: Belknap/Harvard University Press, 2004), p. 111.

21 Welsh, *Medical Histories of the Confederate Generals*, p. 23.

22 S. Robertson, *Age of Consent Laws* [website] <https://chnm.gmu.edu/cyh/case-studies/230>, and <https://chnm.gmu.edu/cyh/primary-sources/24>, accessed September 2016; *The New York Times*, July 10, 1860.

23 Lowry, *Sexual Misbehavior in the Civil War*, p. 257.

24 *Official Records*, Series III, Vol. I, pp. 855–58.

25 Lowry, *Sexual Misbehavior in the Civil War*, p. 265.

26 Lowry, *The Story the Soldiers Wouldn't Tell*, p. 160. 28 R. D. Hunt and J. R. Brown, *Brevet Brigadier Generals in Blue* (Gaithersburg, MD: Olde Soldier Books, Inc., 1990), p. 575.

27 R. D. Hunt and J. R. Brown, *Brevet Brigadier Generals in Blue* (Gaithersburg, MD: Olde Soldier Books, Inc., 1990), p. 575.

Chapter 11

1 Adapted from A. A. Nofi, "Who Served? Soldiers' Occupations During the American Civil War," *North & South*, I/1 (1997), pp. 8–9.

2 Hauptman, *Between Two Fires*, pp. x, xii–xiv, 22, 50, 75, 78–85, 92, 113; R. Hartwell (ed.), *The Confederate Reader: How the South Saw the War* (New York, NY: Dover Publications, Inc., 1989), pp. 310–15; J. Monaghan, *Civil War on the Western Border 1854–1865* (Boston, MA: Little, Brown & Co., 1955), p. 250; W. L. Shea and E. J. Hess, *Pea Ridge: Civil War Campaign in the West* (Chapel Hill, NC: The University of North Carolina Press, 1991), p. 102; P. L. Faust (ed.), *Historical Times Illustrated Encyclopedia of the Civil War* (New York,

NY: Harper Perennial, 1986), pp. 381, 556; Lause, *The Collapse of Price's Raid*, p. 5; J. P. Collins, "Native Americans in the Census, 1860–1890," *Prologue*, 38/2 (2006).

3   J. D. Hoptak, *Nicholas Biddle: The Civil War's First Blood* [website] <http://www.historynet. com/nicholas-biddle-first-blood.htm>, accessed April 2016.

4   Pierson, *Lt. Spalding in Civil War Louisiana*, p. 37.

5   "Affairs in the West; A Negro Regiment in Action," *The New York Times*, November 19, 1862.

6   Grant, *Personal Memoirs*, Chapter XXXVII.

7   B. Tap, *The Fort Pillow Massacre: North, South, and the Status of African Americans in the Civil War Era* (New York, NY: Routledge, 2014), pp. 129–30.

8   J. K. Bryant, II, *The 36th Infantry United States Colored Troops in the Civil War: A History and Roster* (Jefferson, NC: McFarland, 2012), p. 5; A. J. Bailey, *Invisible Southerners: Ethnicity in the Civil War* (Athens, GA: University of Georgia Press, 2006), p. 47.

9   R. D. Cunningham, *The Black Citizen-Soldiers of Kansas, 1864–1901* (Columbia, MO: University of Missouri Press, 2008; D. T. Cornish, *The Sable Arm: Black Troops in the Union Army, 1861–1865* (Lawrence, KS: University Press of Kansas, 1987); J. T. Glatthaar, *Forged in Battle: The Civil War Alliance of Black Soldiers and White Officers* (Baton Rouge, LA: Louisiana State University Press, 2000); J. M. McPherson, *The Negro's Civil War: How American Blacks Felt and Acted During the War for the Union* (New York, NY: Vintage Knopf, 2003); M. Humphreys, *Intensely Human: The Health of the Black Soldier in the American Civil War* (Baltimore, OH: John Hopkins University Press, 2008).

10   D. Blanton and L. M. Cook, *They Fought Like Demons: Women Soldiers in the Civil War* (New York, NY: Vintage Books, 2002); S. R. Wakeman (ed. L. C. Burgess), *An Uncommon Soldier: The Civil War Letters of Sarah Rosetta Wakeman, alias Pvt. Lyons Wakeman, 153rd Regiment, New York State Volunteers, 1862–1864* (New York, NY: Oxford University Press, 1996); L. G. Eggleston, *Women in the Civil War: Extraordinary Stories of Soldiers, Spies, Nurses, Doctors, Crusaders, and Others* (Jefferson, NC: McFarland, 2009); M. R. Cordell, *Courageous Women of the Civil War: Soldiers, Spies, Medics, and More* (Chicago, IL: Chicago Review Press, 2016); S. K. Bierle, *Discovered: Female Soldiers At Gettysburg* [website] <https://emergingcivilwar. com/2016/07/03/discovered-female-soldiers-at-gettysburg/>, accessed August 2016.

11   McCurry, *Confederate Reckoning*, p. 87, note 3; D. Blanton, "Women Soldiers of the Civil War," Part 3, *Prologue Magazine*, 25/1 (spring 1993), available at [website] <http://www. archives.gov/publications/prologue/1993/spring/women-in-the-civil-war-1.html>, accessed January 2016.

12   Bailey, *Invisible Southerners*, p. 47.

13   J. A. Martinez, *Confederate Slave Impressment in the Upper South* (Chapel Hill, NC: University of North Carolina Press, 2013); C. E. Woodward, *Marching Masters: Slavery, Race, and the Confederate Army During the Civil War* (Charlottesville, VA: University of Virginia Press, 2014); B. Levine, *Confederate Emancipation: Southern Plans to Free and Arm Slaves during the Civil War* (New York, NY: Oxford University Press, 2007); Brasher, *The Peninsula Campaign and the Necessity of Emancipation*; A. W. Bergeron, Jr., "Free Men of Color in Gray," *Civil War History*, 32/3 (September 1982), pp. 246–55; McCurry, *Confederate Reckoning*; B. I. Wiley, *Southern Negroes, 1861–1865* (New Haven, CT: Yale University Press, 1938); G. Baylor, "The Army Negro," *Southern Historical Society Papers*, 31 (1903), pp. 365–69; J. J. Zaborney, *Slaves for Hire: Renting Enslaved Laborers in Antebellum Virginia* (Baton Rouge, LA: Louisiana State University Press, 2012); J. H. Brewer, *The Confederate Negro: Virginia's Craftsmen and*

Military Laborers, 1861–1865 (Durham, N C: Duke University Press, 1969); J. H. Segars and C. K. Barrow (eds.), *Black Southerners in Confederate Armies: A Collection of Historical Accounts* (Gretna, LA: Pelican Publishing, 2007); Levine, *Confederate Emancipation*.

14   *Army Regulations, Adopted for the Use of the Army of the Confederate States, in Accordance with Late Acts of Congress* (Atlanta, GA: Gaulding & Whitaker, 1861), p. 163; *Regulations for the Army of the Confederate States* (Richmond, VA: J. W. Randolph, 1863), p. 3.

15   Jones, *A Rebel War Clerk's Diary*, p. 247.

16   *Militia Law of Louisiana, Adopted by the State Legislature, January 23, 1862* (Baton Rouge, LA: Tom Bynum, 1862), p. 3.

17   See, for example, *Official Records*, Series I, Vol. XV, p. 138.

18   J. W. Binsfield, W. C. Davis, B. Maryniak, and J. I. Robertson, Jr., *Faith in the Fight: Civil War Chaplains* (Mechanicsburg, PA: Stackpole Books, 2003), p. 88, note 8.

19   C. L. Brown and P. D. Morgan (eds.), *Arming Slaves: From Classical Times to the Modern Age* (New Haven, CT: Yale University Press, 2006), p. 277.

20   "Old Dick, the Drummer," Richmond *Daily Dispatch*, January 2, 1862; "Dick Slate, Colored Drummer of 18th VA. Inf. Sold," *Petersburg Express*, December 16, 1863.

21   J. G. Hollandsworth, Jr., Black Confederate Pensioners After the Civil War [website] <http://mshistory.k12.ms.us/articles/289/black-confederate-pensioners-after-the-civil-war>, accessed May 2016.

22   Brasher, *The Peninsula Campaign and the Necessity of Emancipation*, p. 27.

23   N. Rosenstein, *Rome at War: Farms, Families, and Death in the Middle Roman Republic* (Chapel Hill, NC: 2004), pp. 22, 98, 244.

24   B. Bloomfield to J. B. Magruder, January 30, 1863, *Official Records*, Series I, Vol. LI, Part 2, p. 458.

25   See, for example, J. F. Gilmer to Robert E. Lee, November 19, 1864, *Official Records*, Series IV, Vol. III, pp. 829–30.

26   Lyman, *Meade's Army*, p. 227.

27   Benjamin Butler to Winfield Scott, May 24, 1861, *Official Records*, Series I, Vol. II, pp. 649–52.

28   W. W. Lester and W. J. Bromwell, *A Digest of the Military and Naval Laws of the Confederate States, from the Commencement of the Provisional Congress to the End of the First Congress Under the Constitution* (Columbia, SC: Evans & Cogswell, 1864), p. 107.

29   D. Mallock, "Cleburne's Proposal," *North & South*, XI/2 (December 2008), pp. 64–72.

30   James A. Seddon to Jefferson Davis, November 3, 1864, *Official Records*, Series IV, Vol. III, p. 761.

31   "Georgia and the Confederacy, 1865," *American Historical Review*, I/1 (October 1895), p. 97.

32   J. Marten, *America's Corporal: James Tanner in War and Peace* (Athens, GA: University of Georgia Press, 2014), p. 6.

33   Glatthaar, *General Lee's Army*, p. 22.

34   N. Silber, *Daughters of the Union* (Cambridge, MA: Harvard University Press, 2005), p. 17.

35   C. R. Newell and C. R. Shrader, *Of Duty Well and Faithfully Done: A History of the Regular Army in the Civil War* (Lincoln, NE: University of Nebraska, 2011), p. 339, note 50.

36   C. Lyons, "'Old Abe' and his Comrades: Some Civil War Mascots," *North & South*, XI/3 (June 2009), pp. 13–15.

37   Kelly and Kelly, *Best Little Stories of the Blue and Gray*, p. 40.

38   "China at Gettysburg," *The New York Times*, July 12, 1863.

39 W. D'Arcy, *The Fenian Movement in the United States, 1858–86* (Washington, DC: Catholic University of America Press, 1947); H. Senior, *The Last Invasion of Canada: The Fenian Raids, 1866–1870* (Toronto, Canada: Durdan Press, 1991).

40 *The Civil War: Sex and Soldiers* [website] <http://artsci.case.edu/dittrick/online-exhibits/history-of-birth-control/contraception-in-america-1800-1900/the-civil-war-sex-and-soldiers/>, accessed July 2017.

41 P. D. Jamieson, *Spring 1865: The Closing Campaigns of the Civil War* (Lincoln, NE: University of Nebraska, 2015), p. 4.

42 S. A. Townsend, *The Yankee Invasion of Texas* (College Station, TX: Texas A&M University Press, 2006), p. 131.

Chapter 12

1   G. W. Wingate, *History of the Twenty-Second Regiment of the National Guard of the State of New York* (New York, NY: Edwin W. Dayton, 1896), p. 52.

2   F. R. Freemon, *Gangrene and Glory: Medical Care During the American Civil War* (Bloomington, IN: University of Illinois Press, 2001); H. H. Cunningham, *Doctors in Gray: The Confederate Medical Service* (Baton Rouge, LA: Louisiana State University, 1960); G. W. Adams, *Doctors in Blue: The Medical History of the Union Army in the Civil War* (New York, NY: Schumann, 1952); T. P. Lowry and T. Reimer, *Bad Doctors: Military Justice Proceedings against 622 Civil War Surgeons* (Frederick, MD: National Museum of Civil War Medicine, 2010); Schmidt and Hasegawa, *Years of Change and Suffering*.

3   W. E. Rickenbacher, "The Demise of Stonewall Jackson: A Civil War Medical Case Study," *Journal of Military History*, 79/3 (July 2015), p. 639.

4   A. Guelzo, *Gettysburg: The Last Invasion* (New York, NY: Vintage, 2014), p. 469.

5   Wiley, *The Life of Billy Yank*, pp. 261–62, and *The Life of Johnny Reb*, pp. 50–55; Welsh, *Medical Histories of the Union Generals*, p. 88, and *Medical Histories of the Confederate Generals*, p. 99; Winkworth, "Sex and the Civil War: A Medical Perspective."

6   *Catalogue of the Alumni, Officers and Fellows of the College of Physicians and Surgeons in the City of New York* (New York, NY: Baker & Godwin, 1850), p. 50.

7   L. R. Speer, *Portals to Hell: The Military Prisons of the Civil War* (Mechanicsburg, PA: Stackpole Books, 1997); R. Pickenpaugh, *Captives in Gray: The Civil War Prisons of the Union* (Tuscaloosa, AL: University of Alabama Press, 2009); F. H. Casstevens, *"Out of the Mouth of Hell": Civil War Prisons and Escapes* (Jefferson, NC: McFarland, 2011), pp. 29, 170–73; T. P. Lowry and J. D. Welsh, *Tarnished Scalpels: The Court-martials of Fifty Union Surgeons* (Mechanicsburg, PA: Stackpole Books, 2000), p. 48–50; J. M. Gillispie, *Andersonvilles of the North: The Myths and Realities of Northern Treatment of Confederate Prisoners* (Denton, TX: University of North Texas Press, 2008); Marvel, *Andersonville*.

8   Clark to Hoffman, October 17, 1863, *Official Records*, Series II, Vol. VI, p. 392.

9   Clark to Hoffman, October 26, 1863, *Official Records*, Series II, Vol. VI, pp. 425–26.

10 Clark to Hoffman, November 28, 1863, *Official Records*, Series II, Vol. VI, p. 592.

11 Clark to Hoffman, April 8, 1864, *Official Records*, Series II, Vol. VII, pp. 23–29; Speer, *Portals to Hell*, p. 174.

12 Schmidt and Hasegawa, *Years of Change and Suffering*, p. ix.

13 R. A. Gabriel, *Man and Wound in the Ancient World* (Washington, DC: Potomac Books, 2012), p. 139.

14 R. J. Musto, "The Other Deadly Bullet: Opium," *North & South*, XIII/1 (May 2011), pp. 8–9.

15 M. D. Maher, *To Bind Up the Wounds: Catholic Sister Nurses in the U. S. Civil War* (Baton Rouge, LA: Louisiana State University Press, 2003).

16 Hattaway and Beringer, *Jefferson Davis*, p. 112.

17 *Official Records*, Series I, Vol. 36, Part 1, p. 96.

18 R. S. Holzman, "Sally Tompkins: Captain, Confederate Army," *The American Mercury*, LXXXVIII/422 (March 1959), pp. 127–30.

19 Davis and Robertson, *Virginia at War*, p. 72.

20 Patterson, *Debris of Battle*, p. 103.

21 Humphreys, *Intensely Human*, p. 12.

Epilogue

1 C. E. Janney, *The Lost Cause* [website] http://www.encyclopediavirginia.org/lost_cause_the>, accessed July 2017.

2 Grant, *Memoirs*, Chapter XI.

3 On Longstreet, see in particular W. G. Piston, *Lee's Tarnished Lieutenant: James Longstreet and his Place in Southern History* (Athens, GA: University of Georgia Press, 1987); D. B. Sanger and T. B. Hay, *James Longstreet: Soldier, Politician, Officer Holder, and Writer* (Baton Rouge, LA: Louisiana State, 1952); W. Thomas, *General James "Old Pete" Longstreet, Lee's "Old War Horse": Scapegoat for Gettysburg* (Parsons, VA: McLain, 1979); T. L. Connelly and B. Bellamy, *God and General Longstreet: The Lost Cause and the Southern Mind* (Baton Rouge, LA: Louisiana State University, 1982); R. L. DiNardo and A. A. Nofi (eds.), *James Longstreet: The Man, the Soldier, the Controversy* (Conshohocken, PA: Combined Publishing, 1998).

4 See J. D. Imboden, "The Confederate Retreat from Gettysburg," in Johnson and Buel, *Battle and Leaders of the Civil War*, Vol. III, p. 428; Wert, *General James Longstreet*, p. 200.

5 Robert E. Lee to Secretary of War, March 29, 1865, and Robert E. Lee to J. A. Early, March 29, 1965, *Official Records* Series I, Vol. XLIX, Part 2, p. 1,171.

6 D. S. Freeman (ed.), *Lee's Dispatches: Unpublished Letters of General Robert E. Lee, C.S.A. to Jefferson Davis and the War Department of The Confederate States of America 1862–65* (New York, NY: G. P. Putnam's Sons, 1915), No. 242.

7 W. G. Piston, "Marked in Bronze: James Longstreet and Southern History," in DiNardo and Nofi, *James Longstreet*, p. 209.

8 See, for example, F. Lee, "A Review of the First Two Days' Operations at Gettysburg and A Reply to General Longstreet," *Southern Historical Society Papers*, V (April 1878), pp. 162–94.

9 J. Davis, *The Rise and Fall of the Confederate Government* (New York, NY: D. Appleton, 1881), pp. 441–42.

10 Freeman, *Lee*, Vol. III, pp. 85, 89.

11 T. M. Fink, "Captain Ewell's Fort Buchanan Affliction," *Journal of Arizona History*, 49/1 (spring 2008), pp. 56–57.

12 Grant, *Memoirs*, Chapter 49.

13 K. M. Levin, *Do You Trust Those Lost Causers?* [website] <http://cwmemory.com/2012/04/02/do-you-trust-those-lost-causers/>, accessed January 2016.

14 Rhea, *Cold Harbor*, pp. 358–62.

15 Coski, *The Confederate Battle Flag*.

16 W. G. Piston, "Marked in Bronze: James Longstreet and Southern History," in DiNardo and Nofi, *James Longstreet*, p. 191.

17 *Commemorative Landscapes of North Carolina* [website] <http://docsouth.unc.edu/commland/results/>, accessed May 2016.

18 J. Hitt and M. Mergen, "Set in Stone," *The New York Times Magazine*, October 16, 2015, p. 48.

19 *War Memorials in NYC* [website] <http://www.nycedc.com/blog-entry/memorials-nyc>, accessed May 2016.

20 R. E. Butchart, *Schooling the Freed People: Teaching, Learning, and the Struggle for Black Freedom, 1861–76* (Chapel Hill, NC: University of North Carolina Press, 2010), pp. xii, 54ff., 80ff.

21 G. W. Gallagher, *Lee: The Soldier* (Lincoln, NE: University of Nebraska Press, 1996), p. 21.

22 I. C. Colby, "The Freedmen's Bureau: From Social Welfare to Segregation," *Phylon*, 46/3 (Third Quarter, 1985), pp. 226–27.

23 C. B. Dawsey and J. M. Dawsey (eds.), *The Confederados: Old South Immigrants in Brazil* (Tuscaloosa, AL: University of Alabama Press, 1995), p. 107.

24 M. Nesbitt, *Saber and Scapegoat: J. E. B. Stuart and the Gettysburg Controversy* (Mechanicsburg, PA: Stackpole Books, 2002), p. xix.

25 E. B. Custer, *Following the Guidon* (New York, NY: Harper & Brothers, 1890), p. 311.

26 J. P. Guzman (ed.), *1952 Negro Yearbook* (New York, NY: Wm. H. Wise, 1952), pp. 275–79.

27 M. Gilbert, *Churchill and America* (New York, NY: The Free Press, 2008), p. 11.

28 M. A. Weitz, *More Damning than Slaughter: Desertion in the Confederate Army* (Lincoln, NE: University of Nebraska Press, 2005), p. xv.

29 D. Brook, *The Forgotten Confederate Jew* [website] <http://www.tabletmag.com/jewish-arts-and-culture/books/106227/the-forgotten-confederate-jew>, accessed May 2016.

30 *The New York Times*, December 14, 2012.

31 E. Thalls, "Bomb Squad Destroys Civil War Artillery Shell Found In Prairie Grove," *Ft. Smith-Fayetteville News*, May 28, 2015.

32 A. A. Nofi, "Willie's Room," *North & South*, XIV/4 (November 2012), pp. 8–9.

Further Reading

Standard references

Cullum, G. W., *Biographical Register of the Officers and Graduates of the United States Military Academy at West Point, New York* (New York, NY: J. Miller, 1879)

Dictionary of American Naval Fighting Ships [website] <https://www.history.navy.mil/research/histories/ship-histories/danfs.html>, accessed July 2017

Grant, U. S., *The Personal Memoirs of Ulysses S. Grant* (New York, NY: C. L. Webster & Co., 1885–86)

Heitman, F. B., *Historical Register and Dictionary of the United States Army* (Washington, DC: Government Printing Office, 1903)

Moore, F. (ed.), *The Rebellion Record: A Diary of American Events* (New York, NY: Putnam's, 1861–68), 12 Vols.

Official Records of the Union and Confederate Armies (Washington, DC: Government Printing Office, 1881–1901), 70 vols.

Official Records of the Union and Confederate Navies in the War of the Rebellion (Washington, DC: Government Printing Office, 1894–1922), 30 vols.

Warner, E. J., *Generals in Gray: Lives of the Confederate Commanders* (Baton Rouge, LA: Louisiana State University Press, 1959)

Warner, E. J., *Generals in Blue: Lives of the Union Commanders* (Baton Rouge, LA: Louisiana State University Press, 1964)

General works

Gallagher, G., *The Union War* (Cambridge, MA: Harvard University Press, 2011)

McPherson, J., *The War that Forged a Nation: Why the Civil War Still Matters* (New York, NY: Oxford University Press, 2015)

Simon, J. Y. (ed. G. W. LaFantasie), *The Union Forever: Lincoln, Grant, and the Civil War* (Lexington, KY: University Press of Kentucky, 2012)

Thomas, E. M., *The Dogs of War, 1861* (New York, NY: Oxford University Press, 2011)

Varon, E. R., *Appomattox: Victory, Defeat, and Freedom at the End of the Civil War* (New York, NY: Oxford University Press, 2014)

Soldiers, soldiering, and military service

Armistead, G. A., *Horses and Mules in the Civil War: A Complete History with a Roster of More Than 700 War Horses* (Jefferson, NC: McFarland & Co., 2013)

Davis, W. C., *A Taste for War: The Culinary History of the Blue and the Gray* (Lincoln, NE: University of Nebraska Press, 2011)

Petriello, D. R., *Bacteria and Bayonets: The Impact of Disease in American Military History* (Philadelphia, PA: Casemate, 2016)

Priest, J. M., *"Stand to It and Give Them Hell": Gettysburg as the Soldiers Experienced it: From Cemetery Ridge to Little Round Top, July 2, 1863* (El Dorado Hills, CA: Savas Beatie, 2014)

Sanders, C. W., Jr., *While in the Hands of the Enemy: Military Prisons of the Civil War* (Baton Rogue, LA: Louisiana State University Press, 2005)

Wei-Siang Hsieh, W., *West Pointers and the Civil War: The Old Army in War and Peace* (Chapel Hill, NC: University of North Carolina, 2009)

Wright, John D. Wright, *The Language of the Civil War* (Westport, CT: Greenwood Publishing, 2001);

The navies

Dougherty, K., *Strangling the Confederacy: Coastal Operations in the American Civil War* (Philadelphia, PA: Casemate, 2010)

McPherson, J. M., *War on the Waters: The Union & Confederate Navies, 1861–65* (Chapel Hill, NC: University of North Carolina Press, 2012)

Symonds, C., *Lincoln's Admirals* (New York, NY: Oxford University Press, 2008)

Slavery in America

Bancroft, F., *Slave Trading in the Old South* (Columbia, SC: University of South Carolina Press, 1996)

Berlin, I., *Generations of Captivity: A History of African American Slaves* (Cambridge, MA: Harvard University Press, 2003)

Davis, D. B., *Inhuman Bondage: The Rise and Fall of Slavery in the New World* (New York, NY: Oxford University Press, 2006)

Foner, E., *Gateway to Freedom: The Hidden History of the Underground Railroad* (New York: W. W. Norton, 2015)

Kolchin, P., *American Slavery: 1619–1877* (New York, NY: Hill and Wang, 2003)

The home front and social history

Gallman, J. M., *Defining Duty in the Civil War: Personal Choice, Popular Culture, and the Union Home Front* (Chapel Hill, NC: University of North Carolina Press, 2015)

Garrison, N. S., *With Courage and Delicacy: Civil War on the Peninsula: Women and the U.S. Sanitary Commission* (Boston, MA: Da Capo Press, 1999)

Hettle, W. (ed.), *The Confederate Home Front: A History in Documents* (Baton Rouge, LA: Louisiana State University Press, 2017)

Lowry, T. P., *The Story the Soldiers Wouldn't Tell: Sex in the Civil War* (Mechanicsburg, PA: Stackpole Books, 1994)

Mobley, J. A., *Weary of War: Life on the Confederate Home Front* (Santa Barbara, CA: Praeger, 2008)

Rable, G. C., *Civil Wars: Women and the Crisis of Southern Nationalism* (Champaign, IL: University of Illinois Press, 1989)

Strausbaugh, J., *City of Sedition: The History of New York City during the Civil War* (New York, NY: Grand Central Publishing, 2016)

Diplomacy, espionage, secret missions, and intelligence

Fishel, E. C., *The Secret War for the Union: The Untold Story of Military Intelligence in the Civil War* (Boston, MA: Houghton Mifflin, 1996)

Foreman, A., *A World on Fire: Britain's Crucial Role in the American Civil War* (New York, NY: Random House, 2010)

Reit, S., *Behind Rebel Lines: The Incredible Story of Emma Edmonds, Civil War Spy.* (New York, NY: Harcourt Brace, 1991)

Van Doren Stern, P., *Secret Missions of the Civil War* (New York, NY: Bonanza Books, 1959)

Varon, E. R., *Southern Lady, Yankee Spy: The True Story of Elizabeth Van Lew, a Union Agent in the Heart of the Confederacy* (New York, NY: Oxford University Press, 2003)

Women and the war

Blanton, D. and L. M. Cook, *They Fought Like Demons: Women Soldiers in the Civil War* (New York, NY: Vintage Books, 2002)

Eggleston, L. G., *Women in the Civil War: Extraordinary Stories of Soldiers, Spies, Nurses, Doctors, Crusaders, and Others* (Jefferson, NC: McFarland, 2009)

Giesberg, J., *Army at Home: Women and the Civil War on the Northern Home Front* (Chapel Hill, NC: University of North Carolina Press, 2009)

Wakeman, S. R. (ed. L. C. Burgess), *An Uncommon Soldier: The Civil War Letters of Sarah Rosetta Wakeman, alias Pvt. Lyons Wakeman, 153rd Regiment, New York State Volunteers, 1862–64* (New York, NY: Oxford University Press, 1996)

Whites, L. A. and A. P. Long (eds.), *Occupied Women: Gender, Military Occupation, and the American Civil War* (Baton Rouge, LA: Louisiana State University Press, 2009)

African Americans and the war

Bailey, A. J., *Invisible Southerners: Ethnicity in the Civil War* (Athens, GA: University of Georgia Press, 2006)

Brasher, G. D., *The Peninsular Campaign & the Necessity of Emancipation: African-Americans & the Fight for Freedom* (Chapel Hill, NC: University of North Carolina Press, 2012)

Cornish, D. T., *The Sable Arm: Black Troops in the Union Army, 1861–65* (Lawrence, KS: University Press of Kansas, 1987)

Dobak, W. A., *Freedom by the Sword: The US Colored Troops, 1862–67* (Washington, DC: Center of Military History, 2011)

McPherson, J. M., *The Negro's Civil War: How American Blacks Felt and Acted During the War for the Union* (New York, NY: Vintage Knopf, 2003)

Lincoln

Anderegg, M., *Lincoln and Shakespeare* (Lawrence, KS: University Press of Kansas, 2015)

Foner, E., *The Fiery Trial: Abraham Lincoln and American Slavery* (New York, NY: W. W. Norton & Company, 2010)

McDermott, S. P., *Mary Lincoln: Southern Girl, Northern Woman* (New York, NY: Routledge, 2015)

Oates, S. B., *With Malice Toward None: The Life of Abraham Lincoln* (New York, NY: HarperCollins, 2011)

Pinsker, M., *Lincoln's Sanctuary: Abraham Lincoln and the Soldiers' Home* (New York, NY: Oxford University Press, 2005)

Trudeau, N. A., *Lincoln's Greatest Journey: Sixteen Days that Changed a Presidency, March 24–April 8, 1865* (El Dorado Hills, CA: Savas Beatie, 2016)

Reconstruction, commemoration, memorialization

Baker, B. E., *What Reconstruction Meant: Historical Memory in the American South* (Charlottesville, VA: University of Virginia Press, 2007)

Blight, D., *Race and Reunion: The Civil War in American Memory* (Cambridge, MA: Harvard University, The Belknap Press, 2002)

Coski, J. M., *The Confederate Battle Flag: America's Most Embattled Emblem* (Cambridge, MA: Harvard University Press, 2005)

Foner, E., *Reconstruction: America's Unfinished Revolution, 1863–77* (New York, NY: Harper, 2015)

Horwitz, T., *Confederates in the Attic: Dispatches from the Unfinished Civil War* (New York, NY: Knopf Doubleday, 1999)

Marshall, A. E., *Creating a Confederate Kentucky: The Lost Cause and Civil War Memory in a Border State* (Chapel Hill, NC: University of North Carolina Press, 2013)

Snee, B. J., *Lincoln before Lincoln: Early Cinematic Adaptations of the Life of America's Greatest President* (Lexington, KY: University Press of Kentucky, 2016)

Wetta, F. J. and Novelli, M. A., *The Long Reconstruction: The Post-Civil War South in History, Film, and Memory* (New York, NY: Routledge, 2013)

For younger readers

Cordell, M. R., *Courageous Women of the Civil War* (Chicago, IL: Chicago Review Press, 2016)

Gilbin, J. C., *Good Brother, Bad Brother: The Story of Edwin Booth & John Wilkes Booth* (New York, NY: Clarion Books, 2005)

Herbert, J., *The Civil War for Kids: A History with 21 Activities* (Chicago, IL: Chicago Review Press, 1998)

Herbert, J., *Abraham Lincoln for Kids: His Life and Times with 21 Activities* (Chicago, IL: Chicago Review Press, 2007)

Kamma, A., *If You Lived When There Was Slavery In America.* (New York, NY: Scholastic, 2004)

King, W. A., *Clad in Uniform: Women Soldiers of the Civil War* (Haddon Township, NJ: C. W. Historicals, 1992)

Nofi, A. A., *Spies in the Civil War* (New York, NY: Chelsea House, 2000)

Onomastic Index